The Grand Fleet 1914-1916

The Grand Fleet 1914-1916

Its Creation, Development and Work

John Rushworth Jellicoe

The Grand Fleet 1914-1916: Its Creation, Development and Work by John Rushworth Jellicoe. First published in 1919.

Revised edition published by Bowsprit Books, 2020.

This book or any portion thereof may not be reproduced, scanned, digitized or used in any manner whatsoever without the express written permission of the publisher except for the use of brief quotations in a book review or scholarly journal. All rights reserved.

FIRST PRINTING 2020.

ISBN: 9798612310532.

Contents

1 – The Opening of the War 7
2 - General Navy Strategy in Home Waters 17
3 - The Grand Fleet and Its Bases 35
4 - Declaration of War 79
5 – Mine Menace in the North Sea 102
6 - Incidents at Sea 135
7 - The Dogger Bank Action 162
8 - German Mines and Submarines 190
9 - Controlling the North Sea 214
10 - Attempts to Entice the Enemy 226
11 - The Naval Situation in May 1916 256
12 - The Battle of Jutland 259
13 - The Battle of Jutland (Cont.) 286
14 - The Battle of Jutland (Cont.) 310
15 - Reflection on the Battle of Jutland 326
16 - Lessons of Experience 346
17 - The Submarine Peril 370

1 – The Opening of the War

Early in 1914, whilst serving at the Admiralty as Second Sea Lord, I had been offered and had accepted the command of the Home Fleets, which in the ordinary course would have become vacant in the following December on the expiration of Admiral Sir George Callaghan's term of command, and public announcement was made of the intended appointment.

Sir George Callaghan was my senior by seven years, and he and I had served together in China fourteen years before, when I was Flag Captain to Admiral — afterwards Admiral of the Fleet — Sir Edward Seymour. He had since had what is probably a unique period of sea service, passing from one appointment to another without an interval of half pay. Soon after his promotion to flag rank he had become Rear-Admiral in the old Channel Fleet; thence he had gone on to the 5th Cruiser Squadron in 1907; two years later he became second in command in the Mediterranean, and on the expiration of his term there, in 1910, he returned to take up the appointment of Vice-Admiral commanding the Second Division of the Home Fleets, succeeding to the position of Commander-in-Chief in 1910. The usual period for which the Commander-in-Chief of the Home Fleet was supposed to fly his flag was two years, but in 1913 the Admiralty, accurately interpreting the sentiment of the whole Service, extended Sir George Callaghan's appointment. And it was the approaching termination of this further period of command — to the regret of the Admiralty, for which I can speak from personal knowledge, and to the regret also of the officers and men of the Home Fleets — which led to my nomination in the spring of that year.

In the latter part of July, when the situation in Europe had assumed a threatening aspect, Mr. Churchill, the First Lord, informed me that in the event of hostilities occurring involving this country, it was considered necessary that the Commander-in-Chief of the Home Fleets should have the assistance of a second in command, and he added that I had been selected for the appointment, and it was desired that I should arrange with Sir George as to the ship in which I should fly my flag.

Sir George Callaghan visited the Admiralty very shortly afterwards, and it was decided between us that the battleship Centurion should be my flagship. We discussed the slight reorganisation that this would involve in the Fleet, and I selected my staff, which comprised:

Captain R. W. Bentinck as Chief of the Staff; Lieut. H. Fitzherbert as Flag Lieutenant; Lieut.-Commander E. Hardman Jones as Signal Officer; Lieut.-Commander R. L. Nicholson as Wireless Officer; Lieut.-Commander (N.) A. F. B. Carpenter as War Staff Officer, and Fleet Paymaster H. H. Share as Secretary.

On July 28th, with no premonition of coming events, I was present at a dinner party given by Lord Morley at the United Services Club. The party was interesting, as it comprised Field-Marshal Lord Kitchener, Mr. Churchill, Lord Haldane, Lord Bryce, and others who figured later prominently in the War.

During the two following days conferences took place at the Admiralty as to the disposition of the Fleet, etc., and, in view of the threatening political situation, the work of demobilisation after the King's inspection at Spithead and the subsequent short fleet exercises were suspended, pending further developments. I met Lord Kitchener, who was about to return to Egypt, on one or two occasions at the Admiralty during these days.

On July 30th, I turned over the duties of Second Sea Lord, which I had discharged since December, 1912, to Vice-Admiral Sir Frederick Hamilton, K.C.B., and made my final preparations for joining the Fleet as second in command.

I spent some hours at the Admiralty on the following day, and during a conversation with Mr. Churchill and the Marquis of Milford Haven, the then First Sea Lord, it was intimated to me that, in certain circumstances, I might be appointed Commander-in-Chief in succession to Sir George Callaghan.

This intimation came upon me as a great surprise, and I protested against such an appointment being made on what might possibly be on the very eve of war. Nothing definite was settled. I left, however, with the impression that the change was not one that had been finally decided upon, but that it might take place. I left London the same night by the mail train for Wick, the Commander-in-Chief having informed me that he would send a vessel to meet me there.

The idea that the change might be made occupied my thoughts during the journey to the North. As I thought over the possibility of a transfer of command at such a moment, the stronger appeared the objections. During the ensuing forty-eight hours I sent several telegrams to both the First Lord and the First Sea Lord on the subject. I dwelt strongly upon the danger of substituting, at such a juncture and at such short notice, an admiral who was not in touch with the Fleet, for a Commander-in-Chief with long experience of the Command. I mentioned, also, the strong feeling of admiration and loyalty to the Commander-in-Chief that existed, and suggested as an alternative that I should act as his assistant on board the Fleet-Flagship. I had in mind that I might act somewhat in the capacity of his Chief of the Staff. In spite of the First Lord's reiterated opinion, my views remained unaltered, although it did not occur to me that some anxiety might be felt that Sir George Callaghan's health would not stand the strain of commanding the Fleet in the event of war. That, however, was a matter on which the Admiralty would be better informed than myself, and I had no hesitation in urging the opinions expressed in my successive telegrams.

A thick fog prevailed at Wick, and the Boadicea, the ship in which I made the passage to Scapa Flow, was not able to leave until late in the forenoon of August 2nd, and arrived at Scapa Flow in the afternoon.

When I reported myself to the Commander-in-Chief, the knowledge of the event which was apparently impending made the interview both embarrassing and painful, as I could see that he had no knowledge of the possibility of his leaving the Fleet, and obviously I could not tell him.

We discussed various arrangements, including the question of the defence of Scapa Flow, for which temporary but naturally inadequate measures were being energetically taken with the limited resources at the disposal of the Fleet.

At about 4 a.m. on August 4th, I received Admiralty orders to open a secret envelope which had been handed to me in the train as I was leaving London, by an officer from the Admiralty. This envelope contained my appointment as "Commander-in-Chief of the Grand Fleet" — a new designation which must be explained later.

On this order I was obliged to act, and I proceeded on board the Iron Duke and found that the Commander-in-Chief had received orders to turn over the command to me.

Sir George Callaghan had been my Commander-in-Chief during my command of the 2nd Battle Squadron. He was, in addition, a personal friend, and I, like all those with whom he had been in contact, had the most profound respect and admiration for him. The idea of taking over his command at the moment of his life naturally caused me feelings of the greatest pain, and, moreover, it was impossible to dismiss the fear that the Fleet might conclude that I had been in some measure responsible for the change. This possibility had, of course, been present in my mind from the moment I left London, and it appeared to add to the objections to a change of command at such a juncture, since any idea of this nature prevalent in the Fleet must affect the feeling of loyalty to me as the new Commander-in-Chief.

It is unnecessary to dwell on the matter, but I cannot close this portion of my narrative without paying a warm tribute to the manner in which Sir George accepted the Admiralty decision, which obviously came as a great shock to him. He behaved, as always, as a most gallant officer and gentleman, and his one desire was to make the position easy for me, in entire disregard of his own feelings.

It was decided that I should take over the Command on the following day, but a telegram having been received from the Admiralty ordering the Fleet to proceed to sea at once, I returned to the Iron Duke, and Sir George Callaghan arranged to leave the Fleet in the Sappho before its departure at 8.30 in the morning.

At that hour I took over the Command from Sir George Callaghan, who then struck his flag.

The following ten or fourteen days were a period of great strain and anxiety. To assume so heavy a responsibility as the command of the Grand Fleet at such short notice on the eve of war was in itself a matter not to be taken lightly; it became necessary to gather together the strings of the whole organisation, to ascertain the dispositions already made and those immediately required, and the whole problem was largely complicated by the fact that the port on which the Fleet was based was open to attack both by destroyers and by submarines, the only obstacle to such attack being the navigational difficulties of the Pentland Firth. Though considerable, these were by no means insuperable.

Added to this was my feeling of deep regret at superseding a valued chief and friend at such a moment. The one thing that helped me through this period was the great and most loyal assistance rendered to me by the staff of Sir George Callaghan, who, notwithstanding their intense personal regret at his departure, gave me their very warm support, and concealed from me any trace of the feelings which they must have experienced at my presence amongst them under such exceptional and trying conditions. They behaved as naval officers always behave — in a true spirit of comradeship. The same may be said of the flag officers and captains in the Fleet, and indeed of every officer and man.

Sir George Callaghan left his whole staff with me, with the exception of his flag lieutenant, who accompanied him to London.

This staff included:

Commodore A. F. Everett, C.B., Captain of the Fleet;
Captain R. N. Lawson, Flag Captain;
Commander Roger Backhouse, C.B., Flag Commander;
Fleet Paymaster C. F. Pollard, C.B., Secretary;
Commander the Hon. Matthew Best, War Staff Officer;
Commander R. W. Woods, Signal Officer;
Lieut.-Commander J. S. Salmond, Wireless Officer;
Lieut.-Commander R, M. Bellairs, War Staff Officer;
Lieut. W. D. Phipps, Signal Officer.

(Later, Commodore L. Halsey, C.M.G., became Captain of the Fleet, Captain F. C. Dreyer, C.B., Flag-Captain; Commander C. M. Forbes, Flag-Commander, and Fleet-Paymaster V. H. T. Weekes, Additional Secretary, Fleet-Paymaster H. H. Share having in the meantime succeeded Fleet-Paymaster C. F. Pollard as Secretary)

When it became certain that I was to take command of the Fleet, I asked the Admiralty to appoint Rear-Admiral Charles Madden as Chief of the Staff; and I was thus able to transfer Captain R. W. Bentinck to act as Chief of the Staff to Vice-Admiral Sir George Warrender, the next senior flag officer in the Fleet.

The composition of the Grand Fleet was:

Fleet-Flagship — H.M.S. Iron Duke.
Attached Ships — H.M.S. Sappho, H.M.S. Oak.

BATTLE FLEET

1st Battle Squadron:
Vice-Admiral Sir Lewis Bayly, K.C.B. (in command).
Rear-Admiral H. Evan Thomas (2nd in command).
Battleships Marlborough (Flag), St. Vincent (Rear Flag), Colossus, Hercules, Neptune, Vanguard, Collingwood, Superb, Bellona (attached Light Cruiser), Cyclops (repair ship)
2nd Battle Squadron:
Vice-Admiral Sir George Warrender, Bart., K.C.B. (in command).
Rear-Admiral Sir Robert Arbuthnot, Bart. (2nd in command).
Battleships King George V, (Flag), Orion (Rear Flag), Ajax, Audacious, Centurion, Conqueror, Monarch, Thunderer, Boadicea (attached Light Cruiser), Assistance (repair ship).
4th Battle Squadron:
Vice-Admiral Sir Douglas Gamble, K.C.V.O, (in command).
Battleships Dreadnought (Flag), Temeraire, Bellerophon, Blonde (attached Light Cruiser).
3rd Battle Squadron:

Vice-Admiral E. E. Bradford, C.V.O. (in command).
Rear-Admiral M. E. Browning (2nd in command).
Battleships King Edward VII. (Flag), Hibernia (Rear Flag), Commonwealth, Zealandia, Dominion, Africa, Britannia, Hindustan, Blanche (attached Light Cruiser).

1st Battle Cruiser Squadron:
Vice-Admiral (acting) Sir David Beatty (in command).
Battleships (sic) Lion (Flag), Princess Royal, Queen Mary, New Zealand.

2nd Cruiser Squadron:
Rear-Admiral the Hon. S. Gough-Calthorpe (in command).
Cruisers Shannon (Flag), Achilles, Cochrane, Natal.

3rd Cruiser Squadron:
Rear-Admiral W. C. Pakenham, C.B. (in command).
Cruisers Antrim (Flag), Argyll, Devonshire, Roxburgh.

1st Light Cruiser Squadron:
Commodore W. E. Goodenough (in command).
Light Cruisers Southampton (Flag), Birmingham, Lowestoft, Nottingham.

Destroyer Flotillas
Second Flotilla:
Captain J. R. P. Hawkesley (in command in Active).
Destroyers Acorn, Alarm, Brisk, Cameleon, Comet, Fury, Goldfinch, Hope, Larne, Lyra, Martin, Minstrel, Nemesis, Nereide, Nymphe, Redpole, Rifleman, Ruby, Sheldrake, Staunch.

Fourth Flotilla:
Captain C. J. Wintour (in command in Swift).
Destroyers Acasta, Achates, Ambuscade, Ardent, Christopher, Cockatrice. Contest, Fortune, Garland, Hardy, Lynx, Midge, Owl, Paragon, Porpoise, Shark, Sparrowhawk, Spitfire, Unity, Victor.

Mine Sweeping Gunboats:
Commander L. G. Preston (in command).
H.M. Ships Skipjack (S.O. Ship) (absent at first), Circe, Gossamer, Leda, Speedwell, Jason, Seagull.

Shetland Patrol Force: Forward (Scott) and four destroyers of the River class.

The above vessels formed the Fleet under the immediate command of the Commander-in-Chief at the outbreak of hostilities. In addition, there were in southern waters, and also under the command of the Commander-in-Chief, the following vessels:

THE HARWICH FORCE

This force, although an integral portion of the Grand Fleet, was based on Harwich. It was intended that it should join the Grand Fleet at sea, if possible, in the event of a fleet action being imminent, and for this reason it was included in the organisation of the Fleet for battle; but the force did not in actual fact, ever so join the Fleet, nor did I expect that it would be able to do so. At the outbreak of war it was commanded by Co
mmodore R. Y. Tyrwhitt in H.M.S. Amethyst and comprised:
1st Flotilla
Commanded by Captain W. Blunt in Fearless with 20 destroyers.
3rd Flotilla
Commanded by Captain C. H. Fox in Amphion with 15 destroyers.

Included also in the organisation of the Home Fleets, which Sir George Callaghan had commanded-in-chief, were the Second and Third Fleets:

SECOND FLEET

(under command of Vice-Admiral Sir Cecil Burney, K.C.B., K.C.M.G.).
Fleet-Flagship - Lord Nelson, Rear-Admiral Stuart-Nicholson and Bernard Currey (commanding Battle Squadrons).
5th Battle Squadron:
Prince of Wales (Flag), Agamemnon, Bulwark, Formidable, Implacable, Irresistible, London, Queen, Venerable.
6th Battle Squadron:

Russell (Flag), Cornwallis, Albemarle, Duncan, Exmouth, Vengeance.
5th Cruiser Squadron:
Rear-Admiral A. P. Stoddart (in command).
 Carnarvon (Flag), Falmouth, Liverpool.
6th Cruiser Squadron:
Rear-Admiral W. L. Grant (in command).
Drake, Good Hope, King Alfred, Leviathan.
(These last two Cruiser Squadrons were, however, broken up immediately, and the ships transferred to other duties.)
Minelayer Squadron,
commanded by Captain M. H. Cobbe.
H.M. Ships Naiad (S.O.'s ship), Andromache, Apollo, Intrepid, Iphigenia, Latona, Thetis.

THIRD FLEET

This Fleet comprised the 7th and 8th Battle Squadrons, consisting of our oldest battleships, and the 7th, 9th, 10th, 11th and 12th Cruiser Squadrons, comprising our oldest cruisers.

But the only vessels of this Fleet which were ever associated with the Grand Fleet were the ships of the 10th Cruiser Squadron, which, under the command of Rear-Admiral Dudley de Chair, joined the Grand Fleet shortly after the outbreak of war, the Squadron being employed mainly on blockading duties. It was composed as follows:

Crescent (Flag), Edgar, Endymion, Gibraltar, Grafton, Hawke, Royal Arthur, Theseus.

All submarines, except those of the B and C classes which were detached for the protection of our coast and ports from Rosyth southwards, were worked, in accordance with Admiralty policy, from Harwich, and were not, therefore, under my command. The C class submarines were unfit for oversea work, and our operations in enemy waters were therefore confined to boats of the D and E classes, of which we possessed a total of 8 D's and 9 E's, as against the German total of 28 boats of the U class.

British admiral Sir George Callaghan (1852–1920)

Image: Callaghan as Second-in-Command of the Home Fleet

2 - General Navy Strategy in Home Waters

It is hardly surprising if the work and purpose of the Navy had somewhat faded from public interest during the century that had elapsed since the Napoleonic Wars, the last occasion on which the inhabitants of this country had felt that their safety depended on maritime power. Indeed, it had fallen to the lot of a distinguished officer in a foreign navy, Captain Mahan, to awaken interest in this matter, and to point out the all-important influence which Sea Power had exerted, and would exert, on history.

Associations such as the Navy League had been formed, having as their object the enlightenment of our countrymen, and although a great work was done in this direction, the mere necessity for such work is an indication of the extent to which the nation had forgotten the lessons of the past.

I therefore offer no apology for making some reference to the use and purpose of the British Navy.

The main objects for which our Navy exists may be shortly summed up under four heads:

1. To ensure for British ships the unimpeded use of the sea, this being vital to the existence of an island nation, particularly one which is not self-supporting in regard to food.

2. In the event of war, to bring steady economic pressure to bear on our adversary by denying to him the use of the sea, thus compelling him to accept peace.

3. Similarly in the event of war to cover the passage and assist any army sent overseas, and to protect its communications and supplies.

4. To prevent invasion of this country and its overseas Dominions by enemy forces.

The above objects are achieved in the quickest and surest manner by destroying the enemy's armed naval forces, and this is therefore the first objective of our Fleet. The Fleet exists to achieve victory.

But history has always shown that it is a very difficult matter to impose our will upon a weaker naval adversary, and that, instead of giving us the opportunity of destroying his armed naval forces, he usually keeps the main body of those forces — the Battle Fleet — in positions of safety in fortified harbours, where they are a constant threat to the sea communications of the stronger naval Power, and force upon that Power a watching policy so that the enemy may be engaged, should he put to sea, before he is able to gain any advantage.

The watching policy in the great wars of the Napoleonic era was carried out by keeping our squadrons, through fair or foul weather, in the vicinity of those ports of the enemy in which his fleet lay. Occasionally our ships were driven off by stress of weather, but they regained their stations as soon as conditions permitted.

During this war, however, the advent of the submarine and destroyer, and, to a lesser extent, the use of the mine rendered such dispositions impossible.

No large ship could cruise constantly in the vicinity of enemy bases without the certainty that she would fall an early victim to the attacks of submarines. Destroyers could, it is true, afford some measure of protection, but destroyers have a very limited range of action, and could not keep the sea off the enemy's distant coast even in good weather for a sufficient length of time. Periodical relief of the destroyers was an impossibility, owing to the great numbers that would be required for this purpose.

Moreover, even if the submarine danger could be overcome, the heavy ships would be so open to attack by enemy destroyers at night, if cruising anywhere near enemy bases, that they would certainly be injured, if not sunk, before many days had passed.

These facts had been recognised before the War and a watching policy from a distance decided upon, the watch being instituted for the purpose of preventing enemy vessels from gaining the open sea, where they would constitute a danger to our sea communications. Now a watch maintained at a distance from the port under observation is necessarily only partial, except in circumstances where the enemy has to pass through narrow straits before gaining open water.

The chances of intercepting enemy ships depend entirely on the number of watching vessels and the distance that those on board them can see.

At night this distance is very short — on a dark night not more than a quarter of a mile, and even in daylight, under the average conditions of visibility obtaining in the North Sea, it is not more than six to eight miles.

The North Sea, though small in contrast with the Atlantic, is a big water area of about 120,000 square miles in extent. The width across it, between the Shetland Islands and Norway (the narrowest portion), is 160 miles, and an additional 40 miles (the Fair Island Channel) would need to be watched also if a patrol were established along this line.

A consideration of all the circumstances had led to the adoption by the Admiralty of Scapa Flow in the Orkneys as the main Fleet Base, and the Admiralty had determined upon a naval strategy in Home Waters, in the event of war with Germany, based upon the idea that the Grand Fleet would control the North Sea, and that the Channel Fleet would watch the English Channel, thus, in combination, holding the enemy's main force.

To effect this purpose, it was intended that the main Battle Fleet should occupy, as circumstances permitted, a strategic position in the North Sea where it would act in support of Cruiser Squadrons carrying out sweeps to the southward in search of enemy vessels, and should be favourably placed for bringing the High Sea Fleet to action should it put to sea.

This policy of cruiser sweeps had been adopted as the result of experience in the various naval manoeuvres carried out in previous years in the North Sea. These had demonstrated quite clearly that the alternative policy of stretching cruiser patrol lines across the North Sea for the purpose of watching for the enemy was an impracticable one, it having been shown on many occasions that evasion of a single patrol line during the hours of darkness, or even daylight, under the conditions of visibility that usually prevail in the North Sea, is a very simple matter. Further, a line of cruisers occupying regular patrol positions is always in peril of successful submarine attack; the loss of the cruisers Hogue, Cressy and Aboukir showed this. It is also open to a concentrated attack by surface vessels.

The War Orders issued to the Commander-in-Chief of the Grand Fleet were based, therefore, on this general idea, and when the Grand Fleet proceeded to sea in compliance with Admiralty orders at 8.30 a.m. on August the 4th, 1914, it left with the intention of carrying out this general policy. The Channel Fleet, under the command of Vice-Admiral Sir Cecil Burney, assembled in the Channel in accordance with the general strategic dispositions.

The vessels engaged in this first move of the Grand Fleet comprised the 1st, 2nd, 3rd and 4th Battle Squadrons, with their attached cruisers; the 1st Battle Cruiser Squadron, with its Light Cruiser Squadron, strengthened by the addition of the Falmouth and Liverpool; the 2nd Cruiser Squadron, and the 3rd Cruiser Squadron. These dispositions continued in force for some three weeks, when the strong influence of the submarine on naval strategy began to make itself apparent.

The ideas held in pre-War days as to the capabilities of submarines were found, after a short experience of war, to need modification. In the first place, it became quickly apparent that the German submarines possessed a radius of action and sea-keeping qualities considerably greater than those of our own submarines. It had been, for instance, looked upon as a considerable achievement for our submarines to keep the sea for a period of five to seven days, and they had not operated at any great distance from the coast.

It is true that submarines had on occasion made long voyages such as to Australia, but they were then usually escorted, or even towed, and the number of days from port to port did not approach the length of time for which German submarines remained at sea. Further, it was known that the Germans possessed a considerable superiority in the number of submarines which were capable of operating overseas, and the frequent sighting of enemy submarines as far north as the

Orkney and Shetland Islands early in the War, combined with the fact that it appeared that the enemy had established a regular submarine patrol in the centre of the North Sea, made it evident that the German submarines would constitute a very serious menace to our heavy ships.

The comparative strength in submarines in Home Waters at the outbreak of war was as follows:

German

28 U Boats, of which U 1 to U 4 were hardly fit for oversea work, but were as good as our D class.

British

8 D Class and 9 E Class, of which D 1 was unreliable and the remaining units of the D class were not equal to the U boats.

34 C Class and 3 B Class. Unfit for oversea work and used only for local defence of the coast or in the Channel.

The Germans also had at least 24 submarines under construction, whilst we were building 19, apart from two experimental vessels of which nothing resulted. Of these 19 submarines, several were of new type, in pursuance of a policy introduced by the Admiralty in 1913-14 of widening the area of supply of these vessels. This policy had far-reaching and beneficial results on the subsequent output of this class of vessel, as it enabled us to increase our submarine flotillas more rapidly than would otherwise have been the case.

A change in previous naval practice was considered necessary at an early period, because vessels moving at anything but high speed, particularly in the case of a number of ships in company, ran very considerable risks in waters where we might expect enemy submarines to be operating, unless screened by a strong force of destroyers. This conclusion affected the movements and operations of the Battle Fleet, since the number of destroyers we possessed was quite inadequate to form a screen for a Battle Fleet and a Battle Cruiser Squadron which constantly kept the sea.

The number required, for such a screen to be effective, was at least 40 for the Battle Fleet alone as then constituted, and that number, 40, was all that we had stationed at the Northern Base. The fuel capacity of destroyers was only sufficient for them to remain at sea in company with a fleet for some three days and nights, whereas the Fleet itself could remain out for three or four times that period. Moreover, the destroyers could not be kept nearly so constantly at sea as the large ships owing to their requirements in the way of boiler-cleaning and the refit and adjustment of their more delicate machinery, and the necessity for giving not only the machinery, but the personnel, periods of rest. The heavy ships, then, had two alternatives, either to remain at sea without a destroyer screen or to return to harbour with the destroyers. In the early days the first alternative was adopted, the risk being accepted, but minimised as far as possible, by keeping the ships in the northern part of the North Sea.

A further danger soon made itself apparent. It became evident at an early period, as many naval officers had expected, in view of German language at the Hague Conference, that our enemy intended to throw overboard the doctrines of international law when he could gain any advantage by doing so. He accordingly proceeded at once to lay mines in positions where he thought they would be advantageous to his operations, in utter disregard of the safety, not only of British, but also of neutral merchant ships. It was, therefore, thought very probable that he would elaborate this practice by laying mines in the North Sea in positions where he anticipated they might prove effective against the Grand Fleet, and that he would do this without issuing any warning to neutral countries.

Consequently, if the main Battle Fleet were kept moving continuously in the central and southern waters of the North Sea, in which waters the enemy could easily lay mines with little danger of his operations being witnessed (as he could carry them out under cover of darkness), it was evident that considerable risks might be incurred without our being aware of the fact. The policy of attrition of our Battle Fleet might thus be carried out with such success as to produce equality, or even inferiority, on the part of the British Fleet as compared with the German, in a comparatively short space of time. The only safeguard against such action which we could take would be to keep minesweepers constantly working ahead of the Battle Fleet. But the number of minesweepers that we possessed was wholly inadequate for such a task; and even if this had not been so, to carry out such an operation would have necessitated the speed of the Battle Fleet being reduced to some 10 knots, the maximum sweeping speed of minesweepers, and it would have been forced also to steer a steady course without zigzagging, conditions rendering the battleships exceedingly vulnerable to submarine attack.

The first effect, therefore, of the submarine menace, combined with possible German action in regard to minelaying, was to cause the Battle Fleet to confine its movements under ordinary conditions to the more northern waters of the North Sea, where the risk might be taken of cruising without the presence of a screen of destroyers, and where it was improbable, owing to the depth of water and the distance from enemy bases, that the Germans would be able to lay mines without discovery.

The fact that this course of action would be forced upon us as the submarine and destroyer menace grew had often been present in my mind in pre-War days, when I had expressed the view that the beginning of a naval war would be a conflict between the small craft, whilst the larger and more valuable vessels were held aloof. I have no doubt that this opinion was very generally held by officers of experience.

The northward movement of the Battle Fleet was combined with the establishment of certain cruiser patrol areas in the North Sea. These areas, which were purposely made large, were watched on a regular, organised plan by our Cruiser Squadrons, moving at fairly high speed in such a manner as to reduce the submarine risk to the cruisers to a minimum, whilst at the same time they kept as effective a watch as possible, first, to intercept German war vessels that might be covering a raid on our coasts or transports, or trying to reach the open sea to operate against trade, and, secondly, to ensure that all merchant ships entering or leaving the North Sea should be closely examined in order to enforce the blockade.

This patrol policy was associated with periodical sweeps of cruisers, supported by the Battle Fleet, down into the southern waters of the North Sea, the object being to catch the enemy's fleet at sea, if possible, and in any case, owing to our movements being probably reported to the Germans by neutral merchant ships, to make them feel that they could never move a force to sea without the possibility of encountering our Fleet engaged in one of these southern sweeps, which we carried out at irregular intervals. A typical sweep is illustrated in accompanying plans. On these occasions the Battle Fleet was kept strictly concentrated during the southern movement, and was screened as far as possible by destroyers against submarine attack; and at times minesweepers were directed to work ahead of the Battle Fleet. When this was not possible, owing to the small number of minesweepers available or the state of the weather, some of the older battleships of the 6th Battle Squadron, if they were in company, were stationed ahead of the main Battle Fleet in order that, should a minefield be encountered, these older ships would be the first to strike the mines, thus giving sufficient warning to enable me to maneuver the more valuable ships clear of the field.

This general policy was continued until the attack on the Theseus and loss of the Hawke, belonging to the 10th Cruiser Squadron, by submarine attack on October 15th, 1914, showed that even under the dispositions then adopted, our larger cruisers were being risked to too great an extent when working without destroyers in the central part of the North Sea.

The next move, therefore, was the withdrawal of the cruiser patrols to a safer position farther to the northward and eastward of the Shetland Islands, this being combined with a watch by the smaller craft on the Fair Island Channel, and on the Pentland Firth approaches to the North Sea. Under these conditions the Battle Fleet was often kept either in a position westward of the Orkneys, where it was in support of the cruisers and at the same time formed a second blockade line, or it cruised to the north and east of the Shetland Islands, the cruiser patrols working farther south.

In all the dispositions which were made for a watch on the northern entrance to the North Sea, the principle kept in mind was the necessity for such an organisation of the patrols as to have, in so far as numbers permitted, two lines, or two areas, watched. The two areas were at such a distance apart that vessels moving in or out of the North Sea were forced, so far as all human foresight could provide, to pass through the waters occupied by one of the two groups of ships during daylight hours; the distances apart were regulated according to the length of the night at the different seasons of the year.

As the Battle Fleet worked farther to the northward and westward, it became possible to make use of the heavy ships to assist in blockade work without running undue risks from submarines, and the blockade increased correspondingly in effectiveness. As time went on, however, the provision by the Admiralty of a larger number of armed merchant cruisers enabled us to establish an effective blockade line by the use of these vessels alone, backed up by Cruiser Squadrons when such were available.

The withdrawal of the Battle Fleet to more northern and western waters first took effect when the Fleet Base was shifted temporarily from Scapa to Lough Swilly. When this occurred, it did not affect the policy of frequent cruiser sweeps into the southern portion of the North Sea, supported by the Battle Fleet, which were still continued.

The dispositions that have been described took account naturally of two other very important factors.

The first was the transport of our Expeditionary Force to France. It was highly probable that the enemy would endeavour to interfere with this movement, and in the early days of the War it would not have been a difficult matter for him to cause us some loss. His failure to make at least some attempt in this direction showed a lack of enterprise which surprised me, as I think it surprised most naval officers.

The conditions for him were distinctly favourable. Our main Fleet was based, as he must have been aware, far away to the northward, and if he had timed an attack on the cross-Channel traffic for a period during which he reckoned that the Grand Fleet, or at least the destroyers, were returning to the base to fuel, he would have stood a good chance of making the attack and returning to his base before that Fleet could intervene. Consequently, he would only have had to deal with the comparatively light forces based in southern waters. On the other hand, if our Fleet arrived on the scene without destroyers, the Germans would have possessed no mean advantage.

The enemy was preceded with a large number of modern destroyers, and some of them would have been well expended over a Channel dash, which would in all probability have met with some success. During the transport of the Expeditionary Force the heavy ships of the Grand Fleet kept the sea as far as possible in order to cover the movement, but the destroyers were constantly returning to the base to fuel.

The second factor which had considerable influence on Fleet dispositions was the possibility of an attempt at a raid or invasion by the enemy. Such a move was not very likely in the earliest days of the War, when the nights were comparatively short, and the Expeditionary Force had not left the country. It is also probable that the enemy had few troops to spare for the purpose. But the chances became greater as we denuded the country of men, and the conditions in other respects became more favourable. In October and November 1914, I held and expressed the opinion that, if raids were attempted, landings would probably be effected in the rivers on the East Coast, the entrances to which were either unprotected or inadequately protected. A beach landing on our East Coast can only be carried out in fine weather, and the chances of encountering favourable conditions on arrival off the coast are not great, and I always doubted the attempt being made. In our rivers the opportunities are greater, and are not so dependent on fine weather, and I suggested to the Admiralty that a simple preventive in this case was to place merchant ships in position ready to be sunk across the channels (which are narrow and shallow), the ships being fitted with explosive charges below ready to blow out the bottoms in case of necessity. I mentioned the names of certain retired naval officers who, I felt certain, would make all the necessary preparations in a very few days. I believe that my proposals were carried out.

The danger of raids, however, and the consequent responsibility thrown upon the Admiralty for their prevention, during a period when we had very little military force in the country, led to a division of the Fleet by Admiralty direction, which, however necessary, had certain disadvantages from a strategic point of view.

The 3rd Battle Squadron, consisting of eight ships of the "King Edward VII" class, and the 3rd Cruiser Squadron of four ships of the "County" class, were ordered to be based on Rosyth, together with destroyers for screening purposes. The eventuality that had then to be faced was that of the remainder of the Grand Fleet having to engage the High Sea Fleet, since concentration with the 3rd Battle Squadron could probably not be effected without the risk of losing the opportunity of engaging.

At this time the battle cruisers Princess Royal, Invincible, and Inflexible were in the Atlantic operating against Von Spee's squadron; and the Australia, Indomitable had not joined the Grand Fleet. The Tiger was not yet ready, so that at times our battle cruiser force consisted of only three ships, the Lion, Queen Mary, and New Zealand.

Throughout the War the responsibility of the Fleet for the prevention of raids or invasion was a factor which had a considerable influence on naval strategy.

If the Fleet, with destroyers, carried out a sweep in the North Sea, or if it was at sea for a cruise having exercises for its main object, there was bound to be present in the mind of the Commander-in-Chief the chance that he might be required suddenly to move south to engage the High Sea Fleet which had put to sea to cover a landing. If his destroyers were short of fuel at such a moment very serious consequences might ensue, and therefore all cruiser sweeps or other operations had to be curtailed to prevent such a situation arising.

One other factor exercised a cramping effect upon our naval strategy throughout the War, namely, the bombardment of our undefended towns on the East Coast. Such bombardments were of no immediate military value to the enemy, but, in spite of the fact that the majority of the Press, and the public, realised that the Navy should not be led into false strategy because of these bombardments, it was difficult for the Fleet to ignore them, and I have no doubt that the Germans relied upon this fact.

Whilst the Fleet was based at Scapa Flow, it was quite impossible to ensure that the enemy would be brought to action after such an operation, since to attain this end it would have been necessary for the Fleet, or a portion of it, to be constantly cruising in the southern portion of the North Sea. This was not practicable, even had it been desirable, because of the impossibility of keeping destroyers with the heavier ships, and in any case it was false strategy to divide the Battle Fleet, as such a course might well have resulted in disaster.

The usual course adopted was to base the Battle Cruiser Fleet on Rosyth, and for that Fleet to cruise from that neighbourhood. The speed of the battle cruisers enabled them to get away from a decidedly superior enemy force of battleships if encountered, but there was always some risk in this case of a ship being disabled; the flag officer in command would then have been faced with the unpleasant alternative of abandoning her or of risking his whole force to cover her retreat.

Had we been able to keep an effective look-out off the enemy ports, so as to obtain warning of their ships leaving, the difficulty would not have been so great, but our submarines in those days (the only class of vessel which could be used for such a purpose) were not fitted with wireless installations with which they could signal from the required positions, or indeed from positions anywhere near the enemy's coast, and, in any case, it must be borne in mind that at night the exit of enemy vessels unobserved, even under the conditions of a close submarine look-out, is a comparatively easy matter.

At this stage it is convenient to remark upon the condition of British naval bases. As is well known, the Grand Fleet was moved to Scapa Flow during the latter days of July, 1914, and the defenceless condition of the Base, both against destroyer attack and submarine attack, was brought very strongly into prominence by the presence of so valuable a Fleet at this Base.

The anchorage known as Scapa Flow has three main entrances navigable by all ships, the Hoxa, the Switha, and Hoy Channels, and, in addition, has some more narrow, shallow and tortuous entrances on the eastern side, the main one being Holm Sound. The question of providing gun defences for this Base, which the Admiralty had decided a year or two before the War was to be the main Fleet Base, had been discussed on more than one occasion, after examination by a committee of officers on the spot; but since finance governs defence, and the Admiralty from year to year had insufficient money for even more urgent needs, no action had been taken. Scapa Flow lies some 450 miles from the German naval bases, and was, therefore, open to an attack by enemy's destroyer flotillas as well as, of course, by submarines. Its main, indeed its only, safety against such attacks by submarines lay in the navigational difficulties attendant upon entry into the harbour, combined, as regards destroyer attacks, with the possibility of an enemy's force being intercepted on its outward or homeward passage, or of its being successfully engaged in the vicinity of the base. The sailing directions laid great stress upon the difficulties of navigations in the approaches to this Base, due to the very strong and varying currents, but the Germans were well acquainted with the Orkney and Shetland Islands. They had indeed made it a practice to send ships to visit these islands fairly frequently before the War, and they were, therefore, as well able to judge of the difficulties of entry into Scapa Flow as we were; and seeing that we used it as a main Fleet Base, they could deduce the fact, if they did not know it already, that the difficulties of entry were not insuperable.

Sir George Callaghan, under these conditions, on the arrival of the Fleet at Scapa Flow at the end of July, took immediate steps, with the resources at his disposal in the Fleet, to improvise defences for the Base against destroyer attack. All that he could do was to land some 12-pounder guns from the ships of the Fleet and mount them at the entrances. No searchlights could, however, be provided, so that the guns were not of much value at night. Arrangements were also made for placing light cruisers and destroyers at the various entrances to assist these defences. The further step, of course, was taken when the Fleet was present at the Base of placing patrols to the eastward of the Pentland Firth. It was not felt in the Fleet, however, that these measures gave much security even against destroyer attack on a dark night, and it gave no security whatever against submarine attack. Nothing but obstructions of some kind could give that security. The matter was frequently discussed. Although many brains had been at work, no satisfactory anti-submarine obstruction had been devised. Under the urgent pressure of war the solution was found. The conclusion generally held by experienced submarine officers was that, whilst the least important entrances, such as the Hoy, the Switha and the Holm Sound Channels, would be extremely difficult for the passage of a submarine, entry by the Hoxa Sound Channel was quite practicable by a determined submarine officer. So much for the Base at Scapa Flow.

At Cromarty the conditions were somewhat better. The only entrance to this Base is comparatively narrow, and was defended against the entry of destroyers and larger vessels by guns, which had been mounted by the Admiralty before war broke out. There was, however, no boom protection against the entry of destroyers, and the conditions in regard to submarine attack were the same as at Scapa Flow, there being no obstructions.

At Rosyth the same conditions prevailed as at Cromarty, namely, the harbour was defended by guns only against attack by destroyers. In this case, the guns were manned by the military, and not by marines, as at Cromarty; again the harbour was quite open to submarine attack.

Consequently, the anxiety of officers in command of Fleets or Squadrons at anchor in any of the Bases used by the Grand Fleet was immense. For my part, I was always far more concerned for the safety of the Fleet when it was at anchor in Scapa Flow during the exceedingly brief periods which were spent there for coaling in the early days of the War, than I was when the Fleet was at sea, and this anxiety was reflected in the very short time that the Fleet was kept in harbour. It was also the cause of my taking the Fleet to sea very hurriedly on more than one occasion owing to the reported presence of a submarine in the anchorage, and considerable risks were accepted in getting the Fleet to sea in very thick weather at night on at least one of these occasions.

I have often wondered why the Germans did not make greater efforts to reduce our strength in capital ships by destroyer or submarine attacks on our bases in those early days. They possessed, in comparison with the uses for which they were required, almost a superfluity of destroyers, certainly a superfluity as compared with ourselves, and they could not have put them to a better use than in an attack on Scapa Flow during the early months of the 1914-1915 winter.

In August, 1914, Germany had 96 destroyers in home waters fit for such an operation, all with a speed of, or exceeding, 30 knots, this number being in addition to a total of 48 more destroyers, rather smaller and with speeds varying between 26 and 30 knots, which were quite fit for work in the Baltic or in the vicinity of German bases in the North Sea.

This country had in home waters at the same period only 76 destroyers that could be compared with the German vessels in view of modern requirements, and 33 of these had a speed of only 27 knots. Of the 76 destroyers, 40 were allotted to the Grand Fleet proper, the remaining 36 being based on Harwich. We had in addition 11 large and fast destroyers of the "Tribal" class which, owing to their small fuel capacity, were only of use in southern waters and were appropriated to Dover. And we possessed 25 destroyers of the "River" class, of a nominal speed of only 25 knots, as well as the old 30-knot destroyer; the latter class was only fit for patrol work in the vicinity of the coast.

It may be said that similar reflections to those I have mentioned might be made by the Germans as regards our own movements, and that they were surprised that we did not attack their Fleet at anchor. The answer is obvious to those aware of the conditions. We were very short of destroyers for fleet work, and we were well aware of the thoroughness of the defences of the German naval bases. We knew that they not only possessed the most powerful and ample artillery defences, but we knew also that the Germans had a very efficient mining service, and we were justified in assuming that they had protected their naval bases by extensive minefields. We, on the other hand, were entirely unprovided with this particular form of defence.

In view of the known quality of German artillery and mine defences and the thorough nature of their organisation, my own view was that they also possessed, in all probability, anti-submarine defences. For these reasons, together with the important fact that the German rivers are so shallow that our submarines could not enter them in a submerged condition, it appeared to me that an attack on their ships in harbour would meet with no success, and that we could not afford to expend any of our exceedingly limited number of destroyers, or submarines, in making an attack which would, in all human probability, be foredoomed to failure. Later knowledge of the German defences proved the correctness of this view. I can only imagine that the Germans credited us, also, with possessing harbour defences and obstructions which in our case were non-existent, although we did our best in the Fleet to give the impression that we had obstructed the entrances, for, pending the provision of proper obstructions, we improvised various contrivances. It may have seemed impossible to the German mind that we should place our Fleet, on which the Empire depended for its very existence, in a position where it was open to submarine or destroyer attack.

This view, however, did not relieve the minds of those responsible for the safety of our Fleet from the gravest anxiety whenever the more valuable ships were in the undefended harbours.

A comparison of numbers between the Grand Fleet and the High Sea Fleet in the early part of the War shows the following figures. Only ships that had completed their training and were fit to fight in the line are included:

The above list gives the vessels nominally available.

In comparisons of the strength at Germany's selected and our average moment, the following facts should be remembered, and were necessarily taken into account by me at the time:

(a) We usually had at least two battleships, one or two light cruisers, six destroyers, one or two cruisers, and perhaps one battle cruiser under refit, in addition to any other vessels that might be temporarily disabled.

(b) Germany would see to it that none of her ships was refitting when planning an operation, and she could reinforce her Fleet by several light cruisers and two or more flotillas of destroyers from the Baltic.

(c) The pre-Dreadnoughts were not a very important factor on either side owing to inferiority of speed, and, in the case of our ships, the comparatively short range of their guns, due to the small amount of elevation of which their mountings admitted.

(d) The German Zeppelins, as their numbers increased, were of great assistance to the enemy for scouting, each one being, in favourable weather, equal to at least two light cruisers for such a purpose.

(e) Account is not taken in the British figures of the Harwich force, as this force could not be counted upon to effect concentration with the remainder of the Grand Fleet at the German selected moment.

(f) The British cruisers, not being very modern, lacked the speed necessary for efficiency as scouts. They were very slightly faster than the battleships of the "Dreadnought" type, and, owing to their lack of speed, they were awkwardly placed if they came within range of an enemy Battle Squadron or Battle Cruiser Squadron. On the other hand, they were very superior in fighting qualities to the German light cruisers.

It will be seen from the above statements that the enemy had by far his best opportunity from the naval point of view in the early months of the War, as he was then much nearer equality of strength with the Grand Fleet than at any later period. A carefully laid trap, which included minefields and submarines, with the High Sea Fleet as a bait, might have been very effective at any period of the War in inflicting considerable losses on us. The Germans had their best opportunities between November, 1914, and February, 1915. After April, 1915, the situation got steadily worse for the enemy.

The lesson of vital importance to be drawn from this review of relative naval strength, is that if this country in the future decides to rely for safety against raids or invasion on the Fleet alone, it is essential that we should possess a considerably greater margin of superiority over a possible enemy in all classes of vessels than we did in August, 1914.

The dreadnought battleship HMS *Iron Duke*

Image: November 1913.

3 - The Grand Fleet and Its Bases

The Grand Fleet may be said to have come into being only at the outbreak of the War when it was so christened. As with the name, so with the organisation.

The great majority of the really effective ships in the Grand Fleet were the outcome of the policy initiated by Admiral of the Fleet Lord Fisher of Silverstone when he took up the appointment of First Sea Lord in 1904 in the Administration of the Earl of Selborne. One of Lord Fisher's first acts—and he carried through a number of other changes which reacted favourably on the efficiency of the Fleet for war — was the introduction of the "all-big-gun" type of battleship, of which the Dreadnought, laid down at Portsmouth on October 2nd, 1905, was the earliest example. She was closely followed by the three "all-big-gun" battlecruisers of the "Invincible" class, which were of the same programme — 1905-6. Much criticism was levelled at the Dreadnought, but even more at the principle embodied in the battle-cruisers — ships with the speed of cruisers, but the same calibre armament as battleships. The War has fully justified Lord Fisher's conception.

Our superiority in capital ships at the outbreak of war was due to the efforts of the Boards presided over by Lord Selborne and his successors from 1904 onwards, and Lord Fisher held the post of First Sea Lord for five and a half years of that period. At the beginning of 1909, during Mr. McKenna's tenure of office as First Lord, great efforts were necessary to ensure the maintenance of a sufficient standard of superiority in capital ships over Germany, and to make good our deficiencies in destroyers. The nation has good reason for the most profound gratitude to Mr. McKenna for the very strong attitude he assumed at this highly critical period. Reference to the table on page 31 will show the position that would have arisen if the four additional "Dreadnoughts" had not been included in the 1909-10 building programme. In the later Administration, presided over by Mr. Churchill, continued efforts were necessary, and were made, and steps were also taken with a view to meeting the crying need for modern light cruisers; Lord Beresford had for some years been pointing out how essential it was to add largely to our programmes of light cruisers and destroyers.

So much for construction in pre-War days when the Germans were carrying out their Navy Acts, one following the other in rapid succession.

It is also of interest to note the part which Lord Fisher took in building up the Fleet organisation that existed in 1914. He introduced the system of manning the older ships, not in the first line, with nucleus crews composed of the principal officers and ratings. These ships were thus rendered capable of being put, in a very short time, into a condition in which they were fit to fight. This system superseded the old arrangement, by which ships not in full commission were not manned at all. Although it naturally led to a reduction in the total number of fully-manned ships, a disadvantage which was minimised by reducing squadrons abroad, it is probably accepted now that in the circumstances existing at the time the nucleus crew system is far preferable; it raised the general standard of the whole Navy in British waters and facilitated the use of the Royal Fleet and Naval Reserves on the outbreak of war.

I. The Development of the Grand Fleet

In the organisation existing before the War, the Home Fleets comprised the First, Second and Third Fleets—in fact, practically all ships in home waters which it was intended to mobilise on the outbreak of war. The war organisation, as carried out, divided the Home Fleets into two parts.

The First, the Grand Fleet, included the First Fleet, comprising the latest-built ships; the force stationed at Harwich; four ships of the 6th Battle Squadron; the 6th and 10th Cruiser Squadrons from the Second and Third Fleets respectively; and the minelaying Squadron from the Second Fleet.

The Second, or Channel Fleet, included the older battleships, the 5th, 6th, 7th, and 8th Battle Squadrons, the 5th and 7th Cruiser Squadrons, and a sweeping flotilla with torpedo boats. This force was commanded by Vice-Admiral Sir Cecil Burney until the end of 1914, when he joined the Grand Fleet. It was independent of the Grand Fleet.

Of the ships of the Channel Fleet, the 5th and 6th Battle Squadrons and the 5th Cruiser Squadron were manned before mobilisation with nucleus crews, and were consequently partly trained; these ships assembled at Portland. The ships of the 7th and 8th Battle Squadrons and 7th Cruiser Squadron were not manned until mobilisation, and the crews consequently required training. This training was carried out near Plymouth, and the battleships joined Sir Cecil Burney's command on September 3rd, 1914.

The ships of the 7th Cruiser Squadron were employed as a look-out force in the Straits of Dover during the time that the Channel Battle Fleet was patrolling to guard the passage of the Expeditionary Force. They were subsequently ordered by the Admiralty to another service, and three of them, the Hogue, Cressy and Aboukir, were sunk whilst patrolling the Broad Fourteens off the Dutch coast.

These, then, were the conditions when War opened. It was only natural that war experience should show very quickly the many directions in which we had to recast, or elaborate, our pre-War ideas, or to introduce new arrangements.

Peace manoeuvres, however useful, can never be a substitute for war experience. They are many factors which render peace manoeuvres unreal. In the first place, the available ships have to be divided so as to form the opposing fleet, "an enemy"; secondly, a matter of far greater moment, the manoeuvres occupy much too short a period, and many of the difficulties affecting both materiel and personnel are not experienced; thirdly, the conditions of war cannot be reproduced without serious inconvenience, and even danger, to merchant ships; finally, in our own manoeuvres there was a tendency in the rules to give the torpedo less than its proper value as a fighting weapon.

But, more than all, it was the conditions under which war broke out that made it necessary for us in the Grand Fleet to build up what was almost a new organisation.

(a) The submarine had just become a most formidable weapon; its development during the War was extraordinarily rapid.

(b) The airship as a scout was in its infancy at the start, but it also developed with great rapidity, as did the heavier-than-air machines.

(c) The mine, neglected by us, had been highly developed by the enemy, both defensively and offensively.

(d) The effective range both of the gun and of the torpedo was quickly shown to be much greater than had been considered possible before the War. (In pre-War days our Battle Practice had been carried out at a maximum range of about 9,500 yards, and only on one occasion, when the Colossus fired at a target at 14,000 yards off Portland in 1912, had this range been exceeded.)

(e) Wireless telegraphy developed with great rapidity, and was put to many uses not dreamt of in pre-War days.

On the other hand, we were very fortunate in having the Fleet concentrated at the outbreak of war. People had often pictured war with Germany coming as a bolt from the blue, and even naval officers feared that when the occasion did arise, it would be found, as had previously been the case, that fear of precipitating a conflict might lead the Government to delay concentration with the result that our squadrons would be separated when war was actually declared. Fortunately, the Admiralty in the last days of July, 1914, placed us at once in a strong strategic position. For this action the nation should be grateful to the First Lord and First Sea Lord.

It was curious that, in spite of all the lessons of history, there was general expectation that a great Fleet action would at once be fought. No doubt this arose, partly, from the boastings of German naval officers in pre-War days, and partly from a knowledge of the great sacrifices the enemy would incur unless he could dispute effectively our command of the sea. Most people found it difficult to imagine that the High Sea Fleet (built at vast expense, and rightly considered by the enemy to be an efficient weapon of war) would adopt from the outset a purely passive role, with the inevitable result that German trade would be swept from the seas. But there were two factors tending to make the High Command adopt this course. First, there was the fear that action with the Grand Fleet would so weaken the High Sea Fleet as to cause the command of the Baltic to pass into Allied hands, with a consequent landing of Russian troops on German soil as the result. This fear had been present in the German mind ever since the days of Frederick the Great when Russia threatened Berlin during the Seven Years' War.

The second point, no doubt, was that the German High Command realised that, if Germany adopted a defensive role with her Fleet, it created, by far, the most difficult situation for us. Repugnant as this might be to high-spirited German naval officers, it was unquestionably the worst policy for us, for, whilst the German High Sea Fleet remained "in being" as a fighting force, we could not afford to undertake operations tending to weaken our Grand Fleet, particularly in the earlier period of the War when our margin of superiority at Germany's "selected moment" was not great. The main disadvantage to the Germans, apart from their loss of trade, lay in the inevitable gradual weakening of the morale of the personnel of the Navy, and it is highly probable that this loss of morale was in the end responsible for the series of mutinies which broke out in the High Sea Fleet during 1917 and 1918, culminating in the final catastrophe in November, 1918. In my view, the passive role was carried much too far.

II. The Staff Organization

To pass to the development of the organisation.
Almost the first question was that of Staff and Staff work. In the days before the War, the Staff of the Commander-in-Chief of the Home Fleets consisted of the following officers:

(a) A Personal Staff, comprising a Flag-Commander, Flag-Lieutenant, and Secretary. The Flag-Captain was also, in a sense, on the Personal Staff.

(b) A General Staffs, comprising a Captain of the Fleet with his Secretary, a Wireless officer, a Signal officer, and the clerical staff of the Secretary.

In addition, the organisation provided for the appointment of two War Staff officers, on mobilisation for war.

This was the Staff which, together with an additional Signal officer, I found in the Iron Duke, on assuming command of the Grand Fleet.

It had always been my intention, on relieving Sir George Callaghan in December, 1914 (as was originally arranged before the War broke out, as I have explained), to add to the above, a Captain, for the operational side of the Staff, leaving the Flag-Captain responsible only for the Command of the Fleet-flagship, this being, in my opinion, sufficient work and responsibility to occupy his whole time; and I had prepared an organisation of the Staff of the Fleet-flagship in accordance with which the work should be divided into two distinct branches, the operations and the materiel side, each with a secretariat. I had communicated my views to the officers selected for the Staff. This, in my judgment, was the correct line for any Naval Staff organisation, and it was later introduced by me into the Admiralty Naval Staff.

When informed, just prior to the declaration of War, that I might be required to take over the command of the Fleet, I decided to ask, as the first step, for the services of Rear-Admiral Charles E. Madden as Chief of the Staff.

I had brought with me from London on my own Staff, as Second in Command of the Grand Fleet, a Captain (Captain Bentinck), with the title of Captain on the Staff, a Secretary with assistants, a Flag-Lieutenant, a Signal officer, a Wireless officer, a War Staff officer, and a Signal Boatswain. These, with the exception of Captain Bentinck (who joined Vice-Admiral Sir George Warrender's Staff), I took to the Iron Duke, and my Staff then comprised:

A Rear-Admiral as Chief of the Staff.
A Commodore as Captain of the Fleet.
Two Secretaries, with the necessary clerical staff.
A Flag-Lieutenant.
Three Signal officers.
Three Wireless officers (very soon reduced to two).
War Staff officers.
Two Signal Boatswains.
A Fleet Coaling officer also joined the Staff.

The main difficulty in providing a Flag officer afloat with a suitable staff is that of accommodation, and this difficulty was somewhat serious when I doubled the staff on board the Iron Duke. However, it was successfully overcome.

The Staff was organised into two branches, Operations and Materiel, the former directly under the Chief of the Staff, the latter immediately under the Captain of the Fleet.

On proceeding to sea, however, the work of the Captain of the Fleet became, of necessity, very largely reduced, and he joined the operational side, arrangements being made by which either he or the Chief of the Staff was always on the bridge in my absence, as we soon found under the new conditions, consequent on the advent of the submarine as an important factor in naval warfare, that it was essential that an officer should be constantly on the bridge who could take immediate action in moving the Fleet, or any portion of it, as might be required.

Even so, the presence of the Commander-in-Chief was so frequently required, at a moment's notice, owing to the swiftness with which a modern fleet moves, that I never left my sea cabin, which was under the bridge, to go to the after part of the ship when the Fleet was at sea.

The duties of my Staff afloat were separated, as already stated, under two headings. This division, as is clear from the above remarks, affected their duties in harbour more than when at sea. In the latter case the two branches combined, and the whole staff became "operational."

The Staff work under these conditions was carried out in the war-room, situated under protection, below the conning tower. Here the movements of our own ships were recorded, as well as those of the enemy until we were nearing contact. All intelligence was sent from the bridge to this centre by the Signal officers, and the situation at any moment could be seen by a glance at the charts kept by the War Staff officer on duty.

When we were nearing enemy vessels or enemy waters, the work was shifted from the war-room to the Admiral's shelter on the bridge, so that the situation could be seen by me more readily; and finally, when, as on May 31st and August 19th, 1916, the two fleets were nearing touch with one another, the "plot" of the movements as reported was continually under my observation.

At ordinary times, in harbour, the Staff officers engaged on the operational side were following the movements of such enemy vessels (chiefly, of course, submarines) as were known to be at sea, as well as those of our own vessels. (In the latter case frequent orders to ships were necessary to ensure that they did not meet each other at night when risk of collision would be incurred owing to ships not carrying lights, or in thick weather.) They put into execution the orders given by myself or the Chief of the Staff, and were engaged in elaborating plans of future movements and drawing up the necessary orders for such movements as I had in contemplation. They were also engaged in arranging all gunnery, torpedo and other practices and exercises, and in the constant work of the production, revision and issue of orders for the organisation and tactical working of the Fleet.

On the materiel side, the Staff work comprised that of storing, provisioning and fuelling the Fleet, all questions of instruction, training, personnel, discipline, mails, refits and repairs, etc.

In action each member of the Staff had his own particular duty allotted to him. The secretaries took notes and recorded proceedings; certain officers had as their sole duty that of watching and reporting to me every movement of enemy vessels; one officer was detailed to attend solely to torpedo attacks made by the enemy, keeping me informed of their progress and of their possibilities; another dealt with all questions relating to concentration or distribution of fire, bringing to my notice any signals required to give effect to our preconceived arrangements; each signal officer had his own special duty, one being responsible that all signals for tactical movements made visually were also made by "short distance" wireless telegraphy. One wireless officer worked in the main office and one in the auxiliary office. The Staff was so organised as to leave the Commander-in-Chief free to take a comprehensive survey of the whole position, whilst ensuring that nothing that should be done was left undone. It must, however, be realised that the rapidity of movement of fleets is so great that, at critical moments, the Commander-in-Chief of a fleet, or the Flag Officer Commanding a Squadron, must of necessity make instant decisions; there is no time for consultation or for advice.

III. Preparation of Cruising Orders

One of the earliest steps taken in organising the Grand Fleet after the declaration of War was to lay down definitely the various cruising orders for the Battle Fleet and its "lookout" screen of battlecruisers, cruisers and light cruisers. There had been much discussion for some years before the War as to the best disposition of cruisers ahead of a Battle Fleet. None of the arrangements that had been under discussion was adopted as a whole, but war experience led to a series of diagrams being drawn up giving the cruising stations of all the various classes of cruisers and other light craft under the different conditions that might exist.

These included diagrams showing the cruiser disposition with the fleet moving towards enemy waters, under conditions of ordinary visibility, by day, or in low visibility by day, both with the Battle Cruiser Fleet in company and without it; a similar diagram when moving away from enemy water by day (this being to meet the possible case of an attempted attack by destroyers as the fleet steered away from enemy waters); diagrams were got out for steering towards or away from enemy waters at night; and, finally, diagrams were prepared, both for day and night, for the dispositions of the cruisers and other light forces after an action.

Several different cruising diagrams for the Battle Fleet itself, both by day and at night, were similarly drawn up. Some of these were specially designed to give such safety from submarine attack as was possible to the main body of the Fleet, in the not unlikely event of destroyers being absent, from bad weather, shortage of fuel, or other causes. The dispositions for use at night provided for the use of destroyer attack, and were designed to give safety from collision, due to squadrons inadvertently closing each other in the darkness, when showing no lights; this was a very possible event during the course of a long night when a very slight error in steering, or a slight difference in compasses, will rapidly bring two squadrons together that started the night five miles apart. It was necessary to keep squadrons separated, as a long line of ships greatly facilitated successful submarine attack, whilst a slight dispersal of squadrons gave greater freedom of movement in the case of destroyer attack. At the same time it was necessary to provide for concentrating the Fleet quickly at daylight.

The question of submarine screens was taken up at the commencement of war. This matter had naturally been considered before the War, but was in its earliest stages, and, although an efficient disposition of a screen of destroyers is a comparatively simple matter when there is no lack of destroyers, the case is different when a fleet is very short of the requisite number, as was our experience, and one destroyer had often to be disposed to endeavour to do the work of two.

Diagrams of submarine screens were, therefore, drawn up to meet the different conditions resulting from the presence of varying numbers of destroyers, or a decreased number of ships requiring to be screened, and also providing for the ships being in various formations. In November, 1916, the number of these diagrams was seventeen.

Early in the War the danger of successful submarine attack on warships at sea, whether in company or proceeding singly, had impressed on us the necessity of taking every precaution for safety, and the practice of the fleet steering zigzag courses was devised and generally adopted in accordance with my directions. In the case of a fleet or squadron, the usual practice was to carry out the alterations of course by turning the ships together; occasionally the turn was made "in succession," but this was exceptional. In small squadrons, the turns were occasionally made at fixed time intervals without signal.

Zigzagging had a very beneficial effect on the manner in which officers of watches kept station in a fleet, since there is no better practice than keeping station on a line of bearing, a far more difficult matter to the novice than keeping station astern of another ship. I attribute the excellent manner in which the ships were handled in 1915 and 1916 very largely to this early experience. Much theoretical investigation was instituted to determine the method of zigzagging, both in a fleet and in a single ship, which gave the greatest protection against submarine attack, and actual experiments took place with our own submarines with a view to forming correct conclusions; the flag officers of the fleet rendered me much assistance in this as in all other matters.

The experience of the Grand Fleet was utilised in the instructions subsequently issued to merchant ships, and the value of zigzagging in reducing the danger of submarine attack was clearly shown during the year 1917 by the comparative immunity of merchant ships that complied with the orders as compared with those that did not do so. Occasionally, of course, zigzagging brought a ship into danger, but this was exceptional as compared with the general immunity given.

When the convoying of merchant ships through the submarine zone was instituted in 1917, after I had returned to the Admiralty, the Grand Fleet experience was again of value in the preparation of instructions.

The supremely important question of how best to handle in action the large and increasing Fleet engaged my attention from the commencement. In drawing up the various instructions for the conduct of the Fleet, both when cruising and in action, I availed myself of the advice and assistance of the experienced flag officers commanding the various Squadrons. Much discussion took place on these matters, and many of the dispositions adopted formed the subject of actual experiment at sea before being incorporated in the orders.

The successful and rapid deployment of the Battle Fleet from its cruising formation was a matter of the greatest importance, and constant practice in carrying cut this manoeuvre under every varying condition was given to the Fleet when at sea. Various arrangements were introduced having as their object the simplification and shortening of the manoeuvre, with a view to bringing the heaviest possible fire to bear on the enemy's fleet as quickly as possible. Orders were drawn up to meet cases of deployment in thick weather, when the enemy might be sighted at short range, and immediate independent action by a divisional Flag Officer would be necessary.

In the early part of the War the rapid deployment of the Fleet for action was complicated by the presence of the 3rd Battle Squadron of pre-Dreadnoughts — the vessels of the "King Edward VII." class — as the speed of the ships of this squadron was some three knots less than that of the rest of the Battle Fleet. I endeavoured to solve this problem by practical experience.

Much depended on the tactics likely to be adopted by the enemy's Battle Fleet. The main difficulty lay in the fact that if the 3rd Battle Squadron was placed on one flank of the Battle Fleet when in cruising order and deployment towards that flank became necessary in conformity with an enemy movement, thus placing the slow 3rd Battle Squadron in the van, the fleet speed of the whole Battle Line was necessarily reduced to some 14 knots, in order to have the necessary reserve of speed in hand. If, on the other hand, the 3rd Battle Squadron was placed in the centre of the Fleet, the Fleet speed was again reduced to that attainable by this squadron. It was desirable to devise a cruising order for the Battle Fleet which would admit of the 3rd Battle Squadron being in the rear after deployment, in whichever direction deployment took place. There was still the objection, which had to be accepted, that a turn of 16 points forced upon us by the enemy would place this squadron in the van.

The cruising order eventually adopted placed the pre-Dreadnought Squadron in rear of the Dreadnought Squadrons, with a view to the slow squadron turning in the opposite direction to the remainder on deployment, and eventually taking station in rear of the Dreadnought Fleet. This involved accepting some delay in getting the 3rd Battle Squadron into effective action.

The question was not one of importance subsequent to April, 1915, from which date our superiority in battleships of the Dreadnought type was sufficient to give me confidence that the High Sea Fleet, engaged under suitable conditions, could be crushed in action without the aid of the 3rd Battle Squadron; but during the winter of 1914-15, when our superiority in Dreadnoughts was frequently very slight, and the enemy possessed two pre-Dreadnought Battle Squadrons, our 3rd Battle Squadron was a necessary addition to the Grand Fleet.

The Battle Orders indicated the position to be occupied by our battlecruisers, cruisers, light cruisers and destroyers on deployment, as well as that of the fast 5th Battle Squadron, consisting of ships of the "Queen Elizabeth" class, when that squadron joined the Fleet. The first Battle Orders drawn up and issued shortly after war commenced were modelled on a Battle memorandum which I had prepared when in command, first, of the Atlantic Fleet, and, later, of the 2nd Battle Squadron. But the changing situation soon made alterations and additions necessary, and the Orders were under constant revision.

The tactics to be pursued by the different units of the Fleet in action under all conceivable conditions were provided for as far as possible.

Stress was laid from the beginning on the fact that the Commander-in-Chief of a large fleet could not after deployment control the movements of all the squadrons comprising that fleet under the conditions of modern action when funnel and cordite smoke, and the great length of the line, would hamper his knowledge of events, and increase the difficulty of communication. The necessity for wide decentralisation of command, after the deployment of the fleet for action, was emphasised.

As the Fleet grew in size, increasing stress was laid on this point. Flag officers commanding squadrons were, of course, kept fully acquainted with the general ideas under which the Fleet would act, so that they might be able to interpret my wishes when acting independently. Stress was laid on the necessity for keeping a close watch on the movements of the Commander-in-Chief, so that squadrons could conform to his movements. The general lines on which I intended to engage were defined. These included the range at which it was intended to open the engagement, the range below which it was not intended to close under ordinary conditions, on account of the risks to be apprehended from torpedo fire, and the exceptions to this rule which might become necessary. Emphasis was laid on the supreme necessity for a free use of our own torpedoes when opportunity occurred.

After the experience of the engagement on January 24th, 1915, between the battlecruisers, and especially as our superiority increased and the High Sea Fleet gave no sign of a desire to engage, the conviction became stronger that in any action between the two fleets, the enemy would fight a retiring battle. This is the most difficult form of tactics to counter in these days of submarines, mines and torpedoes since a retiring fleet is in a position of great tactical advantage in the employment of these weapons. The Tactical Board was in constant use for a consideration of this problem, both by myself and the other flag officers.

In the earliest stages of the War, when the German submarine strength was not great, one of the main problems to be considered in regard to a fleet action was the employment of our destroyers and light cruisers to attack the enemy's Battle Fleet with torpedoes and to counter his similar attacks, which, owing to his great superiority in destroyers, was a matter of supreme importance. The knowledge, too, that his light cruisers and destroyers, as well possibly as some of his heavier ships, were fitted for minelaying (which was not the case with us) made it necessary to take into account the probability that he would use this form of attack at the commencement of a general action, or during the stages leading up to it. Later, when his submarines increased in number, the method of countering the use of such vessels by the enemy, in the preliminary stages of a fleet action, had also to be considered, particularly as it was not until 1916 that the Grand Fleet was provided with any submarines of this type, and not until 1917 that submarines which could maintain the Fleet-speed at sea became part of the organisation.

The comparative immunity of the van from torpedo attack by the enemy, if the fleets were approximately abeam of one another, and the risks run by the centre and rear were pointed out, as were the different conditions produced in the case of a retiring enemy, or one which had a position of torpedo advantage.

The influence of the torpedo on tactics became greater as the War progressed, owing to the advance made in the technique of these weapons. Before the opening of hostilities, for instance, torpedoes had a maximum range of about 10,000 yards. We made many improvements in our torpedoes as the War progressed, including a great increase in range, and we had every reason to believe that the Germans were making similar progress, and that the range of their torpedoes was as much in excess of the pre-War range as was that of our own weapons.

The threat of successful torpedo attack even from battleships in the line was, therefore, an important factor to be taken into account, with the ships of the opposing fleets formed in single line at the close intervals which are necessary for successful co-operation and the concentration of power afforded by a shortened line. Investigation into possible alternative formations for fighting a fleet action was constantly proceeding, but the single line, or a modification of it, was, under most conditions, the best that could be devised.

It was pointed out that, although our Fleet would be manoeuvred for advantage in gunnery position, it might be necessary to engage under unfavourable gunnery conditions in order to prevent the enemy reaching his own waters.

Several new manoeuvres were introduced and practised by the Fleet with a view to countering possible tactics on the part of the enemy. These included a "turn away" or a "turn towards" to counter a serious attack by torpedoes; a quick method of reversing the course of the Fleet without impairing its organisation to meet enemy tactics necessitating such a move; rapid methods of re-forming single line; etc. Other new tactical methods were introduced as time progressed to meet the changing conditions of modern warfare.

Detailed orders were drawn up in regard to the conduct of the Fleet after an action, so far as it was possible to foresee the conditions that might arise. The object was to arrange to continue the attack by light craft, whilst safeguarding the heavy ships against counterattack by light forces.

In the orders which were issued for the guidance of the destroyers both before, during, and after an action, endeavour was made to provide for all these contingencies. The stations of the flotillas, including the Harwich flotillas, if they were present, were laid down, and each had its particular duties assigned to it. General directions were given for the employment of the destroyers, wide latitude being reserved to the officers commanding flotillas.

The treatment of disabled ships was legislated for.

The duties of each class of vessel, battle-cruiser, cruiser and light cruiser when in cruising order, or in action, or after an action, were defined, particular emphasis being laid on the necessity for ships in the van, when in action, gaining a position of torpedo advantage in regard to the enemy's Battle Fleet, whilst at the same time engaging enemy vessels of a similar class and preventing torpedo attacks on our own Battle Fleet from developing.

Thus it was laid down as the leading principle in the General Cruiser Instructions, that after gaining touch with the enemy the first essential was to maintain that touch. Instructions were also given that in the event of the enemy's advanced forces becoming engaged with our Battle Cruiser Fleet, the cruisers in our advanced line were to push on and gain touch with the enemy's Battle Fleet. It will be seen later that this situation arose during the Jutland battle.

The Instructions for battle cruisers laid down the principle that in action their primary function was the destruction of the similar enemy vessels if present, and, after their destruction or in their absence, to attack the van of the enemy's Battle Fleet. Prior to action their duty was defined as giving information as to the enemy's Battle Fleet, whilst denying similar information to the enemy. The Vice-Admiral commanding the Battle Cruiser Fleet was given a free hand to carry out these general instructions.

The Instructions for the 5th Battle Squadron (the ships of the "Queen Elizabeth" class) were drawn up to provide for the battlecruisers being either absent or present. In the former event, this squadron took the place, and the duties, of the battle-cruisers; with our battle-cruisers present and in the van, the 5th Battle Squadron was ordered to take station ahead of the remainder of the Battle Fleet in the case of a deployment towards Heligoland, and in rear of the Battle Fleet in the case of deployment away from Heligoland. The object of this latter disposition was to place the High Sea Fleet at a disadvantage should it execute a 16-point turn after deployment. In order to enable the 5th Battle Squadron to carry out its functions in action, it was stationed between the Cruiser Line and the main Battle Fleet when in cruising order.

The Instructions to the light cruisers defined their duties in action as being to attack the enemy's light cruisers and torpedo craft, to support our destroyers, and to attack the enemy's battle line with torpedoes. For this purpose most of the light cruiser squadrons were required to be in the van on deployment.

The Instructions for destroyers laid emphasis on the fact that they should carry out an early attack on the enemy's Battle Fleet, commencing their attacks in clear weather as soon as the Battle Fleet were engaged. Under conditions of low visibility, they were instructed to attack without waiting for the Battle Fleets to be engaged. It was pointed out that destroyers closing the enemy's Battle Fleet for the purpose of an attack were also in the best position for preventing successful attacks on our own fleets.

As soon as submarine flotillas were attached to the Grand Fleet, in 1916, instructions for their conduct before, during, and after action were drawn up. Instructions for two other classes of vessel, namely, minelayers and seaplane carriers, had been issued earlier, vessels of the minelaying type, but of a slow speed, having been attached to the Fleet from the commencement of War, and seaplane carriers, possessing, however, but slow speed and inferior arrangements, having joined during 1916.

IV. The Training of the Fleet

Inseparable from the question of the management of the Fleet before and during action was that of the working together of its units at sea by day and at night. This matter was, of course, one to which great attention had been devoted by Sir George Callaghan, who, when he handed over the Fleet to me, gave me a fighting machine trained to a very high pitch of perfection by an officer who was a past master in fleet training.

But it was inevitable that war conditions should make even greater demands on the skill of the personnel than had previously been necessary, and in no direction was this more necessary than at night, the number of ships in company being far greater than had previously been usual; and the necessity of abstaining from signalling added to the difficulties. Further, under peace conditions, fleets cruising on dark, stormy nights without showing any lights, did so for comparatively short periods, during which the more experienced officers could, to a certain extent, remain on deck.

Under war conditions no ships at sea ever showed more than a very dim light at the stern, and frequently not even that, adding greatly to difficulties of fleet cruising. Consequently provision had to be made for ensuring safety whilst cruising under these conditions, and considerable foresight and great skill on the part of officers was necessary

Single ships and squadrons that might by any possibility pass close to one another during hours of darkness were warned beforehand of the danger, and arrangements made so that they should be aware of each other's positions. Destroyers, especially, were given directions so as to enable them to keep clear of larger vessels which otherwise might open fire upon them. Patrol craft of all sorts were similarly warned so far as this was possible, but in their case the conditions, owing to difficulties of communication, were frequently much more embarrassing.

Finally, the methods of disposing the Fleet at night had to be such as to reduce to a minimum the necessity for signals, whilst giving freedom of action in an emergency. What applied to conditions of darkness applied equally to fog. The ordinary means adopted for ensuring safety in a fog at sea, the use of the steam siren, could not as a rule be employed, since the blasts might give warning to the enemy and place the Fleet open to attack by enemy destroyers or submarines.

On the other hand, the necessity for our destroyers being in close company with the larger ships for screening purposes against submarines led, in the case of sudden fog, to a difficult situation, as, before the Fleet could safely carry out any manoeuvre, it was essential to get the destroyers clear. The sudden descent of fog during zigzagging by the large ships was also embarrassing. Orders were issued to meet all these conditions, and the best testimony to the training of the Fleet prior to the War was the remarkable freedom from accident during the early months after the opening of hostilities. The manner in which newly commissioned ships (in many cases ships which were by no means handy vessels in a fleet) fell into the organisation, was also a source of great gratification to me, and must have been most satisfactory to the officers and men concerned.

The gradual increase in the size of the Fleet, particularly in light craft, the higher speeds attained by its units, the extreme importance of reducing signalling by wireless at sea to an absolute minimum, except in the presence of the enemy, all tended to concentrate attention on the question of the efficiency of our signal arrangements. Wireless signalling by ships at sea had to be stopped, because by means of directional wireless stations the positions of ships using wireless telegraphy could be determined by the enemy. As time went on, we felt that the enemy might be able to ascertain the class and in some cases even the name of the ship so signalling. This we deduced from the fact that we ourselves made progress in this direction. The fact of a German fleet being at sea, for instance, could hardly be disguised if much use was made of wireless signals. We naturally concluded that the enemy could similarly locate any of our squadrons using the same means of communication. That was an inevitable inference.

The foregoing considerations made it necessary, in the first place, to endeavour, by means of carefully compiled and elaborate orders, to reduce the amount of signalling that would ordinarily be required after the Fleet had left its bases. Printed orders were prepared for the Fleet leaving its bases under all the varying conditions that could be anticipated, and whilst this made the orders somewhat lengthy so as to meet every possibility, the object was achieved.

Similarly, when the Fleet was in cruising order at sea in daylight, arrangements were made to pass signals in and out between the most advanced cruisers and the Fleet Flagship by searchlight, except in the presence of the enemy, and good organisation gradually reduced the time occupied in this process very considerably. All Fleet manoeuvring when much to the southward of the latitude of Kinnaird Head, on the coast of Aberdeen, was also carried out by visual signalling.

Owing to the danger of disclosing the position of the Fleet to enemy submarines or destroyers, it was not possible to use visual signalling at night, except with carefully shaded lamps which were only visible at a distance of about a quarter of a mile, and then only by the ship addressed, and this problem thus became complicated at night, in fogs or in very thick weather. Occasional resort had then to be made to wireless, but by signalling before dark all expected movements during the night, and by arranging the course of the Fleet so that few alterations were necessary, we succeeded in keeping almost absolute wireless silence. It had to be used, however, when important information from the Admiralty and elsewhere was to be transmitted to the Fleet-Flagship, or to senior officers of squadrons, or to single ships when at sea engaged in operations, etc., and early in the War we had to devise a method by which this could be done without calling up the ships in question by wireless, thus necessitating a reply from them, and thus possibly acquainting the enemy of their position.

After a time a satisfactory and ingenious system of communicating the required information without causing the ship herself to divulge her position was devised by the Fleet Wireless officer, Lieutenant-Commander R. L. Nicholson. This plan worked excellently and gradually was greatly extended during the later stages of the War.

It must not be thought that, because wireless signalling at sea was restricted, it was not intended to make full use of it when necessary and when silence was no longer required, such as when the fleets were within sight of one another. On the contrary, a great advance was made during the War in the use of wireless telegraphy for manoeuvring the Battle Fleet, as well as in every other direction. So proficient did the ships become under the organisation introduced by Lieutenant-Commander Nicholson, assisted as he was by the very efficient wireless officers and wireless personnel, that in 1916 I could handle the Battle Fleet by wireless with as much ease and rapidity as by visual signals. At the beginning of the War ten minutes to a quarter of an hour would elapse before I could be sure that all ships had received a manoeuvring wireless signal addressed to the whole Battle Fleet. In 1916 the time rarely exceeded two to three minutes. This great improvement was due to new methods introduced, as well as to incessant practice in harbour.

Our advance in the use of wireless telegraphy was very considerable indeed, and I owed a great debt of gratitude to Lieutenant-Commander Nicholson, the other wireless officers of the Fleet-Flagship, and the wireless officers and personnel of the whole Fleet. The progress was the more remarkable since, owing to extreme shortage of wireless personnel for the expanding Fleet and the large number of auxiliary vessels commissioned, we were forced to discharge many of the best operators in the Fleet as the War progressed and to replace them by boys trained in the Wireless School established by the Fleet at Scapa Flow.

A point which war experience brought into considerable prominence was the difficulty of distinguishing, with sufficient rapidity, enemy vessels from our own ships both before, and, more particularly during, action. The difficulty applied to all classes of vessels, but was greatest in the case of torpedo craft and submarines. Steps were taken to deal with it, and satisfactory arrangements made for certain distinguishing marks visible at long distances to be worn during daylight by our own surface vessels. The question of identification at night was more difficult, and although we effected improvement in this respect also, the results were not so satisfactory.

Of the original experimental work carried out by the Fleet at Scapa Flow none was more important than that connected with the safety of ships from mines. Early in the War it had become obvious that there was danger of a serious weakening of the Grand Fleet by successful mine attack, and no safeguard existed beyond the work of the minesweepers; these vessels could not work far afield, and in bad weather could not work even close to their bases, whereas the Fleet might be required to proceed to sea when minesweeping was impracticable.

A solution of this difficulty was required. Commander Cecil V. Usborne, of the Colossus, in these circumstances proposed to me the trial of an apparatus which he suggested should be towed from the bows of ships; it was intended to fend off any mine encountered, provided the ship did not strike it absolutely "end on." I ordered immediate trials; all the necessary materiel was provided with Fleet labour and appliances, and starting with trials in a picket boat, they were continued until a series of experiments commenced in large ships, battleships and cruisers. I placed Rear-Admirals A. L. Duff and A. C. Leveson in charge of the experiments and great progress was made, although absolute success was not obtained.

Lieutenant Dennis Burney, the son of Admiral Sir Cecil Burney, visited the base at this juncture, and, knowing his inventive turn of mind, I discussed the matter with him at considerable length. Lieutenant Burney soon afterwards put forward proposals for effecting the required object. His idea was to utilise apparatus which he had devised earlier for other purposes. His scheme was of a more elaborate nature than that devised by Commander Usborne, and necessitated the manufacture of appliances by outside manufacturers. I urged the Admiralty to take up the question at once; this was done, and the experiments, started at Portsmouth, were transferred to Scapa Flow as soon as preliminary success had been obtained.

The two devices were then tried over a considerable period at Scapa Flow, still under the immediate direction of Rear-Admirals Duff and Leveson, who threw themselves wholeheartedly into the task, Rear-Admiral E. F. A. Gaunt taking up this work in their occasional absence. After many disappointments the Burney system was proved to be successful, and I at once requested that manufacture on a large scale should be proceeded with. The device was of an elaborate character, and many persons at first were sceptical as to its value, owing partly to early difficulties in manipulation. But Rear-Admirals Duff and Leveson rendered the greatest assistance in overcoming objections, and gradually it came to be seen in the Fleet that we had become possessed of a most valuable safeguard. By the time I relinquished the Command a very large number of battleships, battlecruisers, and cruisers, and some light cruisers had been fitted, and the gear was working well. Owing to Lieutenant Burney's efforts, improvement was constantly being effected, with the result that during 1917 the fitting was universal. During that year it was instrumental in saving several warships from damage by mines, and in 1918 the number of ships saved was also considerable.

The initial idea was that of Commander Usborne, and both he and Lieutenant Burney displayed much energy in working out their respective devices. But it was through Lieutenant Burney's ingenuity that final success was achieved. Rear-Admirals Duff and Leveson eventually brought the appliance to perfection, with the result that it was generally adopted. A modified arrangement of the same nature was fitted to merchant ships during 1917 and 1918, and proved of very great value.

As was inevitable, my thoughts turned at an early stage of my Command to the necessity for constant improvement in the fighting efficiency of the Grand Fleet. My knowledge of the German Navy, which was considerable, left me under no delusions as to its character. I had made it my business to keep myself very fully acquainted with German progress. I had first been brought into close touch with the modern German Navy during service in China from 1899 to 1902, which included the Boxer campaign, when I saw a great deal of its officers and men. I had then formed a high estimate of its efficiency, and subsequent touch on many occasions with the German Fleet had convinced me that in materiel the Germans were ahead of us, and that the personnel, though lacking the initiative and resource and seamanlike character of the British, was highly disciplined, and well educated and trained. I knew also that the German Fleet was in no way short of officers; this was the case with us owing to the constant political pressure in the years before the War, and I expected that this shortage of officers would be a great handicap to us as the War progressed. The branch of the German Navy from which I expected very good work was the destroyer service. I had seen German destroyers manoeuvring.

Finally I knew, perhaps better than most of our officers, how efficient was the gunnery and torpedo work of the High Sea Fleet, and how rapid had been its advance in the year or two before the War. A great increase had been made in the allowance of ammunition for practice. Before the War this was much higher than our own, and there was no doubt in my mind that the German allowance would be well expended. Indeed, we had obtained information which placed this beyond question.

I was well acquainted personally with many of the flag officers and captains in the German Navy and had some idea of their views on naval warfare. Amongst those whom I knew best were Admiral von Ingenohl, the then Commander-in-Chief of the High Sea Fleet, Vice-Admiral von Lans, commanding a Battle Squadron, Admiral von Pohl, the Chief of the Naval Staff, who later succeeded Admiral von Ingenohl, Grand-Admiral von Tirpitz, Admiral von Holtzendorff, a former Commander-in-Chief of the High Sea Fleet, who succeeded Admiral von Pohl as chief of the Naval Staff, and Admiral von Usedom, who did conspicuous work in the shore batteries during the Dardanelles operations. My knowledge of these officers led me to expect good work in the High Command, and I also expected that they would be well supported.

It is interesting to record that I took part in a Conference of Allied naval officers in a pagoda at the end of the Great Wall of China in company with Admiral von Holtzendorff (the then German Flag Captain in China) after the capture of the Shanhai-Kwan forts, in 1900, and that Admiral von Usedom succeeded me as Chief of the Staff to Admiral — afterwards Admiral of the Fleet — Sir Edward Seymour, when I was wounded during the international expedition for the relief of the Peking Legations. I had met both these officers on several subsequent occasions, as well as Admiral von Lans, who was in command of the Iltis at the capture of the Taku forts by the Allies in the Boxer campaign.

My knowledge of the German Navy was a strong reason, had no others existed, for making me desirous of doing all that was possible to increase our own gunnery and torpedo efficiency.

The Germans possessed an excellent practice ground in Kiel Bay, with every appliance for carrying out gunnery exercises, and I felt sure that they had rendered it safe from any hostile attack, and that the German Fleet would be able to maintain and improve its efficiency as time progressed.

We were not in so fortunate a position. There had been no recent opportunity for carrying out gunnery and torpedo exercises and practices; Scapa Flow had not been used as a base for such work in peace time, except for destroyers, and consequently no facilities existed there, although the proximity of Cromarty, which had been a Fleet practice base, neutralised this disadvantage to a certain extent at a later period. But there was no protected area outside the harbour where practices could be carried out in safety, and the harbour itself was not at first secure against submarine attack.

Much use, however, was made of the Moray Firth outside Cromarty later when submarine obstructions had been provided, and the Germans had obligingly laid a minefield which protected the practice area from seaward. At the commencement of the War, then, it was necessary to depend on fleet resources for the provision of targets for gunnery practices, and the practices themselves were carried out under conditions which laid the ships open to submarine attack. This was most unsatisfactory, and the work suffered considerably as the result. The opportunity provided by constant sea work in the first months of the War was, however, utilised to carry out such gunnery practices as the conditions admitted.

At first the custom was for the Fleet to use small targets which the ships carried with them. These were unsuitable; their small size rendered them frequently invisible at even moderate ranges in any sea, and I felt that the Fleet could not make progress under such conditions.

Practice at rocks or small islands was next resorted to, but no really suitable rocks existed, and, in any case, practice at them eventually involved too much risk of submarine attack, as the German submarines began to find their way to the westward of Scotland. Towards the end of 1915 it became possible, owing to the increase in the number of destroyers attached to the Fleet, and to the provision of submarine obstructions at Cromarty, to carry out gunnery practices at long ranges at targets in the Moray Firth, and real improvement dated from that period.

Later still, battle practice targets were brought to Scapa Flow, and the long-range firing was carried out in the Pentland Firth, a still more convenient place.

Meanwhile Scapa Flow itself had been developed for all the preliminary gunnery practices which could be carried out with guns up to 6-inch in calibre, and also for night firing and for torpedo work. The fine stretch of water was secure from submarine attack after the obstructions had been provided, and ships could practise by day and night without danger of attack. The Flow was simply invaluable for this purpose. Ships were firing, running torpedoes, practising fire control exercises, carrying out experiments and exercising in dealing with attacks by destroyers, day after day, from daylight until dark.

After dark, night firing was frequently carried out, and occasionally a division of battleships was exercised in steaming in company, without lights, in order to give the officers of watches practice. When the constant sea work of the earlier months of the War gave place to occasional cruises, the seagoing and fighting efficiency of the Fleet was maintained at a remarkably high standard as a result of the work in Scapa Flow.

During the period 1914-16 a marked advance was undoubtedly made in gunnery efficiency. At an early period of the War a memorandum was issued pointing out the necessity for increased attention to drill and organisation. Absolute perfection was insisted upon, and it was obtained, by the strenuous efforts of officers and men. I knew that we had to deal with an enemy who would be as perfect as constant drill could ensure.

A great extension of the system of Director Firing, by which one officer or man could lay and fire all the guns, was made. The situation in this respect before the War was that a few ships had been fitted for the system, which had been devised by Admiral Sir Percy Scott. But a very large number of officers were sceptical as to its value compared with the alternative system; there was considerable opposition to it, and the great majority of the ships were not fitted. In some cases the system was not favoured even in the ships provided with it.

It had fallen to my lot in 1912 to carry out competitive trials of the Director System and the alternative system already in use, and the results of these trials had fully confirmed me in my previous opinion of the great value of the Director System. I was able to press these views on my return to the Admiralty at the end of 1912 as Second Sea Lord, and it was then decided to provide all the later ships with the arrangement. Little progress had, however, been made when the War broke out, only eight battleships having been fitted.

Early in 1915 arrangements were made, with the assistance of Sir Percy Scott and the warm support of Lord Fisher, then First Sea Lord, by which the battleships and battlecruisers were supplied with this system, without being put out of action or sent to a dockyard for the purpose. The necessary instruments were manufactured at various contractors' shops, and the very laborious task of fitting them, and the heavy electric cables, on board the ships was carried out by electricians sent to the various bases. The complicated work naturally took a considerable time, and many vexatious delays occurred; but gradually all ships were fitted. Sir Percy Scott rendering invaluable assistance at headquarters.

As a first step, the system was fitted to the heavy guns mounted in turrets, and by the date of the Battle of Jutland there were few ships that were not supplied with the system, although six of those last fitted had not had much experience with it.

The conditions under which that action was fought converted any waverers at once to a firm belief in the Director System, and there was never afterwards any doubt expressed as to its great value.

Further efforts were made later to accelerate the work, and the system was extended to smaller vessels. This had been the intention even before the action, but there were then still many who were unconvinced. However, during the remainder of 1916 and 1917 the work was pressed forward, and the system became universal for all guns and in all classes of ships.

The improvement in what may be termed the application of existing methods of fire control may now be mentioned. Throughout the War we had gradually, as the result of practice, increased greatly the effective range at which ships could engage, and stress had been laid on the necessity for bringing the fire rapidly on to the target in order to obtain early hits. Improvement was perhaps most rapid in the five or six months following the Jutland action. In this action the Fire Control Instruments, as adopted in the Service, which were the outcome of the work of naval officers, were found to meet the gunnery requirements most successfully. The only important improvement that was made was the provision of additional means for keeping the observation of Fire Instruments trained on the correct enemy ship. Various committees were formed immediately after the battle in order that full advantage might be taken at once of our experience. The result was the introduction of new rules for correcting gunfire; these, in addition to greatly increasing the volume of fire from a ship, also rendered it difficult for the enemy vessels to evade punishment by dodging tactics.

In order to cope more successfully with the latter development, more experiments were ordered, having as their object the determination of the inclination of the enemy vessel to the line of bearing from us, and various methods of obtaining this inclination were recommended to the Fleet. The most promising at the time that I relinquished command of the Fleet was that proposed by Lieutenant J. W. Rivett-Carnac, R.N., the range-finding expert of the Grand Fleet, who had investigated this inclination problem for some years. A great increase in the rapidity with which the fall of shot were "spotted on" to a target resulted from all this work. It is not too much to say that the interval between opening fire and the moment at which the salvoes began to "straddle" the target was certainly halved, and the rapidity of fire when the enemy was "straddled" was very greatly increased. The new firing rules, by standardising the system of correcting fire, produced a marked increase in the efficiency of the methods by which the fire of two ships was concentrated on to one target and generally paved the way for the solution of many gunnery problems which the Fleet had previously been unable to solve completely.

The use of smoke screens was closely investigated as a result of our experience of the German use of this device. Prolonged experiments were carried out at Scapa Flow to ascertain the possibilities and the best method of using smoke screens, and they were also used during battle tactics, and during range-finder exercises. The trials included the use of smoke shell as well as funnel and artificial smoke.

In another direction efforts were made to increase efficiency. The Jutland battle convinced us that our armour-piercing shell was inferior in its penetrative power to that used by the Germans, and immediately after the action I represented this with a view to immediate investigation. A Committee sat to consider the matter. In 1917, as First Sea Lord, I appointed a second Committee.

With one of the old type of armour-piercing shells of a particular calibre as used at Jutland the shell would, with oblique impact at battle range, break up whilst holing a certain thickness of plate, and the shell could not, therefore, reach the vitals of the enemy's ships. A shell of the new type, as produced by the 1917 Committee, of the same calibre would at the same oblique impact and range pass whole through a plate of double the thickness before exploding and could therefore with a delay action fuse penetrate to the magazines of a capital ship. Had our ships possessed the new type of armour-piercing shell at Jutland, many of the enemy's vessels, instead of being only damaged, would probably not have been able to reach port. The manufacture of these new type shells for the Fleet was well advanced before the end of 1917.

The value of the torpedo as a fighting weapon in action, from ships, from destroyers, and from submarines, was also greatly increased. The torpedo practices at Scapa Flow, which were of a realistic character, were of the greatest possible use.

The real cause underlying the improvement was the great keenness displayed by officers and men. Their one idea was to strive for the highest efficiency, and there was never apparent the least sign of weariness or staleness in repeating time after time exercises and practices with which they were so familiar. No tribute that I can pay to the personnel of the Grand Fleet in this connection could be sufficiently high. I know that under my successor the improvement in fighting efficiency continued.

Owing to the collapse of the moral of the personnel of the German Navy, culminating in the surrender for internment of the majority of their capital ships, the Grand Fleet was given no opportunity of testing in action the methods adopted as a result of our experience during the first two years of war, and perfected by two years' further training. Had the German fleet come out to battle a terrible punishment awaited it!

Mention has been made of the development of aircraft during the War. The possibilities resulting from the use of the air for reconnaissance work, for assisting in the direction of gunfire, and, finally, for offensive operations, were fully recognised in the Grand Fleet; but for a considerable period the lack of suitable machines hindered development. The first decisive step taken was the fitting out of the Campania, a passenger ship of the Cunard Line, as a seaplane carrier to be attached to the Battle Fleet. Prior to that, the Harwich Force and, later, the Battle Cruiser Fleet had been provided with smaller vessels, the Vindex and Engadine, carrying a few seaplanes. They had been used in operations in the Heligoland Bight, but without much success, owing to the difficulty experienced in getting seaplanes to rise from the water except in the finest weather.

With the arrival of the Campania at Scapa, we were able to investigate the difficulties attending the use of aircraft from ships as then fitted and to indicate the direction in which improvement was desirable and possible. It was apparent that little improvement could be expected so long as we were dependent on the machines rising from the water. The first step, therefore, was to improve the arrangements for flying off from the deck of the Campania. The ship returned to Liverpool at the end of 1915 in order that the necessary alterations might be effected; these were not completed until the late spring of 1916; during the alterations, the Campania was also, at my request, fitted to carry a kite balloon.

The advantages to be obtained from the use of kite balloons had been demonstrated during the Dardanelles operations, and the Menelaus, kite balloon ship, was sent to the Grand Fleet. But it was soon obvious that we could not make profitable use of kite balloons in a fleet action unless they were flown from the ships themselves, and experiments were carried out, under the direction of Vice-Admiral Sir Doveton Sturdee, commanding the 4th Battle Squadron, having as their object the best method of fitting and using kite balloons from warships. Many difficulties were experienced, the principal one being that of providing wire of sufficient strength to stand the tension of the balloon during strong winds. The Kite Balloon Section at Roehampton gradually solved the difficulties, and by the end of 1916 the majority of the flagships leading divisions of the Fleet were provided with kite balloons, and were experiencing their utility. From this beginning, great developments took place in providing vessels of all classes, including light cruisers, destroyers, P boats, and trawlers, with kite balloons; the balloon was used in the case of the smaller vessels for anti-submarine reconnaissance work, whilst in the heavy ships it was used for observation and correction of fire.

Meanwhile, the development of the aircraft carrier had proceeded, but not with the same rapidity. It was evident to me in 1916 that for anti-Zeppelin work we should look towards the aeroplane flying from the deck, rather than to the seaplane, although it also could rise from the deck; but I gathered the time was hardly ripe for the step, owing to the landing difficulty, and the first efforts of the Royal Naval Air Service lay in the direction of providing a type of seaplane that would fly well off the deck and climb quickly. These efforts were fairly successful, but the development of the heavier-than-aircraft machine for use with the Fleet did not begin until the aeroplane was adopted for the work; and this took place in 1917, when progress became rapid, and continued until the end of the War.

There remains the question of the airship, which was also being developed during the period 1914-16, but as this matter was not within the province of the Fleet, it is not necessary to touch upon it here.

V. The Blockade

The story of the development of the Grand Fleet would be incomplete without reference to the Blockade, and, in particular, to the work of the 10th Cruiser Squadron. In the early days of the War, the 10th Cruiser Squadron consisted of the ships of the "Edgar" class — vessels at least twenty years old; and during August, 1914, the Admiralty commissioned three armed merchant ships, the Mantua, Alsatian and Oceanic, to strengthen the squadron for blockade work; the latter ship was lost, by shipwreck in September of that year.

The Blockade in those early days was carried out by the 10th Cruiser Squadron and by the other cruiser squadrons attached to the Grand Fleet. During November, 1914, the ships of the "Edgar" class were withdrawn owing to their unseaworthy condition, and the ships' companies utilised to commission a number of additional armed merchant cruisers. By the end of December, 1914, the squadron consisted of eighteen ships, being raised later to a strength of twenty-four ships. A very large proportion of the officers and men of the reconstituted 10th Cruiser Squadron belonged to the Mercantile Marine.

The advent of so large a squadron of these vessels called for a considerable organisation for their maintenance; they were based on Liverpool for all the heavy work of upkeep, whilst a secondary advanced base at Swarbachs Minn, on the west coast of the Shetland Islands, was gradually developed, and obstructed against submarine attack. The work of organisation was carried out by Rear-Admiral de Chair, who commanded the squadron, ably seconded by Rear-Admiral H. H. Stileman the Senior Naval Officer at Liverpool, to whom we were much indebted for hearty co-operation and efficient organisation at the base.

The work of the squadron consisted in intercepting and boarding all vessels bound into or out of the northern entrance to the North Sea, and this work could obviously not be carried out in the face of the German submarines without heavy risk to the ships. The danger was greatest during the operation of boarding, as the examining vessel was obliged to stop to lower the boarding-boat. As the number of German submarines increased, the squadron was necessarily withdrawn to positions further removed from the enemy submarine bases, and the Blockade line, after the spring of 1915, ran generally from the Orkneys and Shetlands past the

Faroe Islands to Iceland, and when freedom from ice rendered passage round the north of Iceland possible, ships operated in that neighbourhood.

A careful organisation of the movements of the ships was necessary to cover such an immense area of the sea, and to provide that all ships should, as far as possible, be intercepted. Even in the case of ships of such large coal endurance as the armed merchant steamers, it was not possible to keep much more than one-half the number in commission on an average on the patrol line at the same time. The remainder were either in port refitting and refueling, or were en route to and from the bases. The distance from the middle of the patrol line to Liverpool was some 600 miles, so that two days were occupied in the passage each way.

When going to or from Liverpool the ships had to run the gauntlet of enemy submarines, which were passing down the west coast of the Hebrides and Ireland, and as no destroyers were available with which to screen them against attack, the risk was considerable. They had also to face the constant danger of minefields. Several ships of the squadron fell victims to submarines or mines with a resultant heavy loss of life.

Whilst the ships were on patrol, the work of the boarding parties was very arduous. The preliminary examination could not be carried out without boarding, and the manner in which the boats of the squadron were handled in the very heavy weather, almost constant in northern latitudes, was a fine tribute to the seamanship of the officers and men. In this boarding work the fishermen of the Newfoundland Royal Naval Reserve, hardy and experienced seamen, rendered most conspicuous service.

The efficiency of the Blockade increased gradually from its inception, as is well known, and after a time the percentage of vessels that evaded the ships of the 10th Cruiser Squadron became so low as to be almost negligible. The procedure adopted was to send all ships, preliminary examination of which at sea aroused any suspicion, into Kirkwall or Lerwick harbours, where regular examination services were instituted. The ships were taken in under the supervision of an armed guard, sent on board from the boarding-vessel, and these guards underwent many unpleasant experiences. Several lost their lives in ships which were torpedoed by German submarines, and in many cases, particularly in badly found sailing ships, they underwent great hardships. The guards were also the means of saving more than one such ship from shipwreck, by working her themselves when the crew refused to do so any longer, and in all cases great tact and discretion on the part of the officer in charge, usually a junior officer of the Royal Naval Reserve, were necessary in his dealings with the neutral captains. The whole question of the efficiency of the Blockade — as shown by the returns furnished to me from Headquarters — was constantly under review by my Staff and myself.

The fate of the detained ship was decided in London on receipt of the report of examination. As was perhaps natural, the sentence on many ships' cargoes pronounced in London was not accepted without question from the Fleet, and a good deal of correspondence passed with reference to individual ships. We, in the Fleet, were naturally very critical of any suspicion of laxity in passing, into neutral countries bordering on Germany, articles which we suspected might find their way into Germany, and constant criticisms were forwarded by me, first to the Admiralty, and, later, to the Ministry of Blockade, when that Ministry was established.

The difficulties with which the Foreign Office was faced in regard to neutral susceptibilities were naturally not so apparent in the Fleet as to the authorities in London, and though many of our criticisms were perhaps somewhat unjustifiable, and some possibly incorrect, it is certain that in the main they were of use. Indeed, they were welcomed in London as giving the naval point of view. The decisive effect of the Blockade did not become apparent until the end, when the final crash came, and it was seen how supreme an influence on the result of the War this powerful weapon had exercised. Even those who during the War had been asking what the Navy was doing, recognised at the last how victory had been achieved, largely, as the result of the silent pressure of Sea Power.

VI. The Grand Fleet Bases

Mention has been made elsewhere of the unprotected state of the Grand Fleet bases against submarine attack in the early part of the War. The matter was one of supreme importance, and formed the subject of very urgent representations to the Admiralty. Many brains were at work on the problem at the Admiralty, at the bases, and in the Fleet itself.

The first step was that taken under the direction of Captain Donald S. Munro, the King's Harbour Master at Cromarty, who devised a system of submarine obstruction which later formed the pattern for the deep-water obstructions at most of our naval bases. Owing to his energy and driving power, the entrance to Cromarty was rendered fairly secure by October 26th, 1914. Whilst he was working out a defence for Cromarty another officer, Lieutenant Bircham, R.N.V.R., under the command of Admiral Sir Robert Lowry, the Commander-in-Chief of the coast of Scotland, suggested a method for providing an obstruction for the Rosyth base. This was fitted in place by the end of October, 1914, and was also entirely successful.

As soon as the Cromarty scheme was in train, I requested that obstructions on similar lines should be fitted to the three main entrances to Scapa Flow, the Hoxa entrance (by far the most likely to be attempted) being taken in hand first. Exasperating delays in the supply of the necessary material were experienced, and the first line of obstructions in the Hoxa entrance was not completed until December 29th, 1914, the first line in Switha Sound by January 12th, 1915, and that in Hoy Sound by February 19th, 1915. Meanwhile officers and men of the Fleet had improvised obstructions, first at Lough Swilly and Loch na Keal, and later at Scapa Flow, which, while not giving thorough security against a determined attempt at entry, had a psychological value. These obstructions, which were kept in existence even after the completion of the more efficient methods of dealing with the problem, involved much labour.

Towards the end of 1915, or early in 1916, the disadvantages attendant on basing the Fleet so far north as Scapa Flow, were discussed between Sir Henry Jackson (then First Sea Lord) and myself. We both felt that, with the Fleet at the northern base, the difficulties of intercepting the High Sea Fleet during coast raids, and of dealing with landing raids covered by the High Sea Fleet, were so considerable as to make it eminently desirable to base the whole Fleet farther south, if this were feasible. A discussion took place at Rosyth, and as the result I suggested a scheme of submarine obstructions across the Firth of Forth, which would admit not only of berthing the whole Grand Fleet in that anchorage, but would also allow of gunnery and torpedo practices being carried out with a considerable degree of safety in the Forth, so that the Fleet, if based there, could keep up its fighting efficiency. Many senior officers in the Grand Fleet were not in favour of the idea, for two reasons: first, that the Fleet could be mined in by the enemy with much greater ease when in the Forth than when at Scapa; and, secondly, that practices could not be so efficiently carried out in the Forth. There was much weight in both these objections, although the difficulties of carrying out practices in the Forth were exaggerated; but the strategic advantage, in my opinion, outweighed them, and the scheme was proceeded with as proposed.

That part of the scheme which admitted of the safe carrying out of practices was completed by December, 1916, and the whole of the new obstructions were in place by July, 1917, nearly a year later, it is true, than the anticipated date. The result certainly justified the conclusion arrived at. When the conditions made it at all probable that the High Sea Fleet might put to sea for an operation in southern waters, the Grand Fleet assembled in the Firth of Forth, and the undoubted disadvantages of the southern base were neutralised by skilful dispositions on the part of the flag officers responsible.

The protection of the Grand Fleet bases against submarine attack was only one of the many factors necessary for their development. In pre-War days, although it had been decided that the use of northern bases would be necessary in the event of a war with Germany, the bases had not been prepared to meet the new situation. It is, perhaps, desirable to remove any misunderstanding as to the causes of this failure:

(a) The decision had not long been taken, and

(b) The necessary financial provision was lacking.

Under the first of these headings the base at Scapa Flow was affected, and, under the second, that at Rosyth, where for some time progress in the development of the base had been arrested. The Admiralty had taken steps to make some preparations at Cromarty, in so far as the provision of gun defences against attack by surface vessels was concerned, but nothing had been done for the upkeep of a fleet beyond a decision to transfer to Cromarty, during war, one of the floating docks at southern yards.

In fact, the situation was that, whilst we had shifted our Fleet to the north, all the conveniences for the maintenance of that fleet were still in the Channel ports. The first step was the transference of the large floating dock from Portsmouth to Invergordon, in the Cromarty Firth, together with a staff of dockyard workmen, who were housed in a merchant ship captured from the Germans. Workshops were fitted up on shore under the energetic superintendence of Rear-Admiral Edmund R. Pears and his able staff of dockyard officers. It can be said with great emphasis that this floating dock was simply invaluable to the Grand Fleet.

Invergordon gradually developed into a great repairing base. A second and smaller floating dock was purchased early in 1916 at my request and placed there, and by the middle of that year the base had attained large proportions; work of all kinds was carried out with rapidity and success, including the repairs of battleships after the Jutland battle, and the great extension in armoured-deck protection fitted to ships after the same action.

Ordinary refits of battleships had been carried out at Invergordon since the autumn of 1914. At Scapa Flow the same possibilities as a repairing base did not exist, although a floating dock for destroyers, for which many requests had been made, was eventually obtained and placed there.

But the base at Scapa Flow had extended out of all knowledge in other directions. In August, 1914, the base organisation consisted only of the seagoing Fleet repair ships Cyclops and Assistance. At an early stage the Cyclops was connected to a shore telegraph cable off the village of Scapa, and she became at the same time a floating post office and a base for the auxiliary vessels (a few drifters) which were first requisitioned. Rear-Admiral Francis S. Miller was appointed to her as the Senior Naval Officer at the base. The manner in which the great demands on her accommodation were met was a standing wonder to me. In the early part of the War, officers on Admiral Miller's staff and others were obliged to make their sleeping berths, as best they could, on the deck or on top of their writing-tables, and it was surprising that the overcrowding in all directions did not affect health. But the work went on very successfully in the most inconvenient circumstances.

Towards the end of 1914 it became necessary, owing to the weather conditions, to move the base organisations from the north to the southwest side of Scapa Flow. The anchorage at Long Hope was selected, whilst the Fleet itself lay off the north side of the Island of Flotta, and the numerous larger auxiliaries, colliers, oilers, store ships, and the ammunition ships lay between Long Hope and Hoy Sound. Prior to this, the importance of the organisation in the Orkneys and Shetlands had increased to such an extent that I had asked for the appointment of a Senior Flag Officer in general command of the whole district, and of the defences in particular.

So much of my time was being occupied in deciding and pressing forward the work of organisation of the base and its obstructions and defences, in dealing with the numerous questions relating to the patrol of the coast by coast watchers, in arranging for the disposal of merchant ships sent in for reexamination, and for guarding such vessels, in considering questions affecting the occupation of land for the erection of defences, in the requisitioning of trawlers and drifters, etc., that it was becoming difficult to deal with the fast accumulating Fleet work proper. Vice-Admiral Sir Stanley Colville, who suggested that he should waive his seniority in order to serve as my junior officer, was appointed Vice-Admiral Commanding the Orkneys and Shetlands. This left Rear-Admiral Miller free to devote himself to the increasingly heavy work of base organisation proper, relieved me of a mass of work outside the Fleet, and was of the greatest possible benefit in every way. Under Sir Stanley Colville's most able direction, the completion of the organisation for the general defences of the Islands, the work of patrol craft and minesweepers, and the provision of submarine obstructions was effected, and the work pushed forward. Captain Stanley Dean Pitt, R.N., an officer of very wide experience, was appointed to superintend the work of laying the submarine obstructions, and under his able direction, in the face of the greatest difficulties due to bad weather and strong tides, the entrances to Scapa Flow were either blocked by sunken ships or obstructed by nets, mines, and other devices.

The gun defences at Scapa, which at the beginning of the War consisted of 12-pounder and 8-pounder guns landed from the Fleet, were gradually reinforced by four-inch and six-inch guns obtained from abroad, the whole being manned by Royal Marine pensioners under Lieut.-Colonel Gerald N. A. Harris, R.M.A. The garrison was housed in huts, erected temporarily for the purpose, and although with the handiness which characterises a Royal Marine in all circumstances, the officers and men eventually made themselves comfortable even under such weather conditions as are experienced at Scapa Flow, they endured a very considerable amount of hardship in the early days with their accustomed cheerfulness.

And here I cannot fail to mention the endurance and staying qualities of the crews of the trawlers that supported the submarine obstructions, particularly those at Scapa Flow. These trawlers were moored in positions in which they were exposed to the whole fury of northerly and southerly gales; in many cases they were within a few yards of a rocky coast, heavy seas breaking over them and bringing on board tons of water. The skippers knew that they had to stick it out for the sake of the safety of the Fleet and the maintenance of the obstruction, and under these conditions they did their duty in a manner which calls for the highest praise.

Meanwhile the development of the base proper proceeded apace. One of the earlier arrivals was the old cruiser Imperieuse, which was used as a post office, depot, and general overflow ship to the Cyclops. The number of trawlers and drifters, which had their home at Scapa Flow and which were engaged on patrol or minesweeping work, attendance on the Fleet, garrison, or on the mass of Fleet auxiliaries, increased with great rapidity during the winter of 1914-15; on September 1st, 1914, the number was nil, and it reached a total of some four yachts, eighty-five trawlers, and twenty-seven drifters by the summer of 1915. These vessels all looked to the Cyclops, Assistance and Imperieuse for refit, pay, food, and for every conceivable want. Gradually the number of base ships was increased, culminating in the arrival of the old battleship Victorious about March 6, 1916, as the "home" of some 500 dockyard workmen working in the Fleet, fitting the Director System, increasing the protection to decks and magazines, carrying out minor repairs, re-tubing condensers, and many other urgent tasks.

Mention has been made of the large number of colliers, oilers, store ships, ammunition ships, etc., that were used by the Fleet. At one time this caused some criticism, based principally on the time spent by the colliers at the Fleet Base. It may be as well to explain the necessity for this. There were no facilities at the base for the storage of coal, either in lighters or on shore. Consequently, the whole of the coal required at the base was necessarily kept on board the colliers. The actual number of colliers which I deemed it necessary to keep at the base during the first two years of war was determined by the necessity for coaling the Fleet and getting it to sea again with the utmost possible rapidity. We could not contemplate such a situation as the Fleet arriving short of fuel, and being delayed in completing owing to shortage of colliers, with the possibility of information being received simultaneously that the High Sea Fleet was at sea and covering a landing raid on our coast! Rapidity of fuelling was of vital importance to the Empire.

Therefore, in stating my requirements of colliers, I gave the number necessary to enable almost the whole Fleet to be fuelled simultaneously; in other words, the number of colliers was dependent on the number of coal-burning ships in the Fleet, Some slight reduction was found possible, to allow for the probable case of some ships requiring less coal than others, thus admitting of two such ships using one collier in succession; but, broadly speaking, the requirements were as stated. When the cargo of colliers fell below a certain minimum, they returned to Cardiff to refill to economise tonnage.

At Rosyth the situation was eased by the transport of coal by rail to Grangemouth and its transshipment to colliers there. As we needed colliers as coal-storing ships, so also we required ammunition ships to carry a proportion of the reserve ammunition for the Fleet. There were no facilities at Scapa or Cromarty for storage on shore. The number of ships required for this service was, however, much smaller.

Floating storage of all sorts possesses one great advantage over shore storage; should strategic conditions necessitate a change of base, the coal, ammunition and other auxiliaries can move with the Fleet. The same argument applies in a lesser degree to floating docks. A consideration of all these facts connected with the development of fleet bases will show that this question necessarily required a good deal of attention on the part of my Staff and myself, and was incidental to the development of the Grand Fleet.

VII. The Personnel and Its Welfare

Another factor in the development of the Fleet, by no means the least important, was that of the moral and spirit of the personnel. It is, of course, impossible to exaggerate the importance of this question as an element in the efficiency of the Fleet. In the early months of war, when the Fleet was continually at sea, the few hours spent in harbour were fully occupied in coaling and storing the ships; but these conditions could not be continued indefinitely. As the months passed with no sign of enemy vessels at sea and time in harbour increased as compared to that spent at sea, it became necessary to find some diversion for the minds of the officers and men.

The first step taken at Scapa Flow was carried out under the superintendence of Vice-Admiral Sir Lewis Bayly, then commanding the 1st Battle Squadron. Always alive to the necessity for providing occupation, recreation, and exercise for officers and men, he started considerable works on Flotta Island, works of such a divergent nature as batteries for the defence of the submarine obstructions then in progress, football grounds for the men, a golf course for the officers, and landing piers on the beach. These schemes grew and were eventually divided out amongst the various squadrons. A rifle and pistol range were also constructed, and several piers built. The whole of the work was carried out, I may add, by means of Fleet labour. Later a "Canteen" ship, the S.S. Ghourko, was fitted up by the Junior Army and Navy Stores, and this vessel played an important part in the harbour life of the Grand Fleet. She carried stores and provisions of all sorts, available for use by all ships, but particularly of the smaller vessels which could not send their mess stewards far afield in search of a change of diet. She was provided with a stage, and theatrical and cinema entertainments took place on board frequently. She was also fitted with a boxing ring, and squadron boxing competitions were held on board with great frequency. Finally, she was utilised for lectures of all sorts, and for the Church services of Roman Catholics and Nonconformists.

The system of lectures was encouraged to the utmost. Officers lectured on board their ships to the ships' companies on every subject, the War included, and much good resulted.

Education was freely developed. The Admiralty provided, at my request, schoolmasters in large numbers, and classes for the boys and voluntary classes for the men in the evenings in harbour were very well attended.

And, finally, exercise of all sorts was encouraged to the utmost extent possible. This took the form principally of football, rowing regattas, athletic sports and boxing. The keenness displayed in all these sports was a certain indication that the personnel was showing no sign of staleness.

The Englishman's love of sport helps him to tide over periods of tedium and weariness, which are most calculated to undermine discipline. Occupation and interest are the surest antidotes to discontent and unrest, and never during the first two and a half years did I see signs of either. On the contrary, the men, I believe, were thoroughly happy and contented, treated the War as being in the day's work, and looked forward eagerly to the day on which their enemy would give them the opportunity for which they were waiting, and for which they kept themselves thoroughly efficient and fit.

In those days the officers got to know the men even better than they had done before, and the spirit of comradeship between all ranks became correspondingly closer. Certainly no Commander-in-Chief could ever have desired to see in the force under his orders a finer spirit than that which animated the officers and men of the Grand Fleet.

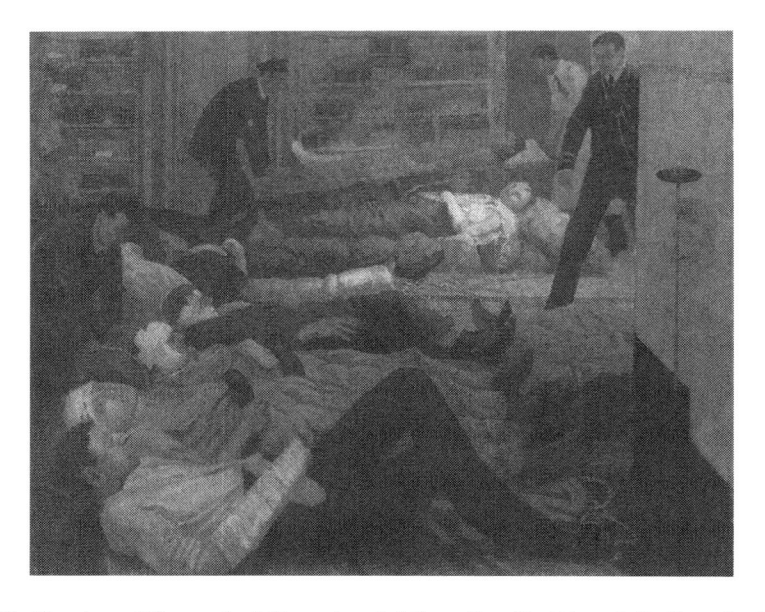

HMS *Castor* - Wounded Received After the Battle of Jutland, 31st May 1916. Painting by Jan (Godfrey Jervis) Gordon, 1917.

4 - Declaration of War

At 8 a.m. on August 4th, 1914, the Grand Fleet proceeded to sea in compliance with Admiralty orders. The ships accompanying the Fleet-Flagship Iron Duke were the vessels of the 1st, 2nd, 3rd and 4th Battle Squadrons, the light cruisers Southampton, Birmingham, Boadicea, Blonde and the destroyers of the 4th Flotilla; the cruisers Shannon, Natal and Roxburgh, and the light cruisers Nottingham, Falmouth and Liverpool, which were at Rosyth with the 2nd Destroyer Flotilla, were directed to meet the Fleet at a rendezvous in Lat. 58.40 N, Long, 1.30 E. The light cruisers Bellona and Blanche were left behind to coal.

A report received from the Admiralty that three German transports had passed the Great Belt on the evening of August 1st had led to the 3rd Cruiser Squadron, with the cruisers Cochrane and Achilles, and the 1st Battle Cruiser Squadron, being ordered to sea on the evening of August 3rd to cruise to the southward of the Fair Island Channel during the night. The orders under which the Fleet acted were to sweep east as far as Long. 2 E. and, then, for the cruisers to carry out a wide sweep to the southward and southwestward.

These orders were in conformity with the general strategical ideas embodied in the War Orders for the Grand Fleet, which, as already indicated, aimed at establishing a blockade; at preventing the enemy forces from getting into the Atlantic to interfere with the operations of our cruisers engaged in protecting our own trade as well as stopping trade on the part of the enemy; and at asserting control of the North Sea and denying it to the enemy. Pursuant to these orders, the 1st Battle Cruiser Squadron and 3rd Cruiser Squadron were directed to sweep the area between Lat. 60 and 61 N., working eastward from the Shetland Islands to Long. 2 E., arriving there at 4 p.m., thence to sweep to the S.E. until 5 a.m. on August 5th, when they were on a line drawn S.W. from Hangesund Light in Lat. 59.25 N. with the eastern ship 20 miles from the coast.

The Antrim and Argyll, being short of fuel, were detached during the evening of August 4th to coal at Scapa.

The sweep was prolonged to the westward by the cruisers and light cruisers from Rosyth; the 2nd Flotilla was detached to Rosyth to fuel. This first sweep was begun in northern waters because the North Sea is narrower at this point, and also because it afforded opportunity of intercepting vessels which might have left German ports two days previously in anticipation of hostilities. The cruiser sweep was supported by the Battle Fleet, which steamed as far as Long. 2 E., turning at 3 a.m. on August 5th to the westward.

The 3rd Battle Squadron which had been compelled to leave Scapa 30 per cent, short of fuel owing to the paucity of colliers, was detached to that base at 8.30 p.m. on the 4th, to complete with coal.

During the night information was received by wireless telegraphy that war had been declared against Germany at midnight, 4th-5th August, and the following gracious message was received from His Majesty the King and was communicated to the Fleet:

"At this grave moment in our National History, I send to you and through you to the officers and men of the Fleet of which you have assumed command, the assurance of my confidence that under your direction they will revive and renew the old glories of the Royal Navy, and prove once again the sure Shield of Britain and of her Empire in the hour of trial."

During daylight on the 5th, the Battle Fleet cruised to the northward of Lat. 57.30 N., in accordance with Admiralty telegraphic orders; the 1st Battle Cruiser Squadron was sent back to Scapa to coal, as well as four light cruisers and the Lowestoft, and the 4th Flotilla was sent to Invergordon for a similar purpose. In the afternoon, the 2nd Cruiser Squadron and the cruiser Devonshire, as well as the 1st Light Cruiser Squadron, were detached to sweep to the eastward, and the Battle Fleet turned to the southward at 8 a.m. on the 6th to meet the 3rd Battle Squadron and 3rd Cruiser Squadron in Lat. 59 N., Long. 1.0 E.

During August 6th the following reports were received:

(a) Two German cruisers were reported passing Trondhjem going north. (This came from the Admiralty.)

(b) Four torpedo-boats had been seen off the northwest end of the Shetlands going north. (This was a local report.)

(c) The German liner Kronprinzessin Cecilie was stated to have passed through the Stronsay Firth, Orkneys, bound east, during the night of the 5th-6th. (Local report.) The destroyer Oak was despatched to search the vicinity of the Stronsay and Westray Firths, but obtained no confirmation of the report.

(d) It was reported that the Germans had established a base in Lat. 62 N. on the Norwegian coast (the exact position unknown).

A search of the coast by cruisers revealed nothing in confirmation of the last report, but a British trawler reported that a large number of German merchant ships had assembled in the West Fiord and in the harbours of the Lofoten Islands on the coast of Norway. Reports as to the Germans having established a base on the Norwegian coast were very persistent during the early days of the War. These reports were probably to some extent due to the ideas prevailing before the War as to German intentions in this respect, these views being naturally coloured by the frequent visits of the German High Sea Fleet in peace time to Norwegian waters, particularly to the vicinity of Trondhjem.

In 1911, when I commanded the Atlantic Fleet, arrangements had been made for me to visit Norwegian ports at the same time as the High Sea Fleet, in order to bring about a meeting between the two navies, with, it was hoped, beneficial results. But the Agadir crisis intervened, and the visit was postponed. The meeting took place in 1914, when a portion of the 2nd Battle Squadron, under the command of Vice-Admiral Sir George Warrender, visited Kiel during the regatta week, very shortly before the outbreak of war.

During daylight of August 6th the Dreadnought Battle Fleet cruised between Lat. 59 N. and 60 N. and Long. 1 E. and 1 W.; the 2nd Cruiser Squadron and the 1st Light Cruiser Squadron swept to the eastward between Lat. 58 N. and 60 N., thence to the northward along the Norwegian coast, and to the

Shetlands and Scapa Flow, the 3rd Battle Squadron being detached to the N.E. to cover them. The 1st Battle Cruiser Squadron rejoined the Battle Fleet at sea after refuelling; the 2nd Flotilla left Rosyth at daylight and swept to the northeastward; and the 4th Flotilla left Invergordon with orders to search the vicinity of the Pentland Firth for submarines prior to the arrival of the Battle Fleet on the 7th.

The Dreadnought Battle Fleet arrived at Scapa at 6 a.m. on the 7th to fuel; the 2nd Cruiser Squadron and the 1st Light Cruiser Squadron arrived at 10 a.m., and during the day the 3rd Cruiser Squadron, with the 2nd Flotilla, carried out a thorough search of the Norwegian coast, being covered by the 1st Battle Cruiser Squadron and 3rd Battle Squadron. No sign of a German base could be discovered, and the force was ordered back to Scapa to fuel.

The fuelling of the Fleet was considerably delayed, owing to the inadequate number of colliers, many of those present being also unsuitable for the work of rapid coaling. The lack of lubricating oil for the 3rd Battle Squadron also caused trouble, but these early difficulties, although a source of considerable anxiety at the commencement of hostilities, were overcome later.

The greatest anxiety constantly confronting me was the defenceless nature of the base at Scapa, which was open to submarine and destroyer attacks. Whilst the Fleet was fuelling the only protection that could be afforded was to anchor light cruisers and destroyers off the various entrances and to patrol outside the main entrance; but these measures were no real defence against submarines, and the position was such that it was deemed most inadvisable to keep the Fleet in harbour longer than was absolutely necessary for fuelling purposes. Accordingly, at 6.30 p.m. on the same day, the Battle Fleet again proceeded to sea, being screened through the Pentland Firth to the westward until dark by the 4th Flotilla, and course being then shaped to pass round the Orkneys into the North Sea. In order to provide some protection against destroyer attack, a request was forwarded to the Admiralty asking that two of the older battleships might be sent up to defend the main entrances. This measure was approved, and a reply was received that the Hannibal and Magnificent were being despatched.

The Russell, Albemarle and Exmouth, of the 6th Battle Squadron, belonging originally to the Channel Fleet, arrived at Scapa to join the Grand Fleet on the night of the 7th-8th.

At 9.30 p.m. on the 8th the battleships Orion, Monarch and Ajax, were detached to carry out target practice, and the remainder of the Fleet proceeded to the southeastward from Fair Island, carrying out Fire Control Exercises; but, on receipt of a report from the Monarch that a torpedo had been fired at her by a submarine, the practice was stopped and the ships rejoined, one-half of the 2nd Flotilla being directed to search for the submarine. At 6.30 p.m. the officer of the watch on board the Iron Duke sighted a periscope and altered course to ram; the same periscope was shortly afterwards reported by the Dreadnought, but was not seen again.

At 4 a.m. on the 9th, the Fleet was in Lat. 58.31 N., Long. 1.9 E.

Shortly afterwards the Orion reported a strong smell of oil, and bubbles were seen on the surface, and the Birmingham, commanded by Captain A. M. Duff, of the 1st Light Cruiser Squadron, which had been screening ahead of the Fleet with the 2nd Cruiser Squadron, claimed to have rammed and sunk the German submarine U 15, which she had sighted on the surface. This initial success was hailed with great satisfaction in the Fleet. Subsequent information showed that the Birmingham had been handled with great promptitude. During daylight of August 9th, the Battle Fleet and 1st Battle Cruiser Squadron were cruising in company, the noon position being Lat. 58.41 N., Long. 0.15 W., and as the presence of submarines was suspected, the Fleet was constantly zigzagging, the ships altering course by "Blue Pendant" turns, that is, turning together by signal.

At midnight, 9th-10th, the position of the Iron Duke was Lat. 57.51 N., Long. 1.2 E.

On the 9th a telegram was dispatched to the Admiralty requesting that the movements of the Commodore (T) and Commodore (S) might be directed from the Admiralty, whilst the Commander-in-Chief with the Fleet remained in northern waters, as it was not possible to be sufficiently conversant with the conditions in the south for the Commander-in-Chief to control these movements. This plan was adopted and continued throughout the War.

On August 10th, the movements of the Fleet were as follows:

At 5 a.m. the Iron Duke parted company from the Fleet and proceeded to Scapa in order that the Commander-in-Chief might communicate by land wire with the Admiralty and make further arrangements for the work at the fleet bases. The Iron Duke, with the 2nd Cruiser Squadron, and the Falmouth, Liverpool and Bellona, arrived at Scapa at 2.30 p.m., the 2nd Flotilla forming a submarine screen through the Pentland Firth.

The remainder of the Battle Fleet proceeded north under the command of Sir George Warrender to a position to the westward of the Shetlands, in accordance with telegraphic directions received from the Admiralty, where it was considered that the submarine danger in the North Sea was considerable at this time. The 1st Battle Cruiser Squadron was detached to sweep a wide area to northward and westward in advance of the Battle Fleet, which was screened by the 4th Flotilla as far north as Lat. 60 N.; this flotilla was then detached for operations on the Norwegian coast in conjunction with the 3rd Cruiser Squadron and the 1st Light Cruiser Squadron, The latter force was directed to search for a suspected German submarine base in the vicinity of Stavanger Fiord. The Flag officer in command was directed to carry out the operation of endeavouring to locate this base — if it existed — with due regard to the susceptibilities of the Norwegians. Commodore W. E. Goodenough, commanding the 1st Light Cruiser Squadron, visited Stavanger in the Southampton and was assured by the Norwegian authorities that no base had been formed in that vicinity by the enemy.

The 2nd Cruiser Squadron and the Falmouth left Scapa at 10 p.m. on the 10th to co-operate with the 3rd Cruiser Squadron, the Hannibal and Magnificent having arrived at Scapa at

4 p.m. These two battleships were stationed to defend the Hoxa and Hoy entrances to Scapa Flow against attack by destroyers.

Rear-Admiral Miller, who arrived in the Hannibal, was placed in administrative charge of the base and of the local defences, and arrangements were made for the local Territorial Force and other inhabitants of the Orkneys and Shetlands to patrol the coast and watch the harbours. Telephonic communication round the coast was established by degrees.

Reports were received of aeroplanes having been seen over the Orkneys on the evening of the 10th, and the Centurion reported having sighted an airship north of the Shetlands on the same evening. Little credence was attached to these reports, which in the early days of the War were very frequently received.

August 11th. — The Iron Duke left Scapa and rejoined the Battle Fleet at 5 p.m. in Lat. 60.8 N., Long 3.28 W. The Battle Fleet was then exercised in forming line of battle, and also carried out sub-calibre gun practice. The 1st Battle Cruiser Squadron joined after completing its northern sweep and was detached to Scapa to fuel at 8 p.m. The 3rd Cruiser Squadron, 1st Light Cruiser Squadron, and 4th Flotilla, having completed their examination of the Norwegian coast, returned, some to Scapa and some to Cromarty, to fuel. The 2nd Cruiser Squadron returned to a position N.E. by E., 30 miles from Kinnaird Head. The Drake, flying the Flag of Rear-Admiral W. L. Grant, which had joined the Grand Fleet, was dispatched to search the coast of the Faroe Islands for possible enemy bases.

The 10th Cruiser Squadron, consisting of the old cruisers of the "Edgar" class, had by this time been established on a northern patrol area between the Shetlands and the Norwegian coast, under the command of Rear-Admiral Dudley de Chair.

On this day orders were given to establish Loch Ewe, on the northwest coast of Scotland, as a secondary coaling base for the Fleet, and Rear-Admiral Richard P. F. Purefoy was appointed to take charge of the base.

A week of war had now elapsed without any move whatever being made on the part of the High Sea Fleet; the only

German naval activities had been minelaying in southern waters during the first two days of the War, together with some submarine activity in the North Sea. The British Fleet during the week had been largely occupied in boarding all merchant vessels sighted, and in instituting as strict a blockade as was possible.

August 12th. — The Battle Fleet to the westward of the Orkneys (noon position Lat. 59.20 N., Long. 4.12 W.) was exercised during the forenoon and afternoon at battle tactics and carried out gunnery practices between 4 and 8 p.m.; it proceeded then to Scapa Flow to fuel arriving at daylight on the 15th, with the exception of the 3rd Battle Squadron, which went to Loch Ewe to coal, and to test the suitability of this base and its capability for defence against submarine attack.

The 1st Battle Cruiser Squadron, which had been fuelling at Scapa, left before dark on the 12th to cruise west of the Orkneys with orders to economise fuel in view of a projected operation to the southward.

The 2nd Cruiser Squadron and the Falmouth swept 100 miles to the southeastward from Kinnaird Head during the day, and then returned to Cromarty to fuel. The Bellona and Liverpool swept to the southeastward of the Pentland Firth during the day and night of the 12th, together with one-half of the 2nd Flotilla as a guard against destroyer attack on the Fleet whilst coaling.

The 10th Cruiser Squadron remained on the northern patrol. A report was received from Rear-Admiral Grant, in the Drake, that the position in the Faroe Islands was quite satisfactory, neutrality being observed. The Drake remained on patrol to the north-eastward of the Faroe Islands, and two ships of the 10th Cruiser Squadron were sent to assist her in her work of blockade.

Rear-Admiral E. R. Pears was on this date appointed in charge of the Fleet Base at Cromarty.

The Admiralty informed me that a neutral steamer from Hamburg had arrived in England and reported that there were fourteen enemy battleships at Cuxhaven on the 9th inst., together with several minelayers; that there were 30 destroyers between Cuxhaven and Heligoland, and that a large minefield had been laid outside the entrance to the Jade river. This was the first definite news of the enemy's main fleet.

August 13th. — The Dreadnought Battle Fleet was coaling at Scapa during the day, and the 3rd Battle Squadron coaling and storing at Loch Ewe. My object in providing this alternative base was to expedite entry into the bases for fuelling, and also to be prepared with a second base in the event of Scapa Flow becoming untenable by submarine attack.

The Albemarle relieved the Liverpool and Bellona on patrol to the eastward of the Orkneys in the evening, these two ships returning to Scapa to fuel.

The 1st Battle Cruiser Squadron was at sea west of the Orkneys; the 2nd Cruiser Squadron at Cromarty coaling; the 3rd Cruiser Squadron at sea sweeping to the southeastward from the Aberdeenshire coast; and the 1st Light Cruiser Squadron at Scapa coaling. The Falmouth was now attached to this squadron.

The 10th Cruiser Squadron and the Drake were on the northern and Faroe patrols. During the day the Commander-in-Chief held a conference with the Flag officers of the Fleet and explained the operations contemplated on the 15th and 16th inst. At 7.30 p.m. the Dreadnought Battle Fleet proceeded to sea to the westward, except two ships which had not finished coaling, the operation having been again delayed owing to an insufficient number of colliers being provided. They followed later.

Ajax reported a turret defective, and was sent back to effect repairs with the aid of the Cyclops.

August 14th. — During the forenoon the Dreadnought Battle Fleet and battle cruisers were carrying out target practice. Noon position of the Iron Duke, Lat. 59.11 N., Long. 4.27 W.

At 2 p.m. all Battle Squadrons, including the 3rd Battle Squadron from Rosyth and the 6th Battle Squadron, rejoined the Flag, and battle exercises, including deployments, were carried out till 7 p.m.

At midnight the whole Fleet passed through the Fair Island Channel on its way to carry out a sweep in the North Sea.

During the night of the 14th-15th all squadrons were moving towards a concentration rendezvous in the North Sea, that for the 2nd and 3rd Cruiser Squadrons being Lat. 58.52 N., Long. 0.0, and for the 1st Light Cruiser Squadron Lat. 59.0 N., Long. 0.15 E., at 3 a.m. on the 15th; the rendezvous for the 2nd and 4th Flotillas was Lat. 59. 7 N., Long. 0.40 W., at 4 a.m. the 15th; for the minesweepers Lat. 58.40 N., Long. 3.45 E., at 6. p.m. the 15th; four ships of the 10th Cruiser Squadron from the northern patrol joined the Fleet at 6 a.m. on the 15th.

Towards the end of July, 1914, information from a usually reliable source had been received at the Admiralty indicating that the Germans intended carrying out a very extensive minelaying policy in British waters in the event of war between the two countries. The actual positions of many minefields were given by our informant, and it was apparent, provided the information were correct, that the enemy intended to lay mines regardless of their effect on mercantile traffic, whether British, Allied, or neutral.

The proceedings of the minelayer Koningen Louise in the first days of war tended to confirm this view, and consequently it was thought to be quite probable that minefields of an extensive character might be laid in the North Sea, in positions where they might be expected to be effective against any movement of our Fleet, particularly any southward movement.

The small margin of superiority which we possessed over the German fleet, as compared with the immense difference in our naval responsibilities, made it very necessary that precautions should be taken to safeguard the most valuable of our ships from such a menace when operating in waters that might be mined.

It was for this reason that the six minesweepers accompanied the Battle Fleet during this sweep, for, although the speed of the Fleet was necessarily reduced by their presence in order to admit of sweeping operations, and the danger from submarine attack thereby increased, and although the sweeping operations could only be carried out in an exploratory fashion, there was the chance that the danger incurred by taking the whole Fleet over possible minefields might be much reduced.

Later, when it became impossible to take the sweepers to sea as their presence was more necessary in the vicinity of the bases, the practice was introduced of placing one of the older battleships of the 6th Battle Squadron ahead of each squadron of the Dreadnought Fleet in order that these less valuable ships might first discover the mines instead of the Dreadnought battleships. The officers and men of the 6th Battle Squadron named their Squadron the "Mine Bumping Squadron" on this account.

August 15th. — At noon the Iron Duke's position was Lat. 58.16 N., Long. 1.45 E., the whole Fleet being in company in cruising order and steering to the eastward, preparatory to turning south. The plan of operations included a sweep of the southern part of the North Sea by cruiser forces comprising some of the older cruisers, together with the 1st and 3rd Flotillas from Harwich; two of our submarines had been ordered to be off the Ems and two off the Jade by 6 a.m. on the 16th.

During the day three seaplanes and two aeroplanes arrived at Scapa for reconnaissance work from the base.

August 16th. — At 4 a.m. the Iron Duke was in Lat. 56.43 N., Long. 4.5 E. At 8 a.m., no report having been received of the sighting of any German vessels, the Commander-in-Chief directed the cruisers to continue the sweep until 9.30 a.m. At this time the Fleet-flagship Iron Duke's position was Lat. 55.56 N., Long. 4.40 E., the battle cruisers being some 40 to 50 miles ahead of the Battle Fleet. The only enemy vessel seen was one submarine by the New Zealand at 10.35 a.m. in Lat. 55.45 N., Long. 5.26 E.

The weather was very fine with high visibility, and at 9.30 a.m., the cruisers being then well to the southward of the latitude of the Horn Reef, the whole Fleet turned to the northward, the Battle Fleet on a north by west course, at a speed of 12 knots, zigzagging.

Rear-Admiral Christian, of the 7th Cruiser Squadron, reported that the sweep of the southern force had been unproductive.

The cruisers were now disposed on a wide front for a northerly sweep, spreading from the Norwegian coast, for a distance of 150 miles, to the westward, with the Battle Fleet in the centre. The 2nd Cruiser Squadron swept to Lister, on the Norwegian coast, and then along that coast as far as Lat. 60 N., thence towards Kinnaird Head, with the 1st Battle Cruiser Squadron prolonging and supporting. The 3rd Cruiser Squadron extended the front to the westward, supported by the 3rd Battle Squadron.

The 1st Light Cruiser Squadron remained in rear of the Battle Fleet until dusk, and then was stationed 12 miles ahead. The 10th Cruiser Squadron, spread 10 miles apart, covered the area between the Battle Fleet and the 2nd Cruiser Squadron. The 2nd and 4th Flotillas remained with the Battle Fleet, acting as a submarine screen by day, and keeping in rear of the Fleet at night.

The minesweepers, which had swept ahead of the Battle Fleet when on the southerly course, acted as a submarine screen during the passage to the northward. During the night of the 16th-17th the 3rd Cruiser Squadron was detached to Cromarty to coal, the 10th Cruiser Squadron to Scapa to coal, and to resume the northern patrol, and the 6th Battle Squadron, the 2nd Flotilla minesweepers and 3rd Battle Squadron proceeded to Scapa to fuel.

August 17th. — At 7.15 a.m. the Dreadnought Battle Fleet altered course to pass through the Fair Island Channel, and the 1st Battle Cruiser Squadron rejoined, The 4th Flotilla, which had been disposed astern during the night, resumed station as a submarine screen at daylight. The Battle Fleet zigzagged as usual throughout daylight.

At noon the Iron Duke's position was Lat. 58.59 N., Long. 1.35 E. At midnight, Lat. 59.27 N., Long. 2.25 W., and at 8 a.m. the 18th, Lat. 58.44 N., Long. 4.47 W.

The 2nd Cruiser Squadron on the northerly sweep sighted only neutral vessels and proceeded to work in an area designated as No. 5 (eastward from Kinnaird Head). Noon position, Lat. 58.42 N., Long. 3.0 E.

This area. No. 5 was designed to cover the approach to the Pentland Firth, both for blockade purposes and as an outpost position for the Fleet at Scapa.

At this time, the northern and central parts of the North Sea were divided into certain numbered areas in which cruisers could be directed by wireless to work without the necessity of making a long signal.

The various areas were approximately placed as follows:

Area No. 1. — Covering the route round the north end of the Shetland Islands from the southward and eastward.

"No. 2. Covering the Fair Island Channel to southeastward, working down to the line Kinnaird Head — Udsire.

"No. 3. Southeastward from the N.E. end of the Orkneys to Lat. of Kinnaird Head, with a width of about 50 miles from the line Noss Head — Kinnaird Head.

"No. 4. Southeastward 120 miles from the line Kinnaird Head — Udsire Lighthouse between 70 and 140 miles from Kinnaird Head.

"No. 5. Southeastward 120 miles from the line Kinnaird Head — Udsire Lighthouse, between Area 4 and Norwegian territorial waters.

"No. 6. Southeastward 120 miles from the line Kinnaird Head — Udsire lighthouse, between 20 and 70 miles from Elinnaird Head.

"No. 7. Between Lat. 55.20 N. and 57.50 N. and between 50 and 150 miles from the English coast.

The 10th Cruiser Squadron, having coaled, left to resume the northern patrol; the Drake, and the two ships acting with her, were ordered to return to Scapa to coal, and directions were given for the other two ships to rejoin the 10th Cruiser Squadron subsequently. During the day the Orion developed serious condenser defects, necessitating retubing her condensers. A telegram was sent to the Admiralty requesting that new condenser tubes might be sent at once to Loch Ewe, together with dockyard workmen to assist with the retubing.

Meanwhile arrangements were made for giving fleet assistance to the Orion, and for all suitable spare condenser tubes from the fleet to be sent to her on arrival.

The situation as regards the coal supply to the Fleet had by this time become very serious, and was causing me much anxiety; in reply to strong representations to the Admiralty, a telegram was received explaining the position and the efforts being made to rectify matters.

The Admiralty also informed me of the great importance that was attached to the efficiency of the northern patrol, and stated that four armed merchant ships were being sent to reinforce the 10th Cruiser Squadron.

The constant sea work had by this time shown the inadequacy of the engine-room implements of all ships for war conditions, and, in consequence of representations to this effect, 1,000 R.N.R. firemen were sent to Scapa for distribution amongst the various ships. The benefit derived from this measure was very considerable.

Two Fleet messenger vessels, the Cambria and Anglia, arrived at Scapa on the 17th. These ships were used for communications between the bases, for carrying mails and despatches, and for boarding duties.

August 18th. — The Dreadnought Battle Fleet arrived at Loch Ewe to fuel early in the afternoon; it was accompanied by the 1st Light Cruiser Squadron which was without the Falmouth and Liverpool. The attached cruisers were anchored in suitable positions for defending the entrance against submarine attack, so far as they were capable of doing it, and the armed steamboats of the fleet patrolled the entrance.

The 1st Battle Cruiser Squadron had been detached to Scapa at daylight to fuel. A coaling base for the 10th Cruiser Squadron had been by this time established at Lerwick in order to shorten the distance for the ships when proceeding to fuel. The Alsatian, an armed merchant ship, joined the 10th Cruiser Squadron.

The Assistance arrived at Loch Ewe as base repair ship, and was connected to the shore telegraph system.

Aeroplanes were reported off Foula Island, southwest of the Shetlands, during the night of the 18th-19th. Enquiry showed this rumour to be false. The Admiralty informed me on this date that Rear-Admiral Arthur Christian, with his Flag in the Sapphire, had been placed in command of all forces in the southern portion of the North Sea, namely, Cruiser force C, the destroyer and submarine flotillas. As already explained, these forces were acting under direct Admiralty orders and were independent of me, unless ordered to join my Flag.

This organisation was dropped later on, after the loss of the Cressy, Aboukir and Hogue, Cruiser force C being abolished, and the command of the destroyer and submarine forces reverting to their own senior officers.

August 19th, 21st, 22nd.— The Battle Fleet and 1st Battle Cruiser Squadron remained in harbour during the 19th, coaling, storing, cleaning boilers, and taking in additional ammunition up to a maximum storage. With the exception of the Orion, these ships left on the 20th at 6.30 p.m. for an area to the westward of the Orkneys and Shetlands, with orders to carry out target practice on the 21st. The battle cruiser New Zealand was ordered to the Humber to join the Invincible.

As Commodore Keyes reported on this date that our submarines in the Heligoland Bight were being followed and watched by German trawlers fitted with wireless, I informed the Admiralty that I proposed to treat such vessels as men of war. This was approved. The 2nd and 3rd Cruiser Squadrons were directed to work in Patrol Area 1 alternately, and to carry out target practice in the Cromarty Firth, en route to the patrol area.

The practice of the Battle Fleet on the 21st was interfered with by fog and the Fleet did not form up until late at night, and passed through the Fair Island Channel into the North Sea during the early morning of the 22nd. The Battle Fleet was joined off Fair Island by the 1st Light Cruiser Squadron, was exercised in battle tactics during the day, and in the afternoon was joined by the 2nd Flotilla as a submarine screen in Lat. 59.50 N., Long. 1.30 E. The position of the Iron Duke at midnight, 22nd-23rd, was Lat. 59.34 N., Long. 1.58 E., steering to southward.

The 1st Battle Cruiser Squadron, which had been detained at Scapa by fog during the 21st, carried out target practice to the westward of the Orkneys on the 22nd, and then proceeded to a position in Lat. 59.15 N., Long. 1 E., in readiness to support cruisers of the 3rd Cruiser Squadron and the 6th Cruiser Squadron, now comprising the Drake and King Alfred, which were ordered to work between Scotland and Norway in areas to the southward of the position named.

There were no reports of enemy ships being sighted except one submarine in Lat. 55.4 N., Long. 1.35 E., on August 20th. The Admiralty informed me on this date that the Portsmouth floating-dock had left for Cromarty north about, in pursuance of the policy decided on before the War. It was, therefore, suggested that one of the boy artificers' floating workshops should be sent north to work in conjunction with the dock. Steps were taken to carry out this suggestion, but the ship was lost on passage in bad weather near Portland.

August 23rd. — The Battle Fleet remained cruising in the North Sea in support of the Cruiser Squadrons, the weather being misty, with rain. The 3rd Battle Squadron was detached to Scapa to coal, to arrive at daylight, the 24th; the 2nd and 6th Cruiser Squadrons and 1st Light Cruiser Squadron, supported by the 1st Battle Cruiser Squadron, were sweeping to the southward as far south as Lat. 56 N.; the Alsatian was sent with the 6th Cruiser Squadron to look out off Jaederens Point, on the southern coast of Norway, to ascertain if German merchant ships, trying to make their own ports, were leaving territorial waters at this point, and, if so, to capture them. One half of the 2nd Flotilla was screening the Battle Fleet, the second half searching for a submarine reported east of the Orkneys. A submarine was sighted by the Ruby of the 2nd Flotilla with the Battle Fleet at 5 p.m., and course altered to avoid her.

The destroyers Rifleman and Comet collided in a fog, the latter being considerably damaged.

The Sappho was sent to search North Rona Island, a statement having been received indicating that it might possibly have been used by the enemy as a base for aircraft. She reported, after examination, that the island was, as expected, unsuitable for such a purpose.

The Ajaw reported having burnt out a boiler, and the Admiralty was asked to instruct the contractors to send to Scapa men and tubes for retubing it. The King Edward VII reported cracks in the inner A tubes of two of her 12-inch guns.

August 24th. — The Battle Fleet cruised between the Orkneys and the Norwegian coast, and carried out battle tactics during the forenoon, the weather becoming too thick in the afternoon.

The 1st Battle Squadron was detached to Scapa to fuel, as well as the 1st Light Cruiser Squadron, the latter being relieved by the 3rd Cruiser Squadron. The remainder of the cruisers continued their sweeping operations as on the 23rd.

August 25th. — The 3rd Battle Squadron left Scapa to relieve the 1st Battle Cruiser Squadron in immediate support of the cruisers at 6 a.m., and while en route to its position captured an Austrian steamer, the Attila. The remainder of the Battle Fleet left its cruising ground, arriving at Scapa at 7.30 a.m, on the 26th, with the 1st Battle Cruiser Squadron to fuel. The Agincourt, a new battleship which was bought from Turkey when still in an unfinished state, was met off Noss Head and entered with the Fleet. At 5.30 p.m. a submarine was sighted from the bridge of the Iron Duke, and the Fleet manoeuvred clear of the position. One-half of the 4th Flotilla, which had screened the 3rd Battle Squadron to sea, joined the Commander-in-Chief at 5 p.m., and was ordered to search for this submarine, but without result. The Drake, of the 6th Cruiser Squadron, left the Norwegian coast for Scapa at 4 a.m., the 25th, owing to condenser trouble. The Dominion reported two of her 12-inch guns cracked. The King Edward VII left Scapa for Devonport to change her two guns, which had also cracked. Vice-Admiral Bradford shifting his flag to the battleship Dominion. The weather was thick during the night of the 25th-26th, but the fog lifted sufficiently for the Battle Fleet to enter Scapa.

August 26th. — The Iron Duke, the 2nd and 4th Battle Squadrons, 1st Battle Cruiser Squadron, and 2nd Flotilla, were at Scapa fuelling.

The 1st Battle Squadron, with one-half of the 4th Flotilla, left to join the 3rd Battle Squadron at sea, their departure having been delayed for some hours by thick fog.

The 2nd Cruiser Squadron left patrol at 5 p.m. for Rosyth to coal.

The 6th Cruiser Squadron left patrol at 8 p.m. to coal, the King Alfred at Scapa, and the Alsatian at Liverpool; the arrangements in the large merchant-ships were such as to render coaling from colliers a difficult and slow progress.

The 10th Cruiser Squadron, except the Mantua, left the northern patrol to coal at Scapa.

During the day the Admiralty informed me of some operations which the southern forces were intended to carry out in the Heligoland Bight on the 28th, and directed that the 1st Light Cruiser Squadron should join in the operations. I made urgent representations as to the necessity of supporting the force with battle cruisers, and informed the Admiralty that I was sending the 1st Battle Cruiser Squadron to take part. I requested that the Vice-Admiral, 1st Battle Cruiser Squadron, and the Commodore, 1st Light Cruiser Squadron, might be informed direct by the Admiralty of the positions which the other ships would occupy, and that the senior officers of the southern force taking part should also be informed of the presence of the battle cruisers and 1st Light Cruiser Squadron.

On this date 1,000 additional seamen ratings arrived to join the Fleet, experience having shown that the number of deck complements, as well as the engine-room complements, required increasing, principally owing to the heavy guns of the secondary armament being so constantly manned at sea — by day against submarine attack, and by night against destroyer attack.

August 27th. — On this date I wired to the Admiralty proposing the erection of two wireless stations in the Orkneys for local communication, and a directional station to assist in locating the positions of German ships using wireless. The remainder of the Battle Fleet proceeded to sea at 6 p.m. to join the 1st and 3rd Battle Squadrons at 7 a.m. on the 28th to the southeastward of the Orkneys in Lat. 58.20 N., Long. 0.20 W. The 2nd Flotilla accompanied the Fleet as a submarine screen.

On this date a patrol of the eastern approaches to the Pentland Firth was inaugurated by the Minelaying Squadron which was not required at the time for mine laying operations, with the object of ensuring a closer watch on the mercantile traffic through the Pentland Firth, and the Oceanic, an armed merchant cruiser, which had joined the Fleet, was detached to carry out a patrol to the westward of the Fair Island Channel in order to control the traffic at this point.

Information was received from the Admiralty of the existence of mined areas off Harwich, Flamborough Head and Tynemouth. The positions of the two latter minefields appeared to corroborate the information obtained prior to the outbreak of war.

A collision occurred at 9.30 p.m. between the Bellerophon and the S.S. St. Clair, which was passing through the Fleet. The St. Clair was damaged, but the damage to the Bellerophon was not serious.

August 28th. — The weather was misty with a visibility of 4 to 6 miles until the evening, when it cleared slightly. The Battle Fleet during the day proceeded to the southward, the noon position being Lat. 58.19 N., Long. 0.21 E., with cruisers in advance. The Fleet was exercised during the day at battle tactics.

The sweep of light forces into the Heligoland Bight which took place at dawn was successful in bringing enemy light forces to action. The events may be shortly described here. At 6.53 a.m. Commodore Tyrwhitt, commanding the Harwich force, which had swept into the Heligoland Bight during the night to cut off enemy vessels, sighted a destroyer and chased her. From 7.20 to 8 a.m. the Arethusa and the 3rd Flotilla were in action with destroyers and torpedo-boats making for Heligoland, sinking one destroyer. At 7.57 the Arethusa, Commodore Tyrwhitt's flagship, which had been in commission only a few days, sighted two enemy light cruisers, and engaged them, assisted a little later by the light cruiser Fearless. At 8.25 a.m. a hit from the Arethusa wrecked the fore bridge of one of the enemy ships, and they both steamed at once for

Heligoland, which was then sighted, and our ships turned to the westward. The Arethusa had been considerably damaged during the action and had suffered several casualties.

At 10.55 a.m. another German light cruiser was sighted by the Arethusa, and on being attacked by the Fearless and destroyers turned away; she reappeared at 11.5 and engaged the Arethusa and Fearless and was attacked by these ships and by destroyers and again turned away. Meanwhile Commodore Tyrwhitt had informed Sir David Beatty of the position, and that officer proceeded at full speed to his support. The light cruiser Mainz had been attacking the somewhat disabled Arethusa and the Fearless at about 11.30 a.m. and had suffered very severely in the action, being practically disabled. The arrival of the First Light Cruiser Squadron, under Commodore Goodenough, on the scene at about noon secured her destruction.

Between 12.37 p.m and 1.45 p.m. the 1st Battle Cruiser Squadron and 1st Light Cruiser Squadron engaged two other German light cruisers, one of which was sunk; the second was last seen burning furiously and in a sinking condition.

Even thus early in the War the difference between the behaviour of British and German seamen was noticeable. On the British side, in addition to other assistance rendered to the survivors of the Mainz (which had been sunk), Commander Keyes, in the destroyer Firedrake, proceeded alongside and rescued 220 of her crew, many of them being wounded. A German light cruiser opened fire on the British destroyers engaged in picking up survivors from the German destroyer V187 when that vessel was sunk by our craft, thus making it necessary for the destroyers to leave behind the boats carrying out the rescue work. The British submarine E4 afterwards took our officers and men out of these boats and left some unwounded Germans to take the other boats, which contained German wounded, to Heligoland.

In the afternoon of August 28th the 10th Cruiser Squadron was directed to work in Area No. 6, leaving the armed merchant cruisers farther to the northward. The object was to give a better chance of intercepting enemy vessels or neutral ships carrying contraband of war by establishing two patrols on the probable exit or entrance courses, one of which would in all probability be crossed of necessity during daylight hours, even if the second were passed through at night.

August 29th. — This was a bright, fine day, with high visibility. The Dreadnought Battle Fleet remained at sea with three divisions of the 2nd Flotilla, cruising and carrying out battle tactics and other exercises.

The 1st Battle Cruiser Squadron arrived at Scapa to fuel at 7 p.m., in company with the 1st Light Cruiser Squadron, the Liverpool being detached to Rosyth to land the German prisoners captured in the Heligoland Bight on the 28th.

The 2nd Cruiser Squadron was cruising in Area No. 5, which the 3rd Cruiser Squadron left during the day for Cromarty to fuel.

The 6th Cruiser Squadron and 10th Cruiser Squadron were in Area No. 6; the minelayers were in Area No. 3.

During the day the Oak arrived from Scapa with telegrams and despatches for me and returned with similar correspondence for the Admiralty. The Oak was usually employed on this duty while the Iron Duke was at sea during the earlier months of the War, my infrequent visits to a base rendering this essential.

Some risk from submarine attack was naturally involved during the time that the Iron Duke, or any other heavy ship, was stopped to communicate. The risk was recognised, and, as the number of enemy submarines increased, it became undesirable to incur it, and the practice of stopping ships at sea for any such purpose was abandoned; the longer time spent in harbour tended to reduce the necessity for the practice to some extent, but during the early part of the War this was the only means of conveying despatches to the Fleet when it was constantly at sea.

The reported increase in enemy minelaying off our eastern coasts caused me to suggest to the Admiralty at this time the desirability of the patrol flotillas working somewhat farther seaward, and to ask for an increase as soon as possible in the number of fast light craft to work off the northern fleet bases.

A request for 20 drifters to work in the approaches to the Pentland Firth was also forwarded.

The Fleet messenger Cambria was brought out to work with the Battle Fleet for the purpose of boarding merchant ships owing to the shortage of light cruisers for this work.

August 30th. — In the afternoon the Dreadnought Battle Fleet shaped course for Scapa, and arrived at 7 a.m. on the 31st to fuel, the 3rd Battle Squadron being ordered out to the eastward of the Orkneys to support the 2nd Cruiser Squadron, which was searching the eastern portion of Area 5.

The patrol of the 6th and 10th Cruiser Squadrons was continued as usual, the 6th Cruiser Squadron leaving the Area at 3 a.m. on the 31st to fuel at Scapa.

During the day the Assistance returned to Scapa from Loch Ewe as base ship, and the Illustrious arrived there as defence ship for the entrance. I had decided her position during my previous visit.

As a result of inquiries of the Admiralty, I was informed that trawlers were being taken up and armed for patrol duties as rapidly as possible, and that arrangements for the defences of Scapa, which had formed the subject of correspondence between the Admiralty and myself, had been approved, including the laying of certain minefields at the entrances.

August 31st. — A sweep towards the Scottish coast of all vessels at sea, or ready for sea, was carried out in consequence of information having been received pointing to the possibility of minelaying by the enemy in the vicinity of the Pentland Firth or Moray Firth during the night of August 31st-September 1st; the sweep was arranged to intercept the enemy minelayers on their return trip. But it was unproductive, no minelaying having taken place. The squadrons engaged in the sweep were the 1st Battle Cruiser Squadron, 3rd Battle Squadron, 3rd Cruiser Squadron, 10th Cruiser Squadron.

In consequence of urgent representations as to the insufficiency of .303 rifle ammunition for the Army, all ships disembarked 50 per cent of their ammunition of this calibre at the end of August for conveyance to Woolwich.

Later, still more of the rifle ammunition and all but a very small number of rifles, as well as many machine guns, were landed from the Fleet for use by the Army.

A meeting of all the captains of Dreadnought battleships was held on board the Iron Duke on August 31st in order to discuss with them the subject of tactics in action.

5 – Mine Menace in the North Sea

On September 1st, 1914 the Dreadnought Battle Fleet with the 1st Light Cruiser Squadron, the 6th Cruiser Squadron and the 2nd and 4th Flotillas were at Scapa Flow, cleaning boilers, storing, and taking in ammunition, etc. The Fleet was at the usual anchorage off Scapa Pier, on the north side of the Flow; the ships which were fitted with torpedo nets had them out, as was customary, unless colliers or store-ships were alongside.

The Falmouth, of the 1st Light Cruiser Squadron, was anchored to the westward of Holm Sound, and the remainder of this squadron formed the outer or southward line of ships, all at two hours' notice for steam. The weather during the day was dull and misty, with rain at times.

At 6 p.m. the Falmouth reported the periscope of a submarine in sight inside the harbour, and immediately opened fire, four rounds being fired by this ship; she reported having probably hit the submarine. Directly afterwards the Vanguard, one of the outer line of battleships, also opened fire on an object reported as a periscope, as did one of the E class destroyers, which was patrolling between the Fleet and the Hoxa entrance.

The 1st Light Cruiser Squadron was directed to weigh immediately steam was ready, which was at 8.30 p.m., and to endeavour to locate the submarine and keep her under.

The 2nd Flotilla, lying at Longhope, at short notice, was also instructed to weigh at once and search for the submarine. The whole of the ships present were ordered to raise steam with all despatch, and to prepare for torpedo attack, and the small craft, such as drifters, steamboats, motor-boats, yachts, etc., which had steam ready and which could be collected, were at once organised in detachments to steam up and down the lines at high speed and outside the Fleet, with the object of confusing the submarine and endeavouring to ram her, if sighted. Colliers and store-ships which had steam ready were directed to weigh and to go alongside the battleships that were not fitted with torpedo nets, in order to act as a form of protection against torpedoes fired at these valuable vessels. All ships in the outer lines were directed to burn searchlights to locate and confuse the submarine.

At about 6.30 p.m. the Drake reported a submarine in sight from that ship, thus confirming the earlier reports.

The Fleet was directed to weigh by divisions as soon as steam was ready and to proceed to sea. By 9 p.m. the weather was exceedingly thick inside the harbour and considerable difficulty was experienced in getting the Fleet out, as at this time there were no navigational facilities of any sort for leaving the harbour at night or in thick weather; but by 11 p.m. all the ships had left the harbour without accident, and, although there was a dense fog outside, the Fleet cleared the Pentland Firth successfully.

The Assistance was ordered to Loch Ewe, and left after the Fleet, reporting having sighted a submarine in the entrance whilst going out. The 2nd Flotilla was left behind to locate and, if possible, destroy the submarine, and the 4th Flotilla was stationed outside the Hoxa and Hoy entrances during the night, and directed to meet the Fleet at 7 a.m. on the 2nd. The only ship, as distinct from destroyers, remaining in the harbour was the Cyclops, lying off Scapa with the telegraph and telephone cables on board, and directions were given to Rear-Admiral Miller to endeavour to locate, by means of the minesweeping gunboats, the submarine reported sunk by the Falmouth.

No trace of a submarine was discovered, and subsequent investigation showed that the alarm may have been false, the evidence not being conclusive either way.

The incident, however, made it clear that protection against submarine attack was an absolute necessity, as the Fleet could not remain at a base that was as open to this form of attack as Scapa Flow. The only possible action, in the event of an alarm being given of the presence of a submarine, was to take the Fleet to sea, and, in addition to the dangers arising at that time from a hurried departure in thick weather, a feeling of insecurity was created, which would be bad for moral, and the ships were deprived of opportunities for cleaning boilers, refitting machinery, etc., which experience was showing was essential if the steaming efficiency of the Fleet was to be maintained.

The matter was at once represented to the Admiralty and proposals were made for blocking all the entrances to Scapa Flow, except the Hoxa and Hoy entrances, by sinking old merchant ships in the channels. Pending the supply of reliable defences for the main entrance, Rear-Admiral Miller was directed to requisition a large number of net-drifters. The plan was to lay drift nets in the entrance to be watched by the drifters, the nets having indicator buoys attached to them and floating on the surface, so that the presence of a submarine might be indicated by the buoy moving with the net.

The navigational difficulties of the narrower entrances were, meanwhile, the only obstacles to the passage of submarines through them, but it was realised that these were considerable. The opinion was formed, however, that the Hoxa entrance presented no insurmountable difficulty of this nature to a determined submarine commander.

By this date the local defence flotilla of destroyers consisted of vessels of the E class. A request was made for basing a hunting flotilla of 16 trawlers on Kirkwall, these vessels being intended to guard the approaches to the Pentland Firth and to act as submarine hunters generally. It was also suggested that a monetary reward should be offered to the personnel of any trawler through whose agency a submarine was captured or destroyed.

The minesweeping force at Scapa had been strengthened by the addition of a flotilla of trawlers, and the minesweeping gunboats and trawlers were continuously employed in keeping certain fixed channels of approach to the Pentland Firth swept and clear of mines. These vessels were, therefore, not available for anti-submarine work, except to the detriment of their minesweeping duties.

On September 1st the available cruiser squadrons were employed in Area No. 6, supported by the 3rd Battle Squadron and the 1st Battle Cruiser Squadron.

From September 1st to September 5th the Battle Fleet remained at sea, cruising in the area between the north-east coast of Scotland and the coast of Norway, in support of the cruiser squadrons working to the southward, and opportunity was taken to continue the exercises of the Fleet in battle tactics, together with occasional gunnery practice. The Orion, of the 2nd Battle Squadron, was still absent from the Fleet, retubing condensers; the King Edward VII rejoined on the 2nd, after exchanging defective guns; and the Dominion was then detached to Devonport to exchange her damaged 12-inch guns.

The 1st Battle Cruiser Squadron had been strengthened by the arrival of the Inflexible from the Mediterranean, and was employed during this period in support of the cruiser sweeps, the Squadron joining the Battle Fleet on the 3rd for battle exercises.

During the period under review reports from time to time of the sighting of enemy submarines appeared to indicate that they were working on a line Ekersund-Pentland Firth, the line which they were apparently occupying during the first few days of the War, when U 15 was sunk by the Birmingham.

Information received on September 3rd suggested that enemy cruisers might have passed, or might be intending to pass, into the North Sea via the Skagerrak. The 2nd and 3rd Cruiser Squadrons and the 1st Light Cruiser Squadron, supported by the 1st Battle Cruiser Squadron and accompanied by the 2nd Flotilla, were, therefore, directed to sweep to the entrance to the Skagerrak, arriving there by noon of September 4th, starting from a position in Lat. 58 N., Long. 2.86 E., at 4 a.m. that day. From the Skagerrak the 2nd and 3rd Cruiser Squadrons were to make a detour to the south westward with the 1st Battle Cruiser Squadron, the latter proceeding then to Rosyth and the Cruiser Squadrons to Cromarty; and the 1st Light Cruiser Squadron, with the 2nd Flotilla, was directed to sweep on a wide front towards the Pentland Firth on the Ekersund-Pentland line in search of enemy submarines, which it was hoped might be caught on the surface at night. Thence the 1st Light Cruiser Squadron was to proceed to Scapa to fuel, and the 2nd Flotilla to the westward of the Orkneys to search for submarines, returning to Longhope at 9 p.m. on September 6th. The 4th Flotilla, which had been with the Battle Fleet, was directed at the same time to sweep the western portion of the Ekersund-Pentland line for submarines, and then to return to Longhope.

These orders were carried out, but no enemy vessels of any sort were sighted, except that at 6.30 a.m. on the 5th the Thetis, minelayer, working southeastward of the Orkneys, reported a suspicious vessel, thought to be a German cruiser. The 2nd and 6th Cruiser Squadrons and 1st Light Cruiser Squadron closed in on the position, but the ship was eventually identified as one of our own vessels.

The Dreadnought Battle Fleet arrived at Loch Ewe at 4 p.m. on the 5th to coal, two minesweeping gunboats having been previously detached to that base to search the entrance for mines.

During the early days of September frequent reports were received of enemy mines having been discovered on the east coast, and several vessels were sunk, as a consequence, including the gunboat Speedy. It appeared that the enemy was laying the mines from merchant vessels flying neutral or even, possibly, British colours, as well as from regular minelaying ships. The large number of vessels trading on the east coast and of fishing craft at sea, both British and neutral, greatly increased the difficulty of preventing these operations. The task of boarding and examining even a considerable percentage of these vessels involved a heavy strain. Our cruiser sweeps were showing this daily. The Admiralty's attention was drawn to the matter, and the question was raised of establishing some restrictions, particularly as regards the areas in which fishing should be permitted.

The extinction of a large proportion of our coast lights was also proposed, the burning of which enabled the enemy to fix his position accurately when engaged in minelaying operations. This policy of the extinction of lights, thus started, gradually became general, and eventually only the most important lights were exhibited at night, and the large majority of these were only shown when requests were made by men-of-war who required them for entering port, the time of their exhibition being thus reduced to a minimum.

The Dreadnought Battle Fleet remained at Loch Ewe until 6 a.m. on September 7th, and then proceeded to sea. The Orion was left behind to complete work on her condensers and rejoined the Fleet at sea on September 9th, having been absent for twenty-one days.

The Agincourt, the new battleship which since commissioning had been engaged in gunnery and torpedo practices either at Scapa or to the westward of the Orkneys, joined the 4th Battle Squadron at sea on September 7th in order to give her officers experience in working with the Fleet. There had been great difficulty in carrying out her practices because she had not been supplied with "sub-calibre" guns, and this deficiency could not be made good for some months; this caused much delay in raising her battle efficiency. However, she was manned with officers and a ship's company of a very high standard and, in spite of all disadvantages, the early gunnery practices carried out by her in company with the Fleet showed that she would eventually prove to be a most valuable addition to the Fleet.

Representations had been made by me to the Admiralty that the presence of a senior Flag officer in general command of the Orkneys and Shetlands, who would be responsible for the defences of these islands and the Fleet bases, was very necessary, the work of actual administration of the base at Scapa Flow being sufficient fully to occupy the time of Rear-Admiral Miller.

Vice-Admiral the Hon. Sir Stanley Colville accepted the post, and as it was very desirable that the officer holding this position should be junior to the Commander-in-Chief of the Grand Fleet, he paid me the compliment of expressing his desire to be placed junior on the list to myself, a reversal of our proper respective seniorities.

He was, accordingly, appointed, and came to Loch Ewe on September 6th, to confer with me before taking up his appointment. He accompanied me to sea in the Iron Duke on the 7th in order to talk matters over, was embarked on board the Oak to the westward of the Orkneys, and took up his command on arrival. The result was immediately most beneficial.

He was able to devote his whole time to the questions of defence and organisation and relieved me of all these matters which had, as was inevitable under the previous arrangement, occupied so much of my time in harbour and so much of my thoughts at sea.

On September 6th the Portsmouth floating dock arrived safely at Cromarty.

During September 7th the Dreadnought Battle Fleet proceeded northward from Loch Ewe en route to the North Sea, and passed through the Fair Island Channel at 10 p.m., being joined at 4 a.m. by the 3rd Battle Squadron. The 1st Battle Cruiser Squadron left Rosyth after dark on this date and proceeded to the north-eastward, being joined at 4 a.m. on the 8th by the Sappho and four destroyers of the 4th Flotilla. These smaller vessels were intended to carry out boarding duties in order to avoid the danger to the large ships from submarine attack, consequent on stopping for this purpose. The 1st Battle Cruiser Squadron swept to the southeastward of Area 6 during daylight on the 8th, and during the night of the 8th and daylight of the 9th was on a patrol area approximately between Lat. 55 N., Long. 2 E., and Lat. 56.20 N., Long. 2.40 E., with the object of intercepting possible enemy minelayers. The Battle Fleet carried out gunnery practices and exercised battle tactics during the 8th eastward of the Orkneys, and at dark proceeded to the southward to support an extensive sweep into the Heligoland Bight which it had been decided to carry out on September 10th. The dispositions for this sweep were generally as follows:

The 1st and 3rd Flotillas from Harwich, supported by the 1st Light Cruiser Squadron and 1st Battle Cruiser Squadron to the northward, and the 7th Cruiser Squadron to the westward, swept out the Heligoland Bight from east to west, commencing from a position some ten to twelve miles from Heligoland, which position was to be reached one hour before dawn. The Battle Fleet, with the 2nd and 3rd Cruiser Squadrons, spread 20 miles ahead, was in position Lat. 55.9 N., Long. 4.24 E. at 8 a.m. on September 10th, steering S.S.E. at 12 knots speed of advance.

The Battle Fleet, with the 2nd and 3rd Cruiser Squadrons to the southward, cruised to the northwestward of Heligoland until 11 a.m. on the 10th, by which time it was clear that the sweep had been unproductive. No German vessel of any sort was sighted, except one seaplane reported by the 7th Cruiser Squadron. The 2nd Flotilla was stationed with the Battle Fleet as a submarine screen, and to assist the attached cruisers in boarding duties during the day, and the 4th Flotilla, which had been working with the 2nd and 3rd Cruiser Squadrons, principally for boarding duties, was also directed to join the Battle Fleet on the morning of the 10th, but by reason of the thick weather did not do so until 2 p.m. Owing to the large number of trawlers that were met with, nearly all of which were flying neutral colours, the boarding duties were very onerous. Considerable suspicion attached to these trawlers because frequently Telefunken wireless signals were noticed to be very strong after the Fleet had passed these vessels; but close examination failed to reveal anything suspicious in those that were boarded, no wireless apparatus being discovered in any of them.

The conditions on September 10th were very unfavourable for the sweep into the Bight. Thick weather prevailed both before and after daylight, and the visibility varied from between two and five miles. The mist prevented the junction of the 4th Flotilla with the Battle Fleet for eight hours, a circumstance which would have had awkward consequences had the High Sea Fleet been encountered with its full complement of 80 to 100 destroyers, as might have been the case in such close proximity to German ports.

It was noted at the time that the conditions were very unfavourable for a Fleet action owing to the low visibility combined with the glare produced by the occasional sunshine and absence of wind. A passage in the notes made on this occasion referred to such conditions as follows:

"The weather conditions ... were very unfavourable for a general action owing to the low visibility and the glare caused by brilliant sunlight and absence of wind... The conditions make it impossible for the Commander-in-Chief in the centre of the Fleet to know what is going on in the van and rear ...

besides being entirely favourable to tactics largely based on the employment of torpedo craft or minelayers.

"In addition there are great difficulties in concentrating detached ships and flotillas and in forming the Fleet prior to battle, also in the recognition of ships and destroyers."

This passage is of interest because of its bearing on the Jutland battle some two years later when somewhat similar conditions prevailed.

The difficulty of recognition mentioned made so much impression on my mind that special daylight recognition devices which could be seen at a considerable distance were subsequently devised and used by our own light cruisers and destroyers when in the presence of the enemy.

When it became evident that there were no enemy vessels to engage, I organised a sweep to the northward on a large scale, with a view to intercepting any enemy ships that might be at sea and of closely examining all merchant ships and fishing vessels which were met with.

The starting point of the sweep was Lat. 55.30 N., Long. 4.0 E., the dispositions being:

The Invincible (which had now joined the Battle Cruisers) and the Inflexible, to sweep towards Dundee.

3rd Cruiser Squadron towards Aberdeen at 12 knots speed of advance.

1st Light Cruiser Squadron towards Pentland Firth at 11 knots speed of advance.

2nd Cruiser Squadron towards Fair Island at 10 knots speed of advance.

All ships spread as widely as visibility admitted.

The 1st Battle Cruiser Squadron (which now once more included the New Zealand) to be in general support.

The Battle Fleet with divisions spread four miles apart to extend the sweep to the eastward.

These dispositions are shown below:

At 3 a.m. on the 11th the sweep was directed to turn to N. 16 E., and, later, the 2nd Cruiser Squadron was stationed in a new area, No. 7, between Lat. 55.20 N. and 57.30 N., between

50 and 150 miles from the coast. The 3rd Cruiser Squadron was sent to Cromarty to coal; the 1st Battle Cruiser Squadron and 1st Light Cruiser Squadron rejoined the Battle Fleet, and the Invincible and Inflexible were sent to Scapa to coal, as well as the 3rd Battle Squadron, a half flotilla of destroyers screening these vessels into the base.

During the 11th and 12th the Battle Fleet and 1st Battle Cruiser Squadron carried out battle tactics and gunnery exercises, and the Battle Fleet then proceeded to Loch Ewe, and the 1st Battle Cruiser Squadron and 1st Light Cruiser Squadron to Scapa to fuel.

During the passage south and north numerous reports of floating mines were received. The majority proved to be fishermen's bladders which at this time were being frequently reported by merchant ships as floating mines.

The Admiralty now informed me that a patrol of the 3rd meridian of East Long, between the parallels of 55.30 N. and 53.30 N. had been established by the 1st and 3rd Flotilla, the patrol consisting of eight destroyers and one light cruiser, supported by two cruisers of the "Bacchante" class, the object being to catch enemy minelayers. I was also informed that a patrol of the "Broad Fourteens," off the Dutch coast, was being maintained to guard the Eastern Channel and Thames approaches.

On September 11th the Hibernia reported a 12-inch gun cracked, the fifth since the outbreak of war.

On the same day salvage operations on the armed merchant-cruiser Oceanic, which had gone ashore in a fog on Foula Island on September 8th, were abandoned owing to heavy weather. The vessel broke up eventually.

Rear-Admiral E. R. Pears reported that the Portsmouth floating dock would be ready for work on September 21st, a very smart piece of mooring work having been carried out by Captain Munro, R.N., the King's Harbour Master.

The Dreadnought Battle Fleet remained at Loch Ewe coaling, storing and cleaning boilers, etc., from 5 p.m. on September 13th until 6 p.m. on September 17th, and the 1st Battle Cruiser Squadron, except the Inflexible and Invincible, remained at Scapa until September 18th. Meanwhile the usual cruiser sweeps in the North Sea in Areas 3, 6 and 7 were carried out by the 2nd, 3rd, 6th and 10th Cruiser Squadrons and the Minelayer Squadron, supported by the Invincible, Inflexible and 3rd Battle Squadron, which left Scapa on the morning of September 14th for the purpose. The armed merchant cruisers Alsatian and Mantua were patrolling eastward of the Shetlands.

Advantage was taken of the stay at Loch Ewe to make general arrangements with the Admiralty for the defence of that base, and on September 17th the First Lord of the Admiralty, with the Chief of War Staff, the Director of Intelligence Division, Commodores (S) and (T) arrived at Loch Ewe to confer with me. The bombardment and capture of Heligoland was also discussed. The proposals had been previously forwarded to me by Mr. Churchill, and had been carefully examined by myself, Rear-Admiral Charles Madden, the Chief of Staff, and by the Flag officers commanding the Battle Squadrons. The opinions of these officers against the operation were unanimous. It had not been suggested that the Grand Fleet should be used for the operation, except as a supporting force; the older battleships were intended for this purpose.

But the arguments against the operation were overwhelmingly strong. It was pointed out that ships were no match for heavy fortifications such as were known to exist on Heligoland; that direct fire from high velocity guns with a low trajectory would be ineffective against well-placed, heavily protected and well-concealed land guns; that, even if a storming party were able to land and to capture the island, it would be quite impossible to hold it, situated as it was close to German naval bases, for if we could take it in a fortified condition, it would be far easier for the Germans to recapture it with the fortifications demolished; that it would be under continuous attack by sea and air, and that any attempt to hold it, if captured, would involve keeping the Grand Fleet constantly in southern waters, which, owing to the number of small craft then available, was an impossibility. Aircraft spotting, which would be a necessary adjunct, was at that time in its infancy, and we had no vessels especially suited for bombardments at long range, such as the monitors which, later on, carried out such useful work on the Belgian coast. After a conference, at which the Flag officers were present, I thought that the idea would be abandoned.

This was not the case, however, and the matter was taken up later at the Admiralty with Vice-Admiral Sir Cecil Burney, commanding the Channel Fleet. His view coincided with those expressed by the Flag officers at the Loch Ewe conference, although he was of course prepared to carry out any orders that might be given him. The idea was not finally abandoned for some time. The opinions of Sir Cecil Burney and myself were identical, as indeed were those of every Flag officer with whom I discussed the matter, with one single exception, a junior Flag officer.

Another subject touched on during Mr. Churchill's visit was that of operations in the Baltic, but as no large operations of this nature could be attempted without the assistance of Allied battleships, in order to maintain supremacy in the North Sea during such operations, no steps were taken.

By this date a regular programme of dockings and refits for all ships was recognised as necessary, and battleships were now being detached one at a time for this purpose. For some months after the commencement of the War, it was not possible to allow ships more than four days for docking and for the execution of the most urgent work, except in cases of accident or very serious defects, as our margin of superiority was none too large, and we were already experiencing a good deal of trouble with condenser tubes, necessitating ships being laid up for the work of retubing; but the work achieved in the four days was a very fine tribute to the dockyard organisation and to the industry of the dockyard men.

The Battle Fleet left Loch Ewe on the evening of September 17th, the Erin, a new battleship bought, incomplete, from Turkey, being in company for the first time in order to accustom her officers to working the ship with the Fleet. Target practice was carried out to the westward of the Orkneys during the forenoon of the 18th, but was interfered with by bad weather — a frequent experience. The Battle Fleet then proceeded into the North Sea, via the Fair Island Channel, the position at midnight, 18th, being Lat. 59.23 N., Long. 1.13 W., and course south. The 1st Battle Cruiser Squadron left Scapa with the 1st Light Cruiser Squadron on the evening of the 19th, and the 2nd Cruiser Squadron left Cromarty at the same time, all for the southward for a sweep into the Heligoland Bight, supported by the Battle Fleet, in search of the enemy and with a view to carrying out a thorough examination of trawlers suspected of acting as look-out vessels for the enemy.

While on passage south during the September 19th, the Battle Fleet was exercised at battle tactics. At midnight on the 19th the Battle Fleet was in position Lat. 58.3 N., Long. 2.24 E., and at 8 a.m. on the 20th, in Lat. 57.8 N., Long. 3.20 E., having met the 2nd Cruiser Squadron. The 2nd Flotilla had been under orders to leave Scapa in time to meet the Battle Fleet at 8 a.m. on the 21st, but, owing to bad weather, the orders were cancelled and the flotilla returned to Scapa, as did the 4th Flotilla, which was to have accompanied the battle cruisers. During daylight of the 20th the Battle Fleet cruised towards the Norwegian coast to the northward of Lat. 57 N., in support of the battle cruisers engaged in examining trawlers in the vicinity of the Little Fisher Bank; it turned to the southward at 4 p.m. to rendezvous, at 5 a.m. on the 21st, in Lat. 56 N., Long. 3.30 E., with the 3rd Battle Squadron, which had been coaling at Scapa and had left on the 20th to join the Commander-in-Chief.

At 7 a.m. on the September 21st, the Battle Fleet was in position Lat. 55.45 N., Long. 3.30 E., and the Vice-Admiral of the battle cruisers having reported at 6.20 a.m. from a position in Lat. 55.16 N., Long. 4.52 E., that the weather was too bad to admit of the search of trawlers being carried out satisfactorily, the operation was abandoned and the Fleet turned to the northward, as it was considered that an incomplete examination would do more harm than good.

During this period the 3rd Cruiser Squadron was working in Area 7, and the 10th Cruiser Squadron in Area 6, as usual; the Alsatian and Mantua, with the Drake, of the 6th Cruiser Squadron, were sweeping down the Norwegian coast and then returned to resume their patrol east of the Shetlands, where they were joined by the armed merchant ship Teutonic.

The 2nd and 4th Flotillas left Scapa on the 20th and joined the Battle Fleet and the Battle Cruiser Squadron respectively on the 21st.

All wireless telegraphy signalling at sea was stopped between 4 p.m. on the 20th and 4 p.m. on the 21st, in order that the enemy should not become aware of the movements of the Fleet, as such knowledge might prevent the High Sea Fleet from putting to sea and possibly deprive us of our opportunity of catching it.

During the passage of the Fleet to the northward, an extensive sweep was carried out during daylight of the 21st. The Battle Fleet covered a front of 40 miles, and battle cruisers and cruisers prolonged the front to the eastward and westward.

On the evening of the 21st I was informed by wireless telegraphy from the Admiralty of a report that a German force of two light cruisers, with destroyers and submarines in company, had been sighted from Esbjerg on the 20th, proceeding to the northward. The whole Fleet was turned to the southward at midnight on the 21st, and spread at dawn to cover a front of 104 miles from the Norwegian coast westward, sweeping to the northward, to endeavour to intercept the enemy vessels if they had continued a course to the northward. The sweep to the northward was continued until 10 a.m. The Iron Duke was in position Lat. 69 N., Long. 2.35 E., when the line was directed to wheel towards the Orkneys and Shetlands on a course N. 51 W. During the 22nd, visibility was very good, but no enemy vessels were sighted, and the Dreadnought Battle Fleet and battle cruisers passed to the westward of the Orkneys during the night, the 3rd Battle Squadron and 6th Battle Squadron being detached to support the cruisers searching in the North Sea areas.

At 7.45 a.m. on the September 22nd wireless telegraphy signals from the Creasy were intercepted indicating that the Aboukir and Hogue had been sunk by submarines in Lat. 52.18 N., Long. 3.41 E. These vessels were patrolling the "Broad Fourteens," off the Dutch Coast, under Admiralty orders. No further details were received, beyond a wireless signal from Commodore (S), at 11.80 a.m., that he was proceeding in the Fearless with seventeen destroyers to Terschelling to endeavour to intercept the enemy submarines on their way back. The Commander-in-Chief, thereupon, ordered the 2nd Cruiser Squadron (from the southern position of Area 7) to proceed at once to support the Commodore (S). By directions, however, given by the Admiralty these orders were cancelled, and the forces returned.

At 10.30 p.m. I ordered the armed merchant-cruisers to proceed at once to a position off Trondhjem, as a report had been received that the German liner Brandenburg, lying at that port, was likely to sail. Constant reports to this effect were received for several days, and the Brandenburg was heard using her wireless telegraphy on September 25th. The patrol was maintained until September 28th, when contradictory reports were to hand — one that she had been seen at sea on the 27th, and the other that she was being interned by the Norwegian Government. The latter report proved to be correct. The patrol was then moved to a position off the Utvoer Lighthouse, Lat. 61.3 N., Long. 4.30 E., to intercept the German commerce destroyer Prinz Friedrich Wilhelm, said to be leaving a Norwegian port.

During the 23rd the Dreadnought Battle Fleet and battle cruisers attempted to carry out gunnery practices, but thick weather interfered. The force returned to Scapa to fuel, arriving on the 24th; the 3rd Battle Squadron arrived for the same purpose on the 25th,

On September 23rd and 24th, the 2nd Cruiser Squadron proceeded from Area 7 to sweep up the Norwegian coast, thence going to Cromarty to coal. The squadron arrived there on the evening of the 25th.

The Dreadnought Battle Fleet remained at Scapa until the evening of the 25th September, when it proceeded out to the westward of the Orkneys; on the 26th bad weather again prevented target practice, a heavy westerly gale being experienced. This moderated on the morning of the 27th, when the Battle Fleet was to the eastward of the Shetlands, but increased again to a very strong gale during that day, with a wind force of 70 miles per hour and a very heavy confused sea.

A considerable amount of damage was done to wireless masts, topmasts, etc., and several ships had boats damaged or washed away. The ships of the "Iron Duke" class took in large quantities of water through their 6-inch gun ports, due to these guns being mounted at such a low level. The gale continued during the 28th, veering to the northward, and moderated on the 29th, on which date the Battle Fleet, which had moved to the southward during the 28th, returned to Scapa, being met and screened by destroyers which had not been able to join the Fleet at sea owing to the bad weather.

The 1st Battle Cruiser Squadron left Scapa on the morning of the September 26th, and proceeded to the Norwegian coast, sweeping down as far as the Naze in search of enemy ships, particularly the S.S. Prinz Friedrich Wilhelm, reported to be about to leave Bergen. It was also to support the Drake, Nottingham, Falmouth, and two destroyers, which had been sent to the vicinity of the Naze to meet Submarines E1 and E5. The latter vessels had been reconnoitering in the Skagerrak and Kattegat for enemy vessels. The two submarines and the destroyers experienced very heavy weather on their return across the North Sea, and some anxiety was felt for their safety.

The 3rd Cruiser Squadron proceeded to Area 2 on the 26th, and on the 29th was sent to watch off the entrances to Bergen in Norway for the German s.s. Prinz Friedrich Wilhelm. The squadron returned to Cromarty on October 1st. On the 28th the Princess Royal left the 1st Battle Cruiser Squadron (proceeding to Scapa to fuel, en route) to meet, and protect, a convoy of Canadian troops about to leave the Dominion for the United Kingdom. The Invincible and Inflexible, which had been cruising north of the Faroe Islands, joined the 1st Battle Cruiser Squadron at sea on the 29th. For the purpose of supporting the cruisers in the North Sea area, the 3rd Battle Squadron and 6th Battle Squadron sailed from Scapa on the arrival of the Dreadnought Battle Fleet. Additional precautions against attack by submarines were taken during the stay of the Fleet at Scapa on this occasion, as reports indicated the presence of a considerably increased number in the North Sea. These precautions included more numerous patrols by destroyers of the 2nd and 4th Flotillas outside the entrances to Scapa, and necessarily involved a greatly increased strain on the destroyers.

Further precautions against submarine attack were also found necessary in the Firth of Forth, and the arrival of light cruisers at Leith for refit were temporarily suspended by Admiralty orders owing to the presence of submarines in the vicinity. Two torpedoes were fired at the destroyer Stag, and another at a torpedo boat off May Island on the 25th. The destroyer Cheerful was also fired at on the 26th.

The month of October 1914, opened with the Dreadnought Battle Fleet at Scapa, with the exception of the Ajax which was en route to Devonport to refit, and the Audacious, which was on passage from Devonport after refit. The 3rd and 6th Battle Squadrons were at sea supporting the cruisers, except the Exmouth, of the 6th Battle Squadron, which was at Devonport refitting. The 1st Battle Cruiser Squadron, the Invincible, and the Inflexible, were at Scapa; the Princess Royal was cleaning boilers and preparing for her trip to Halifax.

Of the cruisers, the Devonshire, of the 3rd Cruiser Squadron, was refitting at Cromarty; the Theseus, of the 10th Cruiser Squadron, was returning from the White Sea, where she had been to fetch some Russian officers; the Mantua and Alsatian, armed merchant-cruisers, were at Liverpool, coaling and making good defects.

Of the destroyer flotillas, the Active and five destroyers of the 2nd Flotilla, and two of the 4th Flotilla, were absent refitting.

On October 1st regulations were brought into force under which a large number of coastal navigational lights were extinguished, as also were regulations closing the east coast ports to neutral fishing craft; other regulations were issued to control the movements of fishing vessels in certain areas. On October 10th further orders, under which additional coastal navigation lights were extinguished (principally in the North of Scotland), became effective.

The Dreadnought Battle Fleet remained at Scapa until 5 p.m. on October 2nd, and then proceeded into the North Sea. The 1st Battle Cruiser Squadron sailed at daylight, October 3rd, and the newly constituted 2nd Battle Cruiser Squadron, consisting of the Invincible and Inflexible, with the Sappho and three minelayers, left at 2 p.m. on October 3rd.

On October 3rd all the ships of the Grand Fleet took up pre-arranged positions designed to secure a close watch over the northern portion of the North Sea, partly with a view to an interception of all traffic, and partly to ensure that no enemy vessel broke out of the North Sea during the ensuing week. The main object was the protection of an important convoy of Canadian troops, which was crossing from Halifax, and which the battle cruiser Princess Royal and the battleship Majestic had been sent to meet and to protect. The Princess Royal arrived at the rendezvous at 8 p.m. on October 7th, and waited for the convoy, which was two and a half days late.

The Grand Fleet was disposed for this purpose during the period Oct. 3rd-11th approximately as follows:

The 1st Battle Cruiser Squadron was watching the Fair Island Channel from the western side.

The 2nd Battle Cruiser Squadron, with armed merchant-cruisers, the Sappho and three minelayers, was stationed to the northward and eastward of the Shetland Islands.

The 1st Light Cruiser Squadron patrolled the northern portion of Area No. 4.

The 2nd and 3rd Cruiser Squadrons patrolled Area No. 5.

The 10th Cruiser Squadron also patrolled Area No. 5.

The minesweepers patrolled to the eastward of the Fair Island Channel.

The Dreadnought Battle Fleet, with its divisions widely spread, worked to the northward of Area No. 5, and the 3rd Battle Squadron to the northward of Area No. 4, whilst the 6th Battle Squadron was utilised to watch the waters between the Dreadnought Battle Fleet and Norwegian territorial waters.

The destroyers were stationed, some to guard the eastern approaches of the Pentland Firth, some to work off the

Norwegian coast, and the remaining available vessels to work with the Battle Fleet for screening and boarding purposes. They returned to the bases (Lerwick or Scapa) as necessary for refuelling, and for shelter when the weather necessitated this.

The Princess Royal met the Canadian convoy in Lat. 49.45 N., Long. 27.5 W., on October 10th. On the 11th the Dreadnought Battle Fleet passed to the westward of the Orkneys, remaining there until daylight on the 12th, and then returning to Scapa, the 2nd Battle Cruiser Squadron, with the Teutonic being withdrawn from the patrol north of the Shetlands to a patrol line northwest from Sule Skerry lighthouse, Lat. 59.6 N., Long. 4.24 W., during the night of the 11th and remaining there until daylight on the 13th, when they left for Scapa. During October 12th all other vessels engaged in this operation returned to their bases for fuel, except the 3rd Battle Squadron (the ships of which had coaled two at a time during the operation) and the cruiser squadrons, which had been relieved as necessary to fuel.

Whilst the Fleet was engaged on this service the following incidents occurred. On October 2nd the Alsatian took six concealed Germans off a Danish steamer. At 5 a.m. on October 7th a submarine was reported inside Loch Ewe, being sighted by a collier and by the Assistance; she was fired at by the latter ship, in misty weather. On receipt of the report I ordered all vessels to leave Loch Ewe at once, and sent a division of destroyers there from Scapa to search for the submarine. Later investigation indicated that the report was well founded.

On October 9th the Alsatian sighted an enemy submarine in Lat. 61.42 N., Long. 0.50 W.; on the same day at 3 p.m. the Antrim, flagship of the 3rd Cruiser Squadron, when in Lat. 59 N., Long. 4.40 E., was missed by two torpedoes fired at her by a submarine which the Antrim just failed to ram after the attack; numerous reports of enemy aircraft having been sighted on the East and West coasts of Scotland were also received.

On October 10th the Liverpool and one-half of the 4th Flotilla were sent to the Norwegian coast to examine the islands in the vicinity of Udsire light, Lat. 59.19 N., Long. 4.50 E., to ascertain that they were not being used as German submarine bases, in view of the attack on the Antrim in that vicinity on the 9th. The 3rd Cruiser Squadron supported. Nothing was seen that lent colour to this idea.

Ships of the Battle Fleet were detached to the northward, two or three at a time, during the operations, to carry out gunnery practices by day and by night. Thick fogs were prevalent during the whole period, and ships detached from the Fleet experienced very considerable difficulty in rejoining. The foggy weather nearly resulted in a serious collision between a battleship of the 6th Battle Squadron and one of the Dreadnought Battle Fleet, the two ships passing within a few feet of each other on opposite courses.

On the return of the Battle Fleet to Scapa on the morning of October 12th, Admiral Sir Stanley Colville reported that a partial submarine obstruction was in place across the Hoxa entrance. The presence of even a partial obstruction reduced the danger of submarine attack on the Fleet whilst coaling, a matter which had given me much anxiety since the beginning of hostilities.

On arrival in harbour it was found that the condenser tubes of the Iron Duke were in a bad condition, although the ship was quite new, and that the condensers would need either complete, or partial, retubing. The discovery was very disconcerting when taken in conjunction with the case of the Orion, the condensers of which ship had been retubed during September; it naturally led to suspicion being directed to the condenser tubes generally of other ships, from which reports of cases of tubes occasionally giving out were being received.

The whole question was taken up with the Admiralty, requests being made that all available spare tubes should be sent at once to the Northern bases, together with some dockyard fitters who could assist the artificers of the Fleet in the work of retubing. Representations were also made as to the urgent necessity of increasing the stock of reserve tubes in case the defects became general in the Fleet owing to the ships being so constantly under steam at sea. The task of replacing the defective tubes in the Iron Duke's condensers was begun at once, with the help of the artificers of the Fleet, and the

Centurion was detailed as the spare Fleet-Flagship in case of emergency. But at this time the Iron Duke was not kept specially in harbour for retubing work, this being carried out as opportunity occurred, although under considerable difficulties, since the labour of suddenly preparing for sea, with a condenser undergoing retubing, was very appreciable. The manner in which this heavy work was taken in hand and rapidly completed in several ships, largely by Fleet labour, demonstrated the extreme efficiency and very fine spirit of the engine-room departments of the ships of the Grand Fleet.

From the 12th to the 16th October the 1st and 4th Battle Squadrons remained at Scapa, and at 6 p.m. on the 16th they left to carry out target practice to the westward of the Orkneys. The 2nd Battle Squadron left Scapa on the evening of the 18th to support the cruisers in the North Sea; it joined the 3rd Battle Squadron already there, the ships of which were being detached to Scapa two at a time to fuel and to overhaul their machinery. It was found necessary to give these ships, with reciprocating engines, five days off duty periodically in order to carry out necessary adjustments.

The 1st Battle Cruiser Squadron, with the 1st Light Cruiser Squadron and two divisions of destroyers, left Scapa at 5.30 p.m. on the 12th, to carry out a sweep of the southern part of the North Sea. This force swept on the 13th on a broad front down to the Dogger Bank, thence to the Norwegian coast, and to the northward on the 14th in conjunction with the 2nd Cruiser Squadron (which was then prolonging the sweeping line), without sighting any enemy vessels. The battle cruisers and light cruisers took up a position on the 15th to support the cruiser squadrons on patrol, the destroyers proceeding to Lerwick to fuel.

The 2nd Battle Cruiser Squadron remained at Scapa. The 2nd Cruiser Squadron was working the N.E. corner of Area 6, and the 10th Cruiser Squadron at this period was working the southwestern portion of Area No. 6. At 1.15 p.m. on October 15th the Theseus reported that a torpedo, which had missed, had been fired at her in Lat. 57.50 N., Long. 0.33 E.

On receipt of this report orders were given that the ships of the 10th Cruiser Squadron, on patrol, were to be withdrawn to the northern corner of the area, and later, at 8 p.m., orders were sent that they were to join the 2nd Battle Squadron still farther north, and to be used by the battleships (which were spread for the purpose of intercepting trade or enemy's ships) for boarding purposes. Meanwhile the senior officer of the 10th Cruiser Squadron ships operating in Area 6 (H.M.S. Edgar) reported that he could get no reply to wireless signals from the Hawke. The Swift, with a division of destroyers, was ordered to proceed from Scapa at high speed to the last reported position of the Hawke in Lat. 57.47 N., Long. 0.12 E., to search for the ship. Two other divisions of destroyers were sent, later on, to assist the Swift. It is to be noted that a submarine had been reported off Tod Head on the Aberdeen coast at 8.30 a.m. on the 14th, but this report did not reach the Iron Duke until the afternoon of the 15th.

The Swift reported on the 16th having picked up a raft with an officer and 20 men, survivors of the Hawke, which had been sunk by a submarine in Lat. 57.40 N., Long. 0.18 W., on the 15th. Shortly after sighting the raft, the Swift was attacked by the same or another submarine (it was thought by more than one) whilst engaged in her work of rescue, and torpedoes were fired at her. Captain Wintour subsequently stated that he was only able to effect the rescue by manoeuvring at high speed in the midst of the wreckage, etc., using the destroyers with him to screen his movements. His experience was an unpleasant one, as he naturally desired to remain on the spot until he had ascertained with certainty that he had picked up all the survivors, and this he proceeded to do with praiseworthy persistence, bringing them to Scapa.

On the 16th reports were also received that the destroyers Alarm and Nymphe had been attacked by submarines to the eastward of the Pentland Firth, and that the Nymphe had rammed the submarine that had attacked her. Later examination of the Nymphe's bottom by divers showed that her starboard propeller was damaged.

At 4.18 p.m. on the same day, the 16th, it was reported from one of the shore batteries that a submarine was close into the Switha entrance to Scapa Flow. The ships inside were immediately ordered to raise steam with all despatch, and the usual precautions were taken of patrolling the harbour with every available small craft, including destroyers, tugs, trawlers, drifters and picket-boats; and colliers and store-ships were as usual sent alongside the battleships, which were not fitted with torpedo nets, as a precaution.

The scene in the harbour on such occasions was a busy one. Small craft of every nature were patrolling at the sight of a periscope; all guns were manned; torpedo nets, where fitted, were placed in position; and every effort was made to ensure that the Fleet was as adequately guarded by the available patrol craft as circumstances admitted. All large ships except the repair ships Cyclops and Assistance left harbour during the night, the Iron Duke joining the 1st and 4th Battle Squadrons west of the Orkneys.

At noon on October 17th Sir Stanley Colville, who had been requested to organise a careful search for the reported submarine, signalled that a submarine was believed to be inside Scapa Flow and had been hunted, but not actually located. Reports had been received that officers and men on board several of the destroyers, and the gunboat Leda, had seen the periscope of the submarine, and that a torpedo had actually been fired at one of the hunting vessels. It was, however, ascertained subsequently that this torpedo was one which had been accidentally discharged by one of our own destroyers.

The accuracy or otherwise of these reports has never yet been determined with certainty, but many of the officers engaged in the search were convinced at the time that a submarine was actually inside, and that they had seen her. Indeed, a good many rounds were fired during the day at objects which were thought at the time to be a periscope.

The reports signalled to me convinced me that, until the matter was cleared up with certainty, and until some more absolute security against submarine attack on the Fleet at anchor could be provided, it was courting disaster to base battleships or battle cruisers at Scapa Flow. We had seen in the loss of the Hawke that enemy submarines could quite well operate in northern waters, and it was thought to be only a matter of time before they would attempt an attack on the Fleet in Scapa Flow, if indeed the attempt had not already been made.

I decided, therefore, that it was necessary to seek for a temporary base which could be used with safety whilst the submarine obstructions at Scapa were being perfected. The incident that had already occurred at Loch Ewe cast doubt on the safety of that base since it was unprovided with any obstructions at all and the depth of water made it impossible to improvise them with Fleet resources. Accordingly I looked for other and more easily obstructed ports, and eventually decided on Lough Swilly for the main part of the Fleet, and Loch-na-Keal in the Island of Mull for the ships for which berthing-space could not be found at Lough Swilly. Both ports possessed comparatively narrow entrances, and at Lough Swilly the water was so shallow as to make it difficult for a submarine to enter submerged. It was also a "defended port" and therefore possessed an organisation which would be useful for regulating the entry of ships.

The extensive dispositions necessitated by the temporary change of base were at once ordered. Colliers, store-ships, and auxiliaries of one kind and another, which were either en route to, or at, Scapa Flow, were diverted to the new bases; the 2nd Battle Squadron and 1st Battle Cruiser Squadron were ordered to Loch-na-Keal to fuel and to improvise anti-submarine obstructions at the entrance; and the Illustrious was ordered there from Loch Ewe to act as guard ship; the 1st and 4th Battle Squadrons and 2nd Battle Cruiser Squadron were detached to cruise to the northwestward of the Hebrides for blockading purposes, and to carry out practices; and the 1st Light Cruiser Squadron, 2nd Cruiser Squadron and 3rd and 6th Battle Squadrons were sent to Lough Swilly to coal.

The cruiser blockade and look-out line was withdrawn farther to the northward owing to the danger from submarines incurred in operating in the central or southern portions of the North Sea on a regular patrol, and the impossibility of providing destroyers as a screen for the ships. The new line was to the northward of the Shetland Islands, and the 3rd and 10th Cruiser Squadrons and armed merchant-cruisers carried out the patrol. There were, therefore, two lines of blockade, one formed by the heavy ships northwestward of the Hebrides, the second to the northward of the Shetland Islands. The organisation was such that it was probable that vessels attempting to evade the blockade would pass one of the two lines during daylight hours. In making these new dispositions it was still intended to keep the North Sea itself under observation by frequent cruiser sweeps.

Numerous reports of submarines in the Minch at this time led to the Active and two divisions of destroyers being sent there to search for them, and the remainder of the 2nd and 4th Flotillas were divided between blockade duty in the Pentland Firth, work at Scapa Flow, and in the vicinity of the Orkneys and Shetlands, and with the ships at Loch-na-Keal and Lough Swilly.

On October 21st the 2nd Battle Cruiser Squadron arrived a Cromarty to coal. Owing to the receipt of information from the Admiralty early that day, that it was reported that some German cruisers, destroyers and submarines had left Danzig on October 17th for the North Sea, the 1st Battle Cruiser Squadron and 1st Light Cruiser Squadron were ordered to leave their bases that morning, proceed into the North Sea, and sweep down on a broad front to the Skagerrak, screened by the 4th Flotilla of destroyers. The latter had to be sent back to their base on October 22nd owing to heavy weather. The remainder of the force swept up to the Skaw without sighting any enemy vessels, then north along the Norwegian coast, and proceeded, the 1st Battle Cruiser Squadron to Cromarty and the 1st Light Cruiser Squadron to Scapa.

On October 21st a submarine was reported just outside Cromarty by an armed trawler, and another report was received of one having been sighted by the destroyer Lynx. The submarine obstruction at Cromarty, designed by Captain Munro, had now been completed, and the base was considered secure. It would, however, only accommodate a small portion of the Fleet.

The dispositions given above were maintained until October 22nd, when the Iron Duke, 1st and 4th Battle Squadrons, the Active and two divisions of destroyers of the 2nd Flotilla, arrived at Lough Swilly. The 3rd and 6th Battle Squadrons and 2nd Cruiser Squadron took their place to the northwestward of the Hebrides as an outer blockade line and support for the cruiser squadrons.

The 2nd Battle Cruiser Squadron and four destroyers were detached to the southern part of the North Sea on the 23rd to support the Commodore (T) in carrying out aerial operations in the Heligoland Bight. The operations failed owing to the difficulty the seaplanes experienced in rising off the water, and the 2nd Battle Cruiser Squadron returned to Cromarty.

On arrival of the 1st and 4th Battle Squadrons at Lough Swilly, steps were immediately taken to lay an anti-submarine obstruction at the entrance, and this was very smartly completed with the limited resources of the squadrons by 4 p.m. on the 23rd, and for the first time since the declaration of war the Fleet occupied a secure base. Wire hawsers provided by the ships of the Fleet were suspended at varying depths between six colliers which were anchored across the entrance, with target rafts as intermediate supports.

It was a fairly effective obstruction, and armed steamboats from the fleet patrolled near it with destroyers as a support.

The relief to those responsible for the safety of the Fleet was immense, and attention was at once turned to the wellbeing of the personnel, which had been pressed very hard, and to improving the efficiency of the ships in gunnery and torpedo work. Battle practice targets were ordered over from Lamlash, in the Island of Arran, a pre-War practice base, with the intention of carrying out practice in the waters northwest of Ireland. The work of retubing the condensers of the Iron Duke was once more taken in hand, and ships were given the opportunity of overhauling and adjusting machinery, steam being put back to longer notice than had previously been possible. The anti-submarine defence was continually strengthened and improved during the stay of the Fleet, and the colliers supporting it were gradually replaced by trawlers and drifters.

In order to give the men some much-needed diversion and exercise a pulling regatta was organised and held on October 26th, and the men were landed for route marches as frequently as possible during the stay of the ships at Lough Swilly.

On the 26th a submarine was reported inside Cromarty harbour, but Sir David Beatty, who was there with the battle cruisers, stated, after investigation, that he did not consider the report was true.

Discussions took place with the Admiralty during the stay of the Fleet at Lough Swilly on the subject of trawlers for the patrol of the Minches and vicinity, and the requirements were given as thirty-six trawlers for this service, which was considered next in importance to the provision of an adequate patrol force of this nature for the waters in the vicinity of the bases at Scapa Flow and Cromarty.

The stay of the Fleet at Lough Swilly was rendered memorable by the unfortunate loss of the Audacious, then one of our most modern battleships.

Orders had been given to the 2nd Battle Squadron to carry out target practice against the two battle practice targets obtained from Lamlash, and the squadron left Loch-na-Keal on the evening of October 26th for a rendezvous in Lat. 55.45 N., Long. 8.30 W., at daylight on the 27th, where the targets which had left Lough Swilly in tow of two tugs, the Plover and Flying Condor, escorted by the light cruiser Liverpool, were to be met.

The squadron was in Lat. 55.34 N., Long. 8.30 W. at 9 a.m. on the 27th, preparing for the practice, when at that hour the Audacious struck a mine whilst turning. The explosion resulted in the flooding of the port engine-room and partly flooding the centre engine-room. It was not clear at the time whether the ship had been mined or torpedoed. The Monarch having reported sighting a submarine at 11 a.m., a precautionary signal was made to Sir George Warrender to keep the squadron clear of the Audacious.

Meanwhile all available destroyers, tugs, trawlers and other small craft were sent from Lough Swilly and Loch-na-

Keal to assist the Audacious and to prevent the submarine (if one were present) from doing further damage; and the armed boarding steamer Cambria escorted the collier Thornhill (provided with towing hawsers) to the scene. The hospital-ship Soudan was ordered out to give help to survivors in case the Audacious sank or to the injured, and the Liverpool was directed to stand by her, but to keep moving at high speed. The battleship Exmouth was put at "short notice" ready to tow the Audacious in if necessary. Vice-Admiral Sir Lewis Bayly, commanding the 1st Battle Squadron, came on board the Iron Duke to suggest that he should proceed to the scene to render any assistance, an offer of which I very gladly availed myself, as Sir George Warrender, in the 2nd Battle Squadron, could not close the ship whilst the danger of submarine attack existed.

Shortly after the Audacious struck the mine, the s.s. Olympic, on passage from the United States to Liverpool, closed the ship on learning of the disaster, and Captain Haddock, C.B., R.N.R., who was in command, at once volunteered to help in any way possible. Captain Dampier, of the Audacious asked that his ship might be taken in tow and brought into Lough Swilly, and Captain Haddock, disregarding the danger of submarine attack or of being mined, took immediate steps to carry out this request. Unfortunately a considerable sea was running, which increased during the day. In spite of the most magnificent and seamanlike handling of the Olympic by Captain Haddock, and later in the day excellent work on the part of the master of the Thornhill, the hawsers constantly parted, owing to the state of the sea and the weight of the Audacious, the stern of that ship being almost awash by the afternoon. The two ships were worked in a manner which Sir Lewis Bayly reported as beyond praise. The attempts to tow the injured ship had to be abandoned before dark, and Sir Lewis Bayly, Captain Dampier and the few officers and men who had remained on board to work the hawsers, etc., were taken off the Audacious by 7.15 p.m. The remainder of the ship's company had been removed without accident, in spite of the heavy sea, in the course of the day by destroyers, trawlers, and other small craft, and in the boats of the Audacious.

The work of the destroyers on this occasion was, as usual, of the greatest value, and the exceedingly seamanlike handling of the Fury by Lieutenant-Commander Sumner, who, in the teeth of the greatest difficulties, took heavy wire towing hawsers between the Audacious and the towing ships on several occasions, elicited from Sir Lewis Bayly expressions of warm admiration. Arrangements were made for the Liverpool to stand by the Audacious during the night, but at 9 p.m. she suddenly blew up with great violence and sank. The cause of this explosion was never ascertained with certainty. At the time the ship blew up the Liverpool was not far distant, and a good deal of debris fell on the deck of that ship, killing one petty officer. This was the only casualty due to the loss of the Audacious.

Meanwhile, at 1.8 p.m., information reached me from Kingstown that the S. S. Manchester Commerce had been sunk on the night of the 26th by a mine in the vicinity of the disaster to the Audacious, and at 4.40 p.m. a report came from Malin Head that a four-masted sailing vessel, the Caldaff, had also struck a mine in the neighbourhood on the previous night.

These unfortunately belated reports disposed at once of any idea that submarines had attacked the Audacious, and at 5 p.m. the Exmouth sailed from Lough Swilly to attempt to tow her in. Steps had already been taken to warn outward and homeward bound vessels of the existence of the minefield and to divert all traffic clear of it; and all minesweeping gunboats were ordered to Lough Swilly to locate the exact limits of the minefield and to sweep a clear passage along the north coast of Ireland.

On the arrival of the S. S. Olympic at Lough Swilly, orders were given that no communication between the ship and the shore was to take place. I wired to the Admiralty suggesting that the loss of the Audacious should be kept secret for as long as possible, so that the enemy should not learn of it, as the fact would afford him encouragement at a time when the military situation was extremely critical for the Allies, and also because, as a general policy, it was desirable to conceal from the enemy any serious losses of which he could otherwise have no immediate knowledge.

This procedure was approved for the time, because of the military situation, and the Olympic was kept at Lough Swilly for several days. This was necessary as she had on board a considerable number of United States passengers, and it was known that they had taken photographs of the Audacious in a sinking condition. Amongst these passengers was Mr. Schwab, of the Bethlehem Steel Company, and it was made known to me after a day or two that he had come over on very important business connected with War Office contracts, and wished to proceed to London. After an interview with him, this was agreed to, and I asked him to call on Lord Fisher of the Admiralty in connection with the construction of some submarines which I ascertained from him that his firm was in a position to build very rapidly and which would be of the greatest value to us. He did this, and with the most satisfactory results, as ten submarines were constructed — as he promised — in the extraordinarily short space of five months. These vessels were most useful to us later.

The 1st and 4th Battle Squadrons were at Lough Swilly during the remainder of October; the 2nd Battle Squadron proceeded to Lamlash on the 29th to coal, and to Lough Swilly on November 1st; the 3rd Battle Squadron went to Scapa on the 27th; and the 6th Battle Squadron to Lough Swilly.

On October 27th a trawler reported very suspicious movements on the part of a large steamer to the westward of the island of Sule Skerry (west of the Orkneys). It appeared possible that the ship might be a German minelayer, and the 1st Light Cruiser Squadron at Scapa was sent to a position 120 miles from Fair Island on the Fair Island — Heligoland line, to intercept her on returning, with orders that, at daylight on the 29th, she should spread widely and sweep towards Fair Island, then sweeping over to the Norwegian coast near Jaederen's Point, spreading at daylight on the 30th and sweeping up a line approximately N. 15 W. from Heligoland, before returning to Scapa. Destroyers of the 4th Flotilla were also sent out from Scapa on the 28th in search of the suspected vessel, and the 3rd and 10th Cruiser Squadrons were disposed so as to cut her off if she passed to the north of the Shetlands. The ship was not sighted, and no mines had been laid.

The Grand Fleet was considerably weakened at this time apart from the loss of the Audacious. The Ajax had developed condenser defects; the Iron Duke had similar troubles; the Orion had to be sent to Greenock for examination of the turbine supports, which appeared to be defective; the Conqueror was at Devonport refitting, and the New Zealand was in dock at Cromarty. The Erin and Agincourt, having been newly commissioned, could not yet be regarded as efficient, so that the Dreadnought Fleet only consisted of 17 effective battleships and 5 battle cruisers; the German Dreadnought Fleet at the time comprised 15 battleships and 4 battle cruisers, with the Blucher in addition. The margin of superiority was, therefore, unpleasantly small in view of the fact that the High Sea Fleet possessed 88 destroyers and the Grand Fleet only 42.

During the stay of the Fleet at Lough Swilly numerous reports of the presence of submarines on the west coast of Scotland were received, a large number of the reports coming from the coast watchers. Destroyers were sent on many occasions to search the localities from which the reports emanated, and the various harbours that could be used by submarines as a base were frequently examined. At this period it was considered possible that enemy submarines, acting so far from their home ports as the west coast of Scotland, would be working from a shore or from a floating base.

It was not thought — from experience with our own submarines — that they would be self-supporting at this distance, and the best method of limiting their activities, if not destroying the submarines, was to find their base. Later experience, and a closer knowledge of German submarines, however, showed that they were independent of such bases.

It is very doubtful whether any enemy submarines passed to the westward of Scotland during October. We, at any rate, found no certain evidence that they were present, in spite of the very numerous reports of their being sighted. Similarly, reports were constantly being received of aircraft (both Zeppelins and aeroplanes) being seen in the north of Scotland; many of the rumours were of the most circumstantial nature, some coming even from warships. It is quite certain that these reports were founded on optical illusions, and it may be said that little credence was attached to them at the time.

But the currency of many rumours in those early days of the War, sometimes supported by statements of the most plausible character, were not only embarrassing, but frequently involved a great deal of unproductive cruising, for it was impossible to ignore anything which would enable us to find out the enemy's movements or intentions.

At the end of October, news came of the unfortunate wreck of the hospital ship Rohilla off Whitby, with considerable loss of life.

About this time the German land forces occupied the Belgian coast. The effect of this occupation on naval strategy was considered in the Grand Fleet, and Sir Lewis Bayly and I discussed the blocking of Zeebrugge by sinking ships across the channel. Sir Lewis Bayly considered the scheme feasible, and wrote to me on the subject. I then suggested to the Admiralty that such an operation should be carried out. It was not considered practicable by the Admiralty at the time. It is perhaps of interest to note that the subject was discussed as early as 1914.

Some two years later I caused the question to be reconsidered after taking up the appointment of First Sea Lord at the Admiralty (it had been under consideration between 1914 and 1917). More than one plan was discussed between Admiral Bacon (commanding the Dover patrol) and myself; one idea, which I favoured, was to utilise ships of the "Apollo" class, cutting down their upper works to render them less visible during approach. Meanwhile, other schemes for driving the enemy from the Belgian coast were in operation, so the question of blocking was deferred. In September, 1917, when it became clear that the object in view would not be effected by military operations during that year, I gave directions to the Plans Division of the Naval Staff, of which Rear-Admiral Roger Keyes had recently become the head, that plans for blocking Zeebrugge were to be prepared; later, after considering an independent proposal by Sir Reginald Bacon for attacking the mole by landing parties from monitors run alongside it, I decided that the operation was to be combined with the landing on the Zeebrugge mole. The main objective for the landing was the destruction of enemy destroyers known to be lying alongside the mole, and I considered that this landing would also be very useful in creating a diversion to facilitate the approach of the block ships. The scheme was eventually approved by me in November, 1917, and the training of the storming party and selection of the block ships were taken in hand.

6 - Incidents at Sea

Nov. 1 to Dec. 31, 1914

On November 1st I left Lough Swilly to confer at the Admiralty with the First Lord and the First Sea Lord, Lord Fisher, who had relieved the Marquis of Milford Haven in this post. During this conference, held on November 2nd, the requirements of trawlers, drifters, etc., for the patrol of the vicinity of the various fleet bases, the Minches, and the waters surrounding the Orkneys and Shetlands were discussed at length and decisions reached. The defence of the bases was also considered. I stated that the requirements of patrol vessels for the Orkney and Shetland areas were a total of 72, and for the Minches of 36.

The future general naval policy was also discussed, one of the main questions being that of the 3rd and 6th Battle Squadrons joining the Channel Fleet. It was determined that this step should be taken, and the necessary orders were given. I agreed to it with some reluctance, as there was obviously no prospect of the 3rd Battle Squadron being able to join the Dreadnought Fleet before a Fleet action if stationed in southern waters, and a dispersion of the Fleet, which resulted in the main Battle Fleet having but a slender preponderance of strength over the High Sea Fleet, was a measure which was open to considerable objection. The increasing necessity for refitting our ships, which involved sending them as far away as Portsmouth or Devonport, combined with the failures in condenser tubes that were occurring, led to two, or three, or even more battleships being absent at a time, on passage, laid up, or refitting. At the German selected moment, our main Battle Fleet might well at this period have been reduced to 18 ships (all Dreadnoughts), whilst the High Sea Fleet was just rising to a strength of 16 Dreadnoughts and 16 pre-Dreadnoughts.

Later, however, after the raid on East Coast towns, the 3rd Battle Squadron was again detached from the Channel Fleet and based on Rosyth, with the 3rd Cruiser Squadron; the two squadrons arrived there on November 20th after passing west of Ireland and coaling at Scapa. The 6th Battle Squadron remained in southern waters. The object which it was desired to attain by this last distribution, which was ordered from the Admiralty, was to have a naval force based farther south than Scapa, to be more immediately available in the case of an attempt by the enemy to land a hostile force on our east coast.

I returned to Lough Swilly at noon, November 3rd, and found the Fleet under orders from the Admiralty to proceed to Scapa at once. These orders were cancelled after my arrival, and the movements of the Battle Fleet left to my discretion. I proceeded to sea with the 1st, 2nd and 4th Battle Squadrons at 3.45 p.m. and, passing south of Tory Island, made for the vicinity of the Bills Rocks on the coast of Galway, for target practice, which was carried out on the 4th, the Fleet then proceeding to the northward.

The Battle Fleet was screened out of Lough Swilly by the 2nd Flotilla, which then left for Scapa. This flotilla had been employed during the stay at Lough Swilly in providing patrols off the entrance and in hunting for submarines, reports of which were very frequent.

Prior to leaving Lough Swilly, news arrived from the Admiralty that the light cruiser Undaunted, of the Harwich force, was being chased by several German vessels in southern waters, and that hostile battle cruisers had been sighted off Gorleston. These occurrences had, presumably, led to the ordering of the Fleet to Scapa. As it was thought that the operations of the German battle cruisers might be part of a general movement, orders were sent to the 3rd Battle Squadron to join the Commander-in-Chief at Scapa, the 1st and 2nd Battle Cruiser Squadrons being directed to proceed with all dispatch towards Heligoland, with the 1st Light Cruiser Squadron; the 2nd and 6th Cruiser Squadrons were ordered to Scapa to coal, and the 10th Cruiser Squadron to the Shetlands for the same purpose, ready for eventualities. These orders were cancelled when it became apparent that the German movement was local, and that our ships would be too late to intercept the enemy. On this occasion, the German cruiser

Yorck, when returning to port, struck a German mine and sank.

The base at Loch-na-Keal was abandoned when the Fleet left Lough Swilly, and the obstructions removed by the battleship Illustrious.

On November 3rd the Admiralty issued a general notice proclaiming the North Sea as an area in which hostile operations were being carried out, and pointing out the danger incurred by neutral vessels which entered the North Sea without first ascertaining the steps necessary for safety.

On November 5th the Invincible and Inflexible left Cromarty for Devonport by Admiralty orders, prior to proceeding to search for Admiral von Spee's squadron in the South Atlantic. This order, the necessity for which was apparent, and the subsequent results of which were undoubtedly of high value, had, however, the effect of still further weakening the Grand Fleet.

The Iron Duke, with the 1st, 2nd and 4th Battle Squadrons cruised between the Hebrides, Faroe Islands and Shetlands after November 4th, and carried out gunnery practices and battle exercises as opportunity occurred. The 1st Battle Squadron was sent to Scapa to coal on the 7th, the 2nd Battle Squadron on the 8th, and the Iron Duke and 4th Battle Squadron arrived there on the 9th.

The 2nd, 3rd and 10th Cruiser Squadrons were engaged on blockade work during this period.

On November 6th, the 1st Battle Cruiser Squadron, with the 1st Light Cruiser Squadron and one-half of the 4th Flotilla, was sent from Cromarty to carry out a sweep of the North Sea, passing through the following positions, namely:

1. Lat. 56.0 N., Long. 1.30 E.
2. Lat. 57.50 N., Long. 5.0 E.
3. Lat. 60.10 N., Long. 3.15 E.
4. Lat. 61.20 N., Long. 3.0 E.
5. Lat. 61.0 N., Long. 1.0 E.
6. Lat. 58.50 N. Long. 0.0.

thence the Battle Cruiser Squadron and destroyers were to go to Cromarty and the light cruisers to Scapa.

The new battle cruiser Tiger, which had been working up gunnery and torpedo practices at Bantry Bay in the south of Ireland, arrived at Scapa on November 6th to continue her practices and to join the 1st Battle Cruiser Squadron. It was felt that she would prove a very welcome reinforcement when efficient, since the departure of the Invincible and Inflexible had left us in a questionable position with regard to battle cruisers as compared with the Germans.

After the Battle Fleet left Lough Swilly, and in consequence of information sent to me by Admiral Colville as to the slow progress being made with the submarine obstructions, orders were given to the various ships to prepare sections of rope net submarine detectors for use in the entrances to Scapa Flow, and these were rapidly placed in position by the Fleet in Hoxa, Switha and Hoy Sounds when the ships arrived at Scapa, armed trawlers being detailed to watch each section. It was very disappointing to find on returning to the base that so little headway had been made with the supply of material for the permanent submarine wire net obstruction, and that the Fleet was still, therefore, open to submarine attack. The increase in the number of patrol trawlers, however, for service in the vicinity of the base gave some protection to the entrances, and relieved the hard-pressed destroyers to a welcome extent.

At this time the watching and blockading cruisers were disposed in areas between the Shetland Islands, Faroe Islands, and Iceland and to the northwestward of the Hebrides, but the whole of the cruisers were beginning to show signs of overwork.

The Rear-Admiral commanding the 10th Cruiser Squadron reported that all his ships, which were very old, were showing increasing signs of needing thorough repair at a dockyard, and arrangements were put in hand for sending them, three at a time, to the Clyde. In addition, the Antrim, of the 3rd Cruiser Squadron, reported condenser defects; the Drake, of the 6th Cruiser Squadron, was at Scapa making good defects, which were constantly developing, and the King

Alfred and Leviathan, of the same squadron, were refitting at dockyard ports. In spite of these incidents, however, large numbers of steamers were being intercepted daily by cruisers, battleships and destroyers, and sent into Kirkwall for examination.

About this time the increase in the number of patrol craft at Scapa made it necessary to add considerably to the administrative organisation at that base, and requests were sent to the Admiralty to provide depot ships for the local defence destroyers, the patrol trawlers, and the other small craft, as well as adequate administrative staffs.

The Dreadnought Battle Fleet remained at Scapa until November 17th with steam ready at from two to three hours' notice, and on that date the 2nd Battle Squadron, 1st Battle Cruiser Squadron, 2nd Cruiser Squadron, and 1st Light Cruiser Squadron, with a half flotilla as a screen, left their bases to take up positions for preventing a suspected attempt on the part of the enemy to send some ships into the Atlantic. The 2nd Battle Squadron worked to the westward, and the remaining vessels to the eastward of the Shetland Islands. The 1st Battle Cruiser Squadron and 1st Light Cruiser Squadron returned to Scapa on the 20th and the 2nd Battle Squadron and 2nd Cruiser Squadron on the 21st.

A heavy gale was experienced in the northern part of the North Sea and in the waters surrounding the Orkneys and Shetlands from November 11th to November 18th, and all work in the harbour had to be suspended, ships lying with steam up, whilst at sea most of the cruisers were obliged to lay to. At Scapa all the seaplane sheds were wrecked by the gale, and the seaplanes damaged.

During this stay of the Battle Fleet at Scapa the routine was introduced of carrying out gunnery and torpedo practices inside the harbour, two or three ships being under way at a time for the purpose. This routine was subsequently carried out whenever the Fleet, or any portion of it, was at Scapa and the greatest possible benefit was derived from it. It was found possible to carry out practice from all guns, up to and including 6-inch, inside the harbour by day and night, besides the ordinary sub-calibre firing and torpedo practices by ships, and by destroyers attacking ships, or divisions of ships.

On November 11th, the battle cruiser Princess Royal sailed for Halifax, by Admiralty orders, for the purpose of strengthening the North American Squadron in operations against Admiral von Spee's squadron, should it appear in northern waters. I protested, as Commander-in-Chief, against sending so powerful a ship as the Princess Royal, armed with 13.5-inch guns, since her absence left our Battle Cruiser Squadron inferior in strength to the German battle cruiser force. I suggested that the New Zealand, carrying 12-inch guns, was, owing to her economical coal consumption, more suited to the work required and strong enough for the purpose. However, the Princess Royal sailed and remained absent from the North Sea until the beginning of January, 1915.

At this period, reports of enemy submarines being sighted, more particularly by shore observers in the Hebrides, Orkneys and Shetlands, were very numerous, and destroyers and patrol craft were frequently being sent to search suspected bases or sheltered bays in which submarines might be taking refuge. All such searches were, however, fruitless, although in many cases the reports were very circumstantial and convincing.

On November 18th the minesweeping gunboats, whilst searching the Fair Island Channel, sighted a submarine on the surface and chased her at a speed of 18 knots, but could not overhaul her. The submarine subsequently dived. This incident was the first practical proof of the high surface speed possessed by German submarines.

Destroyers were sent out immediately from Scapa to assist in the search, with orders to use their searchlights after dark in order to force the submarine to keep underwater and so exhaust her batteries. The search, however, proved abortive, although continued for 24 hours. The use of searchlights for this purpose, begun on this occasion, became common later on.

A submarine was sighted by the 2nd Battle Squadron at 9 a.m. on the 19th, well to the westward of the Orkneys, and this may have been the vessel chased by the minesweepers.

During the gale on November 12th, the ships of the 10th Cruiser Squadron — the old "Edgar" class of cruisers — which were on patrol between the Shetlands and Faroe Islands had suffered much damage, many of them showing signs of leaking and straining; boats and ventilators were washed away; and water in large quantities found its way below. It became evident that these old ships were not sufficiently seaworthy to withstand the winter gales of northern latitudes without first undergoing a thorough repair, and arrangements were made to send them, three at a time, to the Clyde for survey and refit. The survey of the first three, however, revealed that some months' work would be required to make them efficient for winter blockade duty, and it was then decided by the Admiralty to pay off the whole squadron, and to utilise the crews to commission armed merchant ships, which would be far more suitable, as they could keep the sea for much longer periods.

The ships of the 10th Cruiser Squadron had been using Swarbachs Minn, a harbour in the Shetland Islands, as an occasional coaling base. This was evacuated on November 20th in consequence of the receipt of a report that a submarine attack on the harbours in the Shetland Islands was probable, all of these harbours being, at that time, defenceless against such attack. On leaving the base, the ships of the 10th Cruiser Squadron, not already at a refitting port, were ordered to dockyard ports to pay off.

On November 20th, during practice, a lyddite common shell detonated in one of the 9.2-inch guns of the Achilles, and the muzzle of the gun was blown off, eleven of the gun's crew being injured. This occurrence cast doubt on the safety of the whole of the lyddite shell afloat, and restrictions on their use were issued, but were eventually removed, after the withdrawal of all suspected shell of this nature.

At dusk on November 22nd the Grand Fleet left its bases for the purpose of carrying out a sweep of the North Sea, and to support an aerial operation in the Heligoland Bight. The 3rd Battle Squadron and 3rd Cruiser Squadron, from Rosyth, were included in this movement, and met the remainder of the Fleet at sea at 9.30 a.m. on November 23rd in Lat. 57.40 N., Long. 2.30 E.

The 1st, 2nd, 3rd and 4th Battle Squadrons, 1st Battle Cruiser Squadron, 1st Light Cruiser Squadron, 2nd Cruiser Squadron, 3rd Cruiser Squadron, 6th Cruiser Squadron, and 2nd and 4th Flotillas, took part in the operation, the Fleet proceeding south in cruising order, with destroyers screening the Battle Fleet and 1st Battle Cruiser Squadron against submarine attack by day. The channel eastward of the Pentland Firth was, as usual, searched by the minesweeping gunboats prior to the departure of the Fleet.

The Commodore (T) from Harwich, with three Light Cruisers and eight destroyers, was directed to co-operate in the aerial operations. During daylight on the 23rd opportunity was taken to carry out two tactical exercises.

The Iron Duke's position at midnight was Lat. 56.55 N., Long. 4.11 E. Ships were ordered to be at action stations by dawn on the 24th, and the 1st Battle Cruiser Squadron, with the 1st Light Cruiser Squadron and a division of destroyers, was detached in the afternoon of the 23rd with directions to be in Lat. 55.10 N., Long. 6.20 E. by 5.30 a.m. on the 24th.

The Drake reported her port engine disabled at 1 p.m. on the 23rd, and had consequently to be sent back to Scapa.

During the night the Admiralty informed me that the aerial operations had been abandoned, as it was thought that the enemy had a force present in the Bight, which would be too strong for our detached vessels. I then directed the Commodore (T) to meet the 2nd Cruiser Squadron at its daylight position in Lat. 54.50 N., Long. 7.6 E., and thence to proceed towards Heligoland and endeavour to draw any enemy forces that might be encountered towards our Fleet. The 1st Battle Cruiser Squadron and 1st Light Cruiser Squadron were directed also to proceed to the 2nd Cruiser Squadron to give any necessary support.

The weather on the 24th was fine and bright with high visibility. The Commodore (T) reconnoitered Heligoland and reported at 10.40 a.m. that there was smoke behind the island, and ships steaming to the southward; and that he had sighted a submarine. The Rear-Admiral of the 2nd Cruiser Squadron reported at 11 a.m. that he had only sighted destroyers, and that he could not draw the enemy towards him, and so was returning to the northward with Commodore (T). The Vice-Admiral of the 1st Battle Cruiser Squadron, who was supporting, turned to the northward shortly afterwards, his noon position being Lat. 54.47 N., Long. 6.35 E. The 2nd Cruiser Squadron was attacked at 12.35 p.m. by an aeroplane, which dropped five bombs near the Liverpool, which was in company.

The Battle Fleet cruised in support, the 10 a.m. position of the Iron Duke being Lat. 55.23 N., Long. 5.30 E. At 2 p.m. the Battle Fleet turned to the northwestward, sighting the 1st Battle Cruiser Squadron astern at 3.30 p.m. The battle cruisers and light cruisers were stationed 15 miles to the eastward of the Battle Fleet during the night, and the necessary dispositions were taken to provide against a destroyer attack during the night.

On November 25th two more tactical exercises were carried out. During the afternoon the wind increased, and thick weather set in, and by daylight on the 26th a heavy southerly gale was blowing, so the attached cruisers were sent to the bases for shelter. The 1st Battle Squadron, 1st Battle Cruiser Squadron and the 1st Light Cruiser Squadron, and the destroyers, had been detached at midnight on the 25th for Scapa, Rosyth and Invergordon respectively. The original intention was to take the remainder of the Fleet farther north for target practice, but it was abandoned owing to the bad weather, and the Iron Duke, the 2nd and 4th Battle Squadrons and the 2nd Cruiser Squadron arrived at Scapa on the 27th.

During the absence of the Fleet, the German submarine U 18 was rammed at 12.20 p.m. November 24th by minesweeping trawler No. 96, one mile off the Hoxa entrance to Scapa. U 18 was damaged in the collision, dived, hit the bottom and received further damage. All the available patrol craft were ordered to the spot most promptly by the Vice-Admiral commanding the Orkneys and Shetlands and hunted her. She finally came to the surface and surrendered off Muckle Skerry in the Pentland Firth. The submarine sank as the crew came on deck, the seacocks, probably, having been previously opened. The commanding officer of the submarine, who had apparently intended to try to enter Scapa Flow, expressed great surprise to Admiral Colville at the absence of the Fleet. It seemed possible that he had been deterred from his attempt by the sight of the buoys across the entrance, probably suspecting the presence of an obstruction which, however, was not there. The sinking of the submarine caused the greatest gratification to the local defence forces at Scapa and acted as an incentive to further efforts. It was also, probably, a deterrent to further attacks on the Fleet at Scapa, as the circumstances in which U 18 was sunk were kept most secret in order that the enemy might be led to think that her destruction was due to nets or mines. Indeed, it is very likely that this incident and the secrecy observed had important results in preventing the loss of ships of the Grand Fleet when at anchor in Scapa Flow.

Great submarine activity occurred at this time in the vicinity of the Orkneys and Shetlands. The Dryad sighted a submarine on the 24th in Lat. 58.35 N., Long. 1.45 W.; a second was sighted by an armed trawler off Copinsay on the same day; and a third was sighted from the shore, proceeding to the eastward through the Pentland Firth. On the 25th U 16 was sighted by a collier and trawler in Lat. 58.46 N., Long. 2.15 W., and later by the minesweeping gunboat Skipjack not far from this position.

On the return of the Fleet arrangements were made for constructing, with Fleet resources, net obstructions across the Hoy entrance to Scapa Flow, and, in view of the attempt of U 18, all patrols were stiffened to the utmost extent possible.

During November 27th and 28th the strong gale continued, interfering considerably with the work on the submarine obstructions. Several reports of the sighting of submarines in harbours in the north of Scotland, the Orkneys and Shetlands were received during the last days of November, and destroyers and patrol craft were kept very busy in searching the various bays and harbours. In many cases charges were exploded on the bottom in bays in which it was considered that a submarine might be lying, in the hope of forcing her to the surface. No known result, however, was obtained.

The Fleet remained in the various bases until the end of the month, the ships in Scapa Flow carrying out gunnery and torpedo practices and working at the obstructions. The King George V., which had just returned from refit at a dockyard, developed condenser defects necessitating partial retubing; she was the fourth battleship in which this defect had occurred since the War started, a period of only four months, and it will be realised that such wholesale breakdowns caused me uneasiness.

During November the work of sinking block-ships in all the entrance channels to Scapa Flow, except the Hoxa and Hoy entrances, was carried out. Unfortunately the block-ships had been sent up in a light condition without cement ballast which, I was informed, could not be supplied, and they began in many cases to break up or to shift their position during the winter gales. This fact, combined with the great difficulty experienced in sinking them in the exact positions required owing to the strong tides prevailing (up to at least eight knots in strength), and the very short periods of slack water, rendered the work of blocking only partially effective.

At the end of November the effective state of the Grand Fleet was as follows:

Fleet-Flagship - the Iron Duke.

1st Battle Squadron - 7 ships, the Neptune being away refitting.

2nd Battle Squadron - 7 ships, of which one, the King George V., was disabled, retubing condensers.

3rd Battle Squadron (Pre-Dreadnoughts) - 7 ships, one ship refitting at twelve hours' notice for steam, and the 8th ship returning from a dockyard refit.

4th Battle Squadron - 5 ships (complete).

1st Battle Cruiser Squadron - 4 ships (the Princess Royal having been detached to North America).

2nd Cruiser Squadron - 3 ships. The Shannon was refitting.

3rd Cruiser Squadron - 4 ships (complete).

6th Cruiser Squadron - 4 ships (complete).

1st Light Cruiser Squadron - 5 ships. The Liverpool was refitting.
2nd Flotilla -15 destroyers (5 refitting).
4th Flotilla - 15 destroyers (5 refitting).
10th Cruiser Squadron - Nil (paid off).
Armed Merchant-Cruisers - 2 (2 were coaling at Liverpool).
Minesweeping Gunboats - 5 (3 were refitting).

The two new battleships, the Emperor of India and Benbow the former flying the flag of Rear-Admiral A. J. Duff, CB., had arrived at Berhaven in the south of Ireland on December 1st to "work up" after commissioning. On the same date the Leviathan arrived at Cromarty to act as flagship of the 1st Cruiser Squadron under the orders of Rear-Admiral Sir A. G. W. Moore. His flag was transferred to her from the New Zealand on December 2nd.

On the night of December 2nd a very violent gale sprang up at Scapa Flow, during which several ships dragged their anchors, in spite of two anchors being down and steam up; the gale lasted until the morning of the 4th. All communication between ships in Scapa Flow, even by drifter, was suspended, and the light cruisers at sea on patrol were forced to lie to. An officer and one man were washed overboard from a picket-boat sheltering under the stern of a store-ship and drowned.

On December 3rd Rear-Admiral Dudley de Chair, lately in command of the 10th Cruiser Squadron, hoisted his flag in the armed merchant ship Alsatian to command the merchant cruisers attached to the Grand Fleet, which were now constituted as the new 10th Cruiser Squadron.

At 1.45 p.m. on December 3rd the destroyer Garry, Commander W. W. Wilson, of the local defence force, reported that she was engaging a submarine at the Holm Sound entrance to Scapa Flow. This submarine was possibly sheltering there from the bad weather. Destroyers and trawlers were at once sent out to assist, and the submarine was last reported diving to seaward. Several rounds from her 12-pounder gun were fired by the Garry at the submarine's conning tower, but apparently without effect, and an attempt to ram her also failed owing to the heavy sea and very strong tides. The submarine and the Garry fired torpedoes at one another, the submarine's torpedo passing under the stern of the Garry. All ships were directed to raise steam for leaving harbour on receipt of the first report from the Garry, from which it was not clear whether the submarine had passed through Holm Sound into the harbour, but this order was cancelled when it was ascertained that she was outside.

On December 4th all the minesweeping gunboats attached to the Grand Fleet were sent to Sheerness by Admiralty direction for the purpose of carrying out sweeping operations off the coast of Belgium; trawlers were then the only sweeping vessels left with the Grand Fleet.

On December 5th another heavy gale was experienced, lasting until the following morning, and all small craft at sea were forced to shelter.

In consequence of representations made to the Admiralty of the inadequacy of the minesweeping force at this time attached to the Grand Fleet, owing to the withdrawal of the gunboats, steps were taken to fit out eight small steamers (screw minesweepers) for the purpose, and I was informed that they would arrive on various dates during the month of December. These vessels did not prove very satisfactory as minesweepers in northern waters, and were withdrawn later for use in the Mediterranean.

During the stay of the Fleet in Scapa Flow work on the improvised submarine obstructions was continued by naval parties with all possible speed, and, meanwhile, work on the permanent obstructions was in hand, though progressing but slowly, owing to the difficulty experienced in fitting out the trawlers at Inverness with the necessary winches and providing the required moorings.

On December 6th bad weather was again experienced. Orders were issued on this date for a sweep down the North Sea, but were cancelled on receipt of information from the Admiralty that the recent bad weather had caused a very large number of mines to break adrift in the southern portion of the North Sea. On the same day the light cruiser Sappho and three armed boarding steamers were sent to Loch Ewe and based there with orders to work northwest of the Hebrides for the interception of trade; the force of armed boarding steamers was increased later. These vessels were mostly Irish mail packets. Rather extensive alterations were necessary, after they had been sent up, before they were fit for their duties.

During the early part of December the ships of the 2nd and 6th Cruiser Squadrons and the 1st Light Cruiser Squadron were mainly engaged in Areas 3, 4 and 6; the 3rd Cruiser Squadron was at Rosyth and working to the eastward from that base.

On December 7th Rear-Admiral Sir A. G. W. Moore, K.C.B., assumed command of the newly constituted 1st Cruiser Squadron, and the Leviathan and Duke of Edinburgh arrived at Scapa on that date; the Warrior and Black Prince, with the above ships, comprised the squadron.

On December 7th, two merchant ships, the S.S. Michigan and City of Oxford, disguised as men-of-war, arrived at Scapa. These vessels, with several others, had been fitted out at Belfast by Admiralty orders with dummy turrets and guns, and altered with a view to representing certain British battleships and battle cruisers. The whole of these were formed into a squadron under the command of Commodore Haddock, C.B., R.N.R., of Olympic fame, and termed the Special Service Squadron. The disguise of the ships was carried out very cleverly, though presumably at considerable expense. They would have been of value had it been possible to select vessels of a suitable speed, but the highest speed attainable by any vessel in the squadron was not more than nine to ten knots, whilst the speed of the squadron as a whole did not exceed seven knots. The ships could not under these conditions accompany the Fleet to sea, and it was very difficult to find a use for them in home waters. Commodore Haddock was, later, detached with the squadron to Loch Ewe, where the ships were worked up to carry out fleet movements. This he did most successfully, so that, had the ships possessed the requisite speed, use might have been made of them as a squadron for various decoy purposes. But, under the conditions existing, this was impossible, and eventually the squadron was disbanded with the exception of one vessel; the experiment was tried of sending her to sea disguised as a disabled man-of-war with a considerable heel to one side, and with patrol craft accompanying her as if for protection, in the hope that a submarine might be induced to attack her and so afford the patrols an opportunity of sinking the submarine.

This scheme, however, met with no success. All the vessels were restored to their original conditions for trading purposes, with the exception of some which were sent to the Mediterranean and to North America, where it was reported that they were of some use.

On December 8th another gale was experienced. The Thunderer, which had developed condenser defects, left for Devonport on the 8th for refit and for retubing condensers; yet another case of this defect!

On December 9th the 1st Battle Squadron proceeded to sea to cruise to the northwestward of the Shetland Islands and to carry out gunnery practices as convenient. In consequence of bad weather the Vice-Admiral sent the attached cruiser Bellona back to Scapa for shelter.

On December 10th the new battleships Benbow and Emperor of India arrived from Berehaven to strengthen the 4th Battle Squadron, and proved very welcome additions to the Fleet. They, as well as all other new ships joining, necessarily spent several weeks in practices before becoming efficient to join the Fleet at sea, or to take part in action. Owing to the hurried completion of these two ships, a great deal of fitting work was also required before they were in a proper condition, and this delayed their practices considerably.

On the December 11th another gale was experienced which lasted until the 14th. The weather during this period was very bad, and ships at sea (including the 1st Battle Squadron which returned to Scapa on the 12th) met with very bad weather. Destroyers on patrol were unable to maintain their stations and were forced to run for shelter, and one of them, the Cockatrice, suffered some damage.

On the 12th the work of retubing the port condenser of the King George V. was completed; the starboard condenser was not taken in hand owing to the small margin of superiority of the Battle Fleet over the High Sea Fleet at this time.

During this stay of the Battle Fleet some very necessary work in the ships of the "Iron Duke" class was partially carried out. These ships were the first modern battleships fitted with 6-inch guns for their secondary armament, and the gunports were very low. Early in the War it was found necessary to unship the ports altogether, as the sea washed them away constantly. Water then had free access to the inside of the ship through the opening between the revolving shield and the ship's side, and, except in fine weather, water entered freely. In bad weather the water, as deep as three to four inches, was continually washing about the living decks and finding its way below through the open hatches, to the great discomfort of the ship's company, who were continually wet, and to the detriment of efficiency. Arrangements were devised on board the Iron Duke to overcome this trouble, and steps taken to have all the necessary fittings made at various contractors' yards. A partial bulkhead was fitted in rear of the guns to confine the water which entered the ship, and watertight india-rubber joints provided between the gun shields and the ship's side. The result was satisfactory, and similar changes were made in the ships of the "Queen Elizabeth" class and in the Tiger. The two after 6-inch guns, which were on the main deck level, were removed altogether at the first opportunity, and the ship's side and armour completed in the after embrasure in all these ships, as it was apparent that these guns could never be worked at sea, being only a few feet above the water line. The guns themselves were mounted in new unarmoured casemates on the superstructure deck level. The work connected with the forward 6-inch guns was entirely carried out at Scapa, with the ships at short notice for steam, and in some cases the workmen remained in the ships and continued the work at sea.

On December 12th serious defects in the boilers of the Liverpool became apparent and the speed of the ship was limited to 17 knots. This defect, which first showed itself in this ship, gradually affected the boilers of the same type in all ships so fitted, as they experienced a certain degree of wear, and from this time onwards there was usually one, and occasionally two, light cruisers paid off for the purpose of carrying out the necessary repairs which occupied a period of two or three months. This reduction in the number of efficient light cruisers was serious, at a time when our numbers compared badly with those possessed by the enemy.

On December 14th directions were given to the 2nd Battle Squadron and the 1st Light Cruiser Squadron at Scapa, the 1st Battle Cruiser Squadron at Cromarty and all the available destroyers which were at that base, and the 3rd Cruiser Squadron from Rosyth, to proceed to sea to meet at a rendezvous in Lat. 57.20 N., Long. 0.10 W., at 2.30 p.m. on December 15th, the force then to proceed to the southward with a view to sweeping the western portion of the North Sea. The 2nd Battle Squadron — without the Thunderer, which was refitting, and, therefore, comprising only six ships — left Scapa early on the 15th, but in passing through the Pentland Firth the attached cruisers Blanche and Boadicea were seriously damaged by the heavy sea running as the result of the late exceptional gales, and were forced to return.

The Boadicea had her bridge washed away and lost several men swept overboard and drowned. This ship was sent to the Clyde for repairs; the damage to the Blanche being less was made good at Scapa. The number of destroyers accompanying the force was, unfortunately, very inadequate, the 2nd Battle Squadron being unprovided with any vessels of this class, as the weather conditions in the Pentland Firth made it out of the question for destroyers to go to sea from Scapa. It was decided not to postpone the sweep on this account. I ordered all available destroyers out from Cromarty in the hope that the weather conditions in the Moray Firth might be better than at Scapa; only seven were available, however, and I therefore asked the Admiralty to direct the Commodore (T), with the 1st and 3rd Flotillas from Harwich, to meet the northern force at a southern rendezvous at daylight on December 16th. This proposal was not carried out, however, the Harwich force, which was at sea, remaining a considerable distance to the southward.

Whilst the force was on passage to the southward, the destroyers Lynx, Ambuscade, Unity, Hardy, Shark, Acasta and Spitfire — which had left Cromarty with the battle cruisers and on reaching the rendezvous were stationed 10 miles ahead of the 2nd Battle Squadron — sighted and became engaged before daylight on December 16th with a strong force of enemy destroyers, and, later, with one enemy cruiser and three light cruisers. The destroyers appeared to be screening ahead of the other vessels and both destroyers and cruisers were engaged by our small destroyer force. It was difficult to ascertain the result of the engagement so far as the German vessels were concerned, although the Hardy claimed to have hit a light cruiser at close range; the Hardy's steering-gear was disabled by enemy fire, two men killed and one officer and 14 men wounded.

The Ambuscade and Lynx were also holed, the Lynx having one man wounded. The Hardy finally withdrew under escort of the Lynx. The engagement caused our own destroyers to become scattered and separated from the Battle Squadron, and in the course of the day they proceeded to various east coast ports to repair and refuel, the Hardy being escorted to the Humber by the Spitfire. No report of this engagement reached me at the time. My first information of the presence of enemy forces in the vicinity of our coast was obtained by intercepting at 8.55 a.m. a wireless message from the Admiralty to Vice-Admiral commanding the 2nd Battle Squadron, timed 8.35 a.m., stating that Scarborough was being shelled. The Grand Fleet was at once ordered to raise steam, and left at 12.15 p.m., steering for a position Lat. 57 N., Long. 2.30 E. The weather had now moderated sufficiently to allow of destroyers accompanying the Fleet.

Meanwhile Sir George Warrender, who was in command of the 2nd Battle Squadron and was the senior officer of the forces at sea, on receipt of the Admiralty telegram had turned to the northward to endeavour to intercept the enemy forces on their return passage. Wireless signals were intercepted in the Iron Duke indicating that the scout cruiser Patrol was being engaged by two enemy battle cruisers and that battleships or battle cruisers were off Scarborough and light cruisers off Hartlepool. I knew that a gap between two minefields, laid by the enemy off our coast existed between Lat. 54.20 N. and 54.40 N. and concluded that any enemy forces operating off our coasts would pass through this gap. At 10 a.m., therefore, after intercepting the various messages mentioned above, I reminded the Vice-Admiral of the 2nd Battle Squadron and the Vice-Admiral of the 1st Battle Cruiser Squadron by wireless that this gap existed, and that the enemy would probably emerge there, and Sir George Warrender at 10.26 a.m. directed Sir David Beatty to pass through the gap towards our coast.

The Admiralty at 10.30 signalled, however, to the Vice-Admiral of the 2nd Battle Squadron that the enemy was probably returning towards Heligoland, and that he should keep outside the minefields and steer to cut off the enemy. Sir George Warrender then directed Sir David Beatty to obey this latter order.

I had ordered the 3rd Battle Squadron to sea from Rosyth immediately on receipt of the first news of the enemy, and Vice-Admiral Bradford, whose squadron was at short notice for steam, left at 10 a.m. with directions from me to proceed to lat. 55.50 N., Long. 1.10 W., my object being for this force to intercept the enemy should he pass out to the northward of the German minefields instead of through the gap between them.

Sir George Warrender, with the 2nd Battle Squadron, the 3rd Cruiser Squadron being in company, was informed of these dispositions by me. At 11.40 a.m. he signalled that at 12.30 p.m. he would be in Lat. 54.24 N., Long. 2.0 E. Sir David Beatty, with the 1st Battle Cruiser Squadron and 1st Light Cruiser Squadron, was to the northwestward of the Battle Squadron, and the Commodore (T) some 60 miles to the southward, having been ordered by the Vice-Admiral of the 2nd Battle Squadron, at 10.28 a.m., to steer for a position in Lat. 54.20 N., Long. 1.30 E. The weather throughout the whole morning had been very misty, with a visibility of about five miles, and sufficient sea to cause a great deal of spray when ships were steaming at high speed.

At 11.30 a.m. Commodore Goodenough, in the Southampton (1st Light Cruiser Squadron), sighted an enemy light cruiser and destroyers steering to the southward, gave chase with the Birmingham and engaged them; owing to the spray washing over the ship, and to the mist, no result was visible. Three other enemy light cruisers, or cruisers, were sighted to the southwestward shortly before 11.50 a.m., at about which time touch with these vessels was lost.

At 12.16 p.m., German cruisers and destroyers were sighted in Lat. 54.23 N., Long. 2.14 E. by the 2nd Battle Squadron distant about five miles on a bearing north by west, steering to the eastward, having evidently come out through the gap in the minefields as was anticipated; the 1st Battle Cruiser Squadron at this time was some 15 miles north of the Battle Squadron. It seems probable that the German force passed either between our 2nd Battle Squadron and the 1st Battle Cruiser Squadron, or ahead of the former and astern of the latter. On sighting our Battle Squadron, which turned to close, the enemy steered to the northward and disappeared shortly afterwards in the mist, steaming at high speed, and without being engaged by the 2nd Battle Squadron. The 1st Battle Cruiser Squadron did not sight any enemy forces.

The escape of the enemy's force was most disappointing, seeing that our own squadrons were in a very favourable position for intercepting the raiders. Low visibility was the main reason for their escape, but the absence from the Battle Squadron (through the bad weather in the Pentland Firth) of its attached cruisers and of a sufficient force of destroyers was a contributory cause, as well as the fact of our light cruisers having lost touch with the enemy at 11.50

At 3 p.m. the Vice-Admiral of the 2nd Battle Squadron informed me of the main features of the position, and stated that he was in Lat. 54.43 N., Long. 1.55 E., steering to the northward, with the 3rd Cruiser Squadron, adding that he had ordered the battle cruisers and light cruisers to rejoin him.

At about 2 p.m. the Admiralty informed me that it was thought, from the information given by our directional stations, that other ships of the High Sea Fleet were probably at sea, and at 6.30 p.m. I gave all our forces a rendezvous at which to meet at 6 a.m. on the 17th.

The force from Scapa, consisting of the 1st and 4th Battle Squadrons, with the 2nd Flotilla, and the 1st, 2nd and 6th Cruiser Squadrons, met at this time the force under Sir George Warrender, the 3rd Battle Squadron under Vice-Admiral E. E. Bradford, and the Commodore (T) with three light cruisers, and proceeded to the southward. During the afternoon of the 17th the Admiralty was able to ascertain (by directional wireless telegraphy) and to inform me that the ships of the High Sea Fleet, previously reported, were now in harbour.

Opportunity was then taken of the whole Fleet being in company with the Commodore (T) to carry out a battle exercise. At dusk, the Commodore (T) was detached to Harwich, the 3rd Battle Squadron and 3rd Cruiser Squadron to Rosyth, the 2nd Battle Squadron and 2nd Flotilla to Scapa, and the Marlborough to Rosyth, for the purpose of allowing Sir Lewis Bayly and Sir Cecil Burney to exchange commands in accordance with orders received from the Admiralty by wireless telegraphy when at sea. The light cruiser Bellona and the flotilla leader Broke collided during the battle exercises, and were seriously damaged, being sent to Rosyth under the escort of the Devonshire.

During the 17th wireless messages intercepted in the Iron Duke showed that the enemy raiding force had laid a large number of mines off the Yorkshire coast and that some British and neutral merchant ships had been sunk as a result.

During December 18th the 1st and 4th Battle Squadrons, the 1st Battle Cruiser Squadron and the 1st Light Cruiser Squadron remained at sea to the eastward of the Orkneys, and in the evening the battleships shaped course for Scapa, arriving on the 19th, the 1st Battle Cruiser Squadron and 1st Light Cruiser Squadron reaching Cromarty on the same day. The 1st and 2nd Cruiser Squadrons also proceeded to

Cromarty, and the 6th Cruiser Squadron remained out on patrol.

During the 18th a submarine was reported inside Scapa Flow, and the 2nd Battle Squadron raised steam; but investigation showed that the report was not well founded.

The strength of the 10th Cruiser Squadron had now risen to 18 ships, and directions were given by me to the Rear-Admiral commanding to establish patrols as follows:

Patrol A. — North of the Faroes and to westward of Long. 5.30 W.

Patrol B. — North of the Shetlands and to westward of Long. 1.0 W.

Patrol C. — South of the Faroes and to westward of a line joining Sydero and Sule Skerry lighthouses.

Patrol D. — West of the Hebrides and a line N.½W. from St. Kilda.

The Sappho and the seven armed boarding-steamers, now available, were based on Loch Ewe, and completed the blockade line between Patrol D and the Hebrides. They were, however, shifted later on to Scapa, where they were employed on patrol and boarding duties in the approaches to the Pentland Firth, or at sea with cruiser squadrons.

On December 20th a report was received that the submarine obstruction in Hoxa Sound had been found to be pierced; this led to steam being raised by all ships at Scapa, and the usual search by small craft was ordered; boats were also sent to explode charges on the bottom in the vicinity of the damaged portion of the submarine obstruction, where it was thought a submarine might have been entangled. Another alarm took place later, due to some trawlers inside Scapa Flow mistaking the concussion due to the explosion of these charges for torpedoes and firing warning signals in consequence. The precautions were kept in force until after daylight on the 21st. On that date Vice-Admiral Sir Cecil Burney arrived at Scapa in the Marlborough and assumed command of the 1st Battle Squadron, Sir Lewis Bayly taking over the command of the Channel Fleet.

On the 21st the 1st Battle Squadron and 1st Light Cruiser Squadron left Cromarty for Rosyth in obedience to directions from the Admiralty that the battle cruisers and light cruisers were to be based on the latter port. This change was one result of the Scarborough raid.

The minesweeping gunboats rejoined the Grand Fleet on this date.

On December 23rd the 2nd and 4th Battle Squadrons, with the Iron Duke, proceeded to sea to the westward of the Orkneys, and carried out target practice at the Sulisker Rock, north of the Hebrides, on the 24th, passed through the Pentland Firth at 6 p.m. on that date, and proceeded into the North Sea for a sweep into southern waters.

During daylight of the 25th the 1st Battle Squadron, the 2nd Flotilla and the 6th Cruiser Squadron from Scapa, the 3rd Battle Squadron, the 3rd Cruiser Squadron, the 1st Battle Cruiser Squadron and the 1st Light Cruiser Squadron from Rosyth, and the 1st and 2nd Cruiser Squadrons and 4th Flotilla from Cromarty met the Iron Duke, and the 2nd and 4th Battle Squadrons at given rendezvous between Lat. 56.45 N., Long. 1.30., and Lat. 56.14 N., Long. 3.20 E.

Vice-Admiral Sir Cecil Burney was under treatment on board a hospital ship and too unwell to take his squadron to sea. Admiral Sir Stanley Colville was, therefore, directed to hoist his flag on board the Marlborough and to assume temporary command of the 1st Battle Squadron.

The whole Fleet was together by 1.20 p.m. on the 25th, steering south-southeast at 15 knots. At 1.40 p.m. the Birmingham and Southampton, of the 1st Light Cruiser Squadron, both sighted submarines about 15 miles to the southwestward of the Battle Fleet.

The Battle Fleet was then gradually turned from the south-southeastward course to north-north-eastward until 3 p.m., being then in position Lat. 56.22 N., Long. 3.43 E.

Course was altered to north-northwest at 8.15 p.m. and speed reduced. At 9.15 p.m. the Fleet again turned to the southward, speed having to be reduced owing to the sea becoming too heavy for the destroyers. By midnight a southwesterly gale was blowing.

At 8 a.m. on December 26th the Battle Fleet was in Lat. 55.58 N., Long. 2.16 E., with the 1st Battle Cruiser Squadron and the 1st Light Cruiser Squadron 40 miles to the southward; a speed of 11 knots was the most that the destroyers could keep up without risk of serious damage, and, as the weather was getting rapidly worse, they were detached at 8.10 a.m to their bases.

By 10 a.m. a whole gale was blowing from the southeastward. The sweep was abandoned and course altered to the northward. At 11 a.m. the Rosyth and Cromarty squadrons were ordered to proceed to their bases, the Indomitable, which had joined the Fleet at 8 a.m. from the Mediterranean, being ordered to Rosyth, there to join the 1st Battle Cruiser Squadron. The destroyers and light cruisers suffered somewhat from the gale, the 2nd Flotilla unfortunately losing three men, and from the light cruiser Caroline one man was washed overboard.

Bad weather continued during the passage north with a very rough sea, and on nearing the Pentland Firth the Dreadnought Battle Fleet found the conditions to be exceptionally severe, with a following wind which caused the funnel smoke to obscure objects ahead of the ships. The ships were directed to enter Scapa Flow in the following order: 2nd Battle Squadron, 1st Battle Squadron, 4th Battle Squadron; the 2nd Battle Squadron was timed to enter at 6 a.m. — some time, of course, before daylight, which, at this period of the year at Scapa Flow, is about 8.30 a.m.

As the rear sub-division of the 2nd Battle Squadron approached the entrance, the ships as usual having no lights showing, the Monarch altered course and stopped to avoid a patrol trawler which she suddenly sighted close under her bows. The Conqueror, astern of her, was unable to avoid the Monarch and the two ships collided; the stern of the Monarch and the starboard bow of the Conqueror were very seriously damaged, rendering both ships unseaworthy. They were brought into the harbour and safely berthed.

Meanwhile, the 1st Battle Squadron, following astern of the 2nd Battle Squadron, entered safely. The Iron Duke was leading the 4th Battle Squadron, and, on intercepting the wireless messages indicating that something was wrong, I stood through the Pentland Firth to the westward with the 4th Battle Squadron until the situation had become clearer. The dawn was very late, and a furious gale was blowing, with a very heavy sea and strong tide in the Firth. These conditions made the handling of the battleships very difficult when they turned through 16 points to return to the eastward.

The Iron Duke and 4th Battle Squadron entered at 10 a.m. The whole Fleet remained with two anchors down and steam up on account of the weather until 1 p.m., when the wind and sea moderated, and by the morning of the 28th normal conditions were resumed. As a result of the gale, it was necessary to send the destroyers Hope, Redpole and Ruby to dockyards for repairs.

On the 28th a new Light Cruiser Squadron, termed the 2nd Light Cruiser Squadron, was formed, consisting of the Falmouth (Flag of Rear-Admiral Trevelyan Napier), Gloucester, Yarmouth and Dartmouth.

Vice-Admiral Sir Cecil Burney now resumed command of the 1st Battle Squadron.

Enemy submarines were active at the entrance to the Firth of Forth at this time; a torpedo was fired at T.B. No. 38 and another at T.B. No. 31 on the 25th, and two submarines were sighted during the 28th off the entrance to the Tay.

Temporary repairs to the Monarch and Conqueror were begun as soon as the weather permitted, and the former ship was able to leave Scapa for Devonport for thorough repair on December 29th. It was found necessary to obtain salvage plant and assistance in the case of the Conqueror, which had sustained very extensive underwater injury over a considerable length, and Captain Young, of the Liverpool Salvage Association, for whose services I applied at once, was sent up with the salvage ship Rattler, arriving on December 31st. The Conqueror was taken into Switha Sound and the repair ship Assistance secured alongside her, and excellent temporary repairs were affected by the 18th January, by the staff of the Assistance, Captain Betty, R.N., and by the salvage artificers under Captain Young.

The second condenser of the King George V. was taken in hand for retubing at this time.

At the end of 1914 the condition of the Fleet was:

Fleet-Flagship - the Iron Duke.

1st Battle Squadron - 8 ships (complete).

2nd Battle Squadron - 4 ships (the Conqueror and Monarch being disabled, and the King George V. retubing her second condenser).

3rd Battle Squadron (Pre-Dreadnoughts) - 7 ships (Commonwealth refitting)

4th Battle Squadron - 7 ships (complete); but two new ships, the Benbow and Emperor of India not yet efficient.

1st Battle Cruiser Squadron - 5 ships (Princess Royal was away).

1st Cruiser Squadron - 3 ships. (Black Prince refitting).

2nd Cruiser Squadron - 4 ships (complete).

3rd Cruiser Squadron - 4 ships (complete).

6th Cruiser Squadron - 2 ships (complete).

1st Light Cruiser Squadron - 4 ships (complete).

2nd Light Cruiser Squadron - 2 ships (2 not joined).

10th Cruiser Squadron – 14 ships (4 coaling and refitting).

2nd Flotilla -16 destroyers (4 refitting).

4th Flotilla - 17 destroyers (3 refitting).

The battleship HMS *Victoria* sinking

7 - The Dogger Bank Action

    Developments in the intelligence system at the Admiralty, initiated at the outbreak of war by Rear-Admiral Henry F. Oliver, the Director of the Intelligence Division, and improvements in the efficiency of our directional wireless stations and of wireless telegraphy generally, led to our being able to obtain more reliable knowledge of the movements of enemy vessels. The result was that it had become unnecessary towards the end of 1914 to keep the Fleet so constantly at sea in anticipation of enemy movements. It was very desirable to spare the ships to some extent, since it was increasingly evident that the War would be prolonged, and we had already had several warnings that the strain of constant sea work was telling on the efficiency of the machinery. Two very disquieting examples of this were the failure of condenser tubes on a large scale, particularly in the battleships, and the trouble developing in the boilers of a very considerable number of light cruisers.
    The problem of training personnel was also beginning to prove serious. In order to commission the large number of new ships which had been laid down since Lord Fisher, full of energy and ideas, had taken up the office of First Sea Lord (the number, of all sorts, building and projected, being more than 600), it became evident that it would be necessary to remove trained men from the Grand Fleet and to replace them with boys or untrained landsmen. Under these conditions the individual efficiency of the ships in gunnery and torpedo work, as well as in such matters as signalling (visual and wireless) and the other factors which are essential in a fighting ship, could only be maintained if we could spend sufficient time in harbour, during which regular instruction could be given; this instruction to be followed by frequent practices under way, in conditions where the ships would not be liable to attack by enemy submarines, and need not, therefore, be screened by the overworked destroyers. The organisation for carrying out this work at Scapa Flow was, therefore, greatly elaborated.

Steps were taken to start a school for training young wireless operators at Scapa, first on board each ship, and, later, in a specially fitted merchant ship. The want of wireless operators had been most seriously felt since the War began. In addition to the needs of new warships of all classes in this respect, the requirements for merchant ships, trawlers and other patrol craft were immense and could not be met. In this branch of instruction Lieut. Commander R. L. Nicholson, the Fleet wireless officer on my staff, carried out invaluable work in organising and starting the school. The training of young ratings in visual signal duties was also taken in hand vigorously under Commander A, E. Wood and the signal officers of the Fleet, The Grand Fleet became, in effect, a great school for turning out trained personnel for the Navy as a whole, whilst still keeping watch over the High Sea Fleet, and controlling the North Sea and its northern exit, thus carrying out its role as the centre and pivot of the whole naval side of the War.

Early in 1915 the subject of the instruction and education of the midshipmen also exercised my attention. On mobilisation all the cadets had been removed from Dartmouth and sent to sea, with their training, of course, very incomplete. During the first months of the War, when the ships were either at sea or, if in harbour, were coaling, it was impossible to give these young officers any regular instruction, and, whilst they were learning much that would be invaluable to them in the future, it was evidently highly desirable that their systematic education should be continued as far as was possible during a war.

Steps were accordingly taken in this direction. The first essential was to obtain naval instructors for the ships carrying midshipmen. The policy of the Admiralty, for some years before the War, had been to reduce gradually the number of naval instructors afloat, the idea being that the training at the Colleges and on board the training cruisers rendered the presence of instructors at sea unnecessary. I never held this view personally, but, in any case, it was clear that, as the cadets had gone to sea with less than half their course completed, further instruction at sea was necessary. The specialist officers afloat could not undertake this work under war conditions and strong representations were, therefore, made to the Admiralty on the subject. Eventually a number of gentlemen were entered specially for this instructional work and, after a short course of training in navigation at Greenwich, were sent to the Fleet, where their work proved to be of great value to the rising generation of officers.

The blockade was becoming daily more effective, although the blockading cruisers worked at so great a distance from the German coast. The only interference ever attempted by the enemy was by submarine attack or by mines, and during the year 1915 no great success was achieved by them in this respect when the conditions are considered. The regular blockading squadron, the 10th Cruiser Squadron, was assisted in its work by the sweeps of our cruisers and light cruisers, accompanied occasionally by the Battle Fleet. In addition to the discharge of these duties, the Battle Fleet engaged in periodical cruises, during which battle exercises were carried out for the purpose of maintaining efficiency in the handling of the ships and squadrons and of giving the fresh officers, who were frequently joining the Fleet, to replace others required for the new ships, experience in the work of the Grand Fleet under the novel war conditions.

Pursuant to this general policy, the Dreadnought Battle Fleet remained in harbour until January 10th, and then left for a cruise to the westward of the Orkneys and Shetlands. Gunnery practices were carried out by day and at night, as well as battle exercises, and the Fleet returned to Scapa during the day and the night of the 13th. The 3rd Battle Squadron left Rosyth on the 12th for a cruise in the North Sea, and on the night of the 13th-14th passed to the westward of the Orkneys for gunnery practice, returning to Rosyth on the 15th.

Other events of interest during the first fortnight of January 1915 were the return of the Princess Royal from North American waters on the 1st; a short cruise in the centre of the North Sea by the 1st Battle Cruiser Squadron and the 1st Light Cruiser Squadron between the 3rd and the 5th, and by the 3rd Cruiser Squadron between the 6th and the 8th; a cruise by the 1st Cruiser Squadron to the westward of the Orkneys between the 4th and 6th, and by the 6th Cruiser Squadron between the 6th and the 9th, and the 10th and 14th. On January 4th the King George V. completed the work of retubing her condenser.

On the 9th all ships at Scapa raised steam ready for leaving, in consequence of a report of a submarine being sighted in Hoy Sound, and available destroyers and trawlers were sent to patrol in the vicinity of the Hoy anti-submarine Fleet obstructions until the Battle Fleet left harbour on the 10th.

Gales were experienced at Scapa on the 1st, 13th, 16th and 19th of January.

On January 15th the 2nd Battle Cruiser Squadron was reconstituted, under Vice-Admiral Sir A. G. W. Moore, K.C.B., whose flag was transferred from the Leviathan, of the 1st Cruiser Squadron, to the New Zealand; the 2nd Battle Cruiser Squadron then comprised the New Zealand, Indomitable and Invincible (the last not having yet arrived). Rear-Admiral Sir Robert Arbuthnot, Bart., took command of the 1st Cruiser Squadron in place of Sir Gordon Moore, flying his flag in the Defence, which took the place of the Leviathan; the latter vessel was transferred to the 6th Cruiser Squadron. Rear-Admiral A. C. Leveson, C.B., relieved Sir Robert Arbuthnot as Rear-Admiral in the 2nd Battle Squadron, flying his flag in the Orion.

On the 17th the 1st and 2nd Battle Cruiser Squadrons and 1st Light Cruiser Squadron left Rosyth for a cruise in the centre and southern portions of the North Sea, and on the 19th, at dawn, arrived in position Lat. 55 N., Long. 5.30 E. to support Commodore Tyrwhitt in carrying out a reconnaissance in Heligoland Bight. Nothing was sighted beyond an airship and a seaplane, and the force was ordered to return to its bases and arrived during the night of the 20th-21st.

On the 18th the Admiral commanding at Queenstown reported that a German mine had been washed ashore at Portrush, as well as bodies and wreckage, apparently belonging to the Viknor, an armed merchant cruiser of the 10th Cruiser Squadron. Anxiety had been felt as to the safety of the Viknor for two or three days owing to no reply to wireless signals being received from her, and the ships of the 10th

Cruiser Squadron had been directed to search for her. The report from Portrush pointed to the probability that she had struck a mine off the north coast of Ireland, either in the Audacious minefield or a field further to the southward, and had been lost with all hands in the very heavy weather prevailing at the time in this vicinity. All traffic round the north of Ireland was stopped until sweepers were able to examine the whole area.

At this time a large number of German mines were being constantly reported both in the North Sea and on the west coasts of Scotland and Ireland, having evidently broken adrift from their moorings in the heavy weather which had been generally prevalent. These mines, which were not safe when adrift, as provided for under The Hague Convention, were a source of some danger to ships, particularly at night. On the 18th the battleship Superb, having developed defects in one of her turbines, was sent to Portsmouth. She was absent from the Fleet until March 11th.

On January 19th, the orders for the 10th Cruiser Squadron (blockading squadron) were somewhat modified by me; the new centre lines of patrol positions being:

Patrol A. - A line 80 miles long, 360 degrees from Lat. 62.20 N., Long. 10.0 W.

Patrol B. - A line 80 miles long, 360 degrees from Lat 61.10 N., Long. 1.15 E.

Patrol C. - A line 80 miles long, 360 degrees from Lat 59.40 N., Long. 9.0 W.

Patrol D. - Eastern line of patrol to be 80 miles in the direction 335 degrees from St. Kilda.

The ships were ordered to patrol on east and west courses on each side of the centre line at a speed of at least 13 knots by day, zigzagging.

At the same time four ships were directed to carry out a special patrol of the Norwegian coast between the parallels of 62 N. and 62.20 N. This patrol was maintained until the 22nd. As indicating the growing work of the ships of the 10th

Cruiser Squadron and the efficiency of the blockade, the Rear-Admiral of the 10th Cruiser Squadron reported on January 18th that 80 ships had been intercepted by his squadron since December 26th, 52 of which were eastward-bound. The strength of the 10th Cruiser Squadron had now risen to 21 ships, exclusive of the Viknor, the loss of which ship with her fine ship's company was deeply regretted.

A patrol to the eastward of the Pentland Firth was at this period being worked by the Sappho and five armed boarding-steamers, which were supported at night by one or two cruisers or light cruisers as necessary.

The Monarch returned from being repaired at Devonport on the 20th. Temporary repairs to the Conqueror had been completed about January 18th, but the ship was detained pending more favourable weather conditions; on the 21st she left for a southern dockyard, escorted by four destroyers. On clearing the Pentland Firth, however, she found that the sea was too heavy for the passage to be made with safety in her damaged condition, and the ship returned to Scapa, where further work was taken in hand and it was decided that it would be necessary to dock her in the floating-dock at Invergordon to effect more permanent repairs for the passage south than could be carried out by divers at Scapa. She reached Invergordon on January 24th.

On January 23rd the 1st and 2nd Battle Cruiser Squadrons and the 1st Light Cruiser Squadron at Rosyth left for a sweep in the southern portion of the North Sea, in conjunction with the Harwich force. The remainder of the Grand Fleet acted in support. The 1st and 2nd Battle Cruiser Squadrons (except the Queen Mary, which was absent refitting) and the 1st Light Cruiser Squadron were directed to a rendezvous, where the Commodore (T), with available destroyers and light cruisers, was ordered to meet them.

The 3rd Battle Squadron and 3rd Cruiser Squadron were ordered to the vicinity of the battle cruisers' rendezvous.

The Iron Duke, the 1st, 2nd and 4th Battle Squadrons, the 1st, 2nd and 6th Cruiser Squadrons, and the 2nd Light Cruiser Squadron, available destroyers of 2nd and 4th Flotilla (a total of 28 destroyers) left Scapa during the evening of the 23rd and proceeded towards the same rendezvous.

At 7.20 a.m. the Aurora, of the Harwich force, reported that she was in action with enemy vessels; at 7.30 a.m. Sir David Beatty reported enemy battle cruisers and cruisers in sight in Lat. 54.53 N., Long. 3.32 E., steering east. At 7.55 a.m. Commodore Goodenough, commanding the 1st Light Cruiser Squadron, reported his position as Lat. 55.10 N., Long. 3.32 E., and enemy vessels in sight, consisting of battle cruisers, light cruisers and destroyers, steering between southeast and south. On receipt of these reports the Battle Fleet increased to 19 knots speed, and steered to support the battle cruisers, and the 3rd Battle Squadron and 3rd Cruiser Squadron, which were further to the southward, were ordered to steer for Heligoland at full speed, to act in immediate support. The 2nd Light Cruiser Squadron was also sent on ahead at full speed to join the other forces.

During the early part of the engagement Sir David Beatty kept me informed of his position and proceedings, but at 11.30 a.m. a report was received from Sir Gordon Moore that he was heavily engaged with the enemy battle cruisers in Lat. 54.21 N., Long. 5.4 E. The fact that this report was made by this officer caused me some uneasiness at first, as it implied that the Lion could not signal, but as the Rear-Admiral made no mention of any casualty to the Lion, I concluded the cause was some breakdown in her wireless arrangements and that all was well.

At 11.50 a.m. Commodore Goodenough, commanding the 1st Light Cruiser Squadron, reported the enemy steering southeast at 25 knots, and at noon that he had lost touch with them; at 12.5 p.m. Rear Admiral Sir Gordon Moore reported that he was retiring northwest, and, later, north-northwest, that the Blucher was out of action, and that the remaining enemy battle cruisers were out of sight; he added that the Lion had hauled out of action. He gave his position as Lat. 54.19 N., Long. 5.22 E.

The Dreadnought Battle Fleet's position at noon was Lat. 56.29 N., Long. 3.22 E., with the cruisers 15 miles ahead and the 2nd Light Cruiser Squadron ahead of the cruisers. At 1.15 Rear-Admiral Moore reported in reply to my enquiry that Sir David Beatty was on board the Princess Royal, that the Lion was damaged and detached; Sir David Beatty then reported that the Lion's speed was reduced to 12 knots, that the Blucher had been sunk, and two other enemy battle cruisers seriously damaged, and that he was covering the retirement of the Lion, which was steaming with her starboard engine only.

The hit which disabled the Lion was a piece of luck for the enemy.

At 2 p.m. Vice-Admiral Bradford, commanding the 3rd Battle Squadron, reported that he was turning to the northward, having all the battle cruisers in sight. The 3rd Battle Squadron was sighted from the Iron Duke at 3.30 p.m., and stationed on the Dreadnought Battle Fleet. Sir David Beatty had meanwhile directed the Indomitable at 3.38 p.m. to take the Lion in tow, and this operation was effected by 5 p.m. At 4 p.m. the Iron Duke's position was Lat. 55.15 N., Long. 4.7 E., and at 4.30 p.m. the battle cruisers were in sight from the Iron Duke. The Battle Fleet then turned to the northward, keeping in company with the battle cruisers until dark.

At 7 p.m. the Lion's starboard engine became disabled and the speed was still further reduced.

At dusk, the 1st and 2nd Light Cruiser Squadrons and all destroyers of the 2nd and 4th Flotillas with the Battle Fleet, except those vessels which were short of fuel, had been detached to assist the remaining destroyers in screening the Lion and her escort against destroyer and submarine attack. The heavy ships, battleships and battle cruisers, stood to the northward to be clear of torpedo attack. The night passed without incident, the 1st and 2nd Light Cruiser Squadrons joining the battle cruisers during the darkness. Wireless messages were sent on the 24th to the Senior Naval Officer, Tyne, to send out tugs to meet the Lion, and this was done.

The Dreadnought Battle Fleet and the battle cruisers remained cruising in the North Sea during daylight on the 25th, except the 3rd Battle Squadron and 3rd Cruiser Squadron, which were detached to Rosyth at 8 a.m.

During these operations many floating mines were sighted and sunk.

The battle cruisers proceeded to Rosyth at dusk, and the Battle Fleet to Scapa, except the Iron Duke and Centurion, which were sent to Cromarty, the Iron Duke to dock and refit and the Centurion to act as "stand by" Fleet-Flagship during the refit. The Lion arrived at Rosyth at 6.35 a.m. on the 26th in a dense fog and was taken up harbour for temporary repairs, the Assistance being sent from Scapa to Rosyth to help in the work. The main injury to the Lion was caused by two hits underwater, which pierced the feed tank and displaced an armour plate; the permanent repairs were completed on the Tyne, the work being carried out by the aid of coffer dams, there being no dock there capable of taking the ship. Her casualties consisted of 11 men wounded. The only other battle cruiser that received injury was the Tiger, in which ship Engineer Captain Taylor, a most valuable officer, and five men were killed, 11 being wounded; the material damage to the ship was slight.

The enemy, as the result of this action, suffered the total loss of the Blucher; and two battle cruisers, the Derfflinger and Seydlitz, sustained severe injuries, a serious fire or explosion occurring in one of the after turrets of one ship, which put that, or possibly both after turrets, out of action and caused a large number of casualties amongst the crew. It was ascertained at a later date from German prisoners that the condition of one, if not of both ships on return to harbour was very serious; the casualties, as well as the material injury, were heavy. It was stated subsequently that the Derfflinger had 60 killed and 250 wounded, and the Seydlitz about 100 killed.

One of our destroyers, the Meteor, was damaged in the action, but was towed back to port and repaired.

On the 26th the 6th Cruiser Squadron was reconstituted and composed of the Drake, Leviathan and Cumberland, and a 7th Cruiser Squadron was formed under the command of Rear-Admiral A. W. Waymouth, consisting of the Minotaur (flagship), Hampshire and Donegal. The 1st and 6th Cruiser

Squadrons were sent to Scapa, and the 2nd and 7th to Cromarty.

The Britannia, of the 3rd Battle Squadron, grounded in the Firth of Forth in the fog on her way back to Rosyth, was ashore for 36 hours, and suffered considerable damage, necessitating repairs at a dockyard.

On the 27th January the 1st Cruiser Squadron and a division of destroyers sailed to cruise in the centre portion of the North Sea and returned on the 30th, being relieved by the 2nd Cruiser Squadron. On January 28th the battle cruisers Princess Royal and Queen Mary, with the 1st Light Cruiser Squadron, left Rosyth to support operations being carried out in the Heligoland Bight by Commodore Tyrwhitt and Commodore Keyes on January 30th and 31st. Owing to fog the operations could not be carried out, and the force returned to its bases on the 30th.

A report of a submarine inside Cromarty Harbour on the 29th caused ships to raise steam preparatory to leaving, and all small craft to search for the submarine, but on investigation it was considered that the report was unreliable.

On January 30th enemy submarines appeared in the Irish Sea, one of them opening fire on Walney Island, where the works of Messrs. Vickers, Limited, are situated. At about this date, owing to marked enemy submarine activity in the Irish Sea, the ships of the 10th Cruiser Squadron were directed to coal temporarily at Loch Ewe instead of at Liverpool, and two divisions of Grand Fleet destroyers were detached to the Irish Sea to assist in hunting the submarines.

During January the number of drifting German mines in the North Sea was very considerable. Many were sighted and sunk by the Fleet when at sea; the 2nd Cruiser Squadron alone, when on patrol on the 30th and 31st January sinking 12 mines.

At the end of January the condition of the Grand Fleet was as follows:

BATTLE FLEET

Iron Duke, Fleet-Flagship, refitting.

1st Battle Squadron: 7 ships (Superb was away).

2nd Battle Squadron: 6 ships (Conqueror was unserviceable).

3rd Battle Squadron: 6 ships (Commonwealth and Britannia refitting).

4th Battle Squadron: 7 ships (complete).

1st Battle Cruiser Squadron: 2 ships (Lion was effecting temporary repairs; the Tiger refitting).

2nd Battle Cruiser Squadron: 1 ship (Indomitable refitting after a fire due to defective electric circuits).

1st Cruiser Squadron: 4 ships (complete).

2nd Cruiser Squadron: 3 ships (Natal refitting).

3rd Cruiser Squadron: 3 ships (Roxburgh refitting).

6th Cruiser Squadron: 3 ships (complete).

7th Cruiser Squadron: 3 ships (complete).

1st Light Cruiser Squadron: 4 ships (complete).

2nd Light Cruiser Squadron: 4 ships (Liverpool refitting).

2nd Flotilla: 11 destroyers (5 refitting, 4 detached in the Irish Sea).

4th Flotilla: 11 destroyers (5 refitting, 4 detached in the Irish Sea).

The shortage of destroyers at this period was exceedingly marked.

During February the Battle Fleet remained in harbour. No enemy movements took place or were expected as several changes were being made in the High Sea Fleet commands; the principal of these was the relief of Admiral von Inghenol by Admiral von Pohl as Commander-in-Chief. It was anticipated that the new Flag officers would exercise their squadrons in order to become familiar with them before attempting any operations.

The opportunity was taken of refitting the Iron Duke, and the ship remained at Invergordon, in the Cromarty Firth, until February 23rd. It was becoming desirable to give the officers and men of the Battle Fleet some change from Scapa Flow, where there were no opportunities for landing for exercise or recreation, and arrangements were made by which battle, as well as cruiser squadrons should visit Invergordon periodically for this purpose. The 2nd Battle Squadron accordingly arrived at this base on February 24th.

During the first half of February, 1915, eight destroyers were absent from the Grand Fleet flotillas, working in the Irish Channel against submarines, leaving only a total of 20 to 22 available for the Fleet; an insufficient number for screening purposes. This deficiency made it desirable to keep the Battle Fleet in harbour, except in an emergency.

The enemy's submarine activity became much more marked during February. Early in the month the German Admiralty proclaimed that after February 18th all the waters round the British Isles would be declared unsafe for merchant-ships of all nationalities, and intimated that Allied merchant-ships would be destroyed in these waters and that neutral merchant-ships ran similar risks. Enemy submarines began to operate in increasing numbers in the English Channel, to the westward of the English Channel, in the Irish Sea and off the west coast of Ireland, as well as on the east coast of England, and the losses of merchant-ships from submarine attack became serious. The destroyers of the Grand Fleet that remained at the northern bases were kept fully employed in searching for and hunting reported submarines.

In addition to the maintenance of the blockade by the 10th Cruiser Squadron, cruiser and light cruiser squadrons carried out various patrol and search operations during the month. The 3rd Cruiser Squadron cruised in the centre portion of the North Sea from February 1st to 3rd; the 2nd Cruiser Squadron cruised off the Shetland Islands from the 11th-13th, then swept down the Norwegian coast and returned to Cromarty on the 16th; the new 2nd Light Cruiser Squadron carried out a sweep in the southern portion of the North Sea between the 16th and 20th with destroyers in company; the new 3rd Light Cruiser Squadron cruised to the westward of the Shetlands for exercise between the 15th and 18th, then passed into the North Sea and swept to the southward, returning to Scapa on the 20th; the 1st Cruiser Squadron left Scapa on the 17th for the vicinity of the Norwegian coast, swept down towards the Naze and then returned to patrol north of the Shetlands until the 21st, when the squadron arrived at Scapa; the four light cruisers attached to the Battle Fleet, Bellona, Blanche, Boadicea, and Blonde, with four destroyers, left Scapa on the 18th for a line N. 37 E. 60 miles long from Lat. 57.30 N., Long. 0.30 W., with directions to sweep towards the Naze by day and patrol the line at night; they remained on this duty until the 21st. The 7th Cruiser Squadron cruised to the westward of the Fair Island Channel from the 19th to the 22nd, and available destroyers of the 2nd and 4th Flotillas were patrolling to the eastward of the Fair Island Channel and the Moray Firth respectively during the same period.

The 3rd Cruiser Squadron, with four destroyers, left Rosyth on the 23rd to cover the Fleet minesweepers whilst searching for mines along a projected Fleet track in the North Sea, but, the sea being too heavy for minesweeping, the squadron carried out a patrol instead until the 25th, when the minesweeping operations took place, lasting until the 27th, when the squadron returned to Rosyth.

This searching mine sweep was carried out because of the increasing probability of the enemy laying mines intended to catch our heavy ships when proceeding towards the southern portion of the North Sea, and the consequent necessity for a periodical examination of a route which the Fleet could traverse with some safety. This policy was maintained throughout the period of my command, alternative routes being periodically examined; although it was obviously impossible to carry out this examination frequently, it did afford some chance of a minefield being discovered before serious losses were sustained by the Fleet.

During the month of February a reorganisation of the battle cruiser and light cruiser squadrons was carried out by Admiralty orders, and a "Battle Cruiser Fleet" instituted under the command of Sir David Beatty, with the title Vice-Admiral Commanding the Battle Cruiser Fleet.

The organisation was as follows:

Lion, Fleet-Flagship.

1st Battle Cruiser Squadron: Princess Royal (Flag of Rear-Admiral O. de B. Brock), Queen Mary, Tiger.

2nd Battle Cruiser Squadron: Australia (Flag of Rear-Admiral W. C. Pakenham), New Zealand, Indefatigable.

3rd Battle Cruiser Squadron: Invincible (to be Flag), Inflexible (had not yet joined by the end of February), Indomitable.

1st Light Cruiser Squadron: Galatea (Broad pendant of Commodore E. S. Alexander Sinclair), Cordelia, Caroline, Inconstant.

2nd Light Cruiser Squadron: Southampton (Broad pennant of Commodore W. E. Goodenough), Nottingham, Birmingham, Lowestoft.

3rd Light Cruiser Squadron: Falmouth (Flag of Rear-Admiral Trevelyan Napier), Yarmouth, Gloucester, Liverpool.

The Battle Cruiser Fleet remained an integral portion of the Grand Fleet. In some respects the term "Fleet" was an unfortunate selection, as it implied, incorrectly, an independent organisation. On my taking office as First Sea Lord at the end of 1916, the title was altered to the more appropriate one of Battle Cruiser Force.

The Australia joined the Battle Cruiser Fleet at Rosyth on February 17th, and the Invincible, having concluded the very successful operations in the South Atlantic under Sir Doveton Sturdee, which culminated in the destruction of Admiral von Spee's Squadron of cruisers and light cruisers, arrived at Scapa for gunnery practices during the latter part of February, and joined the Battle Cruiser Fleet at Rosyth early in March; the Indefatigable also arrived on the 24th from the Mediterranean.

The Tiger arrived in the Tyne on February 1st for refit, and left again on the 8th. The Lion reached the Tyne for repairs on February 9th, remaining there for the remainder of the month. The strength of the destroyer force working with the Grand Fleet was increased on February 19th by the addition of the light cruiser Fearless and two divisions of destroyers from the 1st Flotilla. These vessels had been relieved at Harwich by new destroyers of the "M" class. This addition brought the destroyer force actually with the Grand Fleet up to a total of 48, and further additions were now gradually made from the 1st

Flotilla at Harwich as new destroyers were completed to relieve them.

His Majesty the King honoured the Grand Fleet on February 27th by visiting the ships based on Rosyth.

In the course of February the destroyers of the "River" or "E" class, based at Scapa for local defence, were replaced, by Admiralty directions, by destroyers of the "C" class (old 30-knot type). This change, although dictated by the general naval situation, limited considerably the range of activity of the local defence vessels, owing to the poorer sea-going qualities of the destroyers of the "C" class. During the month the destroyer Erne was wrecked off Rattray Head on the Aberdeen coast, and became a total loss; the Goldfinch went ashore in a fog in the north of the Orkneys and was also lost; the Sparrowhawk also went ashore, but was got off, though considerably damaged. The armed merchant cruiser Clan McNaughton, of the 10th Cruiser Squadron, was lost with all hands during the month, the supposition being that she foundered in one of the numerous heavy gales. Although a prolonged search was carried out, only a certain amount of wreckage was found. The loss of this ship and her efficient ship's company brought once more into prominence the excellent work of the 10th Cruiser Squadron and the risks to which the ships were subjected.

The activities of the 10th Cruiser Squadron were daily increasing, and the number of ships passing the blockade line unexamined was becoming very small. During one week in February sixty-seven vessels were intercepted and eighteen of them sent in with prize crews on board. During February the old battleships Hannibal and Magnificent were relieved as guard-ships by the old cruisers Crescent and Royal Arthur.

Vice-Admiral Sir Doveton Sturdee succeeded Vice-Admiral Sir Douglas Gamble in the command of the 4th Battle Squadron during the month; Admiral Gamble's period of command had expired. Sir Doveton Sturdee, who had served as Chief of the Naval Staff early in the War, came to the Fleet fresh from his Falkland Islands victory.

The weather at the northern bases during February was less boisterous than usual. There was a good deal of misty and foggy weather in the early part of the month, and a considerable amount of snow towards the end.

During March the principal movements of the Fleet were as follows:

From March 4th to the 10th, the 6th Cruiser Squadron was, with the Orotava of the 10th Cruiser Squadron, cruising off the Norwegian Coast, From the 7th to the 10th the Dreadnought Battle Fleet was cruising in the northern portion of the North Sea, accompanied by the 1st, 2nd, and 7th Cruiser Squadrons and the 4th Flotilla; and the Battle Cruiser Fleet was also cruising during the same period in the central part of the North Sea. The opportunity was taken of carrying out various battle exercises. The 2nd Battle Squadron and 7th Cruiser Squadron did not return with the remainder of the Battle Fleet on the 10th, but remained at sea until the 11th. The 4th Flotilla was forced to shelter at Lerwick from the 7th to the 9th owing to bad weather.

From March 10th to the 18th the 3rd Battle Squadron and 3rd Cruiser Squadron were cruising in the centre portion of the North Sea.

From the March 16th to the 19th the Dreadnought Battle Fleet again cruised in the northern and central parts of the North Sea, accompanied by the 1st, 2nd, and 7th Cruiser Squadrons, the 3rd Light Cruiser Squadron, and the 2nd Flotilla, The 2nd Flotilla, however, could not remain at sea on the 17th owing to bad weather and was sent back to Scapa. A collision occurred between the Nemesis and Nymphe, which necessitated the docking of both vessels for repairs. The flotilla was ordered out again from Scapa early on the 18th, but only seven destroyers were available, and they reached the Fleet at 2 p.m. on that date.

The Battle Fleet and cruisers carried out a strategical exercise in the early morning of the 18th, and then steered for the bases, a projected second exercise being abandoned as the Fleet was by this time in an area which was not considered safe from submarine attack; the visibility was also very high, and it was suspected that at least one enemy submarine might be in the neighbourhood.

At noon the Battle Fleet was in Lat. 58.21 N., Long. 1.12 E., zigzagging at a speed of 15 knots, and the 4th Battle Squadron had just been detached to proceed to Cromarty, when at 12.18 p.m. Vice-Admiral Sir Cecil Burney commanding the 1st Battle Squadron signalled that a submarine's periscope had been sighted from the Marlborough, the leading ship of the port wing column, and that a torpedo fired by the submarine had passed just astern of the Neptune, the rear ship of the column. The Fleet was at once turned away from the submarine 12 points to starboard (ships turning together) and speed was increased to 17 knots.

At 12.30 p.m. the 4th Battle Squadron was crossing under the stern of the remainder of the Battle Fleet and signals were being made to Vice-Admiral Sir Doveton Sturdee to steer clear of the position in which the submarine was sighted, but before any movement was effected the officer of the watch, Lieutenant-Commander Piercy, of the Dreadnought of that Squadron, sighted a periscope close to, one point on the port bow, the submarine apparently steering a southerly course and zigzagging. Captain Alderson, commanding the Dreadnought, at once altered course direct for the submarine, increased speed, followed, and rammed her. The bow of the submarine came out of the water and her number, U 29, was plainly visible. She sank immediately. The Blanche, which passed close to the spot, reported a large quantity of wreckage, one article of clothing and much oil and bubbles on the surface, but no survivors.

It seems probable that the captain of the submarine, after firing at the 1st Battle Squadron, was confused by the movements of the 4th Battle Squadron crossing astern of the remainder of the zigzagging Fleet, at high speed, and in trying to get clear failed to observe the Dreadnought until too late. The Dreadnought was admirably handled.

On arrival of the Fleet in harbor, I wired to the Admiralty urging that the fate of U 29 should be kept secret. The secrecy regarding the loss of this submarine commanded by

Commander Weddingen, was much resented in Germany, and many accusations of treacherous conduct levelled at the British, probably in the hope that we might give information as to her fate. The policy of secrecy was certainly correct, as it left the enemy entirely ignorant of our methods, and possibly had some effect of the moral of the submarine crews.

The Fleet steered to the eastward until well clear of the area in case other submarines were present, and then shaped course for the bases, arriving on the 19th.

On March 29th the Grand Fleet left its bases with the intention of carrying out a sweep of the North Sea, but the plan was abandoned and the Fleet returned to its bases on the following day.

The principal movements of destroyers during March, additional to the regular patrols and fleet movements, were as follows:

From March 2nd to March 5th search was made by a half flotilla for a number of oil drums reported as moored in certain areas in the North Sea. The report indicated that the enemy might be refuelling submarines in this manner; the search disposed of the supposition.

From March 8th to March 10th the Commander-in-Chief Coast of Scotland, Sir Robert Lowry, in conjunction with Vice-Admiral Bradford, who was the Senior Flag Officer of Grand Fleet ships at Rosyth, and was, therefore, responsible for all movements of these ships from the Rosyth base, organised a search on a large scale for a submarine reported to be operating off the Aberdeenshire coast. The vessels employed in this operation comprised trawler patrols and destroyers of the 1st Flotilla, and they were rewarded on March 10th by forcing the submarine - U 12 - to the surface, when H.M.S. Ariel, very skilfully handled, succeeded in ramming and sinking her. Ten of her crew of twenty-eight were rescued. The Ariel was considerably damaged, and was docked at Leith for repairs.

On March 20th and 21st a division of destroyers hunted a submarine in the Moray Firth without success.

On March 12th the Faulknor and six destroyers were detached from the Grand Fleet flotillas to operate against submarines in the Irish Sea.

In the course of the month the small steamers, specially fitted as minesweepers for the Grand Fleet, were withdrawn for service abroad. The increasing number of mines in the North Sea and the paucity of minesweepers led me to decide on March 22nd to fit eight destroyers each from the 2nd and 4th Flotillas with light mine sweeps, and the work was taken in hand. These vessels were intended to augment the regular force of minesweepers in an emergency, as it was felt that a movement of the High Sea Fleet for an important naval operation would in all probability be preceded by extensive minelaying outside the Fleet bases, and a much stronger sweeping force than we possessed was required to enable a passage for the Fleet to be rapidly cleared.

The Conqueror rejoined the Fleet on March 6th after effecting repairs which had been carried out by Messrs. Cammell Laird at Liverpool with most commendable rapidity.

The 10th Cruiser Squadron experienced a further loss during March, the Bayano being sunk by a submarine off Corsewall Point, Galloway, on March 11th, with considerable loss of life.

In the course of this month Rear-Admiral W. L. Grant succeeded Rear-Admiral W. C. Pakenham in command of the 3rd Cruiser Squadron, the latter succeeding Rear-Admiral Sir Gordon Moore in command of the 2nd Battle Cruiser Squadron; Vice-Admiral Patey transferred his flag from the Australia to the Leviathan to proceed to the West Indies as Commander-in-Chief, and the 6th Cruiser Squadron was broken up, the ships being transferred to service abroad.

The enemy submarines were very active against merchant shipping during March, and our losses were considerable, both from this cause and from mines.

During March, the weather at the northern bases was not very boisterous, but a great deal of mist and fog was prevalent during the first fortnight, and during the last fortnight snow fell on at least seven days.

An average of fifty-six ships per week was intercepted by the ships of the 10th Cruiser Squadron during the month.

During April, 1915, intended Fleet movements were prevented on several occasions by bad weather, and the 10th Cruiser Squadron and other ships at sea experienced exceptional gales; the principal movements carried out were as follows:

From the 5th to the 8th the 3rd Battle Squadron, 3rd Cruiser Squadron and five destroyers of the 1st Flotilla cruised in the North Sea (central portion), and from the 5th to the 9th the Battle Cruiser Fleet with eight destroyers of the 1st Flotilla cruised in the northern portion of the North Sea.

On April 8th the Lancaster, of the 7th Cruiser Squadron, and the Caribbean, of the 10th Cruiser Squadron, were detached to watch the Norwegian coast between Lat. 62 and 64 N.

On April 11th the whole Grand Fleet proceeded to sea; the Battle Fleet met the Battle Cruiser Fleet and 3rd Battle Squadron from Rosyth, and cruised in the centre portion of the North Sea during the 12th and 13th, returning to the various bases on the 14th to fuel. The opportunity was taken of carrying out battle exercises.

Whilst the Dreadnought Battle Fleet was passing down east of the Orkneys at 2.30 p.m., and was being met by the 2nd and 4th Flotillas, which had come out to screen the ships in, the Neptune reported having sighted a submariners periscope, but as the Fleet was steaming at 18 knots and the destroyers were taking up screening stations it was not considered that successful attack was probable, and the Fleet held its course for Scapa.

Submarines were also sighted during the day by the Antrim in Lat. 57.18 N., Long. 1.2 E., and by the Battle Cruiser Fleet in Lat. 58.15 N., Long. 2.40 E., but no successful attack resulted.

The Grand Fleet proceeded to sea again for a sweep in southern waters on the 17th, and at 8 a.m. on the 18th the Dreadnought Battle Fleet, with the 1st, 2nd, and 7th Cruiser Squadrons looking out ahead and the 2nd and 4th Flotillas screening, was in Lat. 57.25 N., Long. 1.4 E., steering at 18 knots' speed for a position in Lat. 56.30 N., Long. 3.30 E., where it was intended to meet the 3rd Battle Squadron and 3rd Cruiser Squadron from Rosyth.

The junction took place at 4 p.m., the Battle Cruiser Fleet, which had been ordered to a position a little farther south, arriving there at this time. No enemy vessels having been sighted, the whole Fleet was turned to the northward shortly before dusk, when in the vicinity of the Little Fisher Bank, to the westward of Northern Denmark. During the night the 3rd Battle Squadron and 3rd Cruiser Squadron were detached to return to Rosyth, and the 2nd and 4th Flotillas to Scapa; the Vice-Admiral, Battle Cruiser Fleet, was directed to cruise independently on the 19th; and the Dreadnought Battle Fleet, with the 1st, 2nd and 7th Cruiser Squadrons, proceeded to the eastward of the Shetlands; target practice was carried out during daylight of the 19th and the night of the 19th-20th, and the Battle Fleet returned to its bases at Scapa and Cromarty during the night of the 20th-21st and fuelled. During the cruise the Achilles, of the 2nd Cruiser Squadron, reported sighting a submarine at 2.40 p.m. on the 18th.

On the 19th the Albemarle and Russell, of the 6th Battle Squadron, which had rejoined the 3rd Battle Squadron from the Channel ports, were detached from Rosyth to Scapa for practices.

The Grand Fleet again proceeded to sea on the night of the 21st for another sweep towards the Danish coast, and at 8 a.m. on the 22nd the forces from Scapa and Cromarty, comprising the 1st, 2nd and 4th Battle Squadrons, Russell and Albemarle, 1st, 2nd and 7th Cruiser Squadrons, and the 2nd and 4th Flotillas, were in position Lat. 58.4 N., Long. 0.27 E.

At 4.30 p.m. the 3rd Battle Squadron and 3rd Cruiser Squadron joined the Commander-in-Chief, and the Battle Cruiser Fleet took station ahead of the cruiser screen. At dusk no enemy ships had been sighted and the Fleet turned to the northward again, the Iron Duke's position being Lat. 57.11 N., Long. 4.53 E.

The 3rd Battle Squadron, 3rd Cruiser Squadron and the Battle Cruiser Fleet were detached to return to Rosyth during the night, and the remainder of the Fleet arrived at the Scapa and Cromarty bases on the 23rd.

During these two southerly sweeps the Fleet sighted a large number of neutral steamers and trawlers which were closely examined, but nothing suspicious was found, although the interception of German wireless messages, when the Fleet was in the vicinity of the trawlers, raised suspicions that they were acting as look-out vessels; this suspicion was strengthened by carrier pigeons being sighted from various ships.

One Norwegian steamer which was found to be carrying magnetic ore to Rotterdam was sent to the Firth of Forth.

Movements of interest of individual ships during April included the arrival of the Lion at Rosyth on the 7th after completion of all repairs, the arrival of the new battleship Warspite, of the "Queen Elizabeth" class, at Scapa on the 18th, and the commissioning on the 26th of four more mercantile vessels to join the 10th Cruiser Squadron.

The Invincible was sent to the Tyne to change some of her 12-inch guns, which had become worn during the Falkland Island engagement.

On April 10th Rear-Admiral Tottenham succeeded Rear-Admiral Waymouth in command of the 7th Cruiser Squadron, the latter officer's health having unfortunately broken down.

On April 7th the patrol areas of the 10th Cruiser Squadron were rearranged somewhat in view of the lengthening of the days:

Patrol Area A was north of the Faroes, the centre line being occasionally shifted.

Patrol Area C had as its centre a line from Cape Sydero in the Faroe Islands to Lat 58.30 N., Long. 8.0 W.

Patrol Area E was north of Iceland.

Patrol Area F was south of Iceland.

Patrol Area G had as its centre the meridian of 3 degrees E. Long, between Lat 62 N. and 63½ N. A cruiser was sent to strengthen the patrol in this area.

(Note: There are no patrol areas B and D listed)

During the month the average number of vessels intercepted weekly by the ships of the 10th Cruiser Squadron was

68, of which an average number of 23 was sent in weekly for examination.

Enemy submarines were very active in April, and destroyers were sent out frequently from the Fleet bases to endeavour to destroy craft reported in the vicinity - particularly in the neighbourhood of the Fair Island Channel - but no success was achieved, except in the case of the Ariel and U 12. The look-out and navigational arrangements for the Pentland Firth were improved during April by the establishment of telephonic communications between Scapa and the Island of Swona. Arrangements were also gradually perfected for obtaining the exhibition of all navigational lights and fog signals in the Pentland Firth on demand by our ships at all times. The weather at Scapa during April was bad.

Gales were experienced on the 4th, 5th, 6th, 7th, 9th and 10th. There was a great deal of mist and fog during the latter part of the month as well as a moderate amount of snow.

The enemy laid a large minefield in the middle of the southern portion of the North Sea during April, thus pursuing the policy which it was expected he would adopt, regardless of the interests of neutrals. Fortunately, information as to its existence was obtained in time to prevent any of our ships from falling victims to the mines. But the minefield was undoubtedly well placed strategically so as to interfere with the freedom of movement of our Fleet in southern waters if it were endeavouring to bring the High Sea Fleet to action, since it necessitated our ships making a wide detour to the eastward or westward to reach the waters to the southward of the minefield; it was doubtless laid with this object in view.

In May the Grand Fleet flotillas were much occupied in endeavouring to locate and destroy enemy submarines, and the movements of the heavy ships were curtailed during the month owing to the absence of destroyers for the purpose of acting as a submarine screen.

The principal work of the destroyers in this connection - officers and men showing a fine spirit in carrying out what were frequently fruitless searches - was as follows:

May 1st-3rd. - The 2nd Flotilla was engaged in operations against enemy submarines reported, first, in the Fair Island Channel and, then, to the eastward and southeastward of the Pentland Firth. The flotilla did not succeed in gaining touch with the submarines.

May 5th-7th. - One half of the 1st Flotilla was searching for a submarine off the Aberdeenshire coast, without result

May 7th. — One division of the 2nd Flotilla was acting against a submarine reported in the Fair Island Channel, and then proceeded to work down the shipping route west of the Hebrides and Ireland in the hope of catching a submarine attacking trade.

May 8th. — Half the 4th Flotilla was searching for submarines off the east coast of the Orkneys.

May 10th-11th – A division of the 4th Flotilla was searching for a submarine reported to be off North Ronaldshay; later, this division was reinforced by all available destroyers from Scapa, with orders that the force was to continue the search during the night, burning searchlights to assist the work and cause the submarine to submerge, thus exhausting her battery power.

May 13th - Six destroyers were searching for a submarine reported west of Thurso.

May 15th. - A division of the 1st Flotilla left Rosyth to operate against a submarine off Aberdeen.

May 16th. - A division of the 4th Flotilla was searching for a submarine reported approaching the Fair Island Channel.

May 19th-20th. - A division of the 4th Flotilla was acting against a submarine reported west of the Orkneys.

The principal Fleet movements during the month were:

May 2nd to May 5th. - Two forces, each consisting of two light cruisers and eight destroyers, were engaged in carrying out a thorough examination of all vessels, especially fishing craft, found in the areas usually traversed by the Fleet during southerly sweeps in order to ascertain whether any were acting as German look-out ships under neutral colours. A considerable number of vessels were examined, especially trawlers, and some were sent in for more detailed examination at the bases, but nothing incriminating was discovered.

Between May 5th and 10th the 3rd Battle Squadron and 3rd Cruiser Squadron cruised in the northern portion of the North Sea, being screened out from Rosyth by a half flotilla. On the return towards Rosyth in Lat. 56.49 N., Long. 0.89 E., and before being met by the screening destroyers, the 3rd Battle Squadron, two torpedoes were fired by a submarine; they were aimed apparently at the Dominion, but both missed. The squadron was in division in line ahead, steaming at 15 knots, and was zigzagging at the time.

On May 6th the minelayer Orvieto and eight destroyers left Scapa to carry out a minelaying operation in the Heligoland Bight. The force ran into a dense fog, and a collision occurred between the destroyers Comet and Nemesis, the latter being seriously damaged. The force was directed to return and left Scapa again on the 8th, carrying out the operation successfully during the night of the 10th-11th; it returned on the 12th.

The light cruisers Phaeton and Royalist left Scapa on May 12th for a position north of the Shetlands, in order to intercept a neutral steamer reported to have left Bremerhaven on May 11th with wireless installations on board. The C Patrol of the 10th Cruiser Squadron was also moved to a position to intercept this vessel, and the light cruiser Sappho and armed boarding steamer Amsterdam were placed on the western side of the Fair Island Channel. The force returned on the 14th, the report proving to be incorrect.

The whole Grand Fleet carried out a sweep of the central part of the North Sea between May 17th and 19th, the forces from Scapa, Cromarty and Rosyth meeting at a rendezvous in Lat. 57.10 N., Long. 0.0 at 7 a.m. on the 8th, and sweeping to the southeastward at a speed of 16 knots until the afternoon, with the Battle Cruiser Fleet some thirty to fifty miles ahead of the Battle Fleet. The Fleet returned to its bases on the 19th, not having sighted any hostile vessels. Battle tactics were exercised during the passage north.

On May 21st the Fleet minesweepers, which had been sent to Aberdeen beforehand in readiness, left with an escort of two light cruisers to examine the minefield reported to have been laid in the centre of the southern portion of the North Sea. Two of the sweepers collided in a fog on leaving Aberdeen, and another went ashore; the remainder proceeded and located the northeast corner of the minefield on the 22nd and 23rd; they returned to Aberdeen on the 24th, after examining en route a position in which it was reported that paraffin barrels were moored. These were destroyed. It was thought that they might be intended for German submarines.

Whilst the Fleet sweepers located the north-east corner of the minefield, paddle sweepers, under the escort of two light cruisers from Harwich, located the southwest corner. The search was subsequently continued under the same conditions, and the limits of the minefield, which covered a large area south of Lat. 56 N. and east of Long. 2.30 E., were determined. The enemy made no attempt to interfere with the sweeping operations, if indeed he was aware of them.

On the 21st the patrol, comprising the Sappho and armed boarding steamers, hitherto maintained in an area east and southeast of the Pentland Firth, was moved temporarily to the west of the Firth on account of submarine activity. Destroyers from the Grand Fleet replaced the original patrol at night, the interception of mercantile traffic being carried out by the armed boarding steamers to the westward. The destroyer Rifleman grounded in a fog on the 22nd, necessitating docking for repairs.

A new form of anti-submarine operation was begun on May 23rd by the Commander-in-Chief Coast of Scotland (Admiral Sir R. Lowry). This consisted of two C-class submarines operating with an armed trawler, the idea being that the trawler should invite attack by a submarine, thus giving our submarines an opportunity of sinking the enemy by torpedo attack.

On May 24th the Admiralty telegraphed that Italy had entered the War on the side of the Allies. On the next day I proceeded in the Iron Duke to Rosyth to confer with Admiral Sir Henry Jackson, who had succeeded Lord Fisher as First Sea Lord. The conference took place on the 26th and was of an important nature. The general naval policy, so far as it concerned the Grand Fleet, was discussed, and arrangements made as to the procedure to be followed in future. Sir Henry Jackson asked that Commodore Everett might join him at the Admiralty as Naval Assistant, and, with the consent of Commodore Everett, this was arranged. His place as Captain of the Fleet was filled by Captain Lionel Halsey, C.M.G., of the New Zealand. It was with great regret that I parted with Commodore Everett; his long experience in the Fleet under Sir George Callaghan and his intimate knowledge of fleet work and unfailing tact had been of the greatest possible assistance. The Iron Duke returned to Scapa on the morning of the 28th. On the 26th Rear-Admiral the Hon. Horace Hood, C.B., had hoisted his flag in the Invincible as Rear-Admiral commanding the 3rd Battle Cruiser Squadron. The battleship Queen Elizabeth arrived at Scapa from the Dardanelles on the same day.

From May 29th to 31st the Grand Fleet carried out another sweep in the North Sea, the direction on this occasion being towards the Dogger Bank. The forces from Scapa and Cromarty concentrated in Lat. 57.35 N., Long. 0.0 at 7.15 a.m. on the 30th, and steered to the southward at 17 knots' speed. The Rosyth force steered for a point farther south and was in sight from the cruiser line at 9.30 a.m., being ordered to keep ahead of the Fleet. The sweep was continued until the Dreadnought Battle Fleet was in the vicinity of the Dogger Bank. No enemy vessel was sighted.

The Fleet then turned to the northward and, owing to a northerly swell, speed had to be reduced on account of the destroyers. During the night the Rosyth force was detached to its base. Speed was increased as the weather improved, and the Scapa and Cromarty forces arrived on the morning of May 31st. The Iron Duke left Scapa for Cromarty during the afternoon of May 31st, and arrived that evening.

During the month the procedure of moving squadrons between Scapa and Cromarty was continued. At this period a second line of submarine obstructions, which was designed to prevent the entry of destroyers, as well as submarines, into Scapa Flow, advanced considerably towards completion. Progress was also made with the laying of minefields at the entrance. The anchorage at Swarbachs Minn, in the

Shetlands, had been selected as a secondary coaling base for the ships of the 10th Cruiser Squadron, and steps were taken to prepare a submarine obstruction for the entrance, and to provide the necessary labour for coaling the ships from colliers.

The blockade work of the 10th Cruiser Squadron continued actively during the month, the average number of ships intercepted per week being 62, and the average number sent into port for closer examination, 16.

The weather at Scapa during the month was misty, fog being experienced on the 5th, 6th, 21st, 23rd, 24th, 27th and 28th, and snow on the 11th and 12th. The wind during the month was not strong.

8 - German Mines and Submarines

In the early summer of 1915 there was a vague impression in some quarters, unsupported, so far as I am aware, by any confirmatory evidence, that the enemy might exhibit greater activity at sea. But during June, so far as could be ascertained by our intelligence system and by our submarine patrols, the Germans made no attempt to move to sea, but concentrated attention on increased submarine activity. The Grand Fleet, for various reasons unconnected with this development, spent the greater part of the time in harbour, exercising in Scapa Flow, the ships from the Rosyth base being sent up in pairs to exercise and carry out gunnery and torpedo practices. The opportunity of this change of base was usually taken for a searching sweep whilst en route between the bases, so that the North Sea was continually under observation.

On June 11th, however, the Grand Fleet went to sea for a cruise in northern waters principally for gunnery practices and battle exercises, which were carried out on a large scale. On this occasion the seaplanes working from the Campania were utilised, so far as I am aware, for the first time in history in observing the movements of the squadrons, which were ordered to represent a large hostile fleet. From this beginning, there was a great development in the work of heavier-than-air craft operating with a fleet. The first step was the provision of a flying-off deck in a ship for seaplanes, as the extreme difficulty experienced by seaplanes in rising from the water, except in very fine weather, rendered the provision of a flying-off deck essential; the next was the substitution of aeroplanes for seaplanes, working from special carriers; and, finally, the provision of flying-off platforms in fighting ships themselves, first in light cruisers, afterwards in battle cruisers, and, eventually, in battleships; these successive developments were rendered possible by the progressive improvement in aircraft. In this way naval power was given the assistance which air power could give it, both in reconnaissance and in making its gunnery more effective.

The Scapa force proceeded to the westward through the Pentland Firth on the 11th. It carried out target practice at special targets towed by colliers to the northwestward of the Shetlands on the 12th, being joined by the Cromarty force (the 1st Battle Squadron and 7th Cruiser Squadron) that evening; the fleet then separated for night-firing.

The Battle Cruiser Fleet, which had also left Rosyth on the 11th, carried out night-firing on the 12th, and the whole Grand Fleet practised battle exercises on the 13th, the Battle Cruiser Fleet afterwards firing at the targets which were towed by colliers, and rejoining my flag at daylight on the 14th. On that day further battle exercises were carried out. The Campania, with her seaplanes, again took part in these exercises, and an improvement in the scouting work of the seaplanes was noticeable. The Fleet then returned to the various bases, the Scapa force passing westward of the Orkneys.

Whilst the main portion of the Grand Fleet was exercising in northern waters, the 3rd Battle Squadron and 3rd Cruiser Squadron, with one-half of the 1st Flotilla, cruised in the central portion of the North Sea.

Other operations during the month included:

From June 1st to the 3rd, and the 5th to the 7th, further minesweeping operations were carried out by the Fleet sweepers and paddle sweepers in connection with the German minefield in the southern portion of the North Sea, the operation being covered by four light cruisers and a force of destroyers. The work of clearing that portion of the minefield, which it was decided to sweep up, was completed on the 7th. On several days during the month a force from Harwich, comprising light cruisers and destroyers, was cruising off the Dutch coast with the object of intercepting and attacking zeppelins. The force did not, however, meet with any success.

From June 4th to the 7th the 1st Cruiser Squadron, with three armed boarding-steamers and three destroyers, operated on the two trade routes, St. Abb's Head to the Skagerrak and Rotterdam to Norwegian ports, examining all vessels encountered; nothing of special interest occurred. But when returning during a thick fog to Scapa the armed boarding-steamer Duke of Albany grounded on the Lother Rock, Pentland Firth, at 4 a.m. on the 7th, remained ashore for seven days, and was considerably damaged.

From June 18th to the 21st the 3rd Cruiser Squadron, with the light cruisers Nottingham and Birmingham, of the 2nd Light Cruiser Squadron, accompanied by four destroyers, swept across the North Sea, steering to the eastward from Rosyth to the entrance to the Skagerrak, thence to the coast of Norway and back to Rosyth. This force was attacked by at least three submarines during the sweep, and torpedoes were fired at the Birmingham on the 19th, and at the Argyll, the Roxburgh (on two occasions), and the Nottingham on the 20th. Two torpedoes were fired at the Nottingham. These ships were proceeding at high speed and all the attacks failed, except the second attack on the Roxburgh (Captain C. R. de C. Foot), which was hit in the bows by a torpedo at 2 p.m. on the 20th in Lat. 56.47 N., Long. 0.38 E. Fortunately, the damage was well forward, and the Roxburgh was able to maintain a speed of 14 knots during her return to Rosyth, all available destroyers of the 1st Flotilla being sent out to meet and screen her in. At the time of the attack the Roxburgh was proceeding at high speed and zigzagging, with one destroyer screening her. The ship was considerably damaged, and her repairs at a dockyard occupied a lengthened period.

The incident furnished an example of the risks run by heavy ships cruising in the North Sea in waters frequented by submarines, unless accompanied by a much stronger screen of destroyers than it was possible to provide owing to the paucity of destroyers and the immense amount of work required of them. It was noted at the time, and considered to be suspicious, that a large fleet of trawlers flying neutral colours was fishing in the neighbourhood of these submarine attacks.

As a result a force comprising three armed boarding steamers and three destroyers was despatched from Scapa on June 26th to examine a fleet of neutral fishing vessels working to the southeastward of the Pentland Firth and on the ordinary track of the Fleet when proceeding to sea. Six vessels were sent in for detailed examination, but nothing suspicious was found on board. The fishing fleet, however, shifted its ground to a position clear of the track of the Fleet.

Operations against enemy submarines carried out by Grand Fleet forces during June included the following:

June 1st to 2nd - A division of destroyers endeavoured, without success, to locate and attack a submarine 60 to 80 miles to the eastward of May Island.

June 4th to 5th. — Two destroyers and two sloops operated against a submarine, with a supposed tender, to the eastward of the Pentland Firth.

June 5th. — The armed trawler Hawk, of the Peterhead area, disabled submarine U 14 by gun fire and sank her by ramming at 7.30 a.m. in Lat. 57.15 N., Long. 0.32 E. One officer and 21 men were rescued. It was a fine exploit, typical of the consistently good work of the vessels of the Peterhead patrol; it was a success that was specially welcome at this time when submarines were very active in northern waters.

There were many other engagements between auxiliary patrols and submarines during the month, but no other certain successes. It was believed that at least one submarine was sunk in a deep minefield which had been laid at my request off Tod Head on the Aberdeen coast.

Appended are notes of further operations against the enemy's underwater craft:

June 18th and 19th. — Anti-submarine operations by three destroyers and sloops were carried out in the Fair Island Channel.

June 20th. — Four destroyers were operating against submarines to the westward of the Orkneys.

June 21st and 22nd. — The Botha and eight destroyers of the 1st Flotilla were operating against submarines in an area between Lat 56.20 and 57.10 N. and Long. 1 E. to 1 W.

June 21st. — Four destroyers and six gunboats were operating to the east of the Pentland Firth against a submarine.

June 23rd. — Submarine U 40 was sunk 50 miles S.E. by S. of Girdle Ness at 9 a.m. by submarine C 24, working in company with a trawler.

June 23rd. — A division of destroyers was sent to operate against a submarine to westward of the Fair Island Channel.

June 24th-26th. — Three sloops were engaged in searching for a submarine to the eastward of Orkneys and Shetlands.

June 26th. — A large force, comprising 20 armed trawlers from Granton in the Firth of Forth, began to operate against submarines in an area round Lat 57 N., Long. 1 E., remaining out until July 7th. Two armed trawlers, with C class submarines in company, were also operating to the southward of this position.

June 30th-July 1st — A force of eight destroyers was operating against submarines in the Fair Island Channel.

The anti-submarine operations by destroyers or sloops met with no success. The invariable difficulty was the provision of a sufficiently large number of vessels to keep the submarine down long enough to cause her to exhaust her battery power, a period of some 48 hours. When destroyers belonging to the Grand Fleet were used for anti-submarine operations at any distance from the base, the disadvantage of their not being available to accompany the Fleet to sea in an emergency had to be accepted. This would have led to awkward results had the Fleet proceeded to sea with any considerable shortage of destroyers for screening purposes on passage south and for Fleet purposes during a Fleet action. The dilemma was one which faced me during the whole period of my command of the Fleet.

My experience convinced me that anti-submarine operations by destroyers in such open waters as existed near the northern bases had but little prospect of success unless undertaken by a considerably larger number of vessels than were usually available at Scapa for such operations; a contributory reason for the shortage of destroyers was that in addition to the operations carried out by the heavy ships, cruisers and light cruisers, for which the presence of destroyers was necessary, there was a constant call on these vessels for escort work during the movements of single ships or of squadrons between bases.

Other events of interest during this month included:

The formation of the 4th Light Cruiser Squadron of new light cruisers under the command of the late Commodore Le Mesurier, C.B., in the Calliope. This squadron was attached to the Battle Fleet, and in cruising order at sea was usually stationed from three to five miles ahead of the Battle Fleet to act as an advanced submarine screen forcing submarines to dive. From this position it could reach the van of the Fleet on deployment for action, and was stationed there for the purpose of attacking enemy destroyers with gunfire and the enemy's Battle Fleet with torpedoes. It was a squadron on which, as Commander-in-Chief, I kept a hold so that I might be certain it would be at my disposal when action with the enemy was joined. Other light cruiser squadrons, which occupied an advanced position in the cruiser screen, could not be depended upon with the same certainty to occupy the van position to which they were allotted during a fleet action, since they might become engaged with enemy vessels of the same class.

The battle cruiser Inflexible joined the Fleet from Gibraltar on June 19th.

The Liverpool left to pay off on the 26th for repair to boilers. Rear-Admiral W. B. Fawckner took charge of the 10th Cruiser Squadron base at Swarbachs Minn on the 18th.

During the month observation minefields at the entrance to Cromarty and off Hoy Sound, Scapa Flow, were completed.

A short visit was paid to the Fleet at Scapa Flow by the Archbishop of York on the 26th. He held a Fleet Confirmation in the Iron Duke, a great open-air service on Flotta Island, many thousands of officers and men attending; there was another service at Longhope, and, in addition, he visited the majority of the ships. He was indeed indefatigable and left amidst the most sincere expressions of regret. To me personally his visit gave the greatest pleasure. From Scapa he passed to Invergordon, where, during a two days' stay, he held a large open-air service, and visited most of the ships based there, moving on to Rosyth, where an impressive open-air service took place in one of the large graving-docks.

The activities of the 10th Cruiser Squadron continued throughout the month, an average of 78 ships being intercepted weekly and 15 sent in for detailed examination.

A serious attack was made by an enemy submarine on the fishing fleet some 50 miles to the eastward of the Shetlands on the night of the 23rd-24th June, about 16 drifters being sunk by bombs and gunfire. This incident emphasised the necessity for better control over the movements of our fishing vessels in northern waters and of providing some form of protection for them. Steps were taken in both directions, although they naturally resulted in some unavoidable reduction in the operations of the fishing fleet.

The weather at Scapa during June was very misty, fog or mist being experienced on the 7th, 8th, 12th, 18th, 26th, 27th, 28th, 29th and 30th.

During July, 1915, fleet movements were kept to the lowest possible minimum owing to a threatened strike in the Welsh coalfields, which eventually took place on the 18th, and caused considerable anxiety as to its effect on Fleet movements.

From July 11th to the 14th the Dreadnought Battle Fleet, the 1st, 2nd and 7th Cruiser Squadrons, the 4th Light Cruiser Squadron, the 2nd and 4th Flotillas, and the Campania cruised in the vicinity of the Shetland Islands and carried out a series of battle exercises during the cruise. The Battle Cruiser Fleet made a sweep between the 11th and 13th down to the Dogger Bank. Whilst the Battle Fleet was at sea the destroyer flotillas were sent into Balta Sound (Shetland Islands) to complete with fuel in case a move south on the part of the Battle Fleet became necessary.

On July 28th the 2nd Battle Cruiser Squadron, with two ships of the 1st Light Cruiser Squadron, the 2nd Light Cruiser Squadron, the 4th Light Cruiser Squadron, and 14 destroyers of the 1st and 4th Flotillas from Rosyth and Scapa, together with Commodore Tyrwhitt and four light cruisers and 12 destroyers from Harwich, left their bases to carry out an operation in the Skagerrak, with the object of intercepting trade and searching for any enemy vessels. Only one German vessel (a trawler) was encountered, and she was sunk after removal of the crew. A Danish steamer was sent into a British port with a guard on board and the force returned to their various bases on the 31st. As the threatened coal strike limited the movements of the coal-burning heavy ships, the oil-burning destroyers were used for anti-submarine work to a greater extent than would have been desirable if greater activity of the Fleet had been anticipated.

Operations against enemy submarines included:

On July 1st the Hampshire reported that a torpedo had been fired at her in the Moray Firth. Twelve destroyers and all available local patrol vessels were sent to endeavour to locate and sink the submarine. The steamboats from the ships at Cromarty were also despatched to operate in the various bays in the Moray Firth, where a submarine might elect to lie on the bottom. The boats exploded a large number of charges on the bottom in the hope of forcing any submarine to the surface. The operations were abandoned on the evening of the 2nd, the submarine not having been located.

On the 4th a division of the 2nd Flotilla hunted for another submarine reported in the Moray Firth.

From the 5th to the 10th the seaplane carrier Campania, with a flotilla leader, eight destroyers, four sloops and a large number of trawlers and net-drifters, operated against submarines that were reported to be passing through the Fair Island Channel, being based on Pierowall Harbour, in the north of the Orkneys. The destroyers, sloops and patrol vessels operated in conjunction with the seaplanes. No success was achieved, however, although these extensive operations covered a large area.

On the night of the 16th a division of destroyers operated against a submarine reported to the southward of the Pentland Firth, off Duncansby Head, but again without result.

From the 15th to the 19th six sloops and seven gunboats were despatched against submarines in the Fair Island Channel and north of the Shetlands, the Campania's seaplanes again assisting from Pierowall Harbour. Destroyers were also helping during a portion of the period covered by the operations. On the 16th the gunboat Speedwell reported having sighted the periscope of a submarine, running her at a speed of 15 knots. The submarine was struck on her starboard quarter at an angle of 10 degrees, but there was, unfortunately, no evidence to show that she was sunk, although it was probable that she was considerably damaged. She was not seen again. On the same day a submarine was reported by the armed yacht Zaza, as being in a drift-net 12 miles east-northeast from Fair Island. Local patrol vessels, gunboats and four destroyers concentrated on the position and explosive charges were fired, but without certain result.

From the 25th to the 27th a sub-division of destroyers searched, fruitlessly, a large area to the northward of the Hebrides for submarines and a reported submarine base ship. They were assisted by four sloops operating in the area from the 26th to the 30th.

On the 18th and 19th a division of destroyers was engaged in moving a neutral fishing fleet away from an area to the eastward of the Firth of Forth where they interfered with Fleet operations. Submarine C 27 had for some little time been operating against submarines in the North Sea from Scapa, in tow of a trawler, to which vessel she was connected by telephone. This idea, which had first been conceived at the Rosyth base, had also been put into operation at Scapa, the arrangements being made under the direction of Admiral Sir Stanley Colville.

On July 20th the trawler Princess Louise, Lieutenant Morton, R.N.R., being in command, with Lieutenant Cantlie, R.N., a submarine officer, on board, was towing Submarine C 27 (Lieutenant-Commander Dobson) in a submerged condition when a German submarine, U 28, was sighted 1 ? miles off on the port bow. C 27 was informed by telephone, telephonic communication then breaking down. U 28 opened fire at a range of 2,000 yards on the Princess Louise. Lieutenant Cantlie, being unable to communicate further with C 27, slipped the tow and proceeded to abandon the trawler with every appearance of haste. U 28 closed to within 600 yards and stopped. Meanwhile, Lieutenant-Commander Dobson, hearing nothing further by telephone, but noticing the splash and explosion of the projectiles in the water, got well clear of the trawler after slipping, and then brought his periscope to the surface for a look around. He sighted U 28 about 900 yards off, closed to a good position for attack within 500 yards, and fired his first torpedo, which missed. His second shot hit; there was a heavy explosion, and U 28 sank; four officers and six men were picked up out of a crew of 34. The whole attack was exceedingly well managed and a very well-deserved success scored, which reflected much credit on all concerned in the operations.

On the 26th a submarine was engaged about 120 miles east of Dundee by the armed trawler Taranaki, which claimed to have sunk her.

On the 27th an engagement took place between the armed trawler No. 830 and a submarine to the southward of St. Kilda, the trawler reporting that the submarine was hit several times by gunfire and considered to have been badly damaged.

Other events of interest during the month included an attempt by the Digby to tow the Norwegian steamer Oscar II, damaged by collision with the Patuca on July 1st, into Stornoway, the destroyers Fury and Staunch being detached from Scapa and local patrol vessels from Stornoway to assist. In spite of perseverance under very bad weather conditions, during which the ships and the destroyers were handled with great ability, the Oscar II sank on the night of the 3rd.

An expedition consisting of the armed merchant-ship Columbella, the sloop Acacia and the two trawlers Arley and Mafeking, left Scapa on July 29th for Bear Island and Spitzbergen to search for a reported German submarine base and wireless station. These vessels carried out as thorough a search as was possible, in face of the icefields in the neighbourhood of the islands; but no trace of a submarine base was discovered, nor could it have been possible for one to operate under such conditions.

The average figures per week for the 10th Cruiser Squadron during the month were: Number of ships intercepted, 62; number of ships sent in with armed guards, 10; number of ships on patrol, 15; number of ships refitting, coaling or on passage to or from base, 9.

German submarines were active in the vicinity of the ships of the 10th Cruiser Squadron during the month, and the Columbella was unsuccessfully attacked on the 21st.

Some armed boarding steamers were detailed to assist the 10th Cruiser Squadron during the month, being withdrawn from the patrol eastward of the Pentland Firth.

The anti-submarine defence of the base at Swarbachs Minn was practically completed during the month.

An event of great interest to the officers and men of the Fleet was a visit from His Majesty the King, who arrived at Scapa on July 7th, crossing from Thurso in the Oak, escorted by a portion of the 2nd Flotilla, During His Majesty's visit he stayed with Admiral Sir Stanley Colville at Longhope and spent two very busy days with the Fleet. His Majesty visited all the flagships, and a large number of the officers and men of the ships of each division of the Battle Fleet and of each vessel in the cruiser squadrons were assembled on board the various flagships and passed before the King.

His Majesty reviewed the officers and men of the smaller vessels, destroyers, sloops, etc., on the island of Flotta, visited hospital ships, and reviewed the great mass of auxiliary vessels anchored in Scapa Flow, being greeted with enthusiastic loyalty by the crews of these vessels; visited the various shore batteries, and inspected the anti-submarine defences and the boom vessels. The weather was bad, but the programme was carried out in spite of these conditions. The officers and men of the Fleet derived the utmost encouragement from His Majesty's gracious visit.

The King made the following signal to the Commander-in-Chief as the Oak left the Fleet, escorted by a portion of the 4th Flotilla:

"I am delighted that I have been able to carry out a long, cherished desire to visit my Grand Fleet. After two most interesting days spent here, I leave with feelings of pride and admiration for the splendid force which you command with the full confidence of myself and your fellow-countrymen.

"I have had the pleasure of seeing the greater portion of the officers and men of the Fleet. I realise the patience and determined spirit with which you have faced long months of waiting and hoping. I know how strong is the comradeship that links all ranks together.

"Such a happy state of things convinces me that whenever the day of battle comes my Navy will add fresh triumphs to its old glorious traditions."

In reply to His Majesty's gracious message, I expressed the appreciation of the officers and men of the Grand Fleet, adding that it was "my conviction that the glorious traditions of the Navy are safe in the hands of those I have the honour to command."

During August the coal strike continued to influence Fleet movements to a certain extent.

On August 2nd the Iron Duke, the 2nd Battle Squadron and the 1st Cruiser Squadron carried out target practice from Cromarty. This was a new departure, the practice hitherto having been limited to firing at a small target towed by other ships or by a collier to the northward or eastward of the Shetlands, or firing at a rock. Both were highly unsatisfactory methods, which did not enable the gunnery efficiency of ships to be either tested or greatly improved. Accordingly I decided to risk sending ships out from Cromarty to fire at a large target of the pattern used in peace practices; it was towed across the Moray Firth, the ships firing, and the towing vessels being protected from submarine attack by destroyers, sloops and gunboats. The system was an improvement, although very expensive in the employment of destroyers, etc. It was continued until practice in the Pentland Firth took its place.

The usual procedure was for two ships, screened by destroyers, to be on the firing ground at a time, firing either independently or with concentrated fire, with two more vessels approaching the firing ground ready to fire when the first pair had finished. On completion of practice the first pair returned to harbour and were met at the entrance by the third pair, to which they turned over their destroyers. Careful organisation insured that ships did not have to wait at the entrance, nor was there delay for the target to be turned round for the return run. A large number of destroyers, sloops or gunboats, patrolled to seaward of the target to prevent submarines from approaching. The total number usually employed screening and patrolling during a day's firing was from 22 to 28.

The Iron Duke, with the 2nd Battle Squadron and the 1st Cruiser Squadron, proceeded to Scapa on completion of the practice, being relieved later by another battle squadron and cruiser squadron in accordance with the routine which had been established of changing bases periodically. The special service ship No. 6 left Scapa for Rosyth, with two destroyers, to endeavour to "draw" submarines to attack her and give the destroyers an opportunity of engaging them; but no attack took place.

From August 5th to the 9th extensive anti-submarine operations were carried out to the westward of the Orkneys by a force consisting of nine destroyers, six sloops, five gunboats and a large number of patrol trawlers. The operations covered a very large area, the general idea being to compel any submarine intending to pass round the Shetland Islands or through the Fair Island Channel to submerge for a period that would exhaust her batteries and eventually bring her to the surface to recharge. The limited duration of darkness in northern latitudes assisted the operations of the hunting vessels. No certain success was attained. A submarine was sighted on the 6th at 7 p.m., and a heavy explosion, underwater, close to the sloop Hollyhock at 9.30 p.m. on the same night might have been due to a submarine coming to grief, while another submarine was sighted at 10.30 a.m. on the 7th. Examination of a sailing vessel found in the vicinity of this latter submarine was unproductive.

The 4th Light Cruiser Squadron left Scapa on August 6th to cruise off the Norwegian coast, and the battleships Albemarle and Russell, of the 6th Battle Squadron, arrived at Scapa for practices, having left the Channel Fleet.

On August 7th I returned in the Iron Duke to Cromarty in order to meet the Prime Minister and Chancellor of the Exchequer who were about to visit Invergordon. At 9 a.m. on the 8th a wireless report was received in the Iron Duke that a submarine was attacking a steamer off Rosehearty on the southern shore of the Moray Firth. The "duty" destroyer division was ordered to sea at once, and the remaining three available destroyers followed shortly afterwards. Meanwhile, the destroyer Christopher, already on patrol in the Moray Firth, reported herself in action at 11 a.m. with the submarine, which had submerged, the report stating that the merchant-ship had been sunk. The second destroyer on patrol, the Midge, assisted in the search for the submarine, as did the remaining destroyers and patrol trawlers, without result. At 10 a.m. the trawler minesweepers, which had been carrying out the usual routine sweep on the southern shore of the Moray Firth, reported the discovery of a minefield to the northward of Banff, and several reports were received during the day of drifting mines being sighted along the coast and in the Firth. All destroyers were ordered in at 4 p.m., except the two on patrol and any others in touch with the submarine, and vessels remaining on patrol were given the limits of the minefield as far as they had then been ascertained.

Such investigation as could be hurriedly carried out during the day, by signal and wireless, revealed the fact that a yacht and a trawler on patrol on the night of the 7th-8th had sighted strange lights, but without identifying the vessel carrying them, and it became apparent that a German surface minelaying vessel had been at work. The night had been somewhat misty. Directions were at once sent by wireless to the 4th Light Cruiser Squadron, still at sea, to proceed at full speed towards the Horn Reef to endeavour to intercept the returning minelayer, and the 1st and 2nd Light Cruiser Squadrons, from Rosyth, were also sent out for the purpose; the Admiralty was also informed, and as a result the Harwich force was sent on the same mission.

As the other squadrons proceeded, the 4th Light Cruiser Squadron was directed to the Skagerrak in case the minelayer endeavoured to return by that route, whilst the remaining light cruiser squadrons made for the Horn Reef. All the minesweepers and the destroyers engaged in the anti-submarine operation mentioned earlier were recalled to fuel with all despatch, and sweeping by the Fleet minesweepers, trawlers and destroyers, organised on a large scale, was begun on the 9th and continued until clear routes for the ships at Cromarty and for merchant ships, gradually extending to 10 miles in width, had been swept on both the northern and southern shores of the Moray Firth. These sweeping operations were greatly delayed by persistent fog, although a clear channel sufficiently wide to admit of the exit of the squadrons at Cromarty was quickly swept. The Campania was sent to Cromarty, so that her seaplanes might assist to locate the mines, but in the rather thick waters of the Moray Firth they were of no use for this purpose.

On the afternoon of August 9th news was received that the destroyer Lynx had been sunk by a mine at 6 a.m. that morning in a position stated to be two miles to the northward of the minefield as then located. It was very regrettable that only three officers and 21 men were saved out of her fine ship's company; those lost included her captain, Commander John F. H. Cole, an officer of great promise. The loss of such a comparatively shallow draft vessel showed that some of the mines had been laid near the surface, and minesweeping operations were suspended near the time of low water.

At 4.30 p.m. Commodore Tyrwhitt, of the Harwich force, reported that the German minelayer Meteor, which had been sighted by his vessels in the vicinity of the Horn Reef, had been abandoned and sunk by her own crew and that he had subsequently rescued four officers and 39 men, survivors of the armed boarding steamer Ramsey, who had been prisoners on board the Meteor.

The Ramsey had been on patrol southeast of the Pentland Firth, and it was ascertained from the survivors later that she had sighted and closed the Meteor, which was disguised as a neutral merchant-ship, shortly after daylight on August 8th, with the intention of boarding her. On closing, however, the Meteor suddenly showed her true character; her powerful armament, hitherto concealed, opened a heavy fire on the Ramsey, which was returned by the latter ship's greatly inferior armament of 12-pounder guns. But the surprise was too complete and the odds too heavy, and the Ramsey was sunk very quickly with her colours flying, four officers and 39 men out of a complement of 97 being picked up by the Meteor.

Acting-Lieut. P. S. Atkins, R.N.R., the senior surviving officer of the Ramsey, came north to report himself to me, and gave full details of his experiences. He stated that when the officers of the Meteor abandoned and sank their ship on sighting Commodore Tyrwhitt's force, the crew, with the British prisoners, went on board a neutral fishing vessel. Shortly afterwards the British light cruisers passed close to the fishing vessel, and Lieut. Atkins signalled to the Commodore, stating that they were survivors of the Ramsey and asked to be taken off. He added that the Commodore, who was at that time being attacked by both aircraft and submarines, replied, "Steer southwest; I will return and pick you up."

Lieut. Atkins thereupon asked the Captain of the Meteor to steer southwest, but the Germans naturally enough objected, as they desired to make their own coast. However, in spite of the fact that the British were unarmed and numerically very inferior, their arguments prevailed, and a southwest course was steered for a short time until another fishing vessel was sighted; the British suggested transferring to her; this was agreed to by the Germans. As the British were leaving, the German captain, Korvetten-Kapitan von Knorr, asked Lieut. Atkins if he had any money, to which he replied, "How could I, seeing that you picked me up in pyjamas?" Captain von Knorr pressed money on him, but Lieut. Atkins said that he did not see that he would require it. However, he eventually took it. Captain von Knorr handing him an English £5 note and other money. It is pleasant to record so gentlemanly and courteous an act, which stands out in strong contrast to the usual behaviour of German naval officers during the War. The money was given to me, and I sent it to the Admiralty, asking that it might be repaid, with the thanks of the British for the courtesy shown to our prisoners of war.

The 1st, 2nd and 4th Light Cruiser Squadrons were ordered to return to their bases on receipt of the news of the sinking of the Meteor.

The minesweeping operations in the Moray Firth on August 9th showed that the minefield was larger than had been at first reported, and additional paddle minesweepers were sent from the Clyde to assist the other vessels.

Mr. Asquith and Mr. McKenna were on board the Iron Duke from the 7th to the 9th, and various matters of importance were discussed. When questioned as to urgent requirements I pressed for the building of a large number of sloops, a class of vessel which had proved most useful, both as minesweepers and as patrol vessels, and which could supplement the numerous destroyers then building, which took much longer to complete.

The persistence of the fog at this period is shown by the fact that the Agincourt, returning to Scapa from Portsmouth, was unable to enter the base for 36 hours after passing Cape Wrath, only 60 miles distant, and was forced to cruise to the westward, making repeated attempts at entry. The Ajax was similarly delayed in entry for 12 hours during the same period.

On August 10th the armed merchant-ship India, of the 10th Cruiser Squadron, was torpedoed and sunk by an enemy submarine off the coast of Norway with considerable loss of life.

Four destroyers were sent on August 13th to locate and engage a submarine that had attacked one of the Fleet minesweepers. They did not succeed in finding her, but on the following day an armed yacht engaged a submarine off the Aberdeen coast and claimed to have hit her by gunfire; and the trawler Shamrock claimed to have run over another submarine.

The 1st Light Cruiser Squadron from Rosyth, the 4th Light Cruiser Squadron from Scapa, and seven destroyers carried out a search between the 16th and 18th for enemy vessels in the northern and central portion of the North Sea, sweeping towards the Skagerrak, and covering a large area by wide zigzags.

The Iron Duke returned to Scapa from Cromarty on the 16th.

From August 18th to the 21st the Lion, with the 1st Battle Cruiser Squadron and 2nd Light Cruiser Squadron, was cruising in the North Sea and carrying out exercises off the

Shetland Islands, proceeding to Scapa for practices on the 21st, and returning to Rosyth on the 23rd.

On August 18th the Fleet minesweeper Lilac, Lieut.-Commander Leslie Fisher, while at work on the Moray Firth minefield, struck a mine. The whole fore part of the ship was destroyed and the wreck of it hung down from the after part, causing her to draw 80 feet of water forward, instead of the usual nine to ten feet. The weather was very bad and a heavy sea running, but by great persistence and good seamanship, aided by very gallant work on the part of her own crew and that of the Hollyhock, Captain Preston, senior officer of Fleet minesweepers, who was in command of the Hollyhock, succeeded in towing her to Peterhead. She was eventually reconstructed and rejoined the Fleet minesweeping flotillas. The value of this class of vessel was clearly shown by the incident.

Eight destroyers from Scapa, with a flotilla leader, were carrying out on August 23rd and 24th anti-submarine operations in the Fair Island Channel, and a division was similarly employed east of May Island, in the Firth of Forth.

Between August 24th and 26th the 3rd and 7th Cruiser Squadrons exchanged bases, between Scapa and Rosyth, carrying out a wide search of the North Sea en route, destroyers screening the ships by day.

On the 24th Rear-Admiral E. F. A. Gaunt, C.M.G., relieved Rear-Admiral Hugh Evan-Thomas in the 1st Battle Squadron, the latter officer being designated to take command of the new 5th Battle Squadron (five ships of the "Queen Elizabeth" class), as it was formed.

On August 30th-31st the 3rd Light Cruiser Squadron, with destroyers, searched to the eastward of May Island for enemy vessels; and from August 31 to September 1st the 2nd Light Cruiser Squadron, accompanied by four destroyers, was cruising between the Firth of Forth and the Dogger Bank for the same purpose.

During the month the 2nd and 4th Battle Squadrons carried out target practice in the Moray Firth, and all battle squadrons and cruiser squadrons proceeded to sea for cruises, independently, from their bases, screened by destroyers.

His Royal Highness the Prince of Wales visited Sir Stanley Colville at Longhope during the month, remaining for six days. He went on board many of the ships of the Grand Fleet.

The 10th Cruiser Squadron report for the month showed the average weekly results as follows: Ships intercepted, 65; ships sent in, 13; number of vessels on patrol, 14; number refitting, coaling or en route to or from patrol, 9.

The weather at Scapa was very misty. Fog or mist was experienced on the 3rd, 6th, 10th, 11th, 12th, 18th, 14th, 15th, 16th, 17th, 23rd, 31st. There were no gales.

On August 3rd the large floating dock from the Medway, which had been towed to the Tyne, was reported as ready for use.

On the 29th the old light cruiser Brilliant arrived at Lerwick to act as guard and depot ship at that base, which was being developed as a secondary examination base for vessels sent in by the 10th Cruiser Squadron.

An extended patrol to the southeastward of the Pentland Firth during the month was maintained by three armed boarding steamers and three destroyers.

The principal events of September, 1915, may perhaps be given most conveniently and briefly in diary form:

On September 1st eight destroyers, fitted for minesweeping, swept the waters to the westward of the Pentland Firth. This was the first occasion on which destroyers were used for this purpose.

September 1st and 2nd. — The Black Prince and four light cruisers, with six destroyers, carried out a sweep to the eastward from Scapa.

September 2nd-5th. - The Dreadnought Battle Fleet, the 1st, 2nd and 3rd Cruiser Squadrons, and the 4th Light Cruiser Squadron were cruising in northern waters. Destroyers screened the Fleet out and back, but did not remain with it during the cruise, being kept at the base, ready fuelled, in case it became necessary to move to the southward. Battle exercises and night-firing were carried out during the cruise, as opportunity offered. The battleship Superb reported sighting the periscope of a submarine.

On September 2nd the Fleet was visited by five French gentlemen of eminence, and a representative of the United States Press, This was the first visit paid to the Grand Fleet base by anyone not immediately connected with the Service, and we were flattered that the occasion should have brought to Scapa Flow representatives of our gallant Allies from across the Channel. The Fleet left immediately after the visit, and an opportunity was afforded our visitors of seeing the ships leave harbour.

September 4th. - Another minesweeping sloop, the Dahlia, Lieutenant G. Parsons, R.N., struck a mine in the Moray Firth minefield during sweeping operations. She was very badly damaged; Lieut. Parsons himself was severely injured. The ship reached Invergordon with the loss of three killed and one missing. She was subsequently repaired.

September 7th. - The 3rd Cruiser Squadron left Scapa, with destroyers, swept down in the direction of the Horn Reef, and arrived at Rosyth on the 9th without sighting enemy vessels. Visibility was low during the sweep.

September 8th. - The 7th Cruiser Squadron left Rosyth, with destroyers, swept out to the eastward, towards the Skagerrak, then turned to the northward and arrived at Scapa on the 10th. Two destroyers were damaged by collision with steamers in a fog on the 8th, necessitating repairs at a dockyard in both cases.

September 10th-12th. - The Lion, with the 1st and 3rd Battle Cruiser Squadrons, the 1st and 2nd Light Cruiser Squadrons and 16 destroyers, was cruising in the North Sea to cover minelaying operations carried out by our minelayers in the Heligoland Bight, the remainder of the Grand Fleet being, as was usual on such occasions, at short notice for steam. The Fearless and a destroyer, part of the force with the battle cruisers, collided while at sea, the former sustaining considerable damage.

September 11th. - The Patia and Oropesa, of the 10th Cruiser Squadron, collided; the Patia was seriously damaged, and was brought into port under convoy of a destroyer and armed trawlers with considerable difficulty, being unsuccessfully attacked by a submarine en route.

September 12th. - Submarine E 16, attached to the Grand Fleet flotilla, was sent to the coast of Norway from Aberdeen to operate against an enemy submarine thought to be operating in those waters. On the 15th E 16 sighted a hostile submarine off the Norwegian coast and sank her with a torpedo. This success, one of the earliest achieved by one submarine operating against another, was very encouraging after the somewhat similar success of C 27 in July.

September 17th. - The 2nd Light Cruiser Squadron, with four destroyers, left Rosyth to sweep to the Skagerrak. They returned on the 19th, without having sighted any enemy vessels.

September 23rd. - The destroyer Christopher was damaged in collision with the armed boarding-steamer King Orry in a fog.

September 26th. - The s.s. Caribbean, which had been fitted out as a receiving-ship for dockyard workmen, encountered very heavy weather whilst en route from her port to Scapa, and got into serious difficulties, taking in a great deal of water. Her wireless distress calls off Cape Wrath were answered by sending to her assistance the light cruiser Birkenhead from Scapa, together with tugs and yachts from Scapa and Stornoway. At 4.45 a.m. on the 27th the Birkenhead and patrol vessels, which were then standing by, took off most of the crew of the Caribbean, which sank at 7.30 a.m., unfortunately with the loss of 15 lives.

During the month the battle and cruiser squadrons carried out independent cruises by day and at night from the Scapa and Rosyth bases, being screened by destroyers during the exercises. The squadrons of the Battle Cruiser Fleet, also, all visited Scapa for the purpose of carrying out gunnery and torpedo practices.

A widely extended patrol by one or more light cruisers with destroyers, working to the southeastward from Scapa, was maintained during the month, in order to guard against any attempt at minelaying in the Pentland Firth by enemy vessels disguised as merchant ships. Similar precautions were taken at Rosyth. This patrol was henceforth regularly established when the conditions of the moon rendered attempted minelaying operations at night probable.

The sweeping operations in the Moray Firth were continued on a large scale throughout the month, and clear channels on each shore were provided. Up to September 19th, 222 mines had been accounted for out of the 450 which survivors of the Ramsey stated had been laid by the Meteor. The Moray Firth minefield, in the centre of the Firth, was purposely left undisturbed, as it formed an excellent anti-submarine defence in that position and reduced the area to be patrolled by our vessels.

The 3rd Cruiser Squadron became non-existent during the month, two ships being detached by the Admiralty on special service, and the remaining two sent into port for somewhat extensive repairs.

The 10th Cruiser Squadron's weekly average for the month worked out at: Ships intercepted, 64; sent in with armed guards, 11; number of vessels on patrol, 13; number absent or en route to or from patrols, 10.

The weather at Scapa showed fog or mist on the 6th, 8th, 9th, 10th, 14th, 18th, 23rd and 24th; a very heavy gale occurred between the 25th and 28th, during which great damage was done to the anti-submarine obstructions at Scapa, and a good deal of damage was suffered on the mainland in the north of Scotland, a portion of the Highland Railway being washed away.

Between June and August, 1915, I had pressed upon the Admiralty my opinion that we should carry out a much more comprehensive mining policy in the Heligoland Bight. I had urged this early in the War, but the view taken at the Admiralty was that mining on any large scale would impede both our submarine operations and also any Fleet operations that might be undertaken in those waters. I felt that unless we adopted one of two policies - namely, either a close watch by surface ships on the exits from the German bases, or an extensive mining policy - we could never feel that we should receive sufficient warning of the exit of enemy forces as to prevent mischief being done. The close blockade by surface ships was not a feasible operation in view of the number of craft at our disposal and the submarine danger; our submarines were too few in number and had not the necessary means of communication to take the place of surface ships.

I could see no alternatives to very extensive mining, limited only by the number of mines that could be produced. The mining proposed by me was intended to hamper the operations of both surface vessels and submarines. I pointed out that earlier in the War the view had been expressed to me by the Admiralty that we should not risk our cruisers too freely in the North Sea owing to the submarine danger, and that, if we adhered to this policy, it was impossible to insure that the exits to the Fleet bases would not be mined by surface minelayers, as the Meteor incident had shown, and as was also indicated by the success of our own infrequent mining excursions to the Heligoland Bight.

The correspondence resulted in increased activity on the part of our minelayers, but the success of our work was unfortunately handicapped by defects in the pattern of mine in use at that time, especially as against submarines.

In 1917, shortly after my return to the Admiralty, I undertook a very extensive mining policy. In the previous year, during Sir Henry Jackson's period as First Sea Lord, a new and much improved mine was designed, the trials of which were carried out after I relieved him. This was one of the replies to the submarine. One hundred thousand of these mines were ordered by me early in 1917 to carry out various schemes for mining the Heligoland Bight and the Straits of Dover. Later in 1917, with the assistance of the United States, provision was made for the large minefield across the North Sea known as the Northern Barrage. It was not until the large supplies of mines became available in the autumn that really effective results against submarines by mining began to be achieved, although the operations of German surface vessels had previously been hampered to a very considerable extent.

The original dreadnought, HMS *Dreadnought*, c. 1906-07

9 - Controlling the North Sea

During the later months of 1915 the Grand Fleet continued to sweep and control the North Sea in spite of the enemy's efforts to effect attrition by submarines and mines. On October 1st the 3rd Light Cruiser Squadron, with destroyers escorting, left Rosyth and proceeded towards the Little Fisher Bank; on reaching that locality the squadron turned to the northwestward and steered towards Scapa, arriving on the 3rd. The line thus swept was the possible course of enemy minelaying or other vessels, proceeding towards, or returning from, the vicinity of Scapa and Cromarty. No enemy ships were sighted.

On October 2nd the battleship Barham, Flagship of the new 5th Battle Squadron, arrived at Scapa.

Commodore Tyrwhitt, with the 5th Light Cruiser Squadron (now comprising six light cruisers) and nine destroyers, left Harwich on the 6th to sweep towards the Skagerrak in search of enemy vessels, particularly fishing trawlers, which were suspected of acting as outpost vessels. The operation on this occasion was fruitful in result; 14 German trawlers were captured and sent in; one was also sunk. As usual during such operations when a supporting force was not actually at sea, the Battle Cruiser Fleet was kept at short notice for steam, to be ready to put to sea if required.

On October 10th the 3rd Light Cruiser Squadron left Scapa and swept down to the Little Fisher Bank, and thence to Rosyth with the same object in view as that of the Harwich force, being met at daylight on the 11th by destroyers from Rosyth, and arriving at that base on the 12th. On this occasion the operation gave no result.

The Dreadnought Battle Fleet, comprising the 1st, 2nd and 4th Battle Squadrons, the 1st, 2nd and 7th Cruiser Squadrons, the 4th Light Cruiser Squadron, and the 2nd and 4th Flotillas, left Scapa on the 13th, and proceeded into the northern portion of the North Sea for a cruise. Owing to bad weather the destroyers were sent back on the 11th, one, the

Mandate, being damaged by a heavy sea; the Ardent and Fortune collided, the former vessel being damaged. The fleet carried out battle exercises during the cruise, and returned to the bases at Scapa and Cromarty on the 15th, on which day the new battleship Canada joined the Grand Fleet.

On October 18th the Harwich force, consisting of the 5th Light Cruiser Squadron and destroyers, sailed to operate off the Danish coast, north of the Horn Reef, against any enemy vessels found there. The Lion, with the 1st Battle Cruiser Squadron and eight destroyers, left Rosyth to support the Harwich force, which closed the Danish coast at daylight on the 19th, then steered to the northwestward, till dark, returning afterwards to Harwich. The search was unproductive, no enemy vessels being sighted. The Lion and 1st Battle Cruiser Squadron proceeded towards Cromarty, but were diverted to Scapa during the night of the 19th-20th, owing to a report of suspicious vessels, possibly minelayers, being sighted off Noss Head. These vessels were subsequently identified as two of our own trawlers.

On October 22nd three divisions of destroyers were sent from Scapa to hunt a submarine off Fair Island, but were forced to return owing to bad weather.

On October 27th the 1st Cruiser Squadron, with two armed boarding-steamers, left Scapa to search the northern portion of the North Sea, returning on the 30th. Nothing was sighted.

On October 30th Commodore Tyrwhitt, with the 5th Light Cruiser Squadron and destroyers, left Harwich for another sweep off the Danish coast. His force passed through a position some 70 miles northwest of Heligoland before daylight on the 21st, steered for the Little Fisher Bank, and thence to Harwich. A portion of the Battle Cruiser Fleet kept steam at short notice during the operation, which was unproductive, except for the interception of an ore-laden neutral steamer which was sent into a British port.

On October 30th the Birkenhead and Liverpool, newly commissioned light cruisers, left Scapa for a searching and exercise cruise in the northern portion of the North Sea, and returned to Scapa on November 1st.

During October squadrons cruised independently in the North Sea from Scapa, as in previous months, by day and at night. The ships of the Battle Cruiser Fleet, as well as the 3rd Battle Squadron from Rosyth and squadrons from Scapa, proceeded to Cromarty, in turn, in order to carry out long-range firing at towed targets in the Moray Firth, being screened from submarine attack by destroyers. Squadrons from Rosyth proceeded also to Scapa to carry out practices.

A patrol, comprising the Sappho and eight armed whalers, based on Peterhead, was instituted as a guard against further attempted minelaying in the Moray Firth. The Peterhead and Cromarty minesweeping vessels, which had been working under the Senior Officer of Fleet minesweepers (Captain Preston) for the clearance of the Moray Firth minefield, reverted to their proper commands, and arrangements were made for a constant sweep by minesweeping trawlers of the channel along the south shore of the Moray Firth, which was that used by ships based on Cromarty when concentrating with the remainder of the Grand Fleet in the North Sea. It was essential to ensure that this channel was kept clear of mines so long as any portion of the Grand Fleet was based on Cromarty.

It may not be out of place here to state the patrol arrangements existing in the vicinity of the Pentland Firth at this time. Usually three armed boarding steamers and three destroyers were patrolling to the eastward of the Firth. They moved to the northward during daylight and worked for a considerable distance to the southeastward of the Firth at night. An extended patrol, usually consisting of a light cruiser and a destroyer, also worked from Peterhead.

A patrol of one or two destroyers was maintained at night off Noss Head on the north shore of the Moray Firth. Destroyers were kept off the entrance to Hoy Sound and Holm Sound, and a large number of trawlers near the Hoxa Sound entrance. In bad weather the eastern destroyer patrol was withdrawn to work between Swona Island and the land to the eastward and to the northwestward. The old local defence destroyers also carried out patrol work off the entrance, and off Kirkwall. These particulars are of interest as conveying some idea of the sea work in a restricted area which had to be carried out in all weathers.

From October 1st to October 11th the Fleet Flagship Iron Duke was refitting at Invergordon.

On October 28th the Argyll, en route from Devonport to Rosyth to rejoin the 3rd Cruiser Squadron, grounded on the Bell Rock, near Dundee, early in the morning in thick weather, and became a total wreck; all hands were taken off in a heavy sea by destroyers from Rosyth. The destroyers were exceedingly well handled under very difficult conditions. On the following day the Arlanza, of the 10th Cruiser Squadron, which had been sent to the White Sea, struck a mine and was seriously damaged, but succeeded in reaching the Yakanski anchorage, in the neighbourhood. Repairs were impossible during the winter and the greater part of her crew was, therefore, brought home in the Orcoma, of the same squadron which had been sent north for the purpose.

From October 29th to October 30th a heavy gale was experienced at Scapa, and considerable damage was done to the anti-submarine defences and to the block-ships at the entrances. Fog or mist was experienced on October 3rd, 4th, 5th, 6th, 9th, 14th, 16th and 30th.

The 10th Cruiser Squadron's work showed as a weekly average the following figures: Ships intercepted, 56; sent in, 16; number on patrol, 14; number absent, 8. The bad weather experienced interfered with the work of the squadron.

On November 2nd the 1st, 2nd, 4th and 5th Battle Squadrons, the 1st, 2nd and 7th Cruiser Squadrons, the 1st Light Cruiser Squadron and the destroyers of the 4th and 11th (old 2nd) Flotilla left for a cruise to the westward of the Orkneys. The destroyers were sent back on the 3rd owing to bad weather. Battle exercises and sub-calibre firing took place during the cruise, which was otherwise uneventful; the Fleet arrived at Scapa and Cromarty on November 5th, being screened in by the destroyers.

On November 6th the 1st and 2nd Light Cruiser Squadrons, with destroyers, left Scapa and Rosyth respectively, to carry out an operation in the Skagerrak.

The force was timed to arrive at the eastern end of the Skagerrak at dawn on the 7th, and to sweep westward during daylight in order that our ships should be between the enemy and his Baltic base if enemy ships were sighted. The Lion, with the 1st and 3rd Battle Cruiser Squadrons and destroyers, left Rosyth in time to be in a supporting position by daylight on the 7th. A large number of vessels were boarded by the destroyers, but nothing suspicious was encountered, and the forces returned to the bases on November 8th.

During the night of November 6th-7th the battleship Hibernia, flying the flag of Rear-Admiral S. Fremantle, with the Zealandia and Albemarle, passed through the Pentland Firth to the westward en route for southern ports and the Mediterranean. A strong wind was blowing against the spring tides, and a very heavy sea was running in the Firth, as was not unusual.

Whilst passing through the Firth the Albemarle, Captain R. A. Nugent, shipped two heavy seas which washed away her fore bridge, with everyone on it, and even displaced the roof of the conning tower; hundreds of tons of water flooded the decks and poured down below. An officer and one man were washed overboard and drowned, and several men injured; Captain Nugent found himself on the upper deck amidst the wreckage of the bridge. The Hibernia, which was ahead, turned to assist the Albemarle, and an urgent signal for assistance was received on board the Iron Duke. One of the emergency cruisers at Scapa was directed to raise steam with all despatch; the Hibernia arrived in with the Albemarle at daylight. The ship presented an extraordinary sight, the sea having made a clean sweep of her bridge and everything on it. In all our experience of the Pentland Firth, we had never witnessed such havoc before. The Zealandia was also obliged to turn back to repair her gunports, damaged by the sea in the Firth.

The next few days were marked only by comparatively trifling incidents. On November 6th the Birkenhead, which had recently been commissioned, completed her practices at Scapa and joined the 3rd Light Cruiser Squadron at Rosyth. Two days later the Princess Margaret laid mines successfully in the Heligoland Bight; on the 9th the Crescent, harbour-defence vessel at Hoy Sound, was withdrawn and left to pay off; and the Matchless, of the 10th Destroyer Flotilla, struck a drifting mine in southern waters, her stern being blown off.

On the 12th Submarine E 17 was sent into the Kattegat to reconnoitre and ascertain whether any German trawlers or other vessels were working there. She returned on the 19th and reported in the negative. On the night of the 15th-16th the S.S. Kristianiafiord, of the Norwegian-American line, a ship which had been endeavouring on other occasions to evade the blockading squadron, was intercepted by the Teutonic in high latitudes; she was steaming fast without lights, and was sent to Kirkwall for examination. In this and in other similar cases the ships ran great risk of being mistaken for enemy vessels and sunk, since the methods employed by the Germans made it very difficult to abstain from opening fire on vessels without running the serious danger of our own ships being sunk by surprise attack. In the case of a ship carrying a large number of passengers, like the Kristianiafiord, the risk taken was very great and could not be justified.

On November 16th the 7th Cruiser Squadron, without the Donegal, but accompanied by the Liverpool and one armed boarding-steamer, left Scapa to patrol an area north of the Shetlands and Faroe Islands, with a view to intercepting possible raiders or other vessels.

At noon on the 18th a report reached me that an enemy three-funnelled cruiser had been seen on the 17th to pass through the Danish Sound going north. The possible objectives of this vessel, if the report were true, appeared to be either minelaying off our bases or an attempt to interfere with the White Sea traffic, the Admiralty having informed me on the 16th that large consignments of arms and ammunition would be passing from France to the White Sea during November and December. In view of the fact that the news had reached me too late to intercept this vessel in southern waters, the dispositions made were as follows:

The Donegal, which had left Scapa on the 17th to cruise along the trade route to the White Sea, was directed to rendezvous with the Orcoma (a ship of the 10th Cruiser Squadron on patrol off the Norwegian coast), and to patrol the parallel of Lat. 66 N. between the meridians of 5.30 E. and 7.30 E.

The 2nd Light Cruiser Squadron sailed from Scapa for a position Lat. 63 N., Long. 4 E., there to meet the 7th Cruiser Squadron, already at sea. Both squadrons, widely spread, were to sweep to the northward along the Norwegian coast, as far as the Rost Islands, and to cruise to the westward of the Lofoten Islands during daylight of the 20th, then returning to their base. The 2nd Cruiser Squadron also left Scapa and proceeded north, the ships spread to cover a wide area to the westward of the 7th Cruiser Squadron, in order to protect the Archangel trade. The 4th Light Cruiser Squadron also left Scapa on the 18th to sweep to the eastward, with orders to return to Cromarty on the 19th.

Strong destroyer patrols were despatched from Scapa and Rosyth to prevent minelaying off the bases, and one Battle Cruiser Squadron was put at short notice for steam. No enemy vessels were sighted, and the Donegal eventually proceeded to the White Sea, being accompanied by the Minotaur as far as the North Cape.

On November 19th three submarines proceeded from Harwich to the Kattegat to obtain information relative to the presence of any enemy vessels.

On November 23rd the Warspite rejoined the 5th Battle Squadron, after having been for some weeks under repair in the Tyne, owing to injuries sustained through grounding in the Firth of Forth.

On November 28th the Battle Cruiser Fleet left Rosyth for a cruise in the northern portion of the North Sea, during which cruiser exercises and gunnery practices were carried out; the squadron returned to Rosyth on December 2nd.

From November 22nd to December 7th, the Donegal and Hampshire were protecting the White Sea trade, working on the trade route and coaling at Alexandrovsk. During the month independent squadron exercise cruises from the bases were continued, as was target practice from Cromarty.

The figures for the 10th Cruiser Squadron gave as a weekly average: Ships intercepted, 30; sent in, 9; number on patrol, 10; absent at ports or en route, 9; on special service, 3. The bad weather experienced during the month interfered considerably with the boarding operations of the squadron and also hampered Fleet movements.

On December 1st the 1st, 2nd, 4th and 5th Battle Squadrons, the 1st and 2nd Cruiser Squadrons, the 4th Light Cruiser Squadron, and the Minotaur of the 7th Cruiser Squadron, proceeded to the westward for a cruise.

Battle exercises were carried out on the 2nd and 3rd, and the Fleet returned to Scapa and Cromarty on December 4th. The exercises were specially intended to represent the conditions that might arise if the High Sea Fleet tried to draw the Grand Fleet over areas in which mines had been laid or in which submarines were operating. During the exercises the Barham and Warspite of the 5th Battle Squadron collided, both being considerably damaged. They were escorted to Scapa for temporary repairs and left later, the Barham for Invergordon and the Warspite for Devonport.

On December 8th the 2nd Light Cruiser Squadron left Rosyth, swept to the eastward to the Little Fisher Bank, and returned on the 10th.

From the 11th to the 18th two ships of the 4th Light Cruiser Squadron were cruising to the eastward of the Fair Island Channel.

On December 12th Submarines D 7 and D 8, which were based temporarily on Blyth, were directed to leave for the Norwegian coast to operate against enemy trade and against enemy submarines. D 7 was directed to make the Ryvingen Light during the dark hours and then to cruise to intercept trade between Ryvingen and Arendal, and between Ryvingen and the west coast of Denmark. It was anticipated that this might draw enemy submarines to the northward from German ports to try to sink D 7, and D 7 was directed to be back at Ryvingen 36 hours after she expected that the first vessel she examined had reached port, so that she might be ready to attack enemy submarines sent after her. D 8 was directed to cruise on a bearing 270 degrees from the Hantsholm Light (coast of Denmark) in order to intercept enemy submarines sent after D 7. Bad weather prevented D 7 leaving before December 15th. The enemy was apparently not drawn, and no success was obtained.

On December 15th the 2nd Cruiser Squadron left Scapa for a sweep to the southeastward, and returned on the 17th.

Two neutral ships, steaming at high speed at night without lights on the 15th and 16th, evidently intending to evade the blockade, were intercepted by the 10th Cruiser squadron and sent into Kirkwall.

On December 20th Commodore Tyrwhitt left Harwich with the 5th Light Cruiser Squadron, to sweep to the Danish coast, and the Battle Cruiser Fleet was kept at the usual short notice for steam during the time that he was absent until the 23rd.

On December 24th the 1st Cruiser Squadron left Scapa to search the central portion of the North Sea, During the day anxiety was felt as to the safety of the destroyers Porpoise and Morning Star, which had been escorting a Russian icebreaker to the northward and which had hove to near the Fair Island Channel in a heavy gale during the 23rd. The 1st Cruiser Squadron was directed to spread and search for them, and the Hampshire and Donegal were also sent from Scapa to endeavour to gain touch. Both the destroyers, however, reached Cromarty in safety, the Porpoise on the 25th, and the Morning Star on the 26th, after having experienced very heavy weather. Many compartments were flooded, and very considerable damage was done. They had been handled with great ability during the exceptionally heavy weather. The 1st Cruiser Squadron, with the Hampshire and Donegal, returned to Scapa on the 26th.

On the 24th, the 3rd Light Cruiser Squadron also proceeded from Rosyth to search the North Sea, down to the vicinity of the Dogger Bank, thence towards the Little Fisher Bank, and back to Rosyth. No enemy vessels were sighted. The weather in the North Sea at this period was very severe, and the Sappho, which was supporting the armed trawler patrol to the north-eastward of Peterhead, lost her rudder in a heavy sea.

On December 30th the 3rd Cruiser Squadron and 1st Light Cruiser Squadron, with destroyers, left Rosyth and carried out a sweep to the southeastward, returning on the 31st.

On the same day, a lamentable disaster occurred, the cruiser Natal (Captain Eric Back) being blown up in Cromarty harbour with great loss of life. Captain Back was amongst those who lost their lives. It was reported by adjacent vessels at 3.25 p.m. that the ship was on fire, and at 3.30 p.m., before any action could be taken, the ship blew up and sank, the explosion taking place in her after magazines. Steps were taken to deal with the situation in case the explosion had been caused by an enemy submarine having entered the harbour, but it soon became evident that this was not the case. Examination of the wreck by divers later showed no signs of any external explosion. A court-martial was subsequently held at Chatham to investigate the causes of the disaster, but the conclusions were not made public.

During the month of December independent exercises from the Fleet bases were continued, as well as target practice from Cromarty. As to the latter, an interesting practice was carried out by the Iron Duke at the range, and under the conditions of battle practice before the War, in order to ascertain, by examining the actual hits made on the canvas of the target, whether the pre-War standard of shooting was being maintained. Some uncertainty existed owing to the great increase in the ranges at which practices were carried out during the War, namely, 16,000 to 19,000 yards, as compared with the 9,500 yards, which was the maximum peace range. The result was very satisfactory and indicated a most decided advance on pre-War accuracy of fire.

On December 13th the first target practice was carried out in the Pentland Firth. This was in the nature of an experiment and, being successful, practice in this locality was later substituted for practice in the Moray Firth; it was far more convenient for the main Fleet base and much less extravagant in the use of screening and protecting destroyers.

On December 16th Vice-Admiral Sir Martyn Jerram, K.C.B., relieved Vice-Admiral Sir George Warrender, Bart., in command of the 2nd Battle Squadron, on the termination of the latter officer's three years' command.

During December patrols seaward of the bases were strengthened and considerably extended during the first and fourth quarters of the moon in order to frustrate any attempted minelaying on the part of the enemy. This "dark night" patrol subsequently became a matter of routine.

The 10th Cruiser Squadron's weekly average showed: Ships intercepted, 35; sent in, 14; number of ships on patrol, 12; number at bases or en route 7; number on special service, 2.

The long nights and bad weather were responsible for the reduction in the number of vessels intercepted.

During December fog or mist were experienced at Scapa on the 15th, 22nd, 25th and 26th; gales on the 6th, 8th and 23rd; and snow on the 3rd, 4th, 8th and 12th. Although the weather at Scapa Flow was fairly good, gales in the North Sea and to the westward of the Orkneys were frequent and violent during the month.

Before turning to the events of 1916 it is of interest to notice the work of the "decoy ships" known later by the name of "Q" ships, fitted out at Scapa during the year 1915. These vessels, five in number, were designed to sink enemy submarines by inducing the latter to close them for the purpose of attack by gunfire or by torpedo. The same system was employed in southern waters, and was developed greatly during the year 1917. At Scapa in 1915 and 1916 the ships were manned principally by volunteers from the Grand Fleet, or from the depot ships at the base. Colliers or store-ships were selected for their size and general suitability for the work, and they were fitted with a very carefully concealed armament, which was kept hidden until the submarine was within point-blank range, so that fire opened on her must be immediately effective; unless the submarine was holed in less than a minute after fire was opened on her she could submerge and escape, and probably torpedo the decoy ship as well.

The five ships, the Prince Charles, Vala, Duncombe, Penshurst and Glen Isla, were fitted up by Captain Farrington of the Cyclops, under the direction of Admiral Sir Stanley Colville and were marvels of ingenuity. Their usual cruising-ground was in the vicinity of the Orkneys, Shetlands, or Hebrides, or towards the Norwegian coast, or the White Sea, or down the east coast of Scotland. They worked on a route that was freely used by merchant ships and altered their appearance according to their route so as to give them the look of vessels usually trading on that route.

Many stories of the "Q" ships have been told in the Press and need not be repeated here, but a high tribute must be paid to the extreme gallantry and splendid discipline of the officers and men who manned these vessels. I had personal knowledge of the work of the vessels operating from Scapa. Their opportunities for engaging submarines successfully were rare, and the work in the small ships in the heavy seas encountered in northern latitudes was very arduous; there was never any lack of volunteers for the duty, the difficulty always being that of selection from the large number of officers and men anxious to serve. It is satisfactory to record that the first submarine sunk by a decoy ship fell a victim to a vessel working from Scapa Flow.

On July 25th, 1915, the Prince Charles (Lieutenant W. P. Mark-Wardlaw - of Admiral Colville's staff - in command) sighted, near North Rona Island, the Danish steamer Louise, stopped and with a submarine close to. When the submarine sighted the Prince Charles she proceeded at full speed towards her and opened fire at 5,000 yards' range. Lieutenant Mark-Wardlaw stopped his engines and went through the usual process of lowering boats in a great hurry. The submarine, which was the U 36, closed to within 500 yards, still on the surface, and at that range the Prince Charles revealed her true character, unmasked her guns, and opened a most accurate fire with her two 6-pounders and two 3-pounders. The U 86 was immediately holed, and two men killed in the conning tower. She was unable to dive and sank stern first; 4 commissioned officers, 2 warrant officers, and 9 men were saved by the Prince Charles.

10 - Attempts to Entice the Enemy

The year 1916 opened and still no general action had been fought in the North Sea, which the Grand Fleet continued to dominate, paying its price - though not so heavy as might have been expected - for the influence it exerted on all the operations - naval, military and economic - to which the country had by that time been committed in face of the active operations pursued by enemy submarines and minelaying craft.

On January 5th the Battle Cruiser Fleet left Rosyth to cruise in the northern part of the North Sea, and returned during the night of the 8th-9th.

The facility with which enemy mines could be laid in the vicinity of naval bases during the long winter nights, when there was little or no moon (as shown, inter alia, by our own minelaying in the Heligoland Bight, which, though not very frequent in 1916, became constant in 1917), led me to extend still further the patrols from the bases at such times; from January 2nd to January 10th inclusive, the patrol vessels (two light cruisers and a destroyer) worked in an area about 140 miles and between bearings 80 and 130 degrees from the Pentland Firth, the ships being in the area by 2 p.m. each day. Similar patrols were ordered to be instituted from the Rosyth base. The enemy, however, instead of mining the exit from the bases to the eastward, selected the western approach to the Pentland Firth for the purpose, possibly because of the considerable mercantile traffic using this route. The patrols in this direction did not extend so far from the base, the sea being very frequently too heavy in the winter months; the practice was to search the route periodically for mines.

The weather early in January had been very bad, and both sweeping and patrol work were impracticable. In these circumstances the enemy raider Moewe, disguised as a neutral merchant-ship, which had probably passed up the Norwegian coast and round the north of the Shetland Islands, laid an extensive and very scattered minefield between Cape Wrath and a position about north from Strathie Point, on the Scottish coast, on the night of January 1st or 2nd. The work of the Moewe was facilitated by the fact that the lights on Cape Wrath and Sule Skerry Island were necessarily exhibited at night for the sake of the large mercantile traffic using the Pentland Firth and the Minches.

On January 6th, at 7 a.m., the pre-Dreadnought battleship King Edward VII., of the 3rd Battle Squadron, left Scapa for Belfast to refit, and at 10.47 a.m., when in Lat. 58.43 N., Long. 4.12 W., a violent explosion occurred under the starboard engine-room. Captain Maclachlan first reported that the ship had been torpedoed, but later came to the conclusion that she had been mined, as was eventually found to be, undoubtedly, the case. The ship heeled at once to starboard, and both engine-rooms filled. A strong westerly wind was blowing at the time with a rising sea.

As soon as the report was received at Scapa the flotilla leader Kempenfelt and 12 destroyers were sent out to assist and to keep the submarine under, if one were present. Tugs were also despatched. Meanwhile the collier Melita, which had arrived on the scene, proceeded to take the King Edward VII in tow, assisted by the Kempenfelt; but the ship was very low in the water and unmanageable, and the tow parted. At 4 p.m., the battleship having by this time a heavy list, Captain Maclachlan decided to abandon her for the night, and the destroyers Musketeer, Marne, Fortune and Nessus were taken alongside her in a heavy sea with great skill; they embarked all hands without loss of life, although the destroyer Musketeer received considerable injury from projections on the side of the battleship. The destroyer Nessus and a tug stood by the King Edward VII. until 8.10 p.m. when she turned over and sank. The Africa, also of the 3rd Battle Squadron, en route from Belfast to Scapa, passed safely through the mined area a few hours before the King Edward VII. was mined - a very fortunate escape!

Steps were at once taken to divert traffic from passing between Cape Wrath and the Pentland Firth, and a large force of minesweepers was detached to ascertain the limits of the minefield and to sweep clear a passage along the coast. The minesweepers were based, some on Loch Eribol, an anchorage between Strathie Point and Cape Wrath, and some on Scapa, but continuous bad weather interfered with the sweeping operations to such an extent that, between January 7th and January 21st, no sweeping was possible except close in shore in sheltered water. On January 14th a German mine drifted ashore in Dunnet Bay, near Thurso, and any doubt as to the cause of the loss of the King Edward VII was thereby removed.

On January 7th the battleship Albemarle left Scapa for Archangel, and, on the 9th, Submarine D 7 left Blyth to operate in the Skagerrak; she returned on the 16th, having met with no success.

On January 12th a very heavy northwesterly gale was experienced at Scapa. The oiler Prudentia drifted across the bows of the Iron Duke during the night and sank, and one ammunition-ship, one store-carrier, a tug and three trawlers went ashore. The wind registered 80 miles an hour at the shore observatory during this gale. The Iron Duke was undamaged.

Between January 20th and 22nd three ships of the 10th Cruiser Squadron on patrol suffered considerable damage from the heavy seas. The month of January, as a whole, was indeed conspicuous for the exceptionally bad weather prevailing in northern latitudes and over the whole North Sea. Great injury was done to all the anti-submarine obstructions at Scapa, many of them being entirely destroyed. In order to make the base temporarily as secure as possible from submarine attack, the Fleet was directed to make and lay improvised net obstructions.

On January 24 the destroyer Talisman reported that a torpedo had been fired at her off Blyth. The Botha and 10 destroyers were sent out from Rosyth to locate and destroy the submarine, but they saw nothing of her.

On January 25th the Ebro, of the 10th Cruiser Squadron, picked up a dismasted Norwegian sailing-ship and towed her to Lerwick, arriving on the 28th.

On January 26th the 1st Light Cruiser Squadron, with six destroyers, and the 2nd Battle Cruiser Squadron, with five destroyers, left Rosyth for operations in the Skagerrak. The 1st

Light Cruiser Squadron and destroyers, during daylight on the 27th, swept through the Skagerrak to the Skaw, the 2nd Battle Cruiser Squadron being in support. The ships then moved to the northward; at daylight on the 28th, the whole force, joined by the 4th Light Cruiser Squadron and three destroyers from Scapa, spread on a line 210 degrees from Udsire Lighthouse and again swept into the Skagerrak. The squadrons then returned to their respective bases. During the operations the remainder of the Battle Cruiser Fleet was at short notice for steam. No suspicious vessels were sighted outside territorial waters, but Commodore Le Mesurier, of the 4th Light Cruiser Squadron, reported a stream of small vessels passing along the Norwegian coast inside territorial waters.

On January 28th the senior officer of the minesweepers reported that he had swept a clear channel along the north coast of Scotland from Cape Wrath to Scapa, between the coast and the Whiten Bank minefield laid by the Moewe. This channel was instituted for warships only for use in daylight. Mercantile auxiliaries were directed to steer to the northward from Cape Wrath, thence to make Noup Head, on the northwest coast of the Orkneys, passing afterwards down the west coast to Scapa; all other vessels were ordered to pass through the Fair Island Channel to their destination.

During the month of January gunnery practices were carried out, both in the Moray Firth and in the Pentland Firth.

The operations of the 10th Cruiser Squadron were much restricted by the bad weather experienced, the weekly average showing: Number of ships intercepted, 21; number sent in, 8; number of ships on patrol, 11; number absent at ports or en route to or from patrol, 10; number on special service, 2.

Gales were experienced at Scapa or the neighbourhood on January 5th, 6th, 7th, 8th, 9th, 12th, 13th, 14th, 15th, 19th, 20th, 22nd, 23rd, 24th and 30th. The weather during the month both at Scapa and in the whole northern area was exceptionally severe, and seriously hampered the work of the 10th Cruiser Squadron and the movements of all small craft.

Independent squadron exercises at sea by day and by night from the various bases were continued in January, as was the change of base of the Rosyth squadrons to Scapa and Cromarty for practices.

At 6 a.m. on February 1st the 1st Cruiser Squadron and four destroyers left Scapa, steering towards the little Fisher Bank, whence the destroyers returned to Scapa, and the squadron proceeded to sweep up the Norwegian coast during daylight hours and thence to Scapa. These sweeps up the coast were undertaken because it was considered probable that enemy raiders, attempting to pass out of the North Sea, would hug the coast on passage.

On February 2nd the 5th Light Cruiser Squadron, from Harwich, was at sea endeavouring to intercept Zeppelins returning from raiding our east coast. The fishing trawler King Stephen on this day sighted Zeppelin L 19 in a sinking condition in the North Sea.

On February 5th Submarine D 8 left Blyth to operate off the Norwegian coast. She returned on the 13th.

On February 7th the 7th Cruiser Squadron proceeded to a position about 150 miles to the southeastward from Scapa for patrol during the night and returned on the 8th, on which date the 1st Cruiser Squadron carried out a similar patrol, returning on the 9th.

On the night of February 10th the 10th Sloop Flotilla, operating from the Humber under the orders of the Rear-Admiral of the East Coast, was attacked by enemy torpedo craft in the vicinity of the Dogger Bank, and the Arabis was sunk. On receipt of the news, and pending further information as to the strength of enemy forces at sea, the Battle Cruiser Fleet left Rosyth during the night of the 10th-11th, and proceeded to the southward; the 5th Light Cruiser Squadron sailed from Harwich; and the remainder of the Grand Fleet left its bases at Scapa, Cromarty and Rosyth to rendezvous in the North Sea and move to the southward. The situation became clear during the 11th, when it was evident that the enemy's force, which had consisted only of destroyers, had returned to its base.

At 10.30 p.m. (the Battle Fleet being then in Lat. 57.57 N., Long. 0.20 E.) orders were given for the Grand Fleet to return to its bases, and the squadrons arrived on the 12th.

From the 17th to the 19th the 3rd Cruiser Squadron, with the armed boarding-steamers Dundee and Duke of Clarence, from Scapa, swept from that base to the Utvoer Lighthouse (Lat. 61.2 N., Long. 40.31 E.), thence down the Norwegian coast and to Rosyth, the armed boarding steamers returning to Scapa. The only vessels sighted were two enemy submarines off the coast of Norway.

On February 18th the new battleship Malaya, the gift of the Federated Malay States, arrived at Scapa and joined the 5th Battle Squadron.

On February 22nd Submarines D 7 and E 30 were sent to the Skagerrak to examine and board merchant vessels with a view to stopping the iron ore trade from Narvik to Rotterdam. Armed guards were sent in the submarines. They were ordered, during the latter part of their cruise, to operate against two enemy submarines reported off the Norwegian coast. They returned on February 28th, not having met, outside territorial waters, the submarines or with any vessels which were engaged in the iron ore trade.

On February 24th two divisions of destroyers were sent without result to operate against a submarine reported in the Fair Island Channel.

On February 26th the Dreadnought Battle Fleet, with the 2nd and 7th Cruiser Squadrons, the 4th Light Cruiser Squadron and flotillas, left Scapa before daylight for a watching and exercise cruise in the northern part of the North Sea. A sweep to the Heligoland Bight, in conjunction with the Harwich force, had been intended, but was abandoned on receipt of a report from Commodore Tyrwhitt that the weather and other conditions were unsuitable for his operations. Battle exercises took place during the afternoon, and the Battle Cruiser Fleet, which left Rosyth at 1.30 p.m. on the 26th, joined the Battle Fleet at 8 a.m. next day. During that day further battle exercises were carried out, including deployments of the whole Grand Fleet from its cruising order, so that the battle cruisers, cruisers, light cruisers and destroyers might become accustomed to taking up the stations assigned to them on deployment under certain conditions. The exercises were of considerable interest. The Fleet returned to its bases on the 28th.

During the absence of the Fleet from Scapa the minesweeping sloops patrolled to the eastward of the Orkneys to prevent minelaying in the approaches to the base.

On February 28th dispositions were made to intercept any enemy vessel that might be attempting to pass out into the North Sea. Information from neutral sources had led to a belief in the possibility of such an attempt being made. As was almost inevitable on such occasions, the information was received after the event, that is, it was reported that the vessel in question had already left German waters. The dispositions were made, therefore, on this assumption, and in making them it was necessary to place our vessels in areas which the enemy might be expected to pass through in daylight.

The dispositions were designed to intercept the ship whether her mission were minelaying near our bases, or an attempt to pass out into the Atlantic. The Patia and Columbella, of the 10th Cruiser Squadron, were directed to patrol a line running north-east from Lat. 61.45 N., Long. 0.50 E., and ships of the same squadron on the C Patrol line were directed to extend this line to the north-eastward. The Alcantara and Andes, of the same squadron, already on a special patrol line, were ordered to remain in their position till further orders. Two ships of the 1st Light Cruiser Squadron and four destroyers left Rosyth at 8 p.m. on the 28th to patrol the area covering the Farn Island — Skaw and the May Island — Skaw trade routes, working to the eastward.

Early on February 29th the Comus and the Calliope, of the 4th Light Cruiser Squadron, which had sailed on the 28th with two destroyers for areas in the vicinity of Lat. 58.38 N., Long. 2.30 E., and Lat. 59.20 N., Long. 3.0 E. respectively, were directed to patrol lines 40 miles long, running 50° to 280° respectively from a position in Lat. 61 N., Long. 1.10 E. The Blanche, which had also sailed, was ordered to a position Lat. 61.30 N., Long. 0.0. The Minotaur and a destroyer were sent to patrol the Fair Island passage during daylight on the 29th. Steps were also taken to cover the approaches to the Pentland Firth against minelaying.

At 8.55 a.m. on the 29th the Andes, Captain G. B. Young, R.N., reported by wireless that an enemy vessel was in sight in Lat. 61.58 N., Long. 1.8 E., and gave her course, speed and description; her enemy character was assumed owing to her movements. The Alcantara, Captain T. E. Wardle, R.N., was not at this time in sight of the Andes, but sighted her at 9.10 a.m. chasing a strange vessel, joined in the pursuit, and, at 9.15 a.m., being then about 6,000 yards from her, ordered her to stop. She complied and informed the Alcantara that she was the Norwegian s.s. Rena from Rio to Trondjhem. She was flying the Norwegian flag, which was also painted on her sides. At 9.40 a.m. the Alcantara, then about 2,500 yards on the quarter of the stranger, began to hoist out a boat for the purpose of boarding. At this moment the other vessel opened a heavy fire from her hitherto concealed armament, throwing her Norwegian ensign and staff overboard and hoisting a German ensign at the main. But she still showed the Norwegian flag on her sides, where it was displayed throughout the action. At the close range at which fire was opened hitting commenced immediately, and as the first hits on the Alcantara cut all her communications, Captain Wardle experienced great difficulty in passing orders to the guns. But the enemy's fire was returned quickly and with effect, in spite of the difficulty of communication. Both ships went ahead, and a hot action ensued; the enemy fired torpedoes, one of which hit the Alcantara between the boiler-rooms at about 10 a.m., causing them gradually to fill.

By 10.15 a.m. the enemy was badly on fire and stopped. A few minutes later, at 10.22 p.m., boats were observed to be leaving her and the Alcantara ceased firing. The latter ship was by this time listing heavily and was abandoned shortly afterwards, sinking at 11.2 a.m. The Andes, which had been engaging the enemy at a longer range than the Alcantara, rendered assistance to the boats of the two ships.

On receipt of the first signal from the Andes, the Calliope, Comus and Blanche had been ordered to the scene at full speed. The Comus, Captain Alan G. Hotham, R.N., the nearest vessel, with the destroyer Munster, arrived on the spot Lat. 61.48 N., Long. 1.40 E., as the Alcantara was sinking. The Munster picked up the crew of the Alcantara, and as the enemy raider still had colours flying the Comus proceeded to sink her by gunfire and to pick up the survivors in her boats. The Calliope and Magic arrived at 1 p.m., but, not being required, returned to their patrol line. The enemy vessel turned out to be the disguised raider Grief, armed with four 5.9-inch guns and two torpedo tubes; she had a complement of 306, of whom 209, including many wounded, were rescued by the Comus and Andes.

The incident showed the great difficulty of carrying out blockade work under modern conditions when dealing with an unscrupulous enemy. A raider disguised as a neutral, and armed with torpedo tubes, is a most difficult customer to deal with, and every neutral vessel had perforce to be treated as "suspect" after an incident of this nature. It is not possible to examine a vessel without boarding her, and, except in very fine weather, it is necessary for the boarding ship to be close to the suspected ship before lowering her boat, as the latter obviously cannot pull long distances.

The experience of the Alcantara showed the danger of closing the ship to be boarded. An attempt to solve the problem was made by informing all neutrals that, when any of our vessels displayed a certain signal, the ship to be boarded should steam towards the boarding boat, this boat being lowered some distance away. But, in order to carry this into effect, we were obviously dependent to a large extent on the co-operation of neutrals, which was not always in evidence.

Modern blockade work undoubtedly bristles with difficulties which did not exist in the days of our forefathers, not the least being the advent of the torpedo and the submarine. The German method of solving such difficulties was to sink vessels at sight, but such methods did not, and never will, appeal to the British mind, or to the mind of any seaman belonging to the Allied nations.

During February, 1916, the somewhat shorter nights, combined with more favourable weather, gave the 10th Cruiser Squadron better opportunities for the blockade, and the average weekly results were: Number of ships intercepted, 39; number sent in. 11; number of ships on patrol, 12; number absent at ports or en route to or from patrol, 9; number detached on special service, 1.

Gales were experienced at Scapa or in the neighbourhood on February 6th, 7th, 8th, 12th, 14th.

The usual exchange of bases for practices and the independent squadron exercises at sea from the bases were carried out during the month.

On March 1st a party of distinguished Russian gentlemen visited the Fleet at Scapa Flow, leaving again in the evening. The party included M. Danchenko, Count Alexis Tolstoy, M. Vladimir Nabakoff, M. Bashmakoff, M. Yiegoroff and M. Chukovsky.

On March 2nd the new battleship Valiant, a vessel of the "Queen Elizabeth" class, arrived at Scapa and joined the 5th Battle Squadron.

Submarine D 7 was despatched on March 5th to the Kattegat to intercept trade and to ascertain the situation there on the chance of any enemy vessels being found. She did not sight any enemy craft. On the same day the 3rd Battle Squadron left Rosyth for a watching and exercise cruise in the centre portion of the North Sea. On the 6th the remainder of the Grand Fleet proceeded into the North Sea for a southerly sweep, concentration being ordered to take place in the vicinity of the "Long Forties," the centre of that area being in Lat. 57.20 N. on the meridian of Greenwich. The weather, however, became very unfavourable for destroyers, and speed had eventually to be reduced to such an extent that the sweep was abandoned, and the Fleet returned to its bases on the 7th.

On March 9th a patrol consisting of one cruiser and one armed boarding-steamer was instituted in an area north of the Shetlands. It was designed to cover the track of vessels en route between the north of Iceland and a point on the Norwegian coast in the vicinity of Stadlandet (Lat 62.10 N., Long. 5.10 E.), as it was considered probable that this route might be taken by enemy raiders as well as by vessels attempting to evade the blockade. The patrol was continued throughout the year, although occasionally modified in details and frequently doubled in strength. It was eventually successful in intercepting and sinking the German raider Wolf, in the spring of 1917, the Achilles (Captain F. M. Leake, R.N.) and the armed boarding-steamer Dundee (Commander Selwyn Day, R.N.R.) being the vessels engaged in this operation. This patrol was also of use for blockade work.

On March 11th the 1st Light Cruiser Squadron, with a division of destroyers of the 1st Flotilla, left Rosyth at 7.30 a.m. for operations off the Norwegian coast, the objective being the capture of any enemy merchant-ships found outside territorial waters between Ekersund and the Naze. It had been ascertained that some of the German merchant-ships engaged in trade with Norwegian ports, and especially Narvik, occasionally ventured outside territorial waters in this locality. It was the only locality, besides the vicinity of Stadlandet, in which they did so venture, and in which, therefore, there was a chance of capturing them. The remainder of the Battle Cruiser Fleet sailed later, on the 11th, for a position to the southward of the Naze for supporting purposes. It was also intended that the remainder of the Grand Fleet should be cruising in the neighbourhood. But an easterly gale sprang up, which prevented the destroyers from accompanying the Battle Fleet, and this portion of the programme was cancelled; Sir David Beatty was informed that, if the weather conditions farther south prevented his destroyers from screening the battle cruisers, the latter should return to their base and a light cruiser squadron be left to support the 1st Light Cruiser Squadron. The conditions being unfavourable for destroyers, this course was adopted. The weather eventually became too bad for the light cruiser squadrons to maintain their speed, and the sweep, which was unproductive, was curtailed.

Submarine E 30 proceeded into the Kattegat on March 14th to intercept contraband trade and for reconnoitering purposes. She did not sight any enemy vessels, but sent in one neutral vessel suspected of carrying contraband.

The 5th Light Cruiser Squadron, from Harwich, was at sea on March 14th and 15th, and the Roxburgh and two destroyers left Rosyth on the 15th for another sweep on the Norwegian coast from Udsire Lighthouse to the Naze. This was again unproductive.

The cruiser Theseus left Barry on the 15th for Alexandrovsk in the White Sea. On the same date the cruiser Crescent, en route from Scapa to the south, was fired at and missed by a submarine south of the Hebrides.

On the 19th the light cruiser Calliope, with two destroyers, left the Tyne, where she had been refitting, with orders to proceed to the Naze and sweep up the Norwegian coast to Udsire; and the Comus and two destroyers left Scapa to proceed to Udsire to sweep down the Norwegian coast to the Naze, the object being again the capture of any German merchant-ships found outside territorial waters in this locality. The Calliope was forced to put into Rosyth owing to a serious fire occurring in her after boiler-room. The Comus completed her sweep in bad weather without sighting any enemy vessels.

On March 24th the Harwich force sailed to carry out aerial operations off the Danish coast, involving an attack on the enemy's Zeppelin shed at Tondern, and the Battle Cruiser Fleet left early that day to cover the operation. In the course of the operations the destroyers of the Harwich force were stationed in positions to pick up returning seaplanes, some of them being despatched to the southward of the Horn Reef for this purpose. Some German outpost trawlers were encountered here by the destroyers; they were engaged and destroyed. But during the engagement the destroyer Medusa was rammed by the destroyer Laverock, being very seriously damaged.

The Medusa was taken in tow, but, the weather becoming very bad, the towing hawser parted, and all attempts to get her in tow again after dark failed. Our vessels were in close proximity to the enemy bases, and it was evident that the enemy would be aware of the incident by means of his directional wireless system, since a good deal of wireless signalling on the part of our ships had been necessary. It was expected, therefore, that he would send out a considerable force of destroyers during the dark hours to attack our vessels. In these circumstances, and in view of the weather conditions, Commodore Tyrwhitt rightly judged it expedient to abandon and sink the Medusa, and gave orders to this effect. The ship's company of the Medusa was taken off in a most seamanlike manner by Lieutenant-Commander Bullen of the Lassoo.

Owing to the bad weather and the darkness it was difficult for Commander Tyrwhitt to ascertain the exact conditions, but during the night of the 25th, having sent his destroyers ahead, he steered with his light cruisers in order to pass to the northward of the enemy's North Sea minefield. At about 10 p.m. two enemy destroyers were sighted on the port bow of the Cleopatra (flying Commodore Tyrwhitt's broad pennant) at a distance of about 800 yards. Their presence was betrayed by the flame from their funnels; they were evidently part of the force which, as anticipated, had been sent out by the enemy.

The Cleopatra at once opened fire and headed for the destroyers, and when it was seen that they were crossing from port to starboard. Captain Loder Symonds of the Cleopatra ported his helm and rammed the second destroyer very neatly amidships, cutting her practically in half. There was a tremendous crash, followed by what seemed to be two explosions, one possibly a boiler explosion, and the second due to either a mine or depth-charge, causing considerable damage to the stern piece of the Cleopatra. The injury was subsequently found to be far too great to have been caused by the impact alone. The sudden alterations of course by the Cleopatra, combined with the gunfire and explosions, had thrown the squadron into some confusion, and, although fighting and navigation lights were all switched on very smartly, the Cleopatra, in separating from the sinking destroyer, found herself across the Undaunted's stern; the latter was somewhat seriously damaged, and reported subsequently that she could only steam at slow speed. The Commodore, therefore, remained near the Undaunted for the night.

Meanwhile the Battle Cruiser Fleet, which had left Rosyth on the 24th to cover the operations, was in the vicinity of the Harwich force, and, on the morning of the 26th, the 5th Light

Cruiser Squadron, except the Undaunted, closed the Battle Cruiser Fleet, and the force swept back towards her position, not sighting any enemy vessels. Three of the light cruisers covered the Undaunted during her passage to the Tyne, where she was sent for repairs. Considerable difficulty was experienced in locating the Undaunted, owing to a difference in "dead reckoning" between the various ships. In order to be prepared for eventualities the remainder of the Grand Fleet proceeded to sea during the night of the 25th-26th, heavy snowstorms being experienced by both the Scapa and Cromarty forces on leaving their bases; the visibility was also very low; a heavy southwesterly gale sprang up when the snow ceased.

During the early afternoon of the 26th the wireless reports from the Vice-Admiral of the Battle Cruiser Fleet, Commodore Tyrwhitt, and the Undaunted cleared up the situation, the latter ship reporting herself as hove to until the weather moderated.

By 4.30 p.m., when the Fleet was in the vicinity of the "Long Forties," the sea had become so heavy and steep that destroyers with the Battle Fleet could not safely steam at 10 knots, and, as the presence of the whole Battle Fleet was no longer necessary in southern waters, and the Undaunted was approaching a safe area, the 5th Battle Squadron was detached at high speed, without destroyers, to assist in covering her passage back to the coast, and the remainder of the Battle Fleet and cruiser squadrons were ordered back to Scapa and Cromarty. The Iron Duke convoyed the destroyer flotillas in order that they could be given their position, as the coast was approached. The weather moderated during the night, and the fleet arrived at its bases on the 27th. Two destroyers collided off Noss Head just before daylight on the 27th, one, the Michael, being somewhat seriously damaged.

By 8 a.m. on the 27th the Undaunted was in Lat 56.35 N., Long. 2 E., and the 5th Battle Squadron returned to Scapa, the Battle Cruiser Fleet arriving at Rosyth on the 27th.

The 1st, 2nd, 4th and 5th Battle Squadrons, the 1st and 7th Cruiser Squadrons, the 4th Light Cruiser Squadron and flotillas again proceeded to sea on March 29th, for a watching and exercise cruise in the northern part of the North Sea. Battle exercises were carried out on the 30th. The Fleet returned to its bases on the 31st, the destroyers having to return independently as they were unable to maintain Fleet speed through bad weather conditions.

During March the system of carrying out target practice in the Pentland Firth off Dunnet Head, instead of in the Moray Firth was regularly instituted, and no further practices took place in the Moray Firth during the year 1916. The new procedure proved to be most satisfactory in every respect, no difficulty ever arising, except that of towing the target in the strong tides of the Pentland Firth.

On March 19th the battleship Hercules, which had been laid up at Scapa with a defective turbine for nearly six weeks, completed her repairs. These were carried out with the assistance of artisans from the engine contractors.

The usual visits to Scapa of the squadrons from Rosyth for the purpose of practices continued.

The 10th Cruiser Squadron's weekly average for March showed: Number of ships intercepted, 43; number sent in, 11; number on patrol, 12; number absent at bases, or en route to or from patrol, 9; number on special service, 1.

A great deal of fog, mist and snow was experienced during the month, and the weather generally in northern waters was bad, gales occurring on the 6th, 11th, 12th, 25th, 26th, 27th, 28th and 29th.

On April 2nd Zeppelins reached the Firth of Forth and attacked Leith and Edinburgh, but did not make any attempt on the Fleet at anchor. The 2nd Light Cruiser Squadron was sent to sea in the hope of intercepting some of them during their return passage, but saw nothing of them.

On April 3rd the Devonshire and two destroyers left Rosyth and proceeded to the Norwegian coast in the vicinity of Udsire lighthouse, and swept thence to the Naze to intercept German merchant-ships, or neutrals with contraband which might be found outside territorial waters. One Swedish steamer was sent in; heavy traffic in territorial waters was reported.

On April 5th three submarines left Blyth to operate against enemy submarines on the route which it was thought was taken by them between the Shetlands and Heligoland. They were directed to work on lines about 30 miles apart, zigzagging across the lines. They did not, however, sight any enemy submarines. Anti-submarine operations of this nature by the submarines attached to the Grand Fleet were carried out at frequent intervals during the remainder of the year 1916 whenever any craft were available for this purpose; the plan of operations was constantly varied. The general scheme was to place our craft in positions through which hostile submarines were expected to pass, or along the routes which they usually took.

On April 6th the Roxburgh left Rosyth with two destroyers, to repeat once again the operation of sweeping down the Norwegian coast from Udsire to the Naze. The search was again unproductive.

On April 12th the armed liner Campania returned from a lengthy refit at Liverpool, during which the ship had, at my request, been provided with a "flying-off" deck for her seaplanes, as experience throughout the War had shown conclusively that it was of little use to depend on seaplanes rising from the water, except under the most advantageous conditions, and that the only system which would give reasonable certainty of the machines being able to get into the air when required was to fly them from the ship. At the same time I formed the conclusion, after consultation with Captain O. Schwann, of the Campania, and pressed it upon the Naval Air Service, that the seaplane should be replaced by aeroplanes flown from ships, since the weight of the floats of seaplanes greatly limited their climbing powers, their radius of action and their speed.

This alteration to the Campania was the commencement of the system, gradually introduced, of providing light cruisers, battle cruisers and battleships with scouting aeroplanes, which could rise from the ship under practically all conditions. I make no apology for referring again to this subject in view of its importance.

The Campania had also been fitted to carry a kite balloon aft, for use for spotting the fall of shot and for reconnaissance purposes. This fitting was the beginning of the arrangement, gradually introduced during 1916, of carrying kite balloons in capital ships. The success in large ships led, before the end of the year, to their being also provided for light cruisers, destroyers, and other small craft, an arrangement which proved to be of great use for anti-submarine and convoy work.

On April 17th the patrol areas of the 10th Cruiser Squadron were modified; "A" and "C" patrols took up a line running from Lat. 56.30 N., Long. 11.30 W. to Lat. 63.30 N., Long. 16.00 W., ships 40 miles apart and steering 70° and 250°. Two ships were also stationed to the northward of Iceland.

On April 20th a force left to carry out an extensive sweep into the Kattegat, designed

(1) to intercept and examine all mercantile traffic,

(2) to operate against enemy vessels in the Kattegat,

(3) to engage any enemy vessels drawn out from North Sea ports by the movements in the Kattegat of the light forces, which it was intended should be sighted from neutral shores in the expectation that they might be reported to the enemy by his agents.

The force included three submarines, which were ordered to positions commanding the northern entrance to the Sound, and the Great and Little Belts, so that enemy forces drawn from the Baltic by the movement might be engaged by them. On April 21st, however, it was decided to move south to the vicinity of the Horn Reef with the whole Grand Fleet, the object being to induce the enemy to keep the ships of the High Sea Fleet in North Sea ports instead of sending them to the Baltic, where they might cause interference with the relaying the Russian minefields, an operation which became necessary at this season of the year after the ice had broken up.

It was thought that the appearance of the Grand Fleet in the vicinity of the Heligoland Bight would probably effect this object better than the operation in the Kattegat. Consequently the Grand Fleet left its bases on the 21st, with orders for the battle and cruiser squadrons to concentrate on the morning of the 22nd in a given position to the eastward of the "Long Forties," whilst the Battle Cruiser Fleet took station some 40 miles ahead of the Battle Fleet in its cruising formation. The 3rd Battle Squadron and 3rd Cruiser Squadron, from Rosyth, were ordered to an area from which they could concentrate later, with the remainder of the Battle Fleet, if required.

At 2.30 p.m. of the 22nd the 4th Light Cruiser Squadron was detached, with three destroyers, to proceed to the Skagerrak, with directions to arrive in the vicinity of the Skaw by daylight on the 23rd, and to sweep out to the westward. The Battle Cruiser Fleet was ordered to push ahead, and at 6 p.m. of the 22nd was in Lat. 56.11 N., Long. 5.26 E., cruising in an area northwest of the Horn Reef until daylight, when it was intended to steer for the Horn Reef, provided the weather, which had become misty, was sufficiently clear. The Battle Fleet, with cruiser squadrons disposed ahead, steered to the eastward from Scapa until shortly before dark, and then altered course to South 18 East for the Horn Reef, to close the Battle Cruiser Fleet by daylight on the 23rd.

The weather had been gradually thickening since 3 p.m., and at 6 p.m. Sir David Beatty reported that the Australia and New Zealand had collided in a fog and had received damage necessitating both ships returning to their base. By 10 p.m. the Battle Fleet and cruisers were also in a dense fog, which continued throughout the night. It was undesirable to close the Danish coast under such conditions with so large a Fleet; the Battle Fleet, cruisers and destroyers, when to the westward of the Little Fisher Bank, were accordingly turned to the northward, the order of turning being rear squadrons first and thence to the van, so as to reduce the danger of collision. Special signals had been introduced to provide for such circumstances, and were of great use on this occasion.

In spite, however, of this precaution, some difficulty was experienced in carrying out the turn in the dense fog that prevailed, especially amongst the destroyers, and three of them, namely, the Garland, Ardent and Ambuscade, were in collision; the Ardent was so seriously damaged forward that it became necessary to tow her back to a repairing-port, stern first. During the night a neutral steamer, in passing through the Fleet in the fog, collided with the battleship Neptune, doing considerable injury to that ship.

The weather cleared somewhat during the morning, and the Fleet cruised to the westward of the Little Fisher Bank until it was certain that the damaged destroyers were safely on their way to their bases. The operations were then abandoned, as the conditions were unsuitable, and the destroyers had not sufficient fuel to admit of the Fleet remaining out for a further twenty-four hours, so as to repeat the sweep to the Horn Reef on the following day.

The whole Fleet returned to its bases during the 24th, fuelled, and again proceeded to sea for another movement south during the evening of that day, the 5th Battle Squadron being sent on in advance of the remainder of the Battle Fleet in order to gain touch with and strengthen the Battle Cruiser Fleet, which was, of course, short of the Australia and New Zealand, damaged in collision.

At 4.6 a.m. on April 25th, however, whilst steering to the southward, a report was received from Commodore Tyrwhitt, who was at sea with the Harwich force, that he had sighted enemy battle cruisers and light cruisers in Lat. 52.24 N., Long. 1.57 E. This report at once influenced the direction of the sweep, and the Battle Fleet increased to full speed, and shaped a course to pass down the searched channel to the westward of the German minefield to support the Battle Cruiser Fleet and the 5th Battle Squadron, which proceeded at full speed on a course designed to intercept the enemy battle cruisers during their expected return passage to their ports. At 4.20 a.m. the Admiralty informed me that the enemy was bombarding Lowestoft, and that the 5th Light Cruiser Squadron was in touch with the enemy's ships; and at 5.40 a.m. the Aldeburgh wireless station reported enemy battle cruisers in sight steaming to the eastward.

At 11 a.m. the Iron Duke, with the Dreadnought Battle Fleet, was in Lat. 56.22 N., Long. 0.0; the 3rd Battle Squadron and 3rd Cruiser Squadron were about 35 miles and the 5th Battle Squadron about 70 miles to the southward, the Battle Cruiser Fleet being well to the southeastward in the direction of Terschelling, and, as appeared later, having evidently only just barely missed cutting the enemy off from his base. The Battle Fleet stood on to the southeastward until the afternoon, when it became evident that the Germans had escaped to their bases, and the Fleet then turned to the northward and shaped course for the bases, arriving on the 26th.

On returning, my opinion was asked by the Admiralty as to the steps which could be taken to minimise the danger of a recurrence of such raids on unfortified towns on the southeast coast as that of the 25th. Although they inflicted no military damage, they were undoubtedly a great annoyance owing to the alarm of the inhabitants, and might result in much loss of life. I suggested that the placing of the 3rd Battle Squadron in the Humber or in the Thames might act as a deterrent, and in any case would make it necessary for the enemy to bring heavy ships, which would give us an opportunity of inflicting injury by submarines or by the ships of the Grand Fleet, if, by good fortune, we happened to be cruising sufficiently far to the southward at the time. The presence of the squadron in southern waters would be useful, also, in the unlikely event of landing raids, and would provide a good backing to the Harwich force, although the difficulties of movement, due to the frequent minelaying by enemy submarines in southern waters, were considerable. I pointed out that since the arrival of the 5th Battle Squadron and the other new ships, the 3rd Battle Squadron was no longer required to strengthen the Grand Fleet; the ships of the "Revenge" class were also approaching completion. The proposal was adopted, and the 3rd Battle Squadron and 3rd Cruiser Squadron sailed for the Humber on the 29th, en route to the Medway. On that port the 3rd Battle Squadron was based in future, the ships of the 3rd Cruiser Squadron being gradually withdrawn for service in foreign waters. The Admiralty also stationed some of the monitors in the more important undefended ports.

During the month of April a policy, suggested by me, of placing the Captains (D) in flotilla leaders instead of in light cruisers, was adopted. This was made possible by the completion of several vessels of the class. The object was to add the light cruisers thus released to our all too slender light cruiser force.

The average weekly figures for the 10th Cruiser Squadron during April were: Number of ships intercepted, 40; number sent in, 10; number of ships on patrol, 12; number absent at ports or en route to or from patrol, 9; number on special service, 1.

A very considerable amount of mist and fog was experienced during the month, and gales on the 8th, 16th and 24th.

On May 2nd forces left for an aerial operation in the vicinity of the Horn Reef. The operation was covered by the Grand Fleet. One of its objects was, as before, to attract the attention of the enemy's naval forces to the North Sea. Even if no enemy force were actually drawn out, it was expected that the presence of the Grand Fleet in southern waters would soon become known to the enemy from neutral sources, with the result that vessels of the High Sea Fleet, intended for operations in the Baltic, might be detained in, or brought back to, North Sea ports. From information obtained subsequently from reliable sources, it appeared that the operation produced the intended result. Between the afternoon of May 2nd and daylight on the 3rd the Fleet left its bases.

The 1st Light Cruiser Squadron, with 16 destroyers convoying the seaplane-carriers Vindex and Engadine, proceeded to a position just north of the Horn Reef, arriving at dawn on May 4th; the objective of the seaplanes was the Zeppelin sheds at Tondern. The minelayer Abdiel proceeded to lay mines on the night of the 3rd-4th to the southward of the Vyl Lightship on the expected track of enemy vessels en route to the North Sea via the Horn Reef. The minelayer Princess Margaret was directed to lay mines on the same night across the expected route taken by enemy vessels if coming out along the route passing the West Frisian Islands. Both minefields were completed without any interference on the part of the enemy.

Three submarines were sent to positions off the Horn Reef, three to positions off the Vyl light vessel, and three to positions off Terschelling, to arrive on the evening of the 3rd. (Two of our submarines collided while submerged off the Horn Reef, one being slightly damaged.)

The Battle Cruiser Fleet and destroyers proceeded to a position for supporting the 1st Light Cruiser Squadron, near the Horn Reef, with directions to arrive at daylight on the 4th, and the Battle Fleet, with its cruiser squadrons, the 4th Light Cruiser Squadron and the destroyer flotillas, to a supporting position to the northward of the Battle Cruiser Fleet. The list of ships absent from the Fleet on this occasion, owing to refit, repair, or to being engaged on other operations, is given below; it is useful as showing the reduction that takes place in the nominal numbers comprising a watching fleet at any given moment:

Battleships, Ajax and Dreadnought; battle cruisers New Zealand, Australia, Invincible; cruisers Black Prince, Warrior, Donegal; light cruisers, Southampton, Gloucester, Blonde; destroyers, 3 from the 1st Flotilla, 6 from the 2nd Flotilla, 3 from the 11th Flotilla.

During the passage south, the 4th Light Cruiser Squadron was detached to endeavour to locate a Zeppelin reported by directional wireless to be in the centre of the North Sea (Zeppelins had been seen off the north-east coast on the night of the 2nd). The search was unsuccessful, but the Zeppelin descended off Stavanger later and was destroyed.

On the morning of the 4th the conditions for seaplanes seemed from the Battle Fleet to be ideal, but, once more, the difficulty of getting these machines to rise from the water was experienced, a slight sea being sufficient to prevent all, except one, from carrying out the attack. This one seaplane reported having dropped bombs on the objective. The remainder were damaged by the sea.

At 10 a.m. a Zeppelin, L7, was sighted by the 1st Light Cruiser Squadron and attacked by gunfire by the Galatea and Phaeton. She was damaged sufficiently to cause her to descend near submarine E 31 in the vicinity of the Vyl Lightship. E 31 completed her destruction and rescued seven survivors.

The Fleet cruised in the vicinity of the Horn Reef during May 4th, no enemy vessels being sighted, and then returned to its various bases. A thick fog was experienced during the return passage, which was made without incident; the Cromarty force was, however, taken to Scapa, as a submarine had been reported off Tarbet Ness in the Moray Firth.

On May 9th the 4th Light Cruiser Squadron left Scapa to carry out another sweep on the Norwegian coast between the Naze and Udsire Lighthouse. The squadron was divided, two ships proceeding to the Naze and two to Udsire, arriving in position at daylight on the 10th and then sweeping towards each other. One neutral steamer, carrying iron ore for Lubeck, was intercepted outside territorial waters and sent in. On the same day the 2nd Light Cruiser Squadron left Rosyth for Scapa, searching the central portion of the North Sea en route.

On the 9th, 11th and 13th the ships on the northern patrol off the Shetlands moved in to Stadlandet for a short period, on the chance of intercepting ships outside territorial waters.

On the 14th an unsuccessful search for a reported submarine was carried out to the southeast of the Pentland Firth.

On the 15th Submarines D 7 and E 30 left for the Kattegat to operate at the northern end of the Sound and off Anholt Island. One German merchant-steamer was intercepted and sunk outside territorial waters off the Kullen on the 22nd by E 30. On the 18th another submarine was sent to operate off Göteborg in Sweden. She returned on the 25th, not having sighted any enemy vessels.

On the same day a reliable report was received that an exceptionally large force of enemy submarines was now operating in the North Sea, and additional precautions were taken at all the bases to strengthen the patrols and to protect inward and outward-bound vessels. The Vice-Admiral of the 10th Cruiser Squadron was warned to be ready to move all his patrol lines to given alternative positions, and on the 19th was directed to move his ships to the most western of these lines. Precautions against minelaying by submarines were also taken, and the waters to the eastward of the "Long Forties" through which the Fleet usually passed when on passage south, were examined by the Fleet minesweepers, protected by destroyers, on the 21st and subsequent days. These vessels searched without result on the 22nd for a submarine which was being chased by a patrol vessel in this neighbourhood.

On May 21st the Donegal and two destroyers were sent to the vicinity of the entrance to Bergen to intercept a steamer which, it was thought, had passed through the 10th Cruiser Squadron blockade during a fog. The ship however, called later at Kirkwall, and the force was recalled.

On the 23rd the first of a series of deep minefields in the Moray Firth, which I had requested might be laid with the object of catching enemy submarines, was placed in position by the minelayer Biarritz.

On the 24th the Donegal and an armed boarding steamer were sent to patrol off Stadlandet with a view to intercepting ships engaged in the iron ore trade from Narvik. This, as before stated, was one of the few positions at which ships were obliged for navigational reasons to leave territorial waters.

On the 24th the 4th Light Cruiser Squadron, with destroyers, which had been at Rosyth, left for another search off the Norwegian coast from the Naze to Udsire, and thence to Scapa. The search was unproductive.

On the 26th two submarines were despatched to operate against enemy submarines off the Norwegian coast, and, on the same date, the 1st Light Cruiser Squadron, with six destroyers, left, via the searched channel, to carry out a reconnaissance to the southward of the German North Sea minefield. The squadron proceeded as far east as Long. 6 E., but, unfortunately, sighted nothing.

The Broke and 12 destroyers left on the 27th May to search for a submarine reported to have been sighted to the eastward of the Pentland Firth, and returned on the 28th, not having seen her; but on the 27th Trawler Unit No. 42, working from Peterhead, reported having engaged and sunk a submarine at 12.45 p.m. in Lat. 57.10 N., Long. 1.20 E., thus adding one more success to the record of this patrol. On the 30th Fleet-sweeper Gentian was missed, in a position about 40 miles due east of the Pentland Firth, by a torpedo fired evidently by the submarine that had been hunted on the 28th. A half flotilla and seaplanes were sent out to search, and a submarine was sighted at 3.45 p.m. near the position given, but she dived and got clear away.

The movements of the Fleet between the time of leaving and returning to the bases in connection with the Battle of Jutland are given in Chapter 11, but some mention may be made of an incident which occurred on the night of May 31st. A report was received at Scapa that an enemy raider might be attempting to escape into the Atlantic. The Vice-Admiral of the 10th Cruiser Squadron was directed to assume a patrol north of the Shetlands in accordance with a plan which had been prearranged to meet such a case. On June 3rd, after the return of the Fleet to its bases, light cruisers were sent out to patrol to the northwestward of the Orkneys, and the 10th Cruiser Squadron was then directed to fall back to a position farther west to form a second patrol line. Nothing came of the matter.

During the month of May the weekly average results of the 10th Cruiser Squadron showed: Number of vessels intercepted, 55, besides 17 trawlers; number sent in, 18; number of ships on patrol, 11; number absent at ports or en route to or from patrol, 9; number on special service, 2.

A good deal of fog and mist was experienced during the month, the worst periods being from the 17th to the 20th, 24th, 26th, and the 28th to 30th.

During the month of May the firing exercises in the Pentland Firth continued, as did the usual exchange of bases between squadrons.

During the months of March, April and May, a flotilla of submarines had been gradually organised as a unit of the Grand Fleet. It was named the 11th Submarine Flotilla, was based on Blyth, with the Titania as parent ship and the Talisman and Trident as attendant destroyers. Separate spheres of activity for the Grand Fleet submarine flotillas and for the submarine flotillas based on Harwich and Yarmouth were also arranged, the dividing line running from a position a little to the southward of the Horn Reef to Flamborough Head. The line was subsequently slightly altered once or twice as the strength of the Grand Fleet submarine flotillas increased, but the general principle was that the Grand Fleet submarines worked to the northward of such a line and the remaining submarines to the southward.

It may not be out of place here to mention the organisation for getting the Grand Fleet to sea from its bases to any desired point of concentration with rapidity and safety, and of bringing the Fleet back into the bases in face of probable submarine or mine attack.

As the Grand Fleet increased in size, and the danger from mine and submarine grew, so the problem of leaving Scapa Flow and re-entering that base with safety became more complicated. The necessity for the Fleet leaving harbour in the shortest possible time and with the fewest possible number of signals was obvious. Similarly on returning the various squadrons had to enter the base with the least practicable delay in order to avoid giving submarines engaged in watching the approaches an opportunity for getting into positions for attacking the squadrons in rear, after having sighted those in the van. The operations, both of departure and entry, were rendered all the more difficult owing to the very strong and erratic tides experienced in the Pentland Firth, while all ships navigating at night had to be navigated without showing lights.

The usual method of departure from Scapa was as follows: A "Preparatory Signal for leaving Scapa" consisting of one word was made as soon as I decided to take the Fleet to sea. On receipt of this "Preparatory Signal" all ships raised steam for 18 knots at two hours' notice. Patrol destroyers were recalled by the Commodore (F) for refuelling. All officers and men absent on patrol duty in drifters were also recalled, and every preparation was made for leaving harbour. The Admiral Commanding the Orkneys and Shetlands warned the outer patrols that the Fleet might be leaving shortly.

Whilst the Fleet was raising steam in readiness to be off at two hours' notice a signal was made which indicated the time at which the first squadron to leave was to move ahead from the anchorage, together with the speed to be maintained after passing the submarine obstructions. No further signals were necessary. The organisation provided for the order in which squadrons were to leave, as well as the interval between squadrons or divisions, which in daylight was usually one mile from the rear ship of one squadron, or division of four ships, to the leading ship of that following, or two miles at night. The organisation also provided for successive squadrons or divisions being taken alternately north or south of the Pentland Skerries if the Fleet proceeded to the eastward, in order that the interval between those following the same course might be increased.

In the strong tides, particularly at night, some such procedure had to be adopted, because the tide was not felt until the ships were clear of Swona Island, and then the effect of it, if running to the westward, and particularly at the period of spring tides, when it has a speed of 10 knots, was to bring a leading squadron or division back on top of that in rear of it. Frequently also a ship, emerging from slack water into the strength of the tide, would be caught by the tide on the bow, and, unless the greatest possible care was taken to watch the steering (and even sometimes in spite of every care), the ship would be turned round through 8, 12 or even 16 points (8 points = 90 degrees) becoming a danger to those astern of her, as she would be almost unmanageable for a time. Such a situation on a dark night, with a large fleet showing no lights, was not pleasant, and it speaks well for the skill shown in handling the ships that no accident occurred from this cause.

The practice in regard to the destroyers, when they accompanied the Fleet (as was necessary after the first twelve months of war), was for the various groups which were detailed by the Commodore (F) to screen the squadrons or divisions of the heavy ships, to meet them just outside the submarine obstruction and screen them from there in daylight, or on moonlight nights, and to form astern on dark nights, in readiness to re-establish the screen at daylight. In the early days of the War, and indeed for the first eighteen months, the practice was for the destroyer flotillas to be stationed some 10 miles from the Battle Fleet at night in order to avoid any chance of their being sighted and mistaken for enemy destroyers; but this procedure caused considerable delay in forming the submarine screen at daylight, and in thick weather the destroyers frequently experienced difficulty in finding the Battle Fleet, Consequently, it became the practice to keep the destroyers actually in company at night, and this procedure was undoubtedly preferable.

After the various squadrons had passed the Pentland Skerries, the organisation provided for their taking certain defined routes; the usual practice was to use three routes with the squadrons divided between them, the routes being about seven miles apart.

A concentration point, which the squadrons would reach at the ordered speed shortly after daylight, was given in the departure signal, and the squadrons closed in on this point at the appointed time, so that the whole Battle Fleet, including detachments coming from Cromarty, was concentrated shortly after daylight, with the cruisers in their assigned positions scouting ahead.

The organisation of the Battle Fleet provided for the strongest squadron being on the eastern flank because it was considered that the enemy would invariably make towards his bases if touch was gained, and it was desired to have our strongest squadron in the van.

The "departure" organisation was carefully worked out by my Staff and very minutely described in the Grand Fleet orders. It was most useful, the whole Fleet, comprising frequently 50 or more battleships, cruisers and light cruisers, and as many as 50 destroyers, being in daylight under weigh in one hour, and clear of the harbour in an hour and a half after the signal was made to proceed; on dark nights this time was lengthened by half an hour.

When returning to Scapa Flow, the usual practice was for the time of entry to be arranged so that the leading squadrons passed the Pentland Skerries shortly before dawn, in order to minimise the danger from submarine attack; but it was not, of course, always possible to arrange the time of entry in this manner. In returning to Scapa, when the arrival was thus timed for dawn, the different squadrons were disposed, as a rule, in two separate lines, the lines being some five miles apart and the squadrons in each line having an interval of about three miles between them. One line would enter the Pentland Firth by passing north of the Pentland Skerries and the other by passing south of these rocks, the object being to confuse any enemy submarines that might be watching the approaches, and also to get the Fleet into the Firth as quickly as possible, as once in the tideway there was little to fear from submarine attack.

If the Fleet entered Scapa Flow during darkness, the ships anchored in the centre of the Flow in certain specified berths, and waited for daylight before taking up their berths in the Fleet anchorage; towards the end of my period of command, however, coloured lights were arranged to be placed as leading-marks for the Fleet anchorage, so that ships could proceed to their final berths under all conditions.

As regards mines, an exploratory search of the channel intended to be used was always carried out, if time permitted, before the Fleet left, and similarly before it returned. Three channels were used, each some 7 to 10 miles in width — one passing up the east side of the Orkneys, one running to the eastward from the Pentland Skerries, and one passing down the Scottish coast for a short distance and then to the eastward. Usually the second of these channels was used. The principal difficulty with which we had, to deal when leaving or returning was fog.

In a really dense fog there was great risk in attempting to leave Scapa with a large fleet, owing to the strong tides to be encountered in the Pentland Firth, and nothing but the gravest emergency would have justified the attempt being made. If it became really necessary, an organisation had been provided to meet the case, and the attempt would have been made. The interval between the various squadrons would have been considerably greater, and the time occupied in leaving would have been correspondingly increased.

The conditions for leaving the other two fleet bases, Cromarty and Rosyth, were, of course, simpler, owing to the absence of the very strong cross-tides, but fog was even more prevalent at Rosyth than at Scapa, and the operation of leaving with a considerable number of ships was not at all an easy one. It was skilfully performed under difficulties on very numerous occasions and with remarkable freedom from accident during my period of command. The approach to the Firth of Forth in thick weather was difficult, and many anxious moments were experienced in making the land when the position of the ships had not been accurately ascertained by sights for some time before approaching the base. These approaches could have been mined by the enemy with great ease by surface ships had they been sufficiently enterprising, and it was a standing wonder to me that the attempt was never made.

11 - The Naval Situation in May 1916

It may not be out of place here to touch upon the general naval situation in the spring of 1916 — that is, on the eve of the Battle of Jutland. What were the strategical conditions? To what extent was it justifiable to take risks with the Grand Fleet, particularly risks the full consequences of which could not be foreseen owing to the new conditions of naval warfare?

The Grand Fleet included almost the whole of our available capital ships. There was very little in the way of reserve behind it. The battleships not included in the Grand Fleet were all of them pre-Dreadnoughts and therefore inferior fighting units. They consisted of seven ships of the "King Edward VII." class, two ships of the "Lord Nelson" class, and four of the "Queen" class, all of these ships being in the Mediterranean except five of the "King Edward VII" class. They were required there either for work with the Italian Fleet or for the operations in the Aegean. Five of our light cruisers were also in the Mediterranean.

The French and Italian Battle Fleets were also in the Mediterranean, but, owing to political considerations and their duty in watching the Austrian Fleet, there was little prospect of their leaving that locality.

It is interesting to compare this situation with that existing a century earlier. In September, 1805, the month before Trafalgar, the disposition of British ships in commission in home waters and the Mediterranean is given in the following table:

In addition to Nelson's force of 26 capital ships and 19 frigates, the Navy had, therefore, in commission in home waters and the Mediterranean a yet more numerous force of 47 capital ships and 50 frigates. The main portion of this force was with Cornwallis off Ushant, and was watching Brest. Between the Shetlands and Beachy Head we had 155 sloops and small vessels.

In 1916, in addition to the Grand Fleet of 39 capital ships (including battle cruisers) and 32 cruisers and light cruisers, we had in commission in home waters and the Mediterranean only 13 capital ships (all of pre-Dreadnought types and, therefore, obsolescent) and 5 light cruisers. Between the Shetlands and Beachy Head we had, exclusive of the Grand Fleet and Harwich force, about 60 destroyers (mostly of old type), 6 P boats, and 88 old torpedo boats.

In September, 1805, we had building 32 ships of the line in England, besides 10 under construction in Russia, and 36 frigates. In May, 1916, we had building five capital ships and about nine light cruisers.

A consideration of these figures will show that the situation at the two periods under review was very different, in that, in 1805, the force engaged at Trafalgar was only a relatively small portion of the available British Fleet, whilst in 1916 the Grand Fleet included the large majority of the vessels upon which the country had to rely for safety.

Earlier in the War, at the end of October, 1914, I had written to the Admiralty pointing out the dangers which an intelligent use of submarines, mines and torpedoes by the Germans, before and during a Fleet action, would involve to the Grand Fleet, and had stated the tactics which I had intended to employ to meet the expected German movement in order to bring the enemy to action in the shortest practicable time and with the best chance of achieving such a victory as would be decisive, I stated that with new and untried methods of warfare new tactics must be devised to meet them.

I received in reply an expression of approval of my views and of confidence in the manner in which I proposed to handle the Fleet in action.

Neither in October, 1914, nor in May, 1916, did the margin of superiority of the Grand Fleet over the High Sea Fleet justify me in disregarding the enemy's torpedo fire or meeting it otherwise than by definite movements deduced after most careful analysis of the problem at sea with the Fleet and on the tactical board.

The severely restricted forces behind the Grand Fleet were taken into account in making this decision. There was also a possibility that the Grand Fleet might later be called upon to confront a situation of much wider scope than that already existing.

The position gradually improved after 1916. During the latter half of that year the remaining ships of the "Royal Sovereign" class joined the Grand Fleet, and greatly increased the ratio of strength of the Fleet as compared with the High Sea Fleet. Early in 1917 it was also possible to withdraw the four battleships of the "Queen" class from the Adriatic. This greatly eased the manning situation. And in April, 1917, the culminating event was the entry of the United States of America into the War on the side of the Entente. In December, 1917, the United States sent a division of battleships to join the Grand Fleet, and it was apparent that we could count upon the whole battleship strength of the United States Navy, if required, to second our efforts.

Finally, and perhaps most important of all, the light cruiser and destroyer forces with the Grand Fleet increased steadily after the Battle of Jutland, and to a very considerable extent reduced the danger of successful torpedo attack on the Grand Fleet in action by surface craft. The inclusion of the K. class submarines — submarines of high speed — in the Grand Fleet in 1917 made it very probable that any losses suffered by us by submarine attack would be more than compensated by enemy losses from the same cause.

In spite of the fact that, in 1918, the situation in regard to battle cruisers was becoming unsatisfactory, the general effect of all these considerations upon the tactics of the Grand Fleet was bound to be overwhelming. The position was assured, and we could have afforded to take risks later on which, in 1916, would have been most unwise.

12 - The Battle of Jutland

On May 31st, 1916, the Grand Fleet and the High Sea Fleet fought the action which has become known as the Battle of Jutland. The despatch describing the battle, as published some weeks later, was not quite in its original form as written by me. After a conference held at the Admiralty, early in June, modifications were made; some of them because it was considered that certain passages might convey useful information to the enemy, and others because it was thought to be undesirable to draw attention to certain features of British design. Amongst the latter was the insufficiency of the armour protection of our earlier battle cruisers.

Throughout the War it had been our policy to cause our battle cruisers, with their attendant light cruisers, to occupy when at sea an advanced position, often at a considerable distance from the Battle Fleet. Battle cruisers were designed and built in order that they might keep in touch with the enemy and report his movements when he had been found; hence the heavy guns which they carried. They were intended to find the enemy for the Battle Fleet and to ascertain the enemy's strength in order to report to the Battle Fleet. Had this policy not been adopted the enemy's battle cruisers could not have been brought to action on such occasions as the engagement of January 24th, 1915. And in the cases of raids on our coast, the battle cruisers were always sent ahead at full speed to endeavour to cut off the enemy battle cruisers.

Bearing in mind our superiority in numbers in the middle of 1916 and the heavier armaments carried by our ships, the real risk involved in this policy was that of our battle cruisers being drawn on to the enemy's Battle Fleet, and one or more of our vessels being disabled. Provided that our ships were not disabled, they would, owing to their higher speed, have no difficulty in clear weather in keeping out of range of the enemy's Battle Fleet, if it were sighted, whilst still maintaining touch with it, and driving off lighter vessels. With the added support of the ships of the 5th Battle Squadron, which had been grouped with the Battle Cruiser Fleet owing to the absence of the 3rd Battle Squadron at Scapa Flow, the tactical advantage of our ships was even stronger, provided always that the 5th Battle Squadron had an excess of speed over the fastest enemy's Battle Squadron.

In these circumstances, when preparing my despatch, I had felt it necessary on the highest grounds, as well as only just to the officers and men of our battle cruisers, to give some explanation of the heavy losses incurred by our ships in the early part of the action, when we were opposing six battle cruisers (supported, though at long range, by four battleships of the "Queen Elizabeth" class, comprising the 5th Battle Squadron) to five enemy battle cruisers, which were not then supported by the German Battle Fleet. Inquiry into this matter showed that one explanation was that our ships were very inadequately protected by armour as compared with the German vessels of the battle cruiser type. It was considered undesirable to draw attention to this publicly while the war was in progress.

The relative values of protection and gun power had frequently engaged my serious attention. It was also a subject of much discussion amongst writers on naval matters, some of whom went to the length of suggesting that all available weight should be put into gun power and that ships should be left practically without armour. Their views were based on the argument that "the best defense is a powerful offensive." Although this argument is very true when applied to strategy, the War has shown its fallacy as applied to materiel.

The loss of the Good Hope, Monmouth, Queen Mary, Indefatigable, Invincible, Defence, and Warrior, and the considerations to which these losses gave rise, convinced naval officers afloat, even if they did not convince others less intimately associated with the Fleet during the War, that ships with inadequate defensive qualities are no match for those which possess them to a considerably greater degree, even if the former are superior in gun power. The conviction was strengthened by the knowledge we obtained, that German ships, far more frequently hit by gunfire, torpedo, or mine than many of our ships that sank, were yet taken safely into port owing, partly, to their defensive qualities, but, partly, to the limitations of our armour-piercing shell at that time.

There has been in the past a tendency in some quarters, when comparing the relative strength of the British and German Fleets for the purpose of future provision of large vessels in the Navy Estimates, to make comparison only on the basis of the gun power of the vessels of the two Navies. Great superiority in fighting qualities on the part of the British Fleet was suggested by this blindness to other considerations. During my pre-War service at the Admiralty this question was often under discussion, and I consistently demurred to this line of argument as being very misleading, and pointed out that the true comparison lay between the displacement of the ships of the various classes, because if we assumed, as War experience has since shown that we were justified in assuming that the German naval designers and constructors were not inferior in ability to our own, it was obvious that, taking ships of equal displacement and equal speed, and about contemporary date, if our vessels possessed superiority in gunfire, the Germans must possess superiority in some other direction. It was well known at the Admiralty that their superiority lay in greatly increased protection, combined with heavier torpedo armament.

We were also aware that the German vessels were fitted with small tube boilers, which were very economical in weight for a given horsepower, and, consequently, the German vessels obtained thereby a further advantage, the weight saved being presumably utilised in giving the ships additional protection. In other words, they adopted a different disposition of the weight available in each ship.

BATTLESHIPS

1. The German ships of any particular period were of considerably greater displacement as compared with contemporary British ships.
2. The German ships carried a much greater weight of armour than their British contemporaries.

3. All German Dreadnoughts were provided with side armour to the upper deck, whilst nine of the earliest British Dreadnoughts were provided with armour protection to the main deck only, thus rendering them far more open to artillery attack. The "Orion" class of battleship and the "Lion" class of battle cruiser, designed during my service at the Admiralty as Controller, were the first of our Dreadnoughts armoured to the upper deck.

4. The main belt and upper belt armour of the German ships was in nearly all cases thicker than in their British contemporaries, whilst the protection at the bow and stern was in all cases considerably greater in the German ships.

5. The deck protection in the German ships was usually greater than in the British vessels and the watertight subdivision more complete.

6. The German ships carried a greater number of submerged torpedo tubes than the British vessels.

BATTLE CRUISERS

1. The earlier German battle cruisers were of greater displacement than their British contemporaries.

2. The German ships carried a greater weight of armour than their British contemporaries.

3. Five out of our nine battle cruisers were without protection above the main deck, the whole of the German vessels being provided with protection to the upper deck.

4. The German vessels possessed thicker armour in all positions, including deck protection, as well as more complete watertight subdivisions.

5. The German ships carried a greater number of submerged torpedo tubes than the British ships.

As against the additional protection of the German ships our vessels of contemporary design were provided in all cases with heavier turret guns, whilst the German ships carried heavier secondary armaments.

A point of considerable interest, which should also be mentioned because it was to prove important, was that the Germans possessed a delay-action fuse which, combined with a highly efficient armour-piercing projectile, ensured the burst of shell taking place inside the armour of British ships instead of outside, or whilst passing through the armour, which was the case with British shells of that date fired against the thick German armour.

The fuel capacity of the ships of the two Navies was not widely different, although the British ships, as a rule, were fitted to carry more fuel. Although I arranged, after the first few months of war, to reduce the amount of fuel carried by our ships very considerably - in fact, by more than 25 per cent. - I was unable to reduce it further in coal-burning ships without sacrificing some of the protection afforded by the coal, since in our case it was necessary to be prepared to do a considerable amount of steaming at high speed, involving expenditure of coal, before obtaining contact with the enemy. It would have been unwise to contemplate meeting the Germans with coal below what I may call the "safety line." On the other hand, it was well known that, as the Germans had no intention of fighting an action far from their bases, they had effected a very much greater reduction in the quantity of fuel carried with consequently a corresponding advantage in speed.

There was yet one other matter of great importance, namely, the vulnerability of the ships of the two Navies in regard to underwater attack. Here the Germans possessed a very real advantage, which stood them in good stead throughout the war. It arose from two causes:

1. The greater extent of the protective armour inside the ships, and in many cases its greater thickness.

2. The greater distance of this armour from the outer skin of the ship and the consequent additional protection to underwater attack afforded thereby.

In regard to the first point, the great majority of our ships only carried partial internal protection, that is, protection over a portion of the length of the ship. The protection was usually confined to the region of the magazine and shell-rooms. In the German ships it ran throughout the length of the vessel.

As to the second point, it was possible to place the protective bulkhead farther "inboard" in the German ships without cramping machinery and magazine spaces, because the ships themselves were of much greater beam. Consequently the explosion of a mine or a torpedo against the hull of the ship was far less likely to injure the protective bulkhead and so to admit water into the vitals of the ships than was the case with a British vessel. The result was that, although it is known that many German capital ships were mined and torpedoed during the war, including several at the Jutland battle, the Germans have not so far admitted that any were sunk, except the pre-Dreadnought battleship Pommern and the battle cruiser Lutzow, whose injuries from shell fire were also very extensive.

On the other hand, British capital ships, mined or torpedoed, rarely survived. The recorded instances of escape are the Inflexible (mined in the Dardanelles) and the Marlborough (torpedoed at Jutland), and in the latter case, although the torpedo struck at about the most favourable spot for the ship, she had some difficulty in reaching port.

The question will be asked why it was that British ships were under this disadvantage. The reply is that the whole of our Dreadnought battleships, designed before the War, were hampered by the absence of proper dock accommodation. The German Emperor once remarked to me at Kiel on this subject, that we had made the mistake of building our ships before we had proper dock accommodation for them, whilst in Germany they had provided the dock accommodation first and had designed the ships subsequently. He was quite right, although, since docks took a long time to construct, the German policy involved delay in shipbuilding, whereas we got ships of a type, and hence our margin of superiority in 1914.

As each successive type of Dreadnought was designed, our constructive staff were faced with the fact that if they went beyond a certain beam the number of docks available would be insufficient; and it was always a matter of great difficulty to obtain money with which to construct adequate docks. Docks make no appeal to the imagination of the public and cost a great deal of money. The result was that August 1914, found us with a superiority in ships, but woefully lacking in dock accommodation; and for this reason alone a Fleet action early in the War, resulting in considerable damage to heavy ships, would have produced embarrassing results.

It is only just to our very able constructive staff at the Admiralty to point this out; it was one of the reasons which led to the German ships being much better equipped to withstand underwater attack than were our own. It is devoutly to be hoped that this lesson will be borne in mind in the future, and adequate dock accommodation provided for the Fleet.

The matter is one of which I have considerable personal knowledge since it came within my province as Controller in 1909-11 and was also given to me to examine whilst Second Sea Lord in 1918. It is needless to say that on both occasions the necessities were pointed out with emphasis. These remarks are not out of place, as will be shown, as an introduction in a consideration of the Battle of Jutland if that action is to be rightly judged.

In following the proceedings of the Fleet it is essential to bear in mind that the time of receipt of signals, especially of reports emanating from the bridge of a ship, is not a true indication of the time at which the officer making the report began his task. A varying but considerable interval is bound to elapse; this includes the time taken to write out the report, transmit it to the wireless office or signal bridge, code it, signal it, decode it on board the receiving ship, write it out and transmit it to the bridge. The interval is greater with wireless than with visual signals.

The Grand Fleet put to sea on May 30th for the purpose of carrying out one of its periodical sweeps in the North Sea. The orders from me under which the Fleet acted were as follows:

Vice-Admiral Sir Martyn Jerram, with the 2nd Battle Squadron from Cromarty, was directed to pass through a position in Lat. 58.15 N., Long. 2.0 E., and to meet the remainder of the Battle Fleet at 2 p.m. on the 31st at position (A) in Lat. 57.45 N., Long. 4.15 E.

Vice-Admiral Sir David Beatty, with the Battle Cruiser Fleet and the 5th Battle Squadron, was directed to proceed to a position in Lat. 56.40 N., Long. 5 E., economising fuel in the destroyers as much as possible; it was expected that he would be in that position by about 2 p.m. on the 31st, after which he was directed to stand to the northward to get into visual touch with the Battle Fleet.

The Iron Duke and the 1st and 4th Battle Squadrons, together with the 3rd Battle Cruiser Squadron, and the newly commissioned light cruisers Chester and Canterbury, which had been carrying out gunnery and torpedo practices at Scapa, left that base during the evening of May 30th, and proceeded towards position (A), Lat. 57.45 N., Long. 4.15 E., having met the 2nd Battle Squadron en route at 11.15 a.m. in Lat. 58.13 N., Long. 2.42 E. Sir David Beatty had been informed before sailing that the Battle Fleet would steer towards the Horn Reef from the position in Lat. 57.45 N., Long. 4.15 E.

At 2 p.m. on May 31st the Battle Fleet was about 18 miles to the northwestward of the position (A), being actually in Lat. 57.57 N., Long. 3.45 E., in organisation No. 5, The Fleet had been slightly delayed for the purpose of enabling the usual and necessary practice of examining trawlers and other vessels met with en route to be carried out without causing the examining vessels to expend unnecessary fuel in regaining station. We had to be on our guard against scouts. The divisions were in line ahead disposed abeam to starboard in the order: 1st-6th Divisions (screened by the 4th, 11th, and 12th Flotillas) with the 4th Light Cruiser Squadron, three miles ahead of the Battle Fleet.

The cruisers, with one destroyer to each cruiser, were stationed 16 miles ahead of the Battle Fleet, spread six miles apart on a line of direction N. 40 E. and S. 40 W.; the cruisers being eight miles apart and their positions being in the order from east to west:

The attached cruisers, the Active, Boadicea, Blanche, and Bellona, were on the flanks of the Battle Fleet, and the 3rd Battle Cruiser Squadron, with the light cruisers Chester and

Canterbury, about 20 miles ahead, the whole steering S. 50 E., and zigzagging, the speed of advance being 14 knots.

The disposition of the Battle Fleet is shown below:

It may be added in further explanation that the flagships of the Battle Fleet were:

Iron Duke, Fleet-Flagship. - Flag of Admiral Sir John Jellicoe (Commander-in-Chief).

King George V. - Flagship of Vice-Admiral Sir M. Jerram, Commanding 2nd Battle Squadron.

Orion - Flagship of Rear-Admiral A. C. Leveson, Rear-Admiral in the 2nd Battle Squadron.

Superb - Flagship of Rear-Admiral A. L. Duff, Rear-Admiral in the 4th Battle Squadron.

Benbow. - Flagship of Vice-Admiral Sir Doveton Sturdee, Commanding the 4th Battle Squadron.

Colossus, - Flagship of Rear-Admiral E. F. A. Gaunt, Rear-Admiral in the 1st Battle Squadron.

Marlborough. - Flagship of Vice-Admiral Sir Cecil Burney, Commanding 1st Battle Squadron and second in command of the Grand Fleet

The Battle Cruiser Fleet and 5th Battle Squadron, with destroyers, were at 2 p.m. in Lat. 5.,46 N., Long. 4.40 E., and had turned to the northward, steering N. by E., speed 19½ knots, in the order:

The Lion and 1st Battle Cruiser Squadron in single line ahead, screened by the light cruiser Champion and 10 destroyers of the 13th Flotilla, with the 2nd Battle Cruiser Squadron in single line ahead three miles E.N.E. of the Lion, screened by six destroyers. (These destroyers belonged to the Harwich force, but happened to be at Rosyth.) The 5th Battle Squadron, in single line ahead, was five miles N.N.W. of the Lion, being screened by the light cruiser Fearless and nine destroyers of the 1st Flotilla. The Light Cruiser Squadrons formed a screen eight miles S.S.E. from the Lion, ships spread on a line of direction E.N.E. and W.S.W., five miles apart in the order from west to east:

It should be added that the flagships were:

Lion - Battle Cruiser Fleet-Flagship of Vice-Admiral Sir David Beatty.

Princess Royal - Flagship of Rear-Admiral O. de B. Brock, commanding 1st Battle Cruiser Squadron.

New Zealand. - Flagship of Rear-Admiral W. Pakenham, commanding 2nd Battle Cruiser Squadron.

Barham. - Flagship of Rear-Admiral H. Evan-Thomas, commanding 5th Battle Squadron.

The Engadine, a seaplane carrier, was stationed between the light cruisers Gloucester and Cordelia, and the light cruiser Yarmouth acted as linking ship between the Lion and the light cruiser screen.

I. – The Battle Cruiser Fleet's Action

Plan 7. Operations of Battle Cruiser Fleet, 2 p. m. to 6.15 p.m., May 31st, 1916

The first report of enemy vessels was received from the Galatea, the flagship of Commodore E. S. Alexander Sinclair, commanding the 1st Light Cruiser Squadron, who, at 2.20 p.m., sighted two enemy vessels to the E.S.E. apparently stopped and engaged in boarding a neutral steamer. Sir David Beatty, recognising the possibilities of the situation, immediately turned his fleet to the S.S.E., the course for the Horn Reef, so as to get between the enemy and his base.

At 2.35 p.m. the Galatea reported a large amount of smoke "as from a fleet" bearing E.N.E., followed by a report that the vessels were steering north. The course of the Battle Cruiser Fleet was then altered to the eastward and N.E. towards the smoke, the enemy being sighted at 3.31 p.m. and identified as five battle cruisers accompanied by destroyers.

Meanwhile the 1st and 3rd Light Cruiser Squadrons changed their direction, and, judging the situation accurately, spread to the east without waiting for orders, forming a screen in advance of the heavy ships. Our Light Cruisers sighted and engaged enemy vessels of a similar class at long range. The 2nd Light Cruiser Squadron, under Commodore W. E. Goodenough, with his broad pendant in the Southampton, came in at high speed towards the battle cruisers and formed ahead of them on an E.S.E. course, and at 3.30 p.m. sighted enemy battle cruisers bearing E.N.E. On receipt of the Galatea's report. Sir David Beatty ordered the Engadine to send up a seaplane to scout to the N.N.E.

This was the first time that seaplanes had been used for reconnaissance work with a fleet in an action, and the event is notable for that reason. The low-lying clouds made observation difficult, but the seaplane, with Flight-Lieutenant F. S. Rutland, R.N., as pilot, and Assistant Paymaster G. S. Trewin, R.N., as observer, was able, by flying low under the clouds, to identify and report four enemy light cruisers, the report being received on board the Lion at 3.30 p.m. The seaplane was under heavy fire from the light cruisers during the observation. By this time the line of battle was being formed, the 2nd Battle Cruiser Squadron forming astern of the 1st Battle Cruiser Squadron, with the destroyers of the 9th and 13th Flotillas taking station ahead. The course was E.S.E., slightly converging on the enemy, the speed 25 knots, and the range 23,000 yards. Sir David Beatty formed his ships on a line of bearing in order to clear the smoke.

The 5th Battle Squadron, which had conformed to the movements of the Battle Cruiser Fleet, was now bearing N.N.W., distant 10,000 yards; the weather was favourable, the sun being behind our ships, the wind S.E., and the visibility good.

Meanwhile, the wireless reports from the Galatea to the Lion had been intercepted on board the Iron Duke, and directions were at once given to the Battle Fleet to raise steam for full speed, the ships being at the time at short notice for full speed. The cruisers had been ordered to raise steam for full speed earlier. At 3.10 p.m. the Battle Fleet was ordered to prepare for action, and at 3.30 p.m., I directed Flag Officers of Divisions to inform their ships of the situation. The earliest reports from the Galatea had indicated the presence of light cruisers and destroyers only, and my first impression was that these vessels, on sighting the British force, would endeavour to escape via the Skagerrak, as they were to the eastward of our vessels and were consequently not in so much danger of being cut off as if they turned to the southward.

The 3rd Battle Cruiser Squadron, which was well placed for cutting the enemy off, had the anticipated move taken place, was ordered to frustrate any such intention; but at 4 p.m., on the receipt of the information of the presence of enemy battle cruisers, it was directed to reinforce Sir David Beatty. About 3.40 p.m. I received a report from Sir David Beatty that he had sighted five battle cruisers and a number of destroyers, and he gave his position at the same time.

As soon as the presence of hostile battle cruisers was reported, course was altered in the Battle Fleet to close our battle cruisers, and speed increased as rapidly as possible. By 4 p.m. the "Fleet Speed" was 20 knots, being higher than had previously been obtained. Zigzagging was abandoned on receipt of the Galatea s first report. The battleships were also directed to keep clear of the wake of the next ahead in order to prevent loss of speed from the wash.

At 3.48 p.m. the action between the battle cruisers began at a range of about 18,500 yards, fire being opened by the two forces practically simultaneously. At the commencement the fire from the German vessels was rapid and accurate, the Lion being hit twice three minutes after fire was opened, and the Lion, Tiger and Princess Royal all receiving several hits by 4 p.m.; observers on board our own ships were also of opinion that our fire was effective at that stage.

At about 4 p.m. it was evident by the accuracy of the enemy's fire that he had obtained the range of our ships, which was then about 16,000 yards. The enemy bore well abaft the beam, and course was altered slightly to the southward to confuse his fire control. Course was altered two or three times subsequently for the same purpose. The German ships frequently zigzagged for the purpose of confusing our fire control.

At this period the fire of the enemy's ships was very rapid and accurate; the Lion received several hits, the roof of one of her turrets being blown off at 4 p.m. At about 4.6 p.m. the Indefatigable was hit, approximately at the outer edge of the upper deck level in line with the after turret, by several projectiles of one salvo; an explosion followed (evidently that of a magazine) and the ship fell out of the line, sinking by the stern. She was again hit by another salvo forward, turned over and sank.

About this time (4.8 p.m.) the 5th Battle Squadron came into action, opening fire at a range between 19,000 and 20,000 yards. This slower squadron was some distance astern of the battle cruisers and, by reason partly of the smoke of the ships ahead of the enemy vessels and partly of the light to the eastward having become less favourable, difficulty was experienced in seeing the targets, not more than two ships being visible at a time. At 4.12 p.m. the range of the enemy's battle cruisers from our own was about 23,000 yards, and course was altered from S.S.E. to S.E. to close the enemy. Fire had slackened owing to the increase in range.

The tracks of torpedoes were now reported as crossing the line of our battle cruisers, and reports of sighting the periscopes of enemy submarines were also made by more than one ship.

In accordance with the general directions given by Sir David Beatty to the destroyers to attack when a favourable opportunity occurred, the Nestor, Nomad, Nicator, Narborough, Pelican, Petard, Obdurate, Nerissa, Moorsom, Morris, Turbulent and Termagant moved out at 4.15 p.m.; at the same time a similar movement took place on the part of an enemy force of one light cruiser and 15 destroyers. Both sides first steered to reach an advantageous position at the van of the opposing battle cruiser lines from which to deliver their attack, and then turned to the northward to attack. A fierce engagement at close quarters between the light forces resulted, and the enemy lost two destroyers, sunk by our vessels; and, in addition, his torpedo attack was partially frustrated; some torpedoes were fired by the enemy, two of which crossed the track of the 5th Battle Squadron, which had been turned away to avoid the attack.

During this action, which reflected the greatest credit on our destroyers, several of our attacking vessels, owing to their having dropped back towards the rear of our line, were not in a good position to attack the enemy's battle cruisers with torpedoes. The Nestor, Nomad, and Nicator, most gallantly led by Commander the Hon. E. B. S. Bingham in the Nestor, were able to press home their attack, causing the enemy's battle cruisers to turn away to avoid their torpedoes. The Nomad was damaged and forced to haul out of line before getting within torpedo range of the battle cruisers, but the Nestor and Nicator succeeded in firing torpedoes at the battle cruisers under a heavy fire from the German secondary armaments.

The Nestor was then hit, badly damaged by the fire of a light cruiser, and remained stopped between the lines. She was sunk later by the German Battle Fleet when that force appeared on the scene, but not before she had fired her last torpedo at the approaching ships. The Nomad was also sunk by the German Battle Fleet as it came up, but this vessel also fired her torpedoes at the fleet as it approached. In both these destroyers the utmost gallantry in most trying circumstances was shown by the officers and men. It is gratifying to record that a considerable proportion of the ship's company of both destroyers was picked up by German destroyers as the German Battle Fleet passed the scene. After completing her attack upon the battle cruisers, the Nicator was able to rejoin her flotilla. The Moorsom also attacked the enemy's Battle Fleet and returned. In the meantime, the Petard, Nerissa, Turbulent and Termagant succeeded in firing torpedoes at long range (7,000 yards) at the enemy's battle cruisers. For his gallantry on the occasion of this destroyer attack Commander the Hon. E. B. S. Bingham, who was rescued from the Nestor and taken prisoner by the Germans, received the Victoria Cross.

Meanwhile the engagement between the heavy ships had become very fierce, and the effect on the enemy battle cruisers began to be noticeable, the third ship in the line being observed to be on fire at 4.18 p.m., whilst our ships of the 5th Battle Squadron were also inflicting and receiving some punishment. The accuracy and rapidity of the fire from the enemy's vessels was deteriorating at this period; our own ships were much handicapped by the decreasing visibility, due partly to the use by the enemy of smoke screens, under cover of which he altered course to throw out our fire.

The flagship Barham, of the 5th Battle Squadron, received her first hit at 4.23 p.m. At about 4.26 p.m. a second disaster befell the British battle cruisers. A salvo fired from one of the enemy's battle cruisers hit the Queen Mary abreast of "Q" turret and a terrific explosion resulted, evidently caused by a magazine blowing up. The Tiger, which was following close astern of the Queen Mary, passed through the dense cloud of smoke caused by the explosion, and a great deal of material fell on her decks, but otherwise the Queen Mary had completely vanished. A few survivors from this ship and from the Indefatigable were afterwards rescued by our destroyers. The loss of these two fine ships with their splendid ships' companies was a heavy blow to the Battle Cruiser Fleet, the instantaneous nature of the disaster adding to its magnitude. (I was not aware of the loss of the Queen Mary and Indefatigable until the morning of June 1st.)

At 4.38 p.m. Commodore Goodenough, in the Southampton, Flagship of the 2nd Light Cruiser Squadron, which had been scouting ahead of the Battle Cruisers, reported that the enemy's Battle Fleet was in sight bearing S.E., and steering to the northward, and gave its position. Sir David Beatty recalled his destroyers, and on sighting the Battle Fleet at 4.42 p.m. turned the battle cruisers 16 points in succession to starboard. This movement was followed by the enemy's battle cruisers, and Sir David Beatty directed Rear-Admiral Evan-Thomas to turn his ships in succession 16 points to starboard. Commodore Goodenough led the 2nd Light Cruiser Squadron to a favourable position from which to observe the movements of the enemy's Battle Fleet, within 18,000 yards' range of the heavy ships, and, in spite of a very heavy fire, clung tenaciously to these ships and forwarded several reports of their position and movements; the skilful manner in which the Commodore, aided by his captains, handled the squadron under this fire undoubtedly saved the ships from heavy loss.

Owing to the constant manoeuvring of the ships of the 2nd Light Cruiser Squadron during the engagement, the position of the Southampton, as obtained by reckoning, was somewhat inaccurate, as was to be expected. This fact detracted from the value of the reports to me; the position of the enemy by latitude and longitude, as reported from time to time to the Iron Duke, was consequently incorrect. This discrepancy added greatly to the difficulty experienced in ascertaining the correct moment at which to deploy the Battle Fleet, the flank on which to deploy, and the direction of deployment. Such discrepancies are, however, inevitable under the conditions.

The necessary move of the battle cruisers to the southward in their pursuit of the enemy, at a speed considerably in excess of that which the Battle Fleet could attain, resulted in opening the distance between the two forces, so that at the time of the turn of Sir David Beatty's force to the northward, the Iron Duke and the Lion were over 50 miles apart, and closing at a rate of about 45 miles per hour.

As soon as the position of the Lion was known after the receipt of the report of enemy battle cruisers being in sight. Rear-Admiral the Hon. H. S. Hood was directed to proceed immediately to reinforce Sir David Beatty's force, whose position, course and speed was signalled to the Rear-Admiral. The latter officer reported his own position and gave his course and speed as S.S.E., 25 knots. At the same time the Battle Fleet was informed that our battle cruisers were in action with the enemy's battle cruisers, and an inquiry was addressed to Rear-Admiral Evan-Thomas to ascertain whether he was in company with Sir David Beatty, a reply in the affirmative being received, with a report that his squadron was in action.

At this time I was confident that, under the determined leadership of Sir David Beatty, with a force of four of our best and fastest battleships and six battle cruisers, very serious injury would be inflicted on the five battle cruisers of the enemy if they could be kept within range.

The report of the presence of the German Battle Fleet, which was communicated to our Battle Fleet, did not cause me any uneasiness in respect of the safety of our own vessels, since our ships of the 5th Battle Squadron were credited with a speed of 25 knots. I did not, however, expect that they would be able to exceed a speed of 24 knots; the information furnished to me at this time gave the designed speed of the fastest German battleships as 20.5 knots only.

Even after making full allowance for the fact that our ships were probably carrying more fuel and stores proportionately than the Germans, and giving the Germans credit for some excess over the designed speed, no doubt existed in my mind that both our battleships and our battle cruisers with Sir David Beatty could keep well out of range of the enemy's Battle Fleet, if necessary, until I was able to reinforce them. I learned later, as an unpleasant surprise, that the 5th Battle Squadron, when going at its utmost speed, found considerable difficulty in increasing its distance from the enemy's 3rd Battle Squadron, consisting of ships of the "Konig" class, and on return to Scapa I received a report from the Admiralty which credited this enemy squadron with a speed of 23 knots for a short period, this being the first intimation I had received of such a speed being attainable by them.

To return to Sir David Beatty. The action between the battle cruisers was renewed during the retirement of our ships to the northward, and the two leading ships of the 5th Battle Squadron, the Barham and Valiant, supported our battle cruisers by their fire, whilst the two rear ships of that force, the Warspite and Malaya, engaged the leading ships of the enemy's Battle Fleet as long as their guns would bear, at a range of about 19,000 yards.

The light cruiser Fearless, with destroyers of the 1st Flotilla, were now stationed ahead of the battle cruisers, and the light cruiser Champion, with destroyers of the 13th Flotilla, joined the 5th Battle Squadron. The 1st and 3rd Light Cruiser Squadrons, which had been in the rear during the southerly course, now took up a position on the starboard, or advanced, bow of the battle cruisers, the 2nd Light Cruiser Squadron being on the port quarter. During this northerly run the fire from our ships was very intermittent, owing to the weather thickening to the eastward, although the enemy was able at times to fire with some accuracy.

From 5 p.m. until after 6 p.m. the light was very much in favour of the enemy, being far clearer to the westward than to the eastward. A photograph taken on board the Malaya at 5.15 p.m. towards the western horizon established this clearly. Our destroyers, shown silhouetted against the bright horizon, were at this time at least 16,000 yards distant.

Our battle cruisers ceased fire altogether for about 30 minutes after 5.12 p.m. owing to the enemy's ships being invisible, fire being reopened at about 5.40 p.m. on the enemy's battle cruisers, three or four of which could be seen, although indistinctly, at a distance of some 14,000 yards. Between 5.42 and 5.52, however, our fire seemed to be effective, the Lion alone firing some 15 salvoes during this period.

At 5.10 p.m. the destroyer Moresby, which had rejoined the Battle Cruiser Fleet after assisting the Engadine with her seaplane, fired a torpedo at the enemy's line at a range of between 6,000 and 8,000 yards from a favourable position - two points before the beam of the enemy's leading battle cruiser.

At 5.35 p.m. the Lion's course was gradually altered from N.N.E. to N.E. in order to conform to the signalled movements and resulting position of the British Battle Fleet. The enemy's battle cruisers also gradually hauled to the eastward, being probably influenced in this movement by reports received from their light cruisers, which were by this time in contact with the light cruiser Chester and in sight of our 3rd Battle Cruiser Squadron led by Rear-Admiral Hood.

The proceedings of these vessels will now be described.

At 4 p.m., in accordance with my directions, the 3rd Battle Cruiser Squadron, under Rear-Admiral Hood, proceeded at full speed to reinforce Sir David Beatty. At 5 p.m. the squadron, comprising the Invincible (Flag), Inflexible, and Indomitable, in single line ahead in that order, with the destroyers Shark, Christopher, Ophelia, and Acasta, disposed ahead as a submarine screen, had the light cruiser Canterbury five miles ahead and the light cruiser Chester bearing N. 70 degrees W., and was steering S. by E. at 25 knots. The visibility was rapidly decreasing. According to the Indomitable's report, objects could be distinguished at a distance of 16,000 yards on some bearings, and on others at only 2,000 yards, and from then onwards, according to the same report, the visibility varied between 14,000 and 5,000 yards, although other reports place it higher at times.

At 5.30 p.m. the sound of gunfire was plainly heard to the southwestward, and the Chester turned in that direction to investigate, and, at 5.36 p.m., sighted a three funnelled light cruiser on the starboard bow, with one or two destroyers in company. The Chester challenged and, receiving no reply, altered course to west to close, judging from the appearance of the destroyer that the vessel was hostile.

As the Chester closed, course was altered to about north in order to avoid being open to torpedo attack by the destroyer on a bearing favourable to the latter. This turn brought the enemy well abaft the port beam of the Chester and on an approximately parallel course. During the turn the Chester sighted two or more light cruisers astern of the first ship, and the leading enemy light cruiser opened fire on the Chester, the latter replying immediately afterwards, at a range of about 6,000 yards. The visibility at this time, judging by the distance at which the enemy's light cruisers were sighted from the Chester, could not have exceeded 8,000 yards. The enemy's fourth salvo hit the Chester, put No. 1 gun port out of action, and killed and wounded a large proportion of the gun crews of Nos. 1, 2, and 3 port guns. The light cruisers sighted by the Chester undoubtedly belonged to one of the enemy's scouting groups stationed on the starboard bow of their battle cruisers.

Captain Lawson of the Chester, in view of the superior force to which he was opposed, altered course to the N.E. and towards the 3rd Battle Cruiser Squadron, bringing the enemy's light cruisers, all of which had opened a rapid and accurate fire, astern of him. The enemy vessels turned after the Chester, and during the unequal engagement, which lasted for 19 minutes. Captain Lawson successfully manoeuvred his ship with a view to impeding the accuracy of the hostile fire, realising that she was in no condition to engage such superior forces successfully in her damaged state.

The Chester closed the 3rd Battle Cruiser Squadron and took station N.E. of this squadron, joining the 2nd Cruiser Squadron at a later phase of the action. The ship suffered considerable casualties, having 31 killed and 50 wounded; three guns and her fire control circuits were disabled; she had four shell holes a little distance above the water line. It was on board the Chester that the second Victoria Cross of the action was earned, posthumously, by Jack Cornwell, Boy 1st Class, who was mortally wounded early in the action. This gallant lad, whose age was less than 16? years, nevertheless remained standing alone at a most exposed post, quietly awaiting orders till the end of the action, with the guns' crew, dead and wounded, all round him.

Meanwhile flashes of gunfire were seen from the 3rd Battle Cruiser Squadron at 5.40 p.m., and Rear-Admiral Hood turned his ships to starboard and brought the enemy light cruisers, which were engaging the Chester, and from which vessels the flashes came, on to his port bow. During this turn the destroyers attached to the 3rd Battle Cruiser Squadron were brought on to the port quarter of the squadron. As soon as Rear-Admiral Hood made out his position he led his squadron with the Canterbury between the enemy and the Chester, on a course about W.N.W., and at 5.55 p.m. opened an effective fire on the German light cruisers with his port guns, at a range of about 10,000 to 12,000 yards. The enemy vessels turned away from this attack and fired torpedoes at the battle cruisers; the tracks of five torpedoes were seen later from the Indomitable. At about 6.10 p.m. the Invincible and Indomitable turned to starboard to avoid these torpedoes, three of which passed very close to the latter ship, and ran alongside within 20 yards of the vessel. The Inflexible turned to port.

Meanwhile more enemy light cruisers were sighted astern of the first group, and the four British destroyers. Shark, Acasta, Ophelia and Christopher, attacked them and the large destroyer force in company with them, and were received by a heavy fire which disabled the Shark and damaged the Acasta. On board the Shark the third V.C. of the action was earned by her gallant captain, Commander Loftus Jones, this award also being, I regret to say, posthumous.

The attack of the British destroyers was carried out with great gallantry and determination, and having frustrated the enemy's torpedo attack on the 3rd Battle Cruiser Squadron, Commander Loftus Jones turned his division to regain his position on our battle cruisers. At this moment three German vessels came into sight out of the mist and opened a heavy fire, further disabling the Shark and causing many casualties on board; Commander Loftus Jones was amongst those wounded. Lieut-Commander J. O. Barron, commanding the Acasta, came to the assistance of the Shark, but Commander Loftus Jones refused to imperil a second destroyer, and directed the Acasta to leave him. The Shark then became the target for the German ships and destroyers. Commander Loftus Jones, who was assisting to keep the only undamaged gun in action, ordered the last torpedo to be placed in the tube and fired; but whilst this was being done the torpedo was hit by a shell and exploded, causing many casualties.

Those gallant officers and men in the Shark who still survived, continued to fight the only gun left in action, the greatest heroism being exhibited. The captain was now wounded again, his right leg being taken off by a shell; but he still continued to direct the fire, until the condition of the Shark and the approach of German destroyers made it probable that the ship would fall into the hands of the enemy, when he gave orders for her to be sunk, countermanding this order shortly afterwards on realising that her remaining gun could still be fought. Shortly afterwards she was hit by two torpedoes, and sank with her colours flying.

Only six survivors were picked up the next morning by a Danish steamer. In recognition of the great gallantry displayed, the whole of the survivors were awarded the Distinguished Service Medal. Their names are: W. C. R. Griffin, Petty Officer, C. Filleul, Stoker Petty Officer, C. C. Hope, A.B., C. H. Smith, A.B., T. O. G. Howell, A.B., T. W. Swan, Stoker.

At this point it is well to turn to the proceedings of our advanced cruiser line, which at 5 p.m. was about 16 miles ahead of the Battle Fleet, the latter being at that time in Lat. 57.24 N., Long. 5.12 E., steering S.E. by S. at 20 knots. It should be noted that, owing to decreasing visibility, which was stated in reports from the cruisers to be slightly above six miles, the cruisers on the starboard flank had closed in and were about six miles apart by 5.30 p.m. The 3rd Battle Cruiser Squadron was about 16 miles due east of the advanced cruiser line, but was steering more to the southward on a converging course at a speed of about five knots faster.

At 5.40 p.m. firing was heard ahead by the cruiser line, and shortly afterwards ships were seen from the Minotaur to be emerging from the mist. Rear-Admiral Heath, the senior officer of the cruiser line, had recalled the ships of the 2nd Cruiser Squadron on hearing the firing and had ordered them to form single line ahead on the Minotaur. He then made the signal to engage the enemy, namely, the ships in sight ahead; but before fire was opened they replied to his challenge and were identified as the ships of the 3rd Battle Cruiser Squadron, engaged with the enemy's light cruisers and steering to the westward.

At 5.47 p.m. the Defence, with the Warrior astern, sighted on a S. by W. bearing (namely, on the starboard bow) three or four enemy light cruisers, and course was altered three points to port, bringing them nearly on a beam bearing. Rear-Admiral Sir Robert Arbuthnot, in the Defence, then signalled "Commence fire." Each ship fired three salvoes at a three-funnelled cruiser. The salvoes fell short, and the Defence altered course to starboard, brought the enemy first ahead, and then to a bearing on the port bow, evidently with the intention of closing. The latter alteration of course was made at 6.1 p.m., and by this time projectiles from the light cruisers were falling in close proximity to the Defence and the Warrior. These ships opened fire with their port guns at 6.5 p.m. and shortly afterwards passed close across the bows of the Lion from port to starboard. One light cruiser, probably the Wiesbaden, was hit by the second salvoes of both ships, appeared to be badly crippled, and nearly stopped. Our ships continued to close her until within 5,500 yards.

From about 6.10 p.m. onwards they had come under fire of guns of heavy calibre from the enemy's battle cruisers, but Sir Robert Arbuthnot, as gallant and determined an officer as ever lived, was evidently bent on finishing off his opponent, and held on, probably not realising in the gathering smoke and mist that the enemy's heavy ships were at fairly close range.

At about 6.16 p.m. the Defence was hit by two salvoes in quick succession, which caused her magazines to blow up and the ship disappeared. The loss of so valuable an officer as Sir Robert Arbuthnot and so splendid a ship's company as the officers and men of the Defence was a heavy blow. The Warrior was very badly damaged by shell fire, her engine-rooms being flooded; but Captain Molteno was able to bring his ship out of action, having first seen the Defence disappear. From diagrams made in the Warrior it appears that the German battle cruisers turned 16 points (possibly with a view either to close their Battle Fleet or to come to the aid of the disabled Wiesbaden), engaged the Defence and Warrior, and then turned back again.

This supposition is confirmed by sketches taken on board the Duke of Edinburgh at the same time. Owing to the smoke and the mist, however, it was difficult to state exactly what occurred. From the observations on board the Warrior it is certain that the visibility was much greater in her direction from the enemy's line, than it was in the direction of the enemy from the Warrior. Although the Defence and Warrior were being hit frequently, those on board the Warrior could only see the ships firing at them very indistinctly, and it is probable that the low visibility led to Sir Robert Arbuthnot not realising that he was at comparatively short range from the German battle cruisers until he was already under an overwhelming fire.

The Warrior passed astern of the 5th Battle Squadron at the period when the steering gear of the Warspite had become temporarily disabled.

The Duke of Edinburgh, the ship next to the westward of the Defence and the Warrior in the cruiser screen, had turned to close these ships when they became engaged with the enemy's light cruisers in accordance with a signal from the Defence. The Duke of Edinburgh joined in the engagement, but, on sighting the Lion on her starboard bow, did not follow the other ships across the bows of the battle cruisers, as to do so would have seriously incommoded these vessels; she turned to port to a parallel course and eventually joined the 2nd Cruiser Squadron.

The Black Prince was observed from the Duke of Edinburgh to turn some 12 points to port at the same time that the Duke of Edinburgh turned, but her subsequent movements are not clear; the German accounts of the action stated that the Black Prince was sunk by gunfire at the same time as the Defence, but she was not seen to be in action at this time by any of our vessels, and, moreover, a wireless signal, reporting a submarine in sight and timed 8.48 p.m., was subsequently received from her. It is probable that the Black Prince passed to the rear of the Battle Fleet at about 6.30 p.m., and that during the night she found herself close to one of the German battle squadrons, and was sunk then by superior gunfire. In support of this theory, the German account mentions that a cruiser of the "Cressy" type was sunk in that manner during the night. None of the ships of this class was present during the engagement, but the Black Prince might well have been mistaken for a ship of this type in the circumstances.

We left the 3rd Battle Cruiser Squadron at about 6.10 p.m. at the termination of their engagement with enemy light cruisers, turning to avoid torpedoes fired at them. At about this time Rear-Admiral Hood sighted the Lion and the 1st Battle Cruiser Squadron, and at about 6.16 p.m. hoisted the signal to his squadron to form single line ahead, and turned to take station ahead of the Lion and to engage the hostile battle cruisers, which at 6.20 p.m. were sighted at a range of 8,600 yards.

A furious engagement ensued for a few minutes, and the fire of the squadron was judged by those on board the Invincible to be very effective. Rear-Admiral Hood, who was on the bridge of the Invincible with Captain Cay, hailed Commander Dannreuther, the gunnery officer in the fore control, at about 6.30 p.m., saying, "Your firing is very good. Keep at it as quickly as you can; every shot is telling." At about 6.34 p.m. the Invincible, which had already been hit more than once by heavy shell without appreciable damage, was struck in "Q" turret. The shell apparently burst inside the turret, as Commander Dannreuther saw the roof blown off. A very heavy explosion followed immediately, evidently caused by the magazine blowing up, and the ship broke in half and sank at once, only two officers, including Commander Dannreuther, and four men being subsequently picked up by the destroyer Badger. The British Navy sustained a most serious loss in Rear-Admiral the Hon. Horace Hood, one of the most distinguished of our younger flag officers, and in Captain Cay and the officers and men of his flagship.

The difficulties of distinguishing enemy ships even at the close range of this engagement is revealed by the fact that the officers in the Invincible and Indomitable were under the impression that they were engaging battle cruisers, whilst officers in the Inflexible, stationed between these two ships in the line, reported that her fire was being directed at a battleship of the "Kaiser" or "Konig" class, and that only one ship could be seen.

Just before the loss of the Invincible, the 3rd Light Cruiser Squadron, commanded by Rear-Admiral Napier, had carried out an effective torpedo attack on the enemy's battle cruisers; both the light cruisers Falmouth and Yarmouth fired torpedoes at the leading battle cruiser. It was thought that one of the torpedoes hit its mark as a heavy underwater explosion was felt at this time.

After the loss of the Invincible, the Inflexible was left as leader of the line, and as soon as the wreck of the Invincible had been passed, course was altered two points to starboard to close the enemy ships, which were disappearing in the mist. A further turn to starboard for the same purpose was made, but at this time, 6.50 p.m., the battle cruisers being clear of the leading battleships (which were bearing N.N.W. three miles distant), Sir David Beatty signalled the 3rd Battle Cruiser Squadron to prolong the line of the battle cruisers, and the Inflexible and Indomitable took station astern of the New Zealand.

The course of events can now be traced with accuracy. The Chester with the 3rd Battle Cruiser Squadron, which by 5.40 p.m. had got ahead of the Battle Fleet's cruiser screen, encountered some of the light cruisers composing the enemy's screen, and engaged them, and, in doing so, drew the enemy's light cruisers towards the 3rd Battle Cruiser Squadron, which, with the Canterbury and destroyers, turned to about W.N.W. to assist the Chester and to engage the enemy vessels.

In the course of this movement a destroyer attack was made by four British destroyers on the enemy's light cruisers. This attack was apparently thought by the Germans to come from the flotillas with the Battle Fleet, as far as can be judged from their report of the action; the ships of the 3rd Battle Cruiser Squadron were undoubtedly mistaken by their vessels for the van of our Battle Fleet, since mention is made in the German report of the British Battle Fleet having been sighted at this time by the German light forces, steering in a westerly or northwesterly direction. The mistaken idea caused the van of the High Sea Fleet to turn off to starboard.

So far from our Battle Fleet being on a westerly course at this time, the fact is that our Battle Fleet held its southeasterly course before, through, and immediately subsequent to deployment, gradually hauling round afterwards, first through south to southwest, and, then, to west, but it was not until 8 p.m. that a westerly course was being steered.

The only point that is not clear is the identity of the light cruiser engaged and seriously damaged by the 3rd Battle Cruiser Squadron. The ship engaged by the Defence and Warrior was apparently the Wiesbaden. It seems to be impossible that the 3rd Battle Cruiser Squadron engaged the same vessel, and it is more likely to have been another light cruiser in the enemy's screen. The two engagements took place at almost the same time, the 3rd Battle Cruiser Squadron opening fire at 5.55 p.m., and the Defence and the Warrior (the 1st Cruiser Squadron) commencing their engagement with the starboard guns at about 5.50 p.m. and continuing it with the port guns at 6.6 p.m. It is hardly possible, even in the conditions of low visibility that prevailed, that the two squadrons could have been engaging the same vessel.

Mention should be made here of the work of the destroyer Onslow, commanded by Lieut.-Commander J. C. Tovey, which at 6.5 p.m. sighted an enemy's light cruiser in a position on the bows of the Lion and favourable for torpedo attack on that ship. The Onslow closed and engaged the light cruiser with gunfire at ranges between 2,000 and 4,000 yards, and then, although severely damaged by shell fire, succeeded in closing a German battle cruiser to attack with torpedoes; she was struck by a heavy shell before more than one torpedo could be fired. Lieut.-Commander Tovey thought that his order to fire all torpedoes had been carried out, and finding that this was not the case, closed the light cruiser and fired a torpedo at her, and then sighting the Battle Fleet fired the remaining torpedoes at battleships. The Onslow's engines then stopped, but the damaged destroyer Defender, Lieut.-Commander Palmer, closed her at 7.15 p.m. and took her in tow under a heavy fire, and, in spite of bad weather during the night and the damaged condition of both destroyers, brought her back to home waters, transferring her on June 1st to the care of a tug.

An English vessel battles with a Barbary ship and two galleys in Tripoli in 1676. Painting by Willem van de Velde the Younger, 1677.

13 - The Battle of Jutland (Cont.)

II. – The Battle Fleet in Action

The "plot" made on the reports received between 5 and 6 p.m. from Commodore Goodenough, of the 2nd Light Cruiser Squadron, and the report at 4.45 p.m. from Sir David Beatty in the Lion giving the position of the enemy's Battle Fleet, showed that we, of the Battle Fleet, might meet the High Sea Fleet approximately ahead and that the cruiser line ahead of the Battle Fleet would sight the enemy nearly ahead of the centre. Obviously, however, great reliance could not be placed on the positions given by the ships of the Battle Cruiser Fleet, which had been in action for two hours and frequently altering course. I realised this, but when contact actually took place it was found that the positions given were at least twelve miles in error when compared with the Iron Duke's reckoning. The result was that the enemy's Battle Fleet appeared on the starboard bow instead of ahead, as I had expected, and contact also took place earlier than was anticipated. There can be no doubt as to the accuracy of the reckoning on board the Iron Duke, as the movements of that ship could be "plotted" with accuracy after leaving Scapa Flow, there being no disturbing elements to deal with.

The first accurate information regarding the position of affairs was contained in a signal from the Black Prince, of the 1st Cruiser Squadron (the starboard wing ship of the cruiser screen), which was timed 5.40 p.m., but received by me considerably later, and in which it was reported that battle cruisers were in sight, bearing south, distant five miles. It was assumed by me that these were our own vessels.

Prior to this, in view of the rapid decrease in visibility, I had directed Captain Dreyer, my Flag-Captain, to cause the range-finder operators to take ranges of ships on bearings in every direction and to report the direction in which the visibility appeared to be the greatest. My object was to ascertain the most favourable bearing in which to engage the enemy should circumstances admit of a choice being exercised. Captain Dreyer reported that the visibility appeared to be best to the southward.

At 5.45 p.m. the Comus (Captain Hotham), of the 4th Light Cruiser Squadron, which was stationed three miles ahead of the Battle Fleet, reported heavy gunfire on a southerly bearing, i.e., three points from ahead, and shortly afterwards flashes of gunfire were visible bearing south-southwest although no ships could be seen.

At about 5.50 p.m. I received a wireless signal from Sir Robert Arbuthnot, of the 1st Cruiser Squadron, reporting having sighted ships in action bearing south-southwest and steering north-east. There was, however, no clue as to the identity of these ships. It was in my mind that they might be the opposing battle cruisers.

At 5.55 p.m. a signal was made by me to Admiral Sir Cecil Burney, leading the starboard wing division in the Marlborough, inquiring what he could see. The reply was: "Gun flashes and heavy gunfire on the starboard bow." This reply was received at about 6.5 p.m.

The uncertainty which still prevailed as to the position of the enemy's Battle Fleet and its formation caused me to continue in the Battle Fleet on the course southeast by south at a speed of 20 knots, in divisions line ahead disposed abeam to starboard, the Iron Duke at 6 p.m. being in Lat. 57.11 N., Long. 5.89 E.

The information so far received had not even been sufficient to justify me in altering the bearing of the guides of columns from the Iron Duke preparatory to deployment, and they were still, therefore, on the beam. The destroyers also were still disposed ahead in their screening formation, as it was very desirable to decide on the direction of deployment before stationing them for action.

At 5.56 p.m. Admiral Sir Cecil Burney reported strange vessels in sight bearing south-southwest and steering east, and at 6 p.m. he reported them as British battle cruisers three to four miles distant, the Lion being the leading ship.

This report was made by searchlight and consequently reached me shortly after 6 p.m., but as showing the interval that elapses between the intention to make a signal and the actual receipt of it (even under conditions where the urgency is apparent, no effort is spared to avoid delay, and the signal staff is efficient), it is to be noted that whereas the report gave the bearing of our vessels as south-southwest, notes taken on board the Colossus placed our battle cruisers one point on the starboard bow of that ship, that is, on a south-southeast bearing and distant two miles at 6.5 p.m.

Shortly after 6 p.m. we sighted strange vessels bearing southwest from the Iron Duke at a distance of about five miles. They were identified as our battle cruisers, steering east across the bows of the Battle Fleet. Owing to the mist it was not possible to make out the number of ships that were following the Lion.

At this stage there was still great uncertainty as to the position of the enemy's Battle Fleet; flashes of gunfire were visible from ahead round to the starboard beam, and the noise was heavy and continuous. Our cruisers ahead seemed to be hotly engaged, but the fact that they were not closing the Battle Fleet indicated to me that their opponents could hardly be battleships.

In order to take ground to starboard, with a view to clearing up the situation without altering the formation of the Battle Fleet, a signal had been made to the Battle Fleet at 6.2 p.m. to alter course leaders together, the remainder in succession, to south (a turn of three points). Speed was at the same time reduced to 18 knots to allow of the ships closing up into station. Immediately afterwards it became apparent by the sound of the heavy firing that enemy's heavy ships must be in close proximity, and the Lion, which was sighted at this moment, signalled at 6.6 p.m. that the enemy's battle cruisers bore southeast. Meanwhile, at about 5.50 p.m., I had received a wireless report from Commodore Goodenough, commanding the 2nd Light Cruiser Squadron, to the effect that the enemy's battle cruisers bore southwest from their Battle Fleet; in other words, that his Battle Fleet bore northeast from his battle cruisers.

In view of the report from Sir Cecil Burney that our battle cruisers were steering east, and observing that Sir David Beatty reported at 6.6 p.m. that the enemy's battle cruisers bore southeast, it appeared from Commodore Goodenough's signal that the enemy's Battle Fleet must be ahead of his battle cruisers. On the other hand, it seemed to me almost incredible that the Battle Fleet could have passed the battle cruisers. The conflicting reports added greatly to the perplexity of the situation, and I determined to hold on until matters became clearer.

The conviction was, however, forming in. my mind that I should strike the enemy's Battle Fleet on a bearing a little on the starboard bow, and in order to be prepared for deployment I turned the Fleet to a southeast course, leaders together and the remainder in succession, and the destroyer flotillas were directed by signal, at 6.8 p.m., to take up the destroyer position No. 1 for battle.

There was, however, a very short interval between this signal to the destroyers and the signal for deployment, and consequently the destroyers did not reach their positions before deployment. The subsequent alterations of course to the southward and westward added to their difficulties and delayed them greatly in gaining their stations at the van of the Fleet after deployment. The correct position for the two van flotillas on deployment was three miles ahead of the Fleet, but slightly on the engaged bow.

At 6.1 p.m., immediately on sighting the Lion, a signal had been made to Sir David Beatty inquiring the position of the enemy's Battle Fleet. This signal was repeated at 6.10 p.m., and at 6.14 p.m. he signalled: "Have sighted the enemy's Battle Fleet bearing south-southwest"; this report gave me the first information on which I could take effective action for deployment.

At 6.15 p.m. Rear-Admiral Hugh Evan-Thomas, in the Barham, commanding the 5th Battle Squadron, signalled by wireless that the enemy's Battle Fleet was in sight, bearing south-southeast. The distance was not reported in either case, but in view of the low visibility, I concluded it could not be more than some five miles. Sir Cecil Burney had already reported the 5th Battle Squadron at 6.7 p.m. as in sight, bearing southwest from the Marlborough.

The first definite information received on board the Fleet-Flagship of the position of the enemy's Battle Fleet did not, therefore, come in until 6.14 p.m., and the position given placed it thirty degrees before the starboard beam of the Iron Duke, or fifty-nine degrees before the starboard beam of the Marlborough, and apparently in close proximity. There was no time to lose, as there was evident danger of the starboard wing column of the Battle Fleet being engaged by the whole German Battle Fleet before deployment could be effected. So at 6.16 p.m. a signal was made to the Battle Fleet to form line of battle on the port wing column, on a course southeast by east, it being assumed that the course of the enemy was approximately the same as that of our battle cruisers.

Speed was at the same time reduced to 14 knots to admit of our battle cruisers passing ahead of the Battle Fleet, as there was danger of the fire of the Battle Fleet being blanketed by them.

During the short interval, crowded with events, that had elapsed since the first flashes and sound of gunfire had been noted on board the Iron Duke, the question of most urgent importance before me had been the direction and manner of deployment.

As the evidence accumulated that the enemy's Battle Fleet was on our starboard side, but on a bearing well before the beam of the Iron Duke, the point for decision was whether to form line of battle on the starboard or on the port wing column. My first and natural impulse was to form on the starboard wing column in order to bring the Fleet into action at the earliest possible moment, but it became increasingly apparent, both from the sound of gunfire and the reports from the Lion and the Barham, that the High Sea Fleet was in such close proximity and on such a bearing as to create obvious disadvantages in such a movement. I assumed that the German destroyers would be ahead of their Battle Fleet, and it was clear that, owing to the mist, the operations of destroyers attacking from a commanding position in the van would be much facilitated; it would be suicidal to place the Battle Fleet in a position where it might be open to attack by destroyers during such a deployment, as such an event would throw the Fleet into confusion at a critical moment.

The further points that occurred to me were, that if the German ships were as close as seemed probable, there was considerable danger of the 1st Battle Squadron, and especially the Marlborough's Division, being severely handled by the concentrated fire of the High Sea Fleet before the remaining divisions could get into line to assist. The 1st Battle Squadron was composed of many of our weakest ships, with only indifferent protection as compared with the German capital ships, and an interval of at least four minutes would elapse between each division coming into line astern of the sixth division and a further interval before the guns could be directed on to the ship selected and their fire become effective after so large a change of course.

The final disadvantage would be that it appeared, from the supposed position of the High Sea Fleet, that the van of the enemy would have a very considerable "overlap" if the deployment took place on the starboard wing division, whereas this would not be the case with deployment on the port wing column. The overlap would necessitate a large turn of the starboard wing division to port to prevent the "T" being crossed, and each successive division coming into line would have to make this turn, in addition to the 8-point turn required to form the line. I therefore decided to deploy on the first, the port wing, division.

The further knowledge which I gained of the actual state of affairs after the action confirmed my view that the course adopted was the best in the circumstances.

The reports from the ships of the starboard wing division show that the range of the van of the enemy's Battle Fleet at the moment of deployment was about 18,000 yards. The fleets were converging rapidly, with the High Sea Fleet holding a position of advantage such as would enable it to engage effectively, first the unsupported starboard division, and subsequently succeeding divisions as they formed up astern. It is to be observed that it would take some twenty minutes to complete the formation of the line of battle.

The German gunnery was always good at the start, and their ships invariably found the range of a target with great rapidity, and it would have been very bad tactics to give them such an initial advantage, not only in regard to gunnery but also in respect of torpedo attack, both from ships and from destroyers.

A subsequent study of the reports and the signals received has admitted of the accompanying plans being drawn up.

The reports on being reviewed fit in very well, and show clearly how great would have been the objections to deploying to starboard. It will be seen that the bearings of the enemy Battle Fleet, as given by the Lion and the Barham at 6.14 and 6.15 respectively, give a fair "cut," and the bearing on which the Marlborough opened fire enables the position of the Battle Fleet to be placed with considerable accuracy.

Assuming that the German Battle Fleet was steaming at 17 knots on an easterly course between 6.14 and 6.31, it will be observed that at the latter time it bore 21 degrees before the starboard beam of the Iron Duke at a range of 12,000 yards. The Iron Duke actually engaged the leading battleship at this time on a bearing 20 degrees before the starboard beam at a range of 12,000 yards. The accuracy of the "plot" is therefore confirmed, so far as confirmation is possible. It appears certain that between about 6.0 p.m. and 6.16 p.m. the German battle cruisers turned 16 points towards their Battle Fleet, and again turned 16 points to their original course. This is borne out by observations on board the Warrior, which ship was being engaged by the starboard guns of enemy vessels. The German account also shows such a turn at this period.

Rear-Admiral Evan-Thomas, commanding the 5th Battle Squadron, had sighted the Marlborough at 6.6 p.m. and the remainder of the 6th Division of the Battle Fleet a little later. Not seeing any other columns, he concluded that the Marlborough was leading the whole line, and decided to take station ahead of that ship. At 6.19 p.m., however, other battleships were sighted, and Admiral Evan-Thomas realised that the

Fleet was deploying to port, the 6th Division being the starboard wing column. He then determined to make a large turn of his squadron to port, in order to form astern of the 6th Division, which by this time had also turned to port to form line of battle. During the turn, which was very well executed, the ships of the 5th Battle Squadron were under fire of the enemy's leading battleships, but the shooting was not good, and our vessels received little injury.

Unfortunately, however, the helm of the Warspite jammed, and that ship, continuing her turn through sixteen points came under a very heavy fire and received considerable injury. The disabled Warrior happened to be in close proximity at this time, and the turn of the Warspite had the effect for the moment of diverting attention from the Warrior, so that the latter vessel got clear.

The Warspite was well extricated by Captain Phillpotts from an unpleasant position and was steered to the northward to make good damages, and eventually, in accordance with directions from Rear-Admiral Evan-Thomas, returned independently to Rosyth, considerably down by the stern owing to damage aft, but otherwise not much injured.

By 6.38 p.m. the remaining ships of the 5th Battle Squadron were in station astern of the Agincourt (1st Battle Squadron), the last ship of the line.

At 6.33 p.m., as soon as the battle cruisers had passed clear, the speed of the Battle Fleet was increased to 17 knots, and this speed was subsequently maintained. The reduction of speed to 14 knots during the deployment caused some "bunching" at the rear of the line as the signal did not get through quickly. The reduction had, however, to be maintained until the battle cruisers had formed ahead.

Experience at all Fleet exercises had shown the necessity for keeping a reserve of some three knots of speed in hand in the case of a long line of ships, in order to allow of station being kept in the line under conditions of action, when ships were making alterations of course to throw out enemy's fire, to avoid torpedoes, or when other independent action on the part of single ships, or of divisions of ships, became necessary, as well as to avoid excessive smoke from the funnels; for this reason the Fleet speed during the action was fixed at 17 knots. The experience of the 1st Battle Squadron, in which some ships had at times to steam at 20 knots, is proof of the necessity for this reserve.

At 6.14. p.m. the enemy's salvoes were falling near ships of the 1st Battle Squadron, and the Marlborough's Division of the Battle Squadron became engaged with some ships of the enemy's Battle Fleet at 6.17 p.m. immediately after turning for the deployment. At this time fire was opened by the Marlborough on a ship stated to be of the "Kaiser" class, at a range of 18,000 yards and on a bearing 20 degrees abaft the starboard beam; this knowledge enables us to deduce the position of the van of the German Battle Fleet at this time.

Our rear ships were now able to make out the enemy's Fleet steering to the eastward, the battle cruisers leading, followed by the Battle Fleet in single line, the order being, four ships of the "Konig" class in the van, followed by ships of the "Kaiser" and "Heligoland" classes, the rear of the line being invisible. A report that had reached me at 4.48 p.m. from the Commodore of the 2nd Light Cruiser Squadron indicated that ships of the "Kaiser" class were in the van of the Battle Fleet. The order of the Fleet may have been changed subsequent to this report, but there is no doubt that ships of the "Konig" class led during the Fleet action. The point is not, however, of importance.

At about 6.38 p.m. the 6th Division was in line and our deployment was complete.

Enemy shells had been falling close to the Colossus and her 5th Division since 6.18 p.m., and these ships opened fire at 6.30 p.m.; but the conditions of visibility made it difficult to distinguish the enemy's battleships.

At 6.23 p.m. a three-funnelled enemy vessel had passed down the line, on the starboard, or engaged, side of our Fleet, apparently partly disabled. Her identity could not at the time be clearly established, but her German colours were flying and she was in a position for attacking the Battle Fleet by torpedoes; at 6.20 p.m. the Iron Duke fired a few turret salvoes at her; she was fired at with turret guns by other vessels and was seen to sink at the rear of the line.

At this time, owing to smoke and mist, it was most difficult to distinguish friend from foe, and quite impossible to form an opinion on board the Iron Duke, in her position towards the centre of the line, as to the formation of the enemy's Fleet. The identity of ships in sight on the starboard beam was not even sufficiently clear for me to permit of fire being opened; but at 6.30 p.m. it became certain that our own battle cruisers had drawn ahead of the Battle Fleet and that the vessels then before the beam were battleships of the "Konig" class. The order was, therefore, given to open fire, and the Iron Duke engaged what appeared to be the leading battleship at a range of 12,000 yards on a bearing 20° before the starboard beam; other ships of the 3rd and 4th Divisions (the 4th Battle Squadron) opened fire at about the same time, and the van divisions (2nd Battle Squadron) very shortly afterwards; these latter ships reported engaging enemy battle cruisers as well as battleships.

The fire of the Iron Duke, which came more directly under my personal observation, was seen to be immediately effective, the third and fourth salvoes fired registering several palpable hits. It appeared as if all the enemy ships at that time in sight from the Iron Duke (not more than three or four, owing to smoke and mist) were receiving heavy punishment, and the second battleship was seen to turn out of the line badly on fire, and settling by the stern. A large number of observers in the Thunderer, Benbow, Barham, Marne, Morning Star and Magic stated afterwards that they saw this ship blow up at 6.50 p.m.

The visibility was very variable and perhaps averaged about 12,000 yards to the southward, though much less on other bearings, but ranges could not at times be obtained from the range-finders of the Iron Duke at a greater distance than 9,000 yards, although at 7.15 p.m., in a temporary clear channel through the mist, good ranges of 15,000 yards were obtained of a battleship at which four salvoes were fired by the Iron Duke before she was again hidden by smoke and mist. The very baffling light was caused principally by low misty clouds, but partly also by the heavy smoke from the funnels and guns of the opposing Fleets. The direction of the wind was about west-southwest with a force 2, causing the enemy's funnel smoke to drift towards our line, thus further obscuring our view of his Fleet.

The visibility at the rear of the battle line was apparently greater than in the centre at about 7 p.m., and the enemy's fire, which was probably being concentrated on our rear ships, was more accurate at this period, but quite ineffective, only one ship, the Colossus, being hit by gunfire, although numerous projectiles were falling new the ships of the 1st and 5th Battle Squadrons.

Whilst observers in ships in the van and centre of the Battle Fleet could see only three or four enemy vessels at any one time, those in the ships of the rear division did occasionally see as many as eight, and were consequently better able to distinguish the formation and movements of the enemy's Battle Fleet. It was not possible, owing to the small number of ships in sight, due to smoke and mist, to distribute the fire of the battleships by signal in the customary manner; the only course to adopt was for the captains to direct the fire of their guns on to any target which they could distinguish.

The course of the Fleet on deployment had been southeast by east, as already stated, but the van had hauled on to southeast without signal shortly after deployment in order to close the enemy, and at 6.50 p.m., as the range was apparently opening, the course was altered by signal to south "by divisions" in order to close the enemy. The King George V., leading the van of the Battle Fleet, had just anticipated this signal by turning to south. The alteration was made "by divisions" instead of "in succession" in order that the enemy should be closed more rapidly by the whole Battle Fleet.

This large turn (of four points) "by divisions" involved some small amount of "blanketing" of the rear ships of one division by the leading ships of that next astern, and at one time the Thunderer was firing over the bows of the Iron Duke, causing some slight inconvenience on the bridge of the latter ship; the "blanketing," however, was unavoidable and the loss of fire involved was inappreciable.

At 6.45 p.m. one or two torpedoes crossed the track of the rear of our battle line, and the Marlborough altered course to avoid one. They were apparently fired, at long range, by enemy destroyers, which were barely visible to the ships in rear and quite invisible to those on board the Iron Duke. They might, however, have been fired by enemy battleships which were within torpedo range, or by a submarine, the Revenge reporting that it was thought that one had been rammed by that ship. The tracks of some of the torpedoes were seen by the observers stationed aloft, and were avoided by very skilful handling of the ships by their captains.

At 6.45 p.m., however, a heavy explosion occurred under the fore bridge of the Marlborough, abreast the starboard forward hydraulic engine-room. The ship took up a list of some seven degrees to starboard, but continued in action so effectively that she avoided three more torpedoes shortly afterwards, re-opened fire at 7.3 p.m., and at 7.12 p.m. fired fourteen rapid salvoes at a ship of the "Konig" class, hitting her so frequently that she was seen to turn out of line.

The signal from Sir Cecil Burney of the damage to his flagship stated that the vessel had been struck by a "mine or torpedo." It was assumed by me that a torpedo had hit the ship, as so many vessels had passed over the same locality without injury from mine. This proved to be the case, the track of this torpedo not having been sufficiently visible to enable Captain Ross to avoid it.

The fact of the tracks of so many of the enemy's torpedoes being visible was a matter of great surprise to me, and I think to other officers. Reports had been prevalent that the Germans had succeeded in producing a torpedo which left little or no track on the surface. The information as to the visibility of the tracks did not reach me until the return of the Fleet to harbour, as although one torpedo was reported by observers on board the destroyer Oak to have passed close ahead of the Iron Duke at about 7.35 p.m., finishing its run 2,000 yards beyond that ship, and a second was observed by the Benbow to pass apparently ahead of the Iron Duke at 8.30 p.m., neither of them was seen on board the flagship by the trained look-outs specially stationed for the purpose.

Some ten minutes after the alteration of course to south, a signal was made to the 2nd Battle Squadron to take station ahead of the Iron Duke and for the 1st Battle Squadron to form astern. This signal had, however, been already anticipated by the vessels ahead of the Iron Duke in accordance with the general battle orders giving discretionary powers to the commanders of squadrons, and the line had been partly reformed before the signal was made.

An incident occurred at about 6.47 p.m. which was an indication of the spirit prevailing in the Fleet, of which it is impossible to speak too highly. The destroyer Acasta, which had been badly hit aft during her attack on enemy light cruisers in company with the Shark and had her engines disabled, was passed by the Fleet. Her commanding officer, Lieut.-Commander J. O. Barron, signalled the condition of his ship to the Iron Duke as that ship passed, leaving the Acasta on her starboard or engaged side. The ship's company was observed to be cheering each ship as they passed. It is satisfactory to relate that this destroyer and her gallant ship's company were subsequently brought into Aberdeen, being assisted by the Nonsuch.

Shortly after 6.55 p.m. the Iron Duke passed the wreck of a ship with the bow and stern standing out of the water, the centre portion apparently resting on the bottom, with the destroyer Badger picking up survivors. It was thought at first that this was the remains of a German light cruiser, but inquiry of the Badger elicited the lamentable news that the wreck was that of the Invincible. It was assumed at the time that she had been sunk either by a mine or by a torpedo, and, in view of the safe passage of other ships in her vicinity, the latter appeared to be the more probable cause of her loss. Subsequent information, however, showed that she was destroyed by gunfire, causing her magazines to explode, as already recorded.

At 7 p.m. Sir David Beatty signalled reporting that the enemy was to the westward.

Our alteration of course to south had, meanwhile, brought the enemy's line into view once more, and between 7.0 and 7.30 p.m. the Battle Fleet was again in action with battleships and also battle cruisers, as they could be distinguished in the haze, which at that period was very baffling. The range varied from as much as 15,000 yards at the van to as little as 8,500 in the rear, this difference in range indicating that the enemy's Fleet was turning to the westward, as shown in the accompanying plan.

In spite of the difficult conditions the fire of many of our battleships was very effective at this period. Some instances may be given. At 7.15 p.m. the Iron Duke, as already mentioned, engaged a hostile battleship at 15,000 yards' range and on a bearing 74 degrees from right ahead. At 7.20 she trained her guns on a battle cruiser of "Lutzow" type, abaft the beam, which hid herself by a destroyer smoke screen; at 7.17 p.m. the King George V. opened fire on a vessel, taken to be the leading ship in the enemy's line at a range of about 18,000 yards; the Orion at a battleship (Calliope reported at 7.18 p.m.: "Two enemy battleships, "Konig" class, engaged by Orion's division, observed to be heavily on fire."); the St. Vincent was "holding her target (a battleship) effectively till 7.26 p.m., the range being between 10,000 and 9,500 yards"; the Agincourt at 7.6 p.m. opened fire at 11,000 yards on one of four battleships that showed clearly out of the mist, and judged that at least four of her salvoes "straddled" the target; the Revenge was engaging what were taken to be battle cruisers, obtaining distinct hits on two of them; the Colossus from 7.12 to 7.20 p.m. was engaging a ship taken to be a battle cruiser, either the Derfflinger or Lutzow, at ranges between 10,000 and 8,000 yards, and observed several direct hits, two being on the water line; whilst the Marlborough, as already mentioned, "engaged a ship of the 'Konig' class."

Other vessels reported being in effective action during this period. The Royal Oak, the ship next astern of the Iron Duke, opened fire at 7.15 p.m. on the leading ship of three vessels taken to be battle cruisers, at a range of 14,000 yards; this ship was hit and turned away, and fire was shifted to the second ship which was lost to sight in the mist after a few rounds had been fired. It was difficult to be certain of the class of vessel on which fire was being directed, but one or more of the enemy's battle cruisers had undoubtedly dropped astern by 7 p.m., as a result of the heavy punishment they had received from our battle cruisers and the 5th Battle Squadron, and were engaged by ships of the Battle Fleet.

Both at this period and earlier in the action, the ships of the 1st Battle Squadron were afforded more opportunities for effective fire than the rest of the Battle Fleet, and the fullest use was made of the opportunities. This squadron, under the able command of Sir Cecil Burney, was known by me to be highly efficient, and very strong proof was furnished during the Jutland battle, if proof were needed, that his careful training had borne excellent results. The immunity of the ships of the squadron from the enemy's fire, whilst they were inflicting on his vessels very severe punishment, bears very eloquent testimony to the offensive powers of the squadron.

At 7.5 p.m. the whole battle line was turned together three more points to starboard to close the range further; immediately afterwards two ships ahead of the Iron Duke reported a submarine a little on the port bow; at 7.10 p.m. a flotilla of enemy destroyers, supported by a cruiser, was observed to be approaching on a bearing S. 50 W, from the Iron Duke, and the Fleet was turned back to south in order to turn on to the submarine and bring the ships in line ahead ready, for any required manoeuvre. A heavy fire was opened on the destroyers at ranges between 10,000 and 6,500 yards. At the latter range the destroyers turned and passed towards the rear of the line in a heavy smoke screen. One destroyer was seen by several observers to sink from the effects of the gunfire.

At a sufficient interval before it was considered that the torpedoes fired by the destroyers would cross our line, a signal was made to the Battle Fleet to turn two points to port by subdivisions. Some minutes later a report was made to me by Commander Bellairs (the officer on my Staff, especially detailed for this duty and provided with an instrument for giving the necessary information) that this turn was insufficient to clear the torpedoes, as I had held on until the last moment; a further turn of two points was then made for a short time. As a result of this attack and another that followed immediately, some twenty or more torpedoes were observed to cross the track of the Battle Fleet, in spite of our turn, the large majority of them passing the ships of the 1st and 5th Battle Squadrons at the rear of the line. It was fortunate that, owing to the turn away of the Fleet, the torpedoes were apparently near the end of their run, and were consequently not running at high speed. They were all avoided by the very skilful handling of the ships by their captains, to whom the highest credit is due, not only for their skill in avoiding the torpedoes, but for the manner in which the ships, by neighbourly conduct towards each other, prevented risk of collision and kept their station in the line. The captains were most ably assisted by the admirable look-out kept by the organisation that existed for dealing with this danger.

The skill shown could not, however, have prevented several ships from being torpedoed had the range been less and the torpedoes consequently running at a higher speed. Frequent exercises carried out at Scapa Flow showed conclusively that the percentage of torpedoes that would hit ships in a line when fired from destroyers at ranges up to 8,000 yards was comparatively high, even if the tracks were seen and the ships were manoeuvred to avoid them. One very good reason is that torpedoes are always a considerable but varying distance ahead of the line of bubbles marking their track, making it difficult to judge the position of the torpedo from its track.

Many ships experienced escapes from this and other attacks; thus the Hercules reported that she "turned away six points to avoid the torpedoes, one of which passed along the starboard side and 40 yards across the bow, and the other passed close under the stern"; the Neptune reported that "the tracks of three torpedoes were seen from the foretop, one of which passed very close and was avoided by the use of the helm"; in the Agincourt's report, a statement occurred that "at 7.8 p.m. a torpedo just missed astern, it having been reported from aloft and course altered"; and again, "at 7.38 p.m. tracks of two torpedoes running parallel were observed approaching;

course altered to avoid torpedoes which passed ahead; and at 8.25 p.m. torpedo track on starboard side, turned at full speed; torpedo broke surface at about 150 yards on the starboard bow"; the Revenge remarked, "at 7.35 p.m. altered course to port to avoid two torpedoes, one passed about ten yards ahead and the other about twenty yards astern, and at 7.43 p.m. altered course to avoid torpedoes, two passing astern"; the Colossus stated, "at 7.35 p.m. turned to port to avoid a torpedo coming from starboard side"; the Barham at this period reported that "at least four torpedoes passed through the line close to the Barham; the Collingwood reported, "torpedo track was seen 20 degrees abaft the beam and coming straight at the ship; large helm was put on and the torpedo passed very close astern; at the same time another was seen to pass about thirty yards ahead." The captain of the Collingwood, in remarking on the destroyer's attack, added, "the great value of this form of attack on a line of ships is, to me, an outstanding feature of the Battle Fleet action."

The first two-point turn was made at 7.23 p.m. and the Fleet was brought to a south by west course by 7.33 p.m. (that is, to a course one point to the westward of the course of the Fleet before the destroyer attack). The total amount by which the range was opened by the turns was about 1,750 yards.

The 4th Light Cruiser Squadron and the 4th and 11th Flotillas had been delayed in reaching their action station at the van until about 7.10 p.m., owing to the turns to the westward made by the Battle Fleet to close the enemy. In accordance with arrangements made previously to counter destroyer attacks, these vessels were ordered out to engage the enemy destroyers, which, according to the report of the Commodore Le Mesurier, commanding the 4th Light Cruiser Squadron, were steering towards the head of the division led by the King George V., the van ship of the Battle Fleet. Although not very well placed for the first attack for the reason given above, they were in a very favourable position to counter the second destroyer attack, which took place at 7.25 p.m. The enemy's flotilla was sighted bearing 30 degrees before the starboard beam of the Iron Duke at a range of 9,000 yards and was heavily engaged by the light forces and the 4th, 1st, and 5th Battle Squadrons.

During this attack three enemy destroyers were reported as sunk by the fire of the battleships, light cruisers and destroyers; one of them, bearing a Commodore's pendant, being sunk at 7.50 p.m. by a division of the 12th Flotilla, consisting of the Obedient, Marvel, Mindful and Onslaught, which attacked them near the rear of our battle line. The Southampton and Dublin, of the 2nd Light Cruiser Squadron, attacked and sank a second destroyer at this period. At least six torpedoes were observed to pass ahead of, or through the track of, the 4th Light Cruiser Squadron during their attack on the German flotilla.

The destroyer attacks were combined with a retiring movement on the part of the enemy's Battle Fleet, the movement being covered with the aid of a heavy smoke screen. Although this retirement was not visible from the Iron Duke owing to the smoke and mist, and was, therefore, not known to me until after the action, it was clearly seen from the rear of our line, as is indicated by the following citations:

The Captain of the Valiant stated in his report: "At 7.23 p.m. enemy's Battle Fleet now altered course together away from us and broke off the action, sending out a low cloud of smoke which effectually covered their retreat and obscured them from further view."

The Captain of the Malaya reported, referring to this period: "This was the last of the enemy seen in daylight, owing to their Battle Fleet having turned away."

Sir Cecil Burney stated in regard to this period: "As the destroyer attack developed, the enemy's Battle Fleet in sight were observed to turn at least eight points until their sterns were towards our line. They ceased fire, declined further action, and disappeared into the mist."

The Captain of the St Vincent said; "The target was held closely until 7.26 p.m. (32 minutes in all), when the enemy had turned eight or ten points away, disappearing into the mist and with a smoke screen made by destroyers to cover them as well"

Rear-Admiral Evan-Thomas remarked: "After joining the Battle Fleet the 5th Battle Squadron conformed to the movements of the Commander-in-Chief, engaging the rear ships of the enemy's battle line, until they turned away and went out of sight, all ships apparently covering themselves with artificial smoke."

The Captain of the Revenge recorded: "A flotilla of destroyers passed through the line and made a most efficient smoke screen. At this period the enemy's fleet turned eight points to starboard and rapidly drew out of sight."

In the German account of the action at this stage, it is stated, in more than one passage, that the British Fleet during this action between the Battle Fleets was to the northward of the High Seas Fleet. This is correct of the earlier stages. The account refers to the attacks on our line by the German destroyer flotillas, and states finally that in the last attack the destroyers did not sight the heavy ships, but only light cruisers and destroyers to the north-eastward. The accuracy of this statement is doubtful since the destroyers were clearly in sight from our heavy ships. But the account then proceeds to state that "the German Commander-in-Chief turns his battle line to a southerly and southwesterly course on which the enemy was last seen, but he is no longer to be found."

This is illuminating. It is first stated that our ships bore north and north-east from the enemy and then that the enemy turned to south and southwest, that is, directly away from the British Fleet. Thus the fact that the German Fleet turned directly away is confirmed by Germans.

No report of this movement of the German Fleet reached me, and at first it was thought that his temporary disappearance was due to the thickening mist, especially as firing could be heard from the battleships in rear, but at 7.41 p.m., the enemy Battle Fleet being no longer in sight from the Iron Duke, course was altered "by divisions" three points more to starboard (namely, to southwest) to close the enemy, and single line ahead was again formed on the Iron Duke on that course.

At this period the rear of our battle line was still in action at intervals with one or two ships of the enemy's fleet, which were probably some that had dropped astern partially disabled, but by 7.55 p.m. fire had practically ceased.

At about 7.40 p.m. I received a report from Sir David Beatty stating that the enemy bore northwest by west from the Lion, distant 10 to 11 miles, and that the Lion's course was southwest. Although the battle cruisers were not in sight from the Iron Duke, I assumed the Lion to be five or six miles ahead of the van of the Battle Fleet, but it appeared later from a report received in reply to directions signalled by me at 8.10 p.m. to the King George V. to follow the battle cruisers, that they were not in sight from that ship either.

At this time the enemy's Battle Fleet seems to have become divided, for whilst Sir David Beatty reported the presence of battleships northwest by west from the Lion, other enemy battleships were observed to the westward (that is, on the starboard bow of the Iron Duke), and the course of the Fleet was at once altered "by divisions" to west in order to close the enemy; this alteration was made at 7.59 p.m.

It will be observed that all the large alterations of course of the Battle Fleet during the engagement were made "by divisions" instead of "in succession from the van, or together." The reason was that in this way the whole Fleet could be brought closer to the enemy with far greater rapidity, and in a more ordered formation, than if the movement had been carried out by the line "in succession."

The objection to altering by turning all ships together was the inevitable confusion that would have ensued as the result of such a manoeuvre carried out with a very large Fleet under action conditions in misty weather, particularly if the ships were thus kept on a line of bearing for a long period.

The battleships sighted at 7.59 p.m. opened fire on the ships of the 4th Light Cruiser Squadron, which had moved out to starboard of the battle line to engage a flotilla of enemy destroyers which were steering to attack the Battle Fleet. The Calliope, the flagship of Commodore Le Mesurier, was hit by a heavy shell and received some damage, but retained her fighting efficiency, and fired a torpedo at the leading battleship at a range of 6,500 yards; an explosion was noticed on board a ship of the "Kaiser" class by the Calliope. (All our battle cruisers had felt this heavy explosion which was clearly concussion underwater, and may have been caused by the Calliope torpedo obtaining a hit.)

The ships sighted turned away and touch could not be regained, although sounds of gunfire could be heard from ahead at 8.25 p.m., probably from our battle cruisers, which obtained touch with and engaged some of the enemy's ships very effectively between 8.22 and 8.25 p.m. The Falmouth was the last ship of the Battle Cruiser Fleet to be in touch with the enemy, at 8.38 p.m.; the ships then in sight turned eight points together away from the Falmouth.

At 8.30 p.m. the light was failing, and the Fleet was turned "by divisions" to a southwest course, thus reforming single line again.

During the proceedings of the Battle Fleet described above, the battle cruisers were in action ahead. At first, touch with the enemy was lost owing to the large alterations of course carried out by the High Sea Fleet, but it was regained at 7.12 p.m., the battle cruisers opening fire at 7.14 p.m., though only for two and a half minutes, and increasing speed to 22 knots. At this period the battle cruisers were steering southwest by south to southwest, and this course took them from the port to the starboard bow of the Battle Fleet by 7.12 p.m. The movements of our battle cruisers, which were at this time between four and five miles ahead of the van of the Battle Fleet, could not be distinguished, owing, partly, to the funnel and cordite smoke from the battle cruisers themselves, but even more to the funnel smoke from the numerous cruisers, light cruisers and destroyers which were attempting to gain their positions ahead of the van.

The movements of the enemy's fleet could not be distinguished from our Battle Fleet owing again to their own funnel and cordite smoke, and, also, to the smoke screens which ships and destroyers were making to conceal their movements.

It will be realised that these conditions, which particularly affected the Battle Fleet, did not apply to the same extent to our ships ahead of our Battle Fleet. They had little but the smoke of the enemy's leading ships to obscure the view. Farther to the rear, the Battle Fleet had the smoke of all our craft ahead of it as well as that of the enemy's long line of ships.

Conditions which were perhaps difficult ahead of the Battle Fleet were very much accentuated in the Battle Fleet. Vice-Admiral Sir Martyn Jerram, in his report, remarked on this point: "As leading ship, in addition to the hazy atmosphere, I was much hampered by what I imagine must have been cordite fumes from the battle cruisers after they had passed us, and from other cruisers engaged on the bow, also by funnel gases from small craft ahead, and for a considerable time by dense smoke from the Duke of Edinburgh, which was unable to draw clear."

The general position at 6.45 p.m. and again at 7.15 p.m. is shown in plans 8 and 9.

At 7.10 p.m., according to remarks from the Minotaur, flagship of Rear-Admiral W. L. Heath, commanding the 2nd Cruiser Squadron, the position as seen from that ship was as follows: "The 2nd Cruiser Squadron was in single line ahead three to four miles on the port side of the King George V., gaining on her slightly, but with all the destroyers and light craft between her and the King George V. The battle cruisers were about four miles distant on the starboard bow of the Minotaur; owing to their higher speed, the battle cruisers rapidly increased their distance from the Battle Fleet to some eight miles."

At 7.5 p.m. according to a report from the Shannon, of the 2nd Cruiser Squadron, the Shannon's course was S. 10 W., "the 2nd Cruiser Squadron endeavouring to take station on the engaged bow of the Battle Fleet; the Battle Fleet still engaged, the battle cruisers not engaged and turned slightly to port." And again at 7.22 p.m. a report says: "The Duke of Edinburgh had now taken station astern of the Shannon, the battle cruisers were engaged and had wheeled to starboard. Leading ships of the 2nd Cruiser Squadron were starting to cross the bows of the Battle Fleet from port to starboard. Battle cruisers firing intermittently, light cruisers making their way through the destroyer flotillas to attack the enemy light cruisers" Rear-Admiral Heath stated:

"At 7.11 p.m. I proceeded with the squadron at 20 knots to take up station astern of the Battle Cruiser Fleet, which was then engaged with the enemy," He added: "One salvo fell short on the starboard bow of the Minotaur and some others in close proximity"; and later says, "even when the salvo referred to in the preceding paragraph fell, no more than the flashes of the enemy's guns could be seen."

Further remarks from the Shannon, at a later stage, were:

"At 8 p.m. Battle Fleet altered course to starboard to close the enemy, and by 8.15 was lost to sight, bearing about north by east."

"At 8.15 p.m. Battle Fleet, out of sight from Shannon, was heard to be in action."

"At 8.30 p.m. the visibility of grey ships was about 9,000 yards." "At 8.45 p.m. King George V. again sighted, bearing north-north-east. Visibility had again improved, and her range was estimated at about 10,000 yards. Conformed to her course S. 75 W. to close enemy."

At 7.20 p.m. the ships engaged by our battle cruisers turned away and were lost to sight. They were located for a moment at 8.20 p.m. with the aid of the 1st and 3rd Light Cruiser Squadrons, and, although they disappeared again at once, they were once more located and effectively engaged between 8.22 and 8.28 p.m. at about 10,000 yards range. They turned away once more and were finally lost to sight by the 3rd Light Cruiser Squadron (the last ships to keep in touch) at 8.38 p.m., steaming to the westward. This was the last opportunity which the battle cruisers had of putting the finishing touch upon a fine afternoon's work. They had, under the very able and gallant leadership of Sir David Beatty, assisted by the splendid squadron so well commanded by Admiral Evan-Thomas, gone far to crush out of existence the opposing Battle Cruiser Squadron.

It will be seen from the above account that our battle cruisers experienced great difficulty in locating and holding the enemy after 7.20 p.m., even when far ahead of the Battle Fleet, with its small craft, and therefore in a position of freedom from the smoke of our own vessels and the enemy's line.

After this time, 7.20 p.m., the battle cruisers were only engaged for some six minutes. The enemy turned away on each occasion when he was located and showed no disposition to fight.

The visibility by this time had become very bad; the light was failing, and it became necessary to decide on the disposition for the night.

HMS *Ark Royal*, c. 1939

Image: British carrier with a flight of "Swordfish" overhead.

14 - The Battle of Jutland (Cont.)

III. The Night Action

The situation, which had never been at all clear to me owing to the fact that I had not seen more than a few ships at a time, appeared to be as follows:

We were between the enemy and his bases, whether he shaped a course to return via the Horn Reef, via Heligoland direct, or via the swept channel which he was known to use along the coast of the West Frisian Islands.

I concluded that the enemy was well to the westward of us. He had been turning on interior lines throughout. We had altered course gradually during the action from southeast by east to west, a turn of 13 points, or 146 degrees, in all, and the result must have been to place his ships well to the westward and ahead of us; although it was possible that ships, which had fallen out owing to damage, might be to the northward.

The possibility of a night action was, of course, present to my mind, but for several reasons it was not my intention to seek such an action between the heavy ships.

It is sufficient to mention the principal arguments against it. In the first place, such a course must have inevitably led to our Battle Fleet being the object of attack by a very large destroyer force throughout the night. No senior officer would willingly court such an attack, even if our battleships were equipped with the best searchlights and the best arrangements for the control of the searchlights and the gunfire at night.

It was, however, known to me that neither our searchlights nor their control arrangements were at this time of the best type. The fitting of director-firing gear for the guns of the secondary armament of our battleships (a very important factor for firing at night) had also only just been begun, although repeatedly applied for. The delay was due to manufacturing and labour difficulties. Without these adjuncts I knew well that the maximum effect of our fire at night could not be obtained, and that we could place no dependence on beating off destroyer attacks by gunfire. Therefore, if destroyers got into touch with the heavy ships, we were bound to suffer serious losses with no corresponding advantage. Our own destroyers were no effective antidote at night, since, if they were disposed with this sole object in view, they would certainly be taken for enemy destroyers and be fired on by our own ships.

But putting aside the question of attack by destroyers, the result of night actions between heavy ships must always be very largely a matter of chance, as there is little opportunity for skill on either side. Such an action must be fought at very close range, the decision depending on the course of events in the first few minutes. It is, therefore, an undesirable procedure on these general grounds. The greater efficiency of German searchlights at the time of the Jutland action, and the greater number of torpedo tubes fitted in enemy ships, combined with his superiority in destroyers, would, I knew, give the Germans the opportunity of scoring heavily at the commencement of such an action.

The question then remained as to the course to be steered. The first desideratum was to keep the British Fleet between the enemy and his bases, so as to be in a position to renew the action at dawn. Daylight was rapidly disappearing; it was necessary to form the Fleet for the night as quickly as possible to avoid visual signalling after dark; and it was also necessary to place our destroyers in a position where the chances of their coming in contact with our own ships was reduced to a minimum, and yet giving them an opportunity of attacking the enemy's capital ships during the night.

The Grand Fleet was formed at the time in practically a single line, steering approximately west-southwest. I considered that a southerly course would meet the situation and would enable me to form the Fleet very quickly, and, if I put the destroyers astern, they would fulfil three conditions: first, they would be in an excellent position for attacking the enemy's fleet should it also turn to the southward with a view to regaining its bases during the night (which seemed a very probable movement on the part of the enemy); secondly, they would also be in position to attack enemy destroyers should the latter search for our fleet with a view to a night attack on the heavy ships; finally, they would be clear of our own ships, and the danger of their attacking our battleships in error or of our battleships firing on them would be reduced to a minimum.

Accordingly, at 9 p.m., I signalled to the Battle Fleet to alter course by divisions to south, informing the Flag officers of the Battle Cruiser Fleet, the cruiser and light cruiser squadrons, and the officers commanding destroyer flotillas, of my movements in order that they should conform. Shortly afterwards I directed the Battle Fleet to assume the second organisation and to form divisions in line ahead disposed abeam to port, with the columns one mile apart.

My object in closing the columns to one mile apart was to ensure that adjacent columns should not lose sight of each other during the night, and that therefore they would not mistake our own ships for those of the enemy.

As soon as the Battle Fleet had turned to the southerly course the destroyer flotillas were directed to take station five miles astern of the Battle Fleet. At 9.32 p.m. a signal was made to the minelaying flotilla leader Abdiel (Captain Berwick Curtis) to proceed to lay a minefield in a defined area some 15 miles from the Vyl Lightship, over which it was expected the High Sea Fleet would pass if the ships attempted to regain their ports during the night via the Horn Reef. The Abdiel carried out this operation unobserved in the same successful manner as numerous other similar operations had been undertaken by this most useful little vessel; from the evidence of one of our submarines, stationed near the Horn Reef, which reported on return to her base having heard several underwater explosions between 2.15 and 5.30 a.m. on June 1st, it was judged that some enemy ships had struck mines.

At 10 p.m. the position of the Iron Duke was Lat. 56.22 N., Long. 5.47 E., course south, speed 17 knots, and the order of the Fleet from west to east was:

Battle Cruiser Fleet (except 2nd Light Cruiser Squadron); Cruiser Squadrons;

Battle Fleet;

2nd Light Cruiser Squadron astern of the 5th Battle Squadron;

4th Light Cruiser Squadron ahead of the Battle Fleet;

11th, 4th, 12th, 9th, 10th and 13th Flotillas disposed from west to east, in that order, astern of the Battle Fleet.

Shortly before the turn of the Fleet to the southward for the night a destroyer attack took place on the 2nd Light Cruiser Squadron at the rear of our Battle line. This was reported to me shortly after 9 p.m., but immediately afterwards a further report stated that the enemy had been driven off to the northwest.

At 10.4 p.m. Commodore Hawkesley, in the Castor, commanding the destroyer flotillas, after dropping astern, sighted three or more vessels at a range of 2,000 yards which he took to be enemy battle cruisers. If the German report is to be believed, the ships were light cruisers and included the Hamburg and Elbing. The enemy at once opened a rapid and accurate fire, and the Castor was hit, and her bridge and wireless telegraphy gear damaged, making it impossible to signal to the 11th Flotilla, which the Castor was leading. The damage to the Castor was slight. The Castor, Magic, and Marne fired torpedoes at the enemy, but the remaining destroyers of the flotilla refrained from doing so, not being certain of the identity of the vessels in sight. The enemy disappeared after a violent detonation, following on the discharge of the torpedoes, had been felt in the engine-rooms of the destroyers near the Castor.

At 10.15 a.m. the Castor sighted a German destroyer on her starboard bow and opened fire with all guns at point-blank range. She was not seen again.

At 10.20 p.m. the 2nd Light Cruiser Squadron sighted and engaged five enemy vessels, apparently a cruiser with four light cruisers, probably of the 4th Scouting Group. The enemy again opened fire with great rapidity and accuracy, and concentrated his fire on our two leading ships, the Southampton and Dublin, at very short range. Both vessels suffered considerable damage during the 15 minutes' engagement and there were fairly heavy casualties; three fires which broke out on board the Southampton were promptly extinguished by fine work on the part of the officers and men, in spite of the fact that the hoses had been much cut up by shell fire.

The enemy squadron disappeared after this short but fierce engagement, and it is probable that the German light cruiser Frauenlob, whose loss was admitted by the enemy, was sunk during this action, which took place in that case between our own 2nd Light Cruiser Squadron and the German 4th Scouting Group.

At 11.30 p.m. the 4th Flotilla sighted and attacked enemy cruisers steering a southeasterly course. Again the vessels sighted opened fire immediately, and the flotilla leader Tipperary, commanded by Captain Wintour, the leader of the flotilla, was severely damaged by gunfire and set on fire forward; the Broke, leader of the 2nd half Flotilla, received injury to her steering-gear, rendering her temporarily unmanageable and causing her to ram the destroyer Sparrowhawk, with the result that it became necessary to abandon the latter destroyer on the following morning after taking off her crew. The destroyer Spitfire (Lieutenant-Commander C. W. Trelawny), next astern of the Tipperary, fired torpedoes at a four-funnelled cruiser which appeared to be hit and in a sinking condition, and the Spitfire then collided with a German light cruiser and, in scraping along her side, carried off some 29 feet of her skin plating.

The remainder of the 4th Flotilla, after this engagement, while steering to the southeastward, came into contact at midnight with the enemy's 2nd Battle Squadron, and one ship (probably the Pommern) was torpedoed and sunk either by the Ardent (Lieutenant-Commander Marsden) or Ambuscade (Lieutenant-Commander G. A. Coles) or Garland (Lieutenant-Commander R. S. Goff). A heavy and accurate fire was opened by the enemy and the destroyer Fortune (Lieutenant-Commander F. G. Terry) was sunk.

The flotilla was again in action a little later with some enemy battleships, and the Ardent attacked, and fired a torpedo, but the result could not be observed as a very heavy fire was concentrated on the Ardent, which sank with colours flying after a very gallant night's work. It is sad to record that Lieutenant-Commander Marsden and one man were the only survivors, being picked up by a destroyer on June 1st after having been five hours in the water.

The 12th Flotilla had formed after dark astern of the 1st Battle Squadron. The 1st Battle Squadron was somewhat astern of the remainder of the Fleet during the night, owing to the Marlborough not being able to keep up 17 knots, although steaming at the revolutions for this speed. Consequently the 1st Flotilla was also more than five miles astern of the main portion of the Battle Fleet. At 11.30 p.m. also this flotilla was obliged for some little time to steer a southeasterly course, owing to the movements of another flotilla on the starboard hand, the identity of which cannot be determined with certainty. The result was that the 12th Flotilla was probably some ten miles to the north-eastward of the 1st Battle Squadron by midnight. The incident was a fortunate one since it brought the flotilla into contact with one of the enemy's battle squadrons.

At 1.45 a.m. Captain Stirling, leading the flotilla in the Faulknor, sighted on the starboard bow this battle squadron, consisting of six ships steering southeast. The leading ships were thought to belong to the "Kaiser" class. Captain Stirling altered his course to one parallel to that of the enemy and increased speed to 25 knots to draw ahead, with the intention of turning to attack on a northwesterly course (the reverse of the enemy's course), in order to give an opportunity of getting into close range. This attack was carried out at 2 a.m. at a range of about 3,000 yards, and all destroyers fired their torpedoes at the second and third ships in the line. Some took effect on the third battleship in the line, the explosion being so violent and the flame reaching to such a height that it appeared to those in our destroyers that the explosion of the torpedoes must have detonated the magazine and destroyed the ship.

Our destroyers were then forced to withdraw by the enemy light cruisers, which were in company with the battle squadron. The destroyer Maenad (Commander J. P. Champion) had, however, not turned to the northwestward with the remainder of the flotilla, as it had been anticipated that the attack would have been made with torpedo tubes bearing to starboard, and her tubes were not ready to fire to port. Commander Champion held on the southeasterly course and, turning later than the rest of the flotilla, fired one port tube, then turned again to southeast, trained his tubes to starboard, and at 2.25 a.m. fired two torpedoes to starboard at the fourth ship in the line at a range between 4,000 and 5,000 yards, one of which took effect. In this case, too, the flame of the explosion reached the mast head, and the ship was not seen again, although those ahead and astern of her were visible.

It is of interest to note that at the time of the first attack on this squadron six battleships were visible. After the first attack only five were seen by Captain Stirling, and twenty-five minutes later five were sighted by the Maenad, and after the Maenad's attack only four were visible. The evidence that at least one of the battleships was sunk was considered at the time to be very strong, particularly as the reports from the Maenad and from Captain Stirling were sent to me quite independently, and Commander Champion was unaware of the fact that Captain Stirling had reported six ships as the original number in the battle squadron, and five as the number remaining after his attack.

When Captain Stirling had located the enemy's battle squadron he reported the fact by wireless, but the signal was, unfortunately, not received by any ship, owing, presumably, to the strong interference caused by German wireless signalling at the time.

The destroyers of the 9th, 10th, and 13th Flotillas took station astern the Battle Fleet in company with the Champion (Captain Farie), leader of the 13th Flotilla; the Fearless, leader of the 9th Flotilla, had not been able to maintain touch with her flotilla. Many of the destroyers of these flotillas lost touch with the Champion during the night, and the flotillas became somewhat scattered.

At 12.30 a.m. a large vessel, taken at first for one of our own ships, crossed the rear of the flotilla at high speed, passing close to the Petard and Turbulent. She rammed the

Turbulent and opened a heavy fire on both the Turbulent and Petard; the Turbulent sank and the Petard was damaged.

At 2.35 a.m. the destroyer Moresby, of the 18th Flotilla, sighted four battleships of the "Deutschland" class, and attacked, firing one torpedo; an explosion was subsequently heard.

It was impossible to state with certainty which of our destroyers were actually successful in their attacks. The enemy, of course, denied that any marked success was obtained by our attacks, but information obtained after the action made it certain that at least four battleships of the "Dreadnought" type were hit by torpedoes, in addition to the pre-Dreadnought battleship Pommern, which was admitted to have been sunk by a torpedo, as was the light cruiser Rostock.

Although the credit for the successful attacks cannot be attributed to particular destroyers, the work of the flotillas as a whole, and particularly of the 4th and 12th Flotillas, was characterised by the splendid dash, skill and gallantry for which our destroyers had been conspicuous throughout the War. They were most ably led and achieved magnificent work under very difficult conditions.

There is no doubt at all that the German organisation for night action was of a remarkably high standard. In the first place, the use of star shell, at that time unfamiliar to us, was of the greatest use to them in locating our destroyers without revealing their own positions; and, secondly, their searchlights were not only very powerful (much more so than ours), but their method of controlling them and bringing guns and searchlights rapidly on to any vessel sighted was excellent. It also appeared that some system of director-firing was fitted to the guns of their secondary armament.

The increased offensive power given by these devices did not, however, prevent our destroyers from inflicting great damage on the enemy during their night attacks, although they led to the loss of some valuable destroyers and still more valuable lives. Captain Wintour, leader of the 4th Flotilla, an officer of wide experience of destroyer work and a fine leader, was a very heavy loss, and other splendid officers perished with their gallant crews. Our destroyer service has, indeed, every reason to be exceedingly proud of the achievements of the flotillas, both during the day action of May 31st and during the night following that action.

Gunfire and underwater explosions were heard at intervals during the night, and, curiously enough, the underwater explosions, four or five in number, were quite clearly recorded on a barograph in the Malaya, a ship well placed for the purpose, as she was in the rear. There is little doubt that these records showed the explosion of our torpedoes against enemy ships.

From the Battle Fleet it was evident shortly after dark that our destroyers were in action. Star shells were fired with great frequency by the enemy, and they produced a very brilliant illumination, leaving the enemy ships in complete darkness and not revealing their positions.

At 11 p.m. the light cruiser Active, astern of the 2nd Battle Squadron, observed a ship coming up from astern, and shortly afterwards saw searchlights switched on and a heavy fire opened against this vessel by a ship, or ships, on her starboard quarter. She appeared to be heavily hit and to sink. It is possible that this ship may have been the Black Prince, which had apparently lost touch with our fleet during the day action.

Shortly after this incident the Active passed over some submerged object which she bumped heavily. Subsequent examination showed that some 15 feet of her bilge keel had been torn away. It was not conceivable that the object struck could have been submerged wreckage from any ship which had taken part in the action, no fighting having taken place in the vicinity, and it seemed possible that the Active had struck an enemy submarine. At 11.30 p.m. the Colossus also passed over some submerged object which was felt to scrape along the bottom of the ship. Subsequent examination showed damage to both starboard propeller blades. Again there is doubt as to what the obstruction could have been; it was certainly not wreckage from any ship that had been in action.

At 2 a.m. on June 1st Vice-Admiral Sir Cecil Burney informed me that the Marlborough could not maintain the Fleet speed of 17 knots any longer, on account of the stress on the bulkheads, and that she had been obliged to ease to 12 knots. I directed him to order the ship to proceed to the Tyne or Rosyth, passing south of the German mined area. Sir Cecil Burney called the light cruiser Fearless alongside the Marlborough, and was transferred in her, with his Staff, to the Revenge, the Fearless being then detached to escort the Marlborough.

Some idea of the area covered by the different engagements which constituted the Battle of Jutland will be gathered from a consideration of the distances steamed by our ships during the operations.

The Battle Cruisers steamed some 64 miles between 3.48 p.m., the time of opening fire, and 6.17 p.m., the time that the Battle Fleet commenced action, and a further distance of some 57 miles to 9 p.m., when the Fleet turned to the southward for the night. The Battle Fleet steamed some 47 miles between the commencement of their engagement with the High Sea Fleet and the turn to the southward at 9 p.m.

The whole Fleet steamed some 85 miles during the period covered by the night action - 9 p.m. to 2 a.m.

At 2.47 a.m., as dawn was breaking, the Fleet altered course to north and formed single line ahead in the order -

2nd Battle Squadron,
4th Battle Squadron,
1st Battle Squadron (less the 6th Division).

The 5th Battle Squadron rejoined at 3.30 a.m. and took station ahead of the 2nd Battle Squadron.

The weather was misty and the visibility even less than on May 31st, being only some three or four miles, and I considered it desirable under these conditions, and in view of the fact that I was not in touch with either my cruisers or destroyers, to accept the danger of submarine attack on a long line in order to be ready to meet the enemy's Battle Fleet, if suddenly sighted. The 6th Division of the Battle Fleet was not in sight at daylight, having dropped astern during the night owing to the reduction in speed of the Marlborough and the change of flag from the Marlborough to the Revenge. Partly on account of the low visibility, and partly because of the inevitable difference in dead reckoning between ships, due to their many movements during the action and during the night, considerable difficulty was experienced in collecting the Fleet. This applied particularly to the destroyer flotillas, which had been heavily engaged, and whose facilities for computing their positions under these conditions were only slight; but the same difficulty was experienced with all classes of ships, and, although awkward, the fact did not cause me any surprise. The cruisers were not sighted until 6 a.m., the destroyers did not join the Battle Fleet until 9 a.m., and the 6th Division of the Battle Fleet with the Vice-Admiral of the 1st Battle Squadron, was not in company until the evening.

The difficulties experienced in collecting the Fleet (particularly the destroyers), due to the above causes, rendered it undesirable for the Battle Fleet to close the Horn Reef at daylight, as had been my intention when deciding to steer to the southward during the night. It was obviously necessary to concentrate the Battle Fleet and the destroyers before renewing action. By the time this concentration was effected it had become apparent that the High Sea Fleet, steering for the Horn Reef, had passed behind the shelter of the German minefields in the early morning on the way to their ports. The presence of a Zeppelin, sighted at 3.30 a.m., made it certain that our position at that time would be known to the enemy, should he be at sea, but the information obtained from our wireless directional stations during the early morning showed that ships of the High Sea Fleet must have passed the Horn Reef on a southerly course shortly after daylight.

At 3 a.m. the destroyer Sparrowhawk, which was lying disabled in Lat. 55.54 N., Long. 5.59 E., sighted a German light cruiser two miles to the eastward, steaming slowly to the northward. After being in sight for about five minutes this vessel slowly heeled over and sank, bows first. The Sparrowhawk was subsequently sighted by the Marksman and others of our destroyers, and, being too seriously damaged for towing back to a base, was sunk by the Marksman.

Shortly after 3.30 a.m. the report of gunfire to the westward was audible in the Battle Fleet, and at 3.38 Rear-Admiral Trevelyan Napier, commanding the 3rd Light Cruiser

Squadron, reported that he was engaging a Zeppelin in a position to the westward of the Battle Fleet. Course was altered "by divisions" to west at 3.44 a.m., as it seemed that the presence of the airship might possibly indicate the presence also of the High Sea Fleet. At 3.50 a.m. a Zeppelin was in sight from the Battle Fleet, but nothing else; course was altered back again to north and fire opened on the airship, which, however, was too high for the fire to be effective. She disappeared to the eastward. She was sighted subsequently at intervals.

At 4.10 a.m. the Battle Fleet was formed into divisions in line ahead, disposed abeam to starboard, in order to widen the front and to reduce the risk of submarine attack. At 4.25 a.m. the cruiser Dublin reported by wireless that she had sighted an enemy cruiser and two destroyers, and she gave her position.

At 5.15 a.m. the Battle Cruiser Fleet joined the Battle Fleet in accordance with orders signalled, and was directed to locate the cruiser reported by the Dublin, whilst the Battle Fleet searched to the southeastward for one of the enemy's battle cruisers which was thought to be in a damaged condition and probably, therefore, still making for a German port. At 4.45 a.m. the Battle Fleet was in Lat. 55.29 N., Long. 6.02 E.; at 5 a.m. the Commodore of the flotillas (Commodore Hawkesley), with destroyers, reported himself as being in Lat. 55.48 N., Long. 6.22 E.; at 5.48 a.m. the Battle Cruiser Fleet was in Lat. 55.45 N., Long. 6.16 E., steering southeast at 18 knots, and at 6.15 a.m. altered course to south.

At 6 a.m., not having met the destroyers, the Battle Fleet altered course to southeast, with the cruisers in company, steaming at 17 knots, and maintained that course until 7.15 a.m., at which time course was altered to north, the Battle Cruiser Fleet altering to north-east at 7.30 a.m. and to north at 8 a.m.

The Dublin was sighted at 7.55 a.m. and reported having lost sight in a fog, in Lat. 55.28 N., Long. 6.32 E., of the cruiser and torpedo boat destroyers she had reported, and, in reply to further inquiries, stated that the cruiser was apparently not disabled and was steaming fast.

At 8.15 a.m. the Battle Fleet was in Lat. 55.64 N., Long. 6.10 E., steering north at 17 knots, turning at 8.52 a.m. to a southwest course.

Between 8 a.m. and 9 a.m. a considerable amount of wreckage was passed, and the bodies of dead German bluejackets were seen in the water. The wreckage of the destroyer Ardent was also passed. Drifting mines in considerable numbers were seen during the whole forenoon of the 1st June, and there were one or two reports of submarines being sighted. At 10 a.m. the Battle Cruiser Fleet was again in sight, ahead of the Battle Fleet, and course was altered to north by west, the destroyers, which had now joined, being stationed to form a submarine screen.

At noon the Battle Fleet was in position Lat. 56.20 N,, Long. 6.25 E., and at 12.30 p.m. the Battle Cruiser Fleet was in Lat. 56.32 N., Long. 6.11 E.

It was now clear that all disabled enemy vessels had either sunk or had passed inside the minefields en route to their bases. It had been evident since the early morning, from the definite information obtained by our directional stations, that the enemy's fleet was returning to port. All our own injured vessels were also en route for their bases, and I decided to return with the whole Fleet, and gave the necessary instructions to the Rosyth force to return independently.

The Harwich force, under Commodore Tyrwhitt, had been kept in port by Admiralty orders on May 31st, and was despatched to sea on the morning of June 1st, when I was informed that it was being sent out to join me and to replace vessels requiring fuel. At 7 a.m. I instructed Commodore Tyrwhitt to send four of his destroyers to screen the Marlborough to her base; he informed me at 2.30 p.m. that he had sighted the Marlborough. At 10.40 a.m. I had reported to the Admiralty that I did not require the Harwich force. I desired Commodore Tyrwhitt to strengthen the Marlborough's escort and told him that I did not need his ships. They would have been of great use at daylight in June 1st had they been on the scene at that time, and it is needless to add how much I should have welcomed the participation of the Harwich force in the action had circumstances admitted of this. I knew well the extreme efficiency and the fine fighting spirit of this force which, under its gallant and distinguished commodore, had rendered such splendid service throughout the War.

The Marlborough reported at 11 a.m. that a torpedo had been fired at her and had missed. Some anxiety was felt about the ship on the morning of June 2nd, as bad weather set in and her pumps became choked; tugs were ordered out to meet her, but she arrived in the Humber at 8 a.m.

The Warrior, which had been taken in tow by the seaplane carrier Engadine, was in Lat. 57.18 N., Long. 3.54 E. at 8 a.m. on the 1st June, but the crew was taken off by the Engadine and the ship abandoned later in the day, as the weather had become bad and it was evident the ship could not remain afloat. The work of rescue was very smartly carried out, the Engadine being skilfully placed alongside the Warrior in a considerable sea way by her Captain, Lieutenant-Commander C. G. Robinson, and the large number of wounded transferred to her. The reports as to the condition of the Warrior were not clear, and it was feared that she might remain afloat, and later fall into the hands of the enemy. Therefore I detached the 2nd Cruiser Squadron, and subsequently the 3rd Light Cruiser Squadron, to search for her. The search continued until the evening of June 23rd, no trace of the ship being found. It became clear from a report received subsequently from the Captain of the Warrior that her condition was such that she must have sunk shortly after having been abandoned.

During the search for the Warrior, one of the cruisers of the 2nd Cruiser Squadron sighted a submarine on the surface at dusk, opened fire, and tried to ram. It was reported quite definitely that the submarine had been sunk. Later evidence showed, however, that the submarine was one of our own vessels of this class, that she had a very narrow escape, but had dived in time to escape injury. This was one instance, amongst others, of our own submarines being mistaken for an enemy, attacked by our own ships, and considered to be sunk. The difficulty of ascertaining definitely the result of an engagement with a submarine was thereby exemplified, and was one of the weighty reasons which led the Admiralty during the War to refrain from publishing any figures giving the results of engagements with submarines.

Some anxiety had been felt as to the safety of the destroyer Broke, and the 2nd Cruiser Squadron was directed to search for that vessel also, assisted by two light cruisers. She, however, arrived safely in the Tyne, having been delayed by bad weather. Other disabled or partially disabled destroyers requiring assistance to reach port were the Acasta, towed by the Nonsuch, and the Onslow, towed by the Defender.

The Fleet arrived at its bases on June 2nd, fuelled, and was reported ready for sea at four hours notice at 9.45 p.m. on that date.

That despatch was sent in under constant pressure for its early receipt and at a time when I, in common with my Staff, was very fully occupied with the arrangements connected with the repair of damaged ships, the constructive alterations which the action had shown to be necessary in our ships, and the various committees which I had formed to report on different subjects in the light of our experience. I was not, therefore, able to give the personal attention to the reports which later opportunities have afforded me, and such slight modifications as I have made are due to a closer study of these reports, and of the signals received during May 31st.

One of my first acts on returning to Scapa was to send to the King on the morning of June 3rd a message of humble duty, respectful and heartfelt wishes on His Majesty's birthday.

The following reply was received from His Majesty, and communicated to the Fleet:

'I am deeply touched by the message which you have sent me on behalf of the Grand Fleet. It reaches me on the morrow of a battle which has once more displayed the splendid gallantry of the officers and men under your command. I mourn the loss of brave men, many of them personal friends of my own, who have fallen in their country's cause. Yet even more do I regret that the German High Sea Fleet in spite of its heavy losses was enabled by the misty weather to evade the full consequences of an encounter they have always professed to desire, but for which when the opportunity arrived they showed no inclination. Though the retirement of the enemy immediately after the opening of the general engagement robbed us of the opportunity of gaining a decisive victory, the events of last Wednesday amply justify my confidence in the valour and efficiency of the fleets under your command. "George R. I."

    The simple duty remained of acknowledging this gracious message, and I added in my telegram to His Majesty that it was "a matter of the greatest gratification to all ranks to receive such an expression of Your Majesty's approval and sympathy for the loss of our gallant comrades."

15 - Reflection on the Battle of Jutland

There has been some discussion on the tactics of the Jutland Battle, and no doubt there will be more. I have endeavoured to give the facts, so that future discussions may take place with adequate knowledge.

It is as well, first, to dispel the illusion, which I have seen expressed, that the Grand Fleet was divided with the object of enticing the enemy out to attack the weaker portion in order to provide the opportunity for a Fleet action. There was no such intention. On May 31st the Battle Cruiser Fleet was scouting to the southward of the Battle Fleet in pursuance of the policy which had been frequently carried out on previous occasions.

Many surmises have been made as to the object with which the High Sea Fleet put to sea on this occasion. The view which I have always held is that the frequent light cruiser sweeps, which had taken place down the Norwegian coast and in the vicinity of the Skagerrak during the spring of 1916, may have induced the German Commander-in-Chief to send out a force with the object of cutting off the light cruisers engaged in one of these operations, and that he took the Battle Fleet to sea in support of this force. There is no doubt that he did not expect to meet the whole Grand Fleet. If confirmation of this were needed it is supplied in the German account of the battle, in which it is stated that "there was no reason for supposing that any enemy forces were about, much less the entire British Fleet."

Consideration of the tactics at Jutland, or indeed of the whole strategy and tactics of the War, leads naturally to the fresh problems which the advent of new weapons had introduced. When I took command of the Grand Fleet one of these problems was that of how to counter a destroyer attack in a day action. It had excited more attention in the two or three years before the War than any other question of tactics, much attention was devoted to it during the War, and for that reason it is desirable to discuss it fully.

It was not, I believe, until the year 1911, during what were then known as "P.Z. Exercises" (that is, actions between Battle Fleets as an exercise), that destroyer attacks were actually carried out in the British Navy on a large scale.

During that year manoeuvres took place between the 3rd and 4th Divisions of the Home Fleets, commanded by Admiral the Marquis of Milford Haven, and the Atlantic Fleet, commanded by myself; and the first phase of the manoeuvres of that year included some Battle Fleet "P.Z. Exercises," during which attacks by considerable forces of destroyers were carried out. Before this date the risk attendant on such exercises, and the fact that our Main Fleet exercises frequently took place without destroyer flotillas being present, had prevented the matter from being made the subject of thorough practical experiment on such a scale as to give reliable guidance. The 1911 exercises brought the question into greater prominence.

The Fleet manoeuvres of 1912 did not throw further light on the question, as no Fleet action took place in which destroyers were engaged; and the subsequent Battle Fleet exercises did not, so far as I recollect, include destroyer flotillas amongst the vessels engaged. During the Fleet action at the close of the 1913 manoeuvres most of the destroyer attacks on the "Red" Fleet were made from towards the rear of the "Blue" battle line, and we did not gain much fresh knowledge from them.

To turn from manoeuvre experience; during the years 1911-14, covering the period of Sir George Callaghan's command of the Home Fleets, destroyer attacks were practised in the smaller Fleet exercises that were constantly being carried out, and officers were impressed with the supreme importance of the whole matter.

This was the position when I took over the command of the Grand Fleet on the outbreak of War, and the matter immediately engaged my attention. The "counter" which had usually been favoured by flag officers commanding Fleets up to the date named, had been the obvious one of an attack by our own light cruisers and torpedo craft on those of the enemy, as the latter advanced to attack. It was difficult to forecast how far such a "counter" would be successful in preventing the destroyers from firing their torpedoes. Much depended on the distance the torpedo could be relied upon to run with accuracy, and on its speed, both constantly increasing figures.

The great number of destroyers possessed by the enemy, the largely increased range of torpedoes, the difficulty which our light cruisers and flotillas might experience in reaching a favourable position for meeting and disposing of the enemy destroyers before the latter could discharge their torpedoes, together with the danger attendant on meeting the enemy's fleet in weather of low visibility, when a destroyer attack could be instantly and effectively launched before such a "counter" could take place, made it essential to consider other means for dealing with the situation.

Some German documents which came into our possession early in the War proved the importance which the enemy attached to this form of attack, and emphasised the gravity of the question.

It was, of course, fully realised that the question had two sides, and that if our own Battle Fleet was open to this form of attack, that of the enemy was equally so, but as against this there were important considerations to which it was necessary to devote attention.

The first was that the element of chance enters very largely into torpedo warfare of this nature. A flotilla of destroyers attacking a Battle Fleet at long range does so with the idea that a certain percentage of the torpedoes fired will take effect on the ships, the remainder passing between the ships.

Obviously a torpedo fired at a range of 8,000 yards having a speed of 30 knots an hour, or, in other words, of 50 feet per second, is not comparable to a projectile from a gun which has a velocity at 8,000 yards of say 2,000 feet per second. The torpedo may run perfectly straight after discharge, but unless the speed and course of the target have been determined with considerable accuracy, the torpedo will not hit.

Let us assume that the target ship X at position A is steaming at 15 knots, and that the destroyer attacks from a favourable position on the bow so that the torpedo with its speed of 30 knots is discharged on a line at right angles to the course of the target at a distance of 8,000 yards. The target ship will advance 4,000 yards along the line AB whilst the torpedo is running 8,000 yards along the line CB. The time occupied in each case is eight minutes.

It will be seen that if the course of the target ship has been misjudged very slightly, or had been altered during the passage from A to B, the torpedo will pass ahead or astern of it. In that case it might hit instead a ship Z ahead or one Y astern of X.

There are no means available on board a destroyer for determining with any real accuracy either the speed or the course of a ship at a distance of four or five miles. Hence the difficulty, and the reason why torpedoes are fired at a ship a little way down a line of ships, in expectation that one of the ships in the line will be hit. The object in view is thus rather to "brown" the enemy, and the chances of achieving this object are naturally proportional to the target presented by a ship as compared with the space between adjacent ships.

In the case of a British line of eight battleships attacked "beam on," the chances of a hit for torpedoes which reach the British line may be assessed roughly at seven to nine, taking the length of a ship as 600 feet, and the distance from the bow of one ship to the bow of her next astern as two and a half cables, that is 1,500 feet, thus giving a total length of ships of 4,800 feet, and the total of the interval between them as 6,300 feet.

A German destroyer usually carries six torpedoes, and at long ranges one may calculate the chances of hits on the above reasoning at between three and four per destroyer, provided all the torpedoes are correctly fired at such a range as to ensure that they reach the British battle line, and provided that the British ships can take no effective steps to avoid the torpedoes. (Few British destroyers carried more than four torpedoes up to the year 1917, although they mounted a much heavier gun armament than their enemies.)

It has been said that the element of chance is a large factor in torpedo warfare of the nature herein discussed. By this it is meant that skill is not a factor that can produce a decisive effect when dealing with torpedoes, as in the case of guns dealing with guns. It is true that skilful manoeuvring may enable a ship to avoid a torpedo, if sufficient warning of its approach is given, and if its position with reference to any track it is leaving can be correctly judged. When experience at the Jutland Battle showed that under favourable weather conditions the track of German torpedoes was visible for some distance, great care was taken to avoid all mention of this in the dispatches so that future use could be made of the fact.

Another factor in this matter was the knowledge that our enemy was almost certain to possess a very considerable superiority over us in the number of destroyers likely to be present during a Fleet action. This was a question which had given rise to anxiety in the minds of the then First Sea Lord and myself before the War; we had discussed it on more than one occasion when the destroyer building programme was being considered.

Our fears were realised, particularly during the first two years of the War. Of the 80 destroyers belonging to the Grand Fleet at the end of May, 1916, 70 were available to go to sea on May 30th (an unusually large proportion). There happened, also, to be on this date at Rosyth eight destroyers belonging to the Harwich force, and these accompanied the battle cruisers to sea, making a total of 78, of which 47 were with the Battle Fleet and cruisers, and 31 with the Battle Cruiser Fleet, including the 3rd Battle Cruiser Squadron. The smaller German Fleet had 88, a far larger proportion to each ship.

This superiority in numbers on the part of the Germans arose from three causes:

(a) The formation, by us, of a light cruiser and destroyer force at Harwich, the presence of which force during a Fleet action was very improbable, owing to the fact that a Fleet action would, if it took place, probably do so at Germany's selected moment and not at ours, and to the difficulty of concentration under such circumstances.

(b) The necessity of utilising a large number of our destroyers for patrol purposes in the Straits of Dover and elsewhere.

(c) We had not built an adequate number of destroyers in the years before the War to meet the many needs that only this class of vessel could fulfil, particularly as the enemy developed his submarine warfare against merchant-ships.

The shipbuilding programmes of 1908-09, and following years up to 1912-13, included provision for twenty destroyers each year. Subsequent to the latter date, the programme of destroyers was somewhat reduced in order to provide for light cruisers, a class of vessel in which we were woefully deficient. In spite of the continual rise in the Estimates, there was never sufficient money to meet all the Admiralty's needs. It was intimated that one or other of the requirements had to give way at a time when the Navy Estimates were mounting up year by year, and as the light cruisers were considered to be even more necessary than the destroyers, the number of the latter class of vessel was reduced.

Although, in spite of the great destroyer programme initiated by Lord Fisher at the end of 1914, the shortage of destroyers was most seriously felt throughout the whole War, the conditions would probably have been even worse had the pre-War programme of light cruisers been sacrificed to maintain the output of destroyers to the standard desired by the Admiralty.

The last consideration that was present in my mind was the necessity for not leaving anything to chance in a Fleet action, because our Fleet was the one and only factor that was vital to the existence of the Empire, as indeed to the Allied cause. We had no reserve outside the Battle Fleet which could in any way take its place, should disaster befall it or even should its margin of superiority over the enemy be eliminated.

The situation was in many respects different from that with which our Navy was faced in the time of the old wars. In those days disaster could only come about by reason of bad strategy or tactics owing to our enemy being in overwhelming strength when met, or handling his force better, and, apart from manoeuvring, the action was invariably decided by gunfire, a well-known and well-tried weapon.

During the recent War two entirely new features of the greatest importance were introduced. First, the torpedo could be fired at very long range, up to 15,000 yards, either from large ships or destroyers, and at shorter range from submarines, and the mine had been developed; the invisibility of these weapons made it difficult for it to be known when they were being employed.

The reasons which make it necessary to be more cautious when dealing with the attack of underwater weapons than with gun attack are the greater damage which one torpedo hit will cause, which damage may well be fatal to many ships, in most cases compelling the ship to reduce speed and leave the line of battle. With the gun, it is usually different; a ship which is being heavily hit can - if her own offensive powers will not save her by crushing the fire of the enemy - so manoeuvre as to derange temporarily the accuracy of that fire. Therein lies the whole necessity for the exercise of care when dealing with the underwater weapon.

These considerations led me to introduce measures for dealing with destroyer attacks on the Battle Fleet other than the counter of attack by our light craft on the enemy's destroyers. These measures involved a turn on the part of the ships, either towards the torpedoes or away from them.

In the first case, the object was to turn the ships so that they would present as small a target as possible to the torpedo, and incidentally that the space between the ships should be correspondingly large. The matter is very technical, and presents many interesting features, one of which may be illustrated by an example:

Generally speaking a safe course to pursue is for ships to steer direct for the attacking destroyers if the moment at which the torpedoes are fired can be ascertained.

This course, although applicable to one attack, leads to difficulties in the case of successive attacks, since further turns towards will bring the battle line within effective range of torpedoes fired from the enemy's battleships; occasions will arise when this risk must be accepted.

If the torpedoes have been fired at the rear squadron instead of the van squadron as supposed, and their objective is the twentieth ship in the line, they will run along the line CD, i.e., directly at the fourth ship in the line.

The target presented is, however, small, and the chances of a flotilla attacking the rear squadron when in a favourable position for attacking the van are not great.

The important point in the case of a turn towards is, however, the necessity for ascertaining the moment of discharge of the torpedoes.

In the second case, that of turning away, the object is to place the ships at such a distance from the attacking destroyers that the torpedoes will not cross their tracks, but if this object is not achieved the ships are in a good position for avoiding the torpedoes if their tracks are visible; the objection to this manoeuvre is that the range of the enemy's battle line is necessarily opened.

It was my intention in a Fleet action to use one or other of the manoeuvres should destroyer attacks take place under conditions which prevented an effective "counter" by our own light craft; both manoeuvres were arranged to be carried out "by sub-divisions" as a turn by divisions of four ships would delay the completion of the manoeuvre to too great an extent.

The Grand Fleet Battle Orders contained a great deal in the way of discussion and instructions on the subject of torpedo attack in a Fleet action. The duties of light cruisers and destroyers in this connection were dealt with at considerable length, and stress was laid on the supreme importance both of making early torpedo attacks on the enemy's line and of immediately countering such attacks, and it was pointed out that an early attack by our own destroyers would not only tend to stop an enemy attack, but would place our attacking vessels in the best position to meet a hostile attack.

The battle stations of both light cruisers and destroyers were so fixed that they should be in the best positions to effect these two objects, such positions being obviously in the van of the Fleet; in order to provide against a 16-point turn on the part of the enemy, or deployment in the opposite direction to that anticipated, one or two flotillas, according to the numbers available, and a light cruiser squadron, were also stationed in the rear.

The probable tactics of the German Fleet had been a matter of almost daily consideration, and all our experience and thought led to the same conclusion, namely, that retiring tactics, combined with destroyer attacks, would be adopted by them. There were many reasons for this belief, and some of them were as follows:

1. On each occasion when German vessels were met, they had immediately retired towards their bases.

2. The tactical advantages of such a move were obvious. They might be enumerated thus:

(a) The retiring fleet places itself in a position of advantage in regard to torpedo attack on the following fleet. The retiring fleet also eliminates, to a large extent, danger of torpedo attack by the following fleet.

(b) Opportunity is afforded the retiring fleet of drawing its opponent over a mine or submarine trap.

(c) Smoke screens can be used with effect to interfere with the observation of gunfire by the following fleet.

(d) Considerations of moral effect will force the stronger fleet to follow the weaker, and play into the hands of the enemy.

We were so certain that the enemy would adopt these tactics that in all the many exercises carried out by the Fleet during the War, it was the invariable rule to indicate beforehand an assumed position of Heligoland, and the Flag officer, representing the Commander-in-Chief of the High Sea Fleet in these exercises, always deployed his Fleet in the direction of Heligoland and adopted retiring tactics. The difficulties resulting from the employment of these retiring tactics and the best method to adopt in the circumstances were, therefore, the subject of constant thought, both by myself and by all the senior officers in the Fleet, and the subject was very frequently discussed and worked out on the tactical board.

The difficulty is, to a certain extent, insuperable if retiring tactics are employed in conjunction with a free and skilful use of underwater weapons.

When, therefore, the two Fleets met on May 31st, 1916, these thoughts were in my mind, and were no doubt present in the minds of all Flag officers in the British Fleet. It has been mentioned that the circumstances of the meeting made it very difficult to ascertain with any degree of certainty the disposition of the enemy's Battle Fleet, and the deployment of our own Fleet took place under these conditions. Even so, however, the course on deployment (that is, southeast by east) was to a certain extent governed by the idea of getting between the enemy and his base on the supposition that he would be making towards it by the shortest route, namely, the Horn Reef Channel.

The arrival of the 3rd Battle Cruiser Squadron in a commanding position on the bow of the enemy caused the enemy to make a large turn to starboard, largely because this squadron - Rear-Admiral Hood's - was mistaken for the British Battle Fleet. The German account, as I have already mentioned, bears out this view, as it is stated that at about 5.45 p.m. "dim shapes of enemy battleships are discerned in a north-easterly direction." These shapes were undoubtedly the 3rd Battle Cruiser Squadron. The German account states that their battle cruisers turned away on sighting these ships. This gave the British Battle Fleet the chance of placing itself between the enemy and his base. Advantage was taken of this opportunity, and the enemy was then forced to pursue his retiring tactics in a westerly direction. In making the large turns required to affect our object, we were inevitably placed in a position of tactical disadvantage owing to the British Fleet working round on a wide circle outside the enemy.

A careful study of the movements of the two Fleets will show this at once. The course of the British Fleet on deployment was southeast by east. Successive turns to starboard brought the course through south by west to southwest and finally to west, a total alteration of 13 points on the outer of two similar arcs, some 12,000 yards apart, the German Fleet moving on the inner of these two circles.

The result was that the "overlap," which the Germans erroneously thought was in favour of the British Battle Fleet, but which was always with the enemy, was accentuated, and the Grand Fleet was gradually brought farther and farther abaft the beam of the High Sea Fleet, placing the latter in a position of tactical advantage in regard to torpedo attack. This advantage was increased by the low visibility, which rendered it difficult to see flotillas approaching to attack until they were at fairly short range.

When the first attack by German destroyers took place and the first of the enemy's flotillas was seen to be approaching on a bearing 30 degrees before the beam of the Iron Duke, and had reached a distance of 9,000 yards or less, the "counter" of a turn "towards" or "away" was essential. Our own flotillas had been using every endeavour to get to the van, but the frequent turns to starboard and the movement of our battle cruisers across the bows of the Battle Fleet had delayed their movement, and it was evident that neither they nor the light cruisers could prevent the attack from developing.

The moment of discharge of torpedoes could not be determined with sufficient accuracy for a turn "towards" and therefore the Battle Fleet was "turned away," in subdivisions.

Although I was not aware of the fact at the time, coincidentally with the destroyer attack the enemy made a very large turn-away from our Fleet, and thus opened the range much farther, disappearing entirely from view even from our rear; this process was repeated on each occasion of our ships getting back into range. The enemy was, therefore, continually refusing action.

It may be asked whether it was necessary to turn the whole line of battle away for this attack, or whether the leading squadron could not have held the original course. Such a movement was provided for in the Battle Orders, but the destroyers were observed at a range of 9,000 yards on a bearing 30 degrees before the beam of the Iron Duke, the leading ship of the centre battle squadron, and therefore the leading Battle Squadron was as open to attack by torpedoes as was the centre or rear squadron; indeed, the destroyers were standing in a direction to attack the van squadron. The rear of the leading Battle Squadron was also not at the time clear of the van of the centre squadron, as the turns that had been made had prevented line ahead being re-formed, and the Iron Duke's

Division could not turn unless the division ahead also turned. These facts strengthened the reasons which led me to make the signal general to the Battle Fleet.

According to the reports of the captains of the ships of the Battle Fleet, a total of at least 20 torpedoes crossed the line of our Battle Fleet during the 7.10 p.m. destroyer attack alone, in spite of the turn. The large majority of these were observed by the ships of the 1st and 5th Battle Squadrons, but one torpedo is known to have crossed the line ahead of the Iron Duke, and at least six crossed the track of the 4th Light Cruiser Squadron, which was moving out to attack the enemy's flotilla.

In the case of a long line of ships there is always danger of the torpedo menace to the ships at the rear being forgotten or minimised by ships that are in the van, owing to failure to realise how dangerous the torpedo fire of ships or destroyers abreast of them may be to vessels a long way in rear, although they themselves are quite immune from this danger.

The Grand Fleet Battle Orders provided for considerable decentralisation of command, and great stress was laid on this point in the general instructions for "Battle Tactics." The opening paragraphs of this section of the Battle Orders emphasised this strongly. It was pointed out that whilst the Commander-in-Chief would control the movements of the whole Battle Fleet before and on deployment (except in the extreme case of very low visibility rendering it necessary for the Flag officer of a wing division to take immediate action), he could not be certain of doing so after deployment, when funnel and other smoke made both vision and communication difficult. The necessity for wide decentralisation of command was then pointed out, combined with a close watch on the movements of the Commander-in-Chief, with which Flag officers should generally conform.

The Battle of Jutland was the first Fleet action since Trafalgar if we except the actions in the Russo-Japanese War, and advantage was naturally taken of the experience to make some changes in the Battle Orders; but there were no surprises in the way of enemy tactics, and, therefore, no radical alterations were necessary. As the Chief of the Staff remarked to me during the Battle Fleet engagement, "This is all going according to expectation." We did, however, obtain confirmation of our views as to the probable retiring tactics that would be adopted by the German fleet.

The principal changes that were made in the Battle Orders were in the direction of laying still further emphasis on the discretionary power which was vested in Flag Officers commanding squadrons, owing to the difficulty, always clearly recognised, and confirmed at Jutland, which the Commander-in-Chief would experience in controlling the movements of the whole Fleet in the heat of action; also in defining still further the different movements that might be adopted to deal with torpedo attacks, whether the torpedoes were fired from battleships or from destroyers.

A very exhaustive analysis of the subject of torpedo attacks in action had been prepared by my Staff during the spring of 1916, and a memorandum, with diagrams, had been written showing the various situations that might arise and the effect of the different counter-movements in each case. It is of interest to note that this memorandum was on the point of issue when the Jutland Battle was fought. It was dated May 27th, 1916, but it had not actually been issued.

The experience gained at Jutland was embodied in the memorandum before it was finally issued to the Fleet. The questions of the use of the torpedo in action and the "counter" measures adopted have been dealt with at considerable length, since this form of attack and its "counter" have been much discussed in the Service since 1911, and it is a subject on which discussion is likely to continue. It is also certain that it will form the subject of much future experiment.

The German attacks at Jutland did not produce any great effect, and their importance should not be exaggerated. The turn of the British Battle Fleet opened the range some 1,750 yards, but it was not this turn which led to the difficulty of keeping touch with the enemy. That difficulty was due to the fact that the German Fleet made a very large turn to the westward under cover of a smoke screen at the moment of launching the earliest destroyer attacks. Neither our battle cruisers in the van which did not turn away at the time, as it was not necessary in their case, nor the Battle Fleet, were able to regain touch until 8.20 p.m. because of the retirement of the enemy.

The instructions as to my intentions as the Commander-in-Chief, in regard to the ranges at which the opening phases of the action should be fought, remained unaltered, and stress was once more laid on the policy of keeping the centre and rear of the Battle Fleet outside torpedo range from the enemy's battle line in ordinary circumstance.

As is very frequently the case when naval actions do not result in overwhelming material losses by one side or the other, or the capture or destruction of a large part of the opposing Fleet, both sides at the time claimed a victory at Jutland, the Germans because they hoped to support confidence at home and encourage a young Fleet, besides influencing neutral, and probably in particular American, opinion.

The Germans apparently based their claim on two grounds, the first being that of having inflicted heavier losses than they received. In order to make good this contention, the Germans claimed to have sunk one battleship, one armoured cruiser, three light cruisers, and five destroyers more than actually were sunk on the British side; and they concealed, until further concealment was impossible, the sinking of the battle cruiser Lutzow and the light cruiser Rostock, besides omitting to mention that the Seydlitz had to be beached to prevent her sinking, thereby slurring over the point that the Seydlitz would undoubtedly have gone to the bottom as our own Warrior did, had the action been fought as far from German bases as it was from British bases.

They also said nothing of at least four German battleships being torpedoed, and of several battleships and all their battle cruisers being so severely damaged by gunfire as to be incapable of further fighting for several months. The case was very different with the British ships, as has been already stated. If these points are borne in mind, the original German claim to victory falls to the ground, even on the material side. After the surrender of the German ships in November, 1918, Captain Persius, a reputable and informed writer on naval matters, stated in the Berliner Tagehlatt of November 18th that "our Fleet's losses were severe," adding that "on June 1st, 1916, it was clear to every thinking person that this battle must, and would be, the last one. Authoritative quarters," he declared, "said so openly".

But a victory is judged not merely by material losses and damage, but by its results. It is profitable to examine the results of the Jutland Battle. With the single exception of a cruise towards the English coast on August 19th, 1916 - undertaken, no doubt, by such part of the High Sea Fleet as had been repaired in order to show that it was still capable of going to sea - the High Sea Fleet never again, up to the end of 1917, ventured much outside the "Heligoland triangle," and even on August 19th, 1916, the much reduced Fleet made precipitately for home as soon as it was warned by its Zeppelin scouts of the approach of the Grand Fleet. This is hardly the method of procedure that would be adopted by a Fleet flushed with victory and belonging to a country which was being strangled by the sea blockade.

Again, in the German account of the "victory" it is remarked that "as the dawn coloured the eastern sky on the historic 1st of June, everyone expected that the rising sun would illuminate the British line deployed in readiness to renew the battle. This expectation was not realised. As far as the eye could reach the horizon was clear. Not until the late morning did our airships, which had gone up in the meantime, announce that a Battle Squadron consisting of twelve ships was approaching from the southern part of the North Sea at full speed on a northerly course. To the great regret of all concerned, it was too late for our Fleet to overtake and attack theirs."

What are the facts? We know now that as the sun rose, the High Sea Fleet (except such portions as were escaping via the Skaw) was close to the Horn Reef, steaming as fast as the damaged ships could go for home behind the shelter of the German minefields. And the Grand Fleet was waiting for them to appear and searching the waters to the westward and northward of the Horn Reef for the enemy vessels; it maintained the search during the forenoon of June 1st, and the airship, far from sighting the Fleet late in the morning, as stated, did so, first at 3.30 a.m., and on several occasions subsequently during the forenoon. And if that airship reported only twelve ships present, what an opportunity for the victorious High Sea Fleet to annihilate them! One is forced to the conclusion that this victorious fleet did not consider itself capable of engaging only twelve British battleships.

I cannot conclude these remarks on the Jutland Battle without mentioning the personnel of the Fleet. From the second in command. Sir Cecil Burney, to the youngest boy, who was possibly young Cornwell in the Chester, the Fleet was imbued with the same high spirit and determination. Sir Cecil Burney was an old and trusted friend, a fine seaman who always handled his squadron - or, in my absence, the Fleet - with marked skill and ability. Sir Martyn Jerram, who held a high reputation as a squadron commander; Sir Doveton Sturdee, the victor at the Falkland Islands, an officer who had made a special study of tactics; Rear-Admiral Evan-Thomas, and the other squadron leaders, including my very old friends and gallant brother officers Sir Robert Arbuthnot and Rear-Admiral Hood, by whose deaths the nation and Fleet lost of their best - were all officers of proved ability, in whom not myself only, but the Fleet, had absolute confidence. In Sir David Beatty the Battle Cruiser Fleet possessed a leader who throughout his Service career had shown fighting qualities of the highest order, and he had imbued his force with his own indomitable spirit. The Flag officers second in command of squadrons had all led divisions for a considerable period, and I was confident that they would handle their divisions as well in action as they did during exercises, as proved to be the case.

The officers commanding Light Cruiser Squadrons and destroyer flotillas had invariably fulfilled every expectation that I had formed of them. I had always admired the manner in which the personnel of these vessels had endured the conditions under which their work was so frequently performed.

Assisted as I was by a brilliant Staff, with Rear-Admiral Sir Charles Madden (my right-hand man throughout) and Commodore Lionel Halsey as its chief members, seconded by such able and experienced Flag officers, and with captains who had on countless occasions shown their skill, I was indeed in a fortunate position.

To the above advantages I must add those obtained by the magnificence of the personnel of the lower ranks. The officers and ships' companies were as keen as any Commander-in-Chief could desire. The long wait had never produced the slightest feeling of staleness. Officers and men were day after day striving to perfect the fighting efficiency of their ships, and well had they succeeded. The engine room staffs had demonstrated early in the War that they would respond magnificently to any demand that I called upon them to make, and they did it on the occasion of the Jutland Battle. The spirit and moral of the Fleet never stood higher than at the time of the Battle of Jutland, and because of that spirit I knew that the Fleet under my command was the most formidable fighting machine in the world.

Of the gallantry shown it is difficult to write with proper restraint. Whenever and wherever there was opportunity, officers and men displayed courage and self-sacrifice of the highest order. There were innumerable instances which proved that the personnel of the present Navy has nothing to learn in this respect from its forefathers. The dead died heroic deaths; the wounded behaved with marvellous fortitude. Forty-four years passed in the Service had given me unbounded faith in, and admiration for, the British officer and bluejacket, but they surpassed all my expectations, and so long as that spirit endures, this country will be fortunate, and with adequate forces will be safe.

It may not be out of place to quote the memorandum issued to the Fleet after the Jutland Battle:

Iron Duke, June 4th, 1916.
H.F. 0022 849.
MEMORANDUM.

I desire to express to the Flag Officers, Captains, Officers and Men of the Grand Fleet my very high appreciation of the manner in which the ships were fought during the action on May 31st, 1916.

2. At this stage, when full information is not available, it is not possible to enter into details, but quite sufficient is already known to enable me to state definitely that the glorious traditions handed down to us by generations of gallant seamen were most worthily upheld.

3. Weather conditions of a highly unfavourable nature robbed the Fleet of that complete victory which I know was expected by all ranks, which is necessary for the safety of the Empire and which will yet be ours.

4. Our losses were heavy, and we miss many most gallant comrades, but, although it is very difficult to obtain accurate information as to the enemy losses, I have no doubt that we shall find that they are certainly not less than our own. Sufficient information has already been received for me to make that statement with confidence.

I hope to be able to give the Fleet fuller information on this point at an early date, but do not wish to delay the issue of this expression of my keen appreciation of the work of the Fleet, and my confidence in future complete victory.

5. I cannot close without stating that the wonderful spirit and fortitude of the wounded has filled me with the greatest admiration.

I am more proud than ever to have the honour of commanding a fleet manned by such officers and men.

J. R. JELLICOE.

Admiral, Commander-in-Chief.

The Flag Officers, Commodores and Officers in command of H.M. ships of the Grand Fleet.

My official despatch on the battle to the Board of Admiralty was forwarded on June 19th, and the following letter was afterwards promulgated to the Grand Fleet:

Admiralty, July 4th, 1916.

Sir, - My Lords Commissioners of the Admiralty have considered your reports on the action off the Jutland Bank between the Grand Fleet under your command and the German High Sea Fleet on the 31st May, together with the report of the Vice-Admiral Commanding the Battle Cruiser Fleet, and those of the various Flag Officers and Commanding Officers of the Grand Fleet.

2. Their lordships congratulate the officers, seamen, and marines of the Grand Fleet on this, the first Fleet action which has occurred since the outbreak of the war, as a result of which the enemy, severely punished, withdrew to his own ports. The events of the 31st May and 1st June gave ample proof of the gallantry and devotion which characterised all who took part in the battle; the ships of every class were handled with skill and determination; their steaming under battle conditions afforded a splendid testimony to the zeal and efficiency of the engineering staff; while individual initiative and tactical subordination were equally conspicuous.

3. The results of the action prove that the officers and men of the Grand Fleet have known both how to study the new problems with which they are confronted and how to turn their knowledge to account. The expectations of the country were high; they have been well fulfilled.

4. My Lords desire me to convey to you their full approval of your proceedings on this occasion.

I am, sir, your obedient servant,
W. Graham Greene.

The Battle of Barfleur, 1692

Image: Artist Richard Paton (1717–1791)

16 - Lessons of Experience

The ships which had received damage in the Jutland Battle had to be repaired without delay. The great majority of the repairs were completed during June or by the first week in July, and, whilst under repair, the opportunity was taken of effecting certain alterations which experience gained in the action had shown to be desirable. The Marlborough was the only large ship whose repairs occupied any considerable length of time, and even she rejoined the Fleet in August, although the work upon her was handicapped to some extent by being carried out in a floating dock moored in a somewhat inconvenient position. The light cruiser Chester was also detained at Hull until July 29th, as her injuries from gunfire were fairly extensive, and a great many alterations were carried out. The principal points affecting materiel to which attention was directed were:

(a) The urgent need for arrangements to prevent the flash of cordite charges, ignited by the explosion of a shell in a turret or in positions between the turret and the magazine, being communicated to the magazine itself. It was probable that the loss of one, if not two, of our battle cruisers was due to this cause, after the armour had been pierced.

(b) Better measures were required to prevent the charges of small guns from being ignited by bursting shell, and to localise any fires due to this cause, in the case of guns of the secondary battery in large ships, and the main armament in small ships.

(c) Increased deck armour protection in large ships had been shown to be desirable in order that shell or fragments of shell might not reach the magazines. This need was particularly felt in all our earlier ships of the Dreadnought type since their side armour was not carried to the upper deck level. The long range at which most modern sea actions are fought, and the consequent large angle of descent of the projectiles made our ships very vulnerable in this respect.

(d) The pressing need for a better armour-piercing projectile with an improved fuze was also revealed.

(e) Improved arrangements for flooding magazines and drenching exposed cartridges had to be made.

Committees were immediately appointed in the Fleet to deal with all questions of this nature, as well as the important matter of possible developments in the fire-control system with a view to improving the methods of correction of fire to enable enemy ships to be "straddled" with greater rapidity. In all these matters, the great gunnery knowledge and experience of Captain F. C. Dreyer, my Flag Captain, were of immense assistance, and he was most ably seconded by the numerous highly skilled gunnery officers on the staffs of the Flag officers and in the ships of the fleet.

The action taken in connection with these matters was prompt, with the gratifying result that before I relinquished the command of the Fleet, the great majority of the heavy ships had been provided with additional deck protection on an extensive scale, and with fittings for rendering their magazines safe. Most of the work was carried out while the ships were at their usual notice for steam, much of it being actually done at Scapa Flow by the dockyard artificers berthed there on board the Victorious: the work carried out by these artificers and by the dockyard staff at Invergordon was executed with most commendable rapidity.

Later, during my period of service at the Admiralty, as First Sea Lord, and under the immediate direction of Captain Dreyer, then Director of Naval Ordnance, a new design of armour-piercing projectile, with a new type of burster and an altered fuse, was introduced for guns of 12-inch calibre and above, which certainly doubled their offensive power.

The investigation into the possibility of further development in fire-correction methods, a subject to which constant attention had been given throughout the War, was at first carried out by two independent committees. Their conclusions were considered by a third Committee, composed of the most experienced and most successful gunnery officers in the Fleet, and modified rules were, as the result, drawn up and passed for adoption in the Fleet; these had already produced a most convincing and most satisfactory advance in accuracy and rapidity of fire before I gave up Command of the Grand Fleet. It is no exaggeration to say that the average time taken to find the gun range of the enemy with these new methods was about one half of that previously required.

Some delay occurred in improving our rangefinders. The majority had been installed in the Fleet before the great increases in the range of opening effective fire had come about, as the result of experience during the War. Our most modern ships at Jutland were provided with rangefinders 15 feet in length, but the majority of the ships present were fitted with instruments only nine feet long. During 1917 successful steps were taken to supply rangefinders up to 25 and 30 feet in length; a series of experiments with stereoscopic rangefinders was also instituted in the same year. It had become known that the Germans used this type of rangefinder. It should be stated, in passing, to prevent any misunderstanding, that the developments introduced in the fire-control arrangements of the Grand Fleet after the Battle of Jutland did not affect the instruments already in use, which fully met our requirements, but the methods of using those instruments and particularly the system of correction of fire.

On June 5th the Battle Cruiser Squadrons and Cruiser Squadrons were reorganised as follows:

Battle Cruiser Squadron
Lion (Fleet-Flagship of Battle Cruiser Fleet).
1st Battle Cruiser Squadron: Princess Royal (Flag), New Zealand, Tiger.
2nd Battle Cruiser Squadron: Australia (Flag), Indomitable, Inflexible.
Cruiser Squadrons
2nd Cruiser Squadron: Minotaur (Flag), Duke of Edinburgh, Cochrane, Shannon, Achilles, Donegal.
3rd Cruiser Squadron: Antrim, Roxburgh, Devonshire.

On June 5th Field Marshal Lord Kitchener arrived at Scapa en route to Archangel. In the morning he crossed from

Thurso in the Oak, and came on board the Iron Duke on arrival at Scapa. He lunched with me, and the Flag officers present were invited to meet him. Before lunch we went round the ship. The officers and men naturally greeted him with much respect, and he can have had no doubt of the admiration in which he was held. During lunch he discussed with me his forthcoming trip, and said once or twice that he was looking forward to it as a real holiday. The strain of the last two years, he confessed, had been very great, adding that he had felt that he could not have gone on without this break, which he welcomed very much.

He was not, however, very sanguine that he could achieve much in Russia. He mentioned the difficulty which he experienced in dealing with questions discussed in the Cabinet, a difficulty felt by most soldiers and sailors, whose training does not fit them to state or to argue a case, and who frequently find great difficulty in doing so. They are, as a rule, accustomed to carry out their ideas without having first to bring conviction to the minds of men who, although possessing great general knowledge and administrative experience, have naturally but little acquaintance with naval and military affairs which in themselves form a lifelong study.

After lunch conversation turned to the Jutland action, and Lord Kitchener evinced much interest in the tactics and the general story of the action. Lord Kitchener impressed me strongly with the idea that he was working to a timetable, and that he felt that he had not a day to lose. He mentioned three weeks as the limit of his absence, and I expressed astonishment at the programme which he had planned to carry out in the restricted period. He was most anxious not to lose a moment on the sea trip and asked me more than once what I thought was the shortest time in which the passage could be made. During the day the weather at Scapa, which had been bad in the morning, gradually became worse, and by the afternoon it was blowing a gale from the north-eastward. It had been originally intended that the Hampshire should take the route which passed up the eastern side of the Orkneys, following the channel ordinarily searched by minesweeping vessels as a routine measure; but as the north-easterly gale was causing a heavy sea on that side, minesweeping was out of the question, and it was also obvious that the escorting destroyers could not face the sea at high speed. I discussed with my Staff which route on the west, or lee, side would be the safest, and finally decided that the Hampshire should pass close in shore, and not take the alternative route passing farther to the westward near Sule Skerry Lighthouse. The reasons which influenced this decision were:

(a) With a north-easterly wind there would be less sea and, therefore, more chance of the destroyers being able to keep up with the Hampshire.

(b) It was practically impossible that this route could have been mined by any surface minelayer owing to the dark period in Northern latitudes being confined to a couple of hours, during which no ship could expect to approach the shore for minelaying without having first been sighted.

(c) The route was one used by Fleet auxiliaries, and was, therefore, under frequent observation.

At this date, minelaying by enemy submarines had been confined to water well to the southward of the Firth of Forth, presumably because of their small radius of action. Danger from this source was, therefore, considered to be very remote.

Finally the weather itself was a protection against submarine attack which was at that time more to be feared than the danger from submarine laid mines. Minesweeping on either side of the Orkneys had not been practicable for three or four days owing to the weather conditions.

At about 4 p.m. Lord Kitchener proceeded on board the Hampshire, accompanied by his Staff comprising Brigadier-General Ellershaw, Sir F. Donaldson, Colonel FitzGerald, Mr. O'Beirne of the Foreign Office, Mr. Robertson of the Munitions Department, and Second-Lieutenant McPherson, Cameron Highlanders. The Hampshire sailed at 5.30 p.m. escorted by two destroyers. Her orders were to proceed at a speed of at least 16 knots, if the weather permitted, and to send the destroyers back if they could not maintain the Hampshire's speed. Experience had proved that high speed was a valuable protection against submarines.

At about 7 p.m. Captain Savill, commanding the Hampshire, ordered the two destroyers back to Scapa, as they were unable to face the heavy seas at the speed of the Hampshire. Between 7.30 and 7.45 p.m. the Hampshire struck a mine about 1½ miles offshore, between the Brough of Birsay and Marwick Head; she sank in 15 minutes, bows first. The incident was witnessed by observers on shore, and a telephone message was sent to the Vice-Admiral Commanding Orkneys and Shetlands that the cruiser was in difficulties. He at once ordered out patrol vessels and informed me, with the result that destroyers were sent to the scene immediately.

The evidence of the few survivors of the Hampshire showed that Lord Kitchener was below when the ship was mined, and that an officer escorted him on deck. Captain Savill was heard to give directions from the bridge for a boat to be prepared for Lord Kitchener and his Staff, and Lord Kitchener was seen subsequently on deck, but was not seen after the ship sank. The weather conditions prevented any boats being hoisted out or lowered, although four boats floated clear as the ship sank.

The scene of the disaster was searched during the night by destroyers and patrol craft, but the only survivors were twelve men who drifted ashore on a Carley raft, although many bodies were picked up by the searching vessels, and many drifted ashore.

The body of Lord Kitchener was not recovered.

At the time of the disaster the Hampshire was steaming at 13½ knots, the wind being north-northwest, with a force of 50 miles an hour. The cold water and the very heavy sea were against even the strongest swimmers surviving for any time. The wind, which was north-east at 4 p.m. at Scapa, had become north-northwest by the time the Hampshire was outside, and there was, therefore, no lee on the west side of the Orkneys, as had been anticipated.

The hours that passed after the receipt of the report of the Hampshire being in difficulties were most anxious ones. In spite of the fact that the destroyers had been sent back, it seemed almost incredible that the wind and sea could have risen to such an extent as was actually the case, as the conditions in Scapa Flow were not so bad as to indicate so extremely heavy a sea off the Brough of Birsay; and even when it was reported that the Hampshire had sunk (a report which took some time to come through), there was hope that, at any rate, Lord Kitchener and his mission would be saved by boat. As the hours passed and no news was received of the rescue of any survivors, the anxiety became intense. With the arrival of daylight, and the certainty that this great man, who had served his country so faithfully and well in its greatest emergency, had met his death when under the care of the Navy, the anxiety turned to consternation and grief.

Lord Kitchener had inspired the Service with confidence and trust. The Navy had frequently worked under him in Egypt and in South Africa, and he had been one of the outstanding figures in the European War on the side of the Entente. Everyone in the Grand Fleet felt the magnitude of the disaster that had fallen upon the nation, and it can well be imagined that the feelings of the Fleet generally were intensified in me, on whom lay the main responsibility for his safe passage to Archangel, so far as such safety could be ensured.

I have often wondered since that fatal day whether anything could have been done that was not done, but short of postponing the departure of the Hampshire altogether, until weather conditions admitted of a channel being swept ahead of her, nothing could have been done. Such a decision would have resulted in two or three days delay in starting, and would never have been agreed to by Lord Kitchener. Moreover, with the knowledge then at my disposal as to enemy minelaying possibilities, I did not consider the delay necessary as I should not have hesitated, if need had arisen, to take the Grand Fleet to sea on the same night and by the same route as that traversed by the Hampshire.

My own sorrow for the incident was overwhelming. There was, at first, doubt in the minds of some people as to whether the loss of the Hampshire was due to a mine or to a submarine, but these doubts were set at rest by the sweeping operations which were undertaken as soon as the weather admitted. They resulted in the discovery of moored mines of the type laid in southern waters by enemy submarines, these mines being easily distinguishable from those laid by surface vessels.

During the month of June cruisers were kept constantly patrolling the route to Archangel to protect shipping against possible enemy raiders, as the traffic was very heavy at this period. The Donegal, Antrim, Devonshire and Roxburgh were the vessels employed. They visited the Norwegian coast in the vicinity of Stadlandet, en route to and from patrol, with a view to intercepting vessels carrying ore from Narvik.

The submarines of the 11th Submarine Flotilla were employed in watching the waters in the Kattegat and cruised in the Skagerrak and off the Norwegian coast, looking for enemy submarines and surface craft. A regular submarine patrol was also begun off the Horn Reef, and was continued up to the time of my relinquishing command of the Fleet. At first two, and later, three, submarines were used for this patrol, which was of great utility in giving information of the movements of the few enemy surface vessels that ever ventured so far from their base, and also proved of use for attacking enemy submarines. At the commencement, the efficiency of our submarines for patrol and look-out purposes was very inferior as compared with that of the German submarines, by reason of their bad wireless equipment, which admitted of a range of some 60 miles only. As soon as submarines were attached to the Grand Fleet, I represented strongly the absolute necessity of effecting an improvement in this particular, stating that I was quite prepared to sacrifice some of the torpedo armament should this be necessary, but that it was a vital matter to install efficient wireless apparatus in the only class of vessel that could carry out a watching patrol in the vicinity of German bases. Eventually arrangements were made to provide them with a wireless installation which gave a range of 300 to 400 miles.

When our submarines had been equipped in this way we were at once able to establish an efficient chain of outposts off the Horn Reef by the Grand Fleet submarines; and from Terschelling to the northward the Harwich submarines were on duty, with the result that in daylight, at any rate, it was very difficult for the enemy to put to sea unobserved and unreported. The comparative inefficiency of the wireless installation in our submarines, and to a lesser extent in our destroyers, was one of the disadvantages which we had to face during the first two years of War. It should be added that while patrolling in the Kattegat, submarine G 4 sank by gunfire on June 19th, outside territorial waters, the German steamship Ems, on passage from Christiania to Lubeck with oil, zinc and copper. The crew were rescued.

The cruiser and light cruiser movements during the month, other than the usual patrols, were as follows:

The 1st Light Cruiser Squadron, with destroyers, left Rosyth on the 14th for the Naze, thence steered up the Norwegian Coast to Udsire, and returned to Rosyth.

The Comus and Constance left Scapa on the 25th, swept down the Norwegian coast and returned on the 27th.

The 3rd Light Cruiser Squadron and destroyers carried out a similar sweep from Rosyth between the 29th June and July 1st.

On June 22nd the first mines from a British submarine minelayer were laid by E 41 in the German Bight.

His Majesty the King honoured the Grand Fleet with a visit on the 14th, arriving at Scapa from Thurso in the Oak, at 5 p.m., being escorted by the destroyers of the 11th Flotilla. After steaming round the Fleet in the Oak, His Majesty proceeded on board the Iron Duke, where he spent the night. On the following day the King visited all the flagships, on board of which a large percentage of officers and men from the various squadrons were assembled, and left for Thurso in the Oak at 5 p.m., proceeded to Invergordon, and thence to Rosyth, honouring the squadrons at each of these bases with a visit.

His Majesty addressed a representative gathering of officers and men from the ships at Scapa, who had been assembled on board the Iron Duke on the morning of the 15th in the following terms: -

"Sir John Jellicoe, officers, and men of the Grand Fleet, you have waited for nearly two years with most exemplary patience for the opportunity of meeting and engaging the enemy's fleet.

"I can well understand how trying has been this period, and how great must have been the relief when you knew on May 31st that the enemy had been sighted.

"Unfavourable weather conditions and approaching darkness prevented that complete result which you all expected, but you did all that was possible in the circumstances. You drove the enemy into his harbours, and inflicted on him very severe losses, and you added yet another page to the glorious traditions of the British Navy.

"You could not do more, and for your splendid work I thank you."

The average weekly report of the 10th Cruiser Squadron during June, gave as the figures: - No. of ships intercepted, 55 and 22 trawlers; No. sent in, 20; No. on patrol, 13; No. absent at ports or en route to a given patrol, 8; No. on special service, 1.

A great deal of fog and mist was experienced during the month - especially in the latter half - and this interfered somewhat with the work of the 10th Cruiser Squadron. A very dense fog prevailed in the Pentland Firth on June 22nd and 23rd. Strong winds, principally from the northward, were prevalent during the first portion of the month, and a northerly gale occurred on the 5th.

No large Fleet movements took place during June, as it was known that the greater part of the High Sea Fleet was under repair as the result of the Jutland action.

During July the Battle Fleet as a whole only engaged in one cruise, namely, from the 17th to the 20th. The 1st, 2nd, 4th and 5th Battle Squadrons, 2nd and 3rd Cruiser Squadrons, 4th Light Cruiser Squadron, the Campania, with seaplanes, and destroyer flotillas left Scapa between noon and 1.30 p.m. on the 17th, and proceeded to the northward and eastward of the Shetlands. The opportunity was taken of carrying out a series of battle exercises on the 18th and 19th; they were based on the experience gained of enemy tactics during the Jutland action. Some of the flotillas were re-fuelled at Lerwick during the cruise, and the Fleet returned to Scapa and Cromarty during the forenoon of the 20th. Fog was met with as the ships approached the Pentland Firth, making entry somewhat difficult.

Cruiser movements during the month comprised:

(a) A regular patrol of the Archangel route by Grand Fleet Cruisers to protect trade against raiders.

(b) The establishment on the 7th of a regular patrol of two cruisers and two destroyers in an area well to the northward of the Shetlands, this patrol taking the place of that of a cruiser and armed boarding-steamer which had been previously placed there.

(c) Extensive dispositions were made on the 9th to intercept a German raider reported from neutral quarters, as about to leave for the Atlantic. These dispositions included a close patrol by two light cruiser squadrons and eight destroyers from Rosyth of an area 80 to 100 miles off the Norwegian coast through which it was expected the enemy would pass; a further patrol by the 4th Light Cruiser Squadron and six destroyers was established farther north to ensure a daylight intercept of hostile vessels; two cruisers were ordered to patrol north of the Shetlands, local patrol vessels being between these cruisers and the Shetlands; a half flotilla of destroyers patrolled the Fair Island Channel. (The dispositions remained in force until the 14th, no enemy vessels being sighted; the report was probably incorrect.)

(d) Two light cruisers and six destroyers left Rosyth on the 12th and swept up the Norwegian coast and back, returning on the 15th.

(e) On the 17th two more light cruisers and six destroyers repeated the sweep, returning on the 20th.

(f) On the 21st two light cruisers and four destroyers left Rosyth and swept to the southward in the direction of the Horn Reef from a position near the Naze, returning on the 23rd, not having sighted anything.

(g) Two light cruisers and four destroyers repeated the sweep of the Norwegian coast on the 24th.

(h) The 2nd Light Cruiser Squadron, with four destroyers, left Rosyth on the 26th, and proceeded to a position to the westward of the Little Fisher Bank, thence swept during daylight to the Naze on the lookout for enemy raiders or Zeppelins, reports having been received of the frequent presence of Zeppelins on this line; the force turned to the northward from the Naze and swept along the 100-fathom line to Lat. 59 N., proceeding thence to Scapa. The sweep was again uneventful.

The submarines of the 11th (Grand Fleet) Flotilla were active during the month in the Kattegat and patrolling off the Horn Reef. They reported on the 20th that nothing but enemy submarines and aircraft were visible.

The attacks by enemy submarines on warships reported during July were:

The minesweeping sloop Rosemary of the Southern Force was torpedoed on the 4th, but was towed into the Humber.

The light cruiser Galatea was missed by a torpedo on the 12th, in Lat. 57.48 N., Long. 1.14 E.

The armed boarding-steamer Duke of Cornwall was missed by two torpedoes on the 18th, whilst engaged in boarding a ship southeast of the Pentland Skerries.

The light cruiser Yarmouth was missed by a torpedo on the 26th.

Three armed trawlers of the Peterhead patrol were sunk by the gunfire of four enemy submarines, on the 11th, in Lat. 57.14 N., Long. 1.11 E., their guns being entirely outranged by the 4-inch guns with which the submarines are armed. This combined attack on the trawlers of the Peterhead patrol, although resulting in the regrettable loss of the three trawlers, was a great and well-deserved tribute paid by the enemy to the work of that patrol which had been uniformly successful, and had proved a great annoyance to the German submarines.

Attempts were made to locate and destroy enemy submarines on the 7th, to the eastward of the Pentland Firth; on the 12th, two divisions of destroyers were sent from Scapa to attack the submarine that had fired at the Duke of Cornwall, the Musketeer dropping a depth charge close to the periscope of the submarine, and it was thought considerably damaging her; on the 15th, destroyers and seaplanes from Scapa were sent after a submarine reported by the armed boarding steamer Dundee as sighted 10 miles east-southeast of the Pentland Skerries, but she was not seen again; on the 29th, a division of destroyers again attempted to locate a submarine in that vicinity, but failed to do so.

Mines laid by an enemy submarine were discovered by the sweeping trawlers in the southern channel in the Moray Firth on the 26th, and were swept up by trawlers and fleet sweepers before any damage was done.

The weekly average of the 10th Cruiser Squadron showed: No. of vessels intercepted, 62 and 34 trawlers; No. sent in, 23; No. on patrol, 13; No. absent at ports or en route to or from patrol, 10; No. on special service, 0.

The armed merchant-steamer Arlanza, after temporary repairs at Alexandrovsk, arrived at Belfast in July for refit.

The weather during July was very foggy, fog or mist being experienced at Scapa or in the neighbourhood on the 2nd, 3rd, 15th, 18th, 23rd, 24th and 25th.

During the month of August the principal cruiser movements, apart from those in connection with the Battle Fleet, were as follows:

(a) The patrol of two cruisers and two destroyers in an area well to the northward of the Shetlands was continued.

(b) The "dark night" light cruiser extended patrol seaward of the Fleet bases was maintained.

(c) The patrol of a cruiser on the Archangel route was continued.

(d) Light cruiser sweeps were carried out as follows:

On the 1st, two light cruisers and four destroyers left Rosyth for a sweep down the Norwegian coast, returning on the 3rd, having sighted nothing of interest; on the 8th, two light cruisers and four destroyers from Rosyth swept from Lat. 60 N., Long. 2 E., to Lat. 57.30 N., Long. 5.0 E., and returned to their base on the 10th, without result. On the 12th the 4th Light Cruiser Squadron, with four destroyers, left Scapa and proceeded towards Udsire Lighthouse, where they met a convoy of 10 British merchant-ships which had been brought out of the Baltic. These vessels were escorted across the North Sea to Rattray Head. The convoy arrived safely on the 14th.

On the night of the 15th the armed boarding-steamers Dundee and King Orry, which had been disguised as merchant-ships, left Scapa for operations off the Norwegian coast. It was hoped that they would be able to close enemy and neutral vessels carrying contraband without exciting suspicion, and that they would stand a better chance of capturing them than any vessel having the appearance of a warship. The Dundee operated between Udsire and Lister, and the King Orry off Stadlandet, both being localities in which ships were in the habit of leaving territorial waters. The light cruiser Constance and two destroyers were sent to support the Dundee, keeping well to seaward of her, as that ship was operating in waters in which enemy warships might be found. The operation resulted in a Norwegian steamer, carrying a cargo of magnetic iron ore for Rotterdam, being sent in.

On the 30th the Abdiel left Scapa to lay mines in the vicinity of the Horn Reef. She carried out the operation successfully, and without being observed, on the night of the 31st-1st.

The work of the 11th Submarine Flotilla in the Kattegat and in the vicinity of the Horn Reef continued. The submarines, returning on the 17th, reported having been attacked by a German decoy trawler in the Kattegat. On the 30th submarine E 43 sailed to operate against this vessel, but met with no success.

Casualties to war-vessels during the month included: The light cruiser Cleopatra, of the Harwich force, which was mined on the 4th near the Thornton Ridge off the Dutch coast, and reached the Nore to be repaired; the destroyer Lassoo, also of the Harwich force, was sunk by mine or submarine near the Maas Lightship off the Dutch coast on the 13th; the armed boarding-steamer Duke of Albany was sunk by a submarine on the 24th, 20 miles to the eastward of the Pentland Skerries, with considerable loss of life, including Commander G. N. Ramage, R.N.R. Sixteen destroyers, seaplanes, and an airship were sent out from Scapa at once to hunt this submarine, but saw nothing of her, although the armed boarding-steamer Duke of Clarence which had stood by the Duke of Albany and rescued the survivors reported that she had passed over and struck a submerged object. The light cruiser Blonde went ashore on the Lowther Rock, Pentland Firth, in thick weather on the 10th, but was lightened and towed off on the 11th, having sustained considerable injuries; the battleships Warspite and Valiant collided in the Scapa Flow on the night of the 24th, whilst, respectively, returning from and proceeding to the night firing area, both ships being considerably damaged, with the result that they had to be docked.

On August 3rd mines were laid off the Longstone by an enemy submarine, and the departure of the Marlborough from the Tyne was thereby delayed; the coincidence that mines were frequently laid in this neighbourhood when warships were due to leave the Tyne after repairs, led to suspicion that enemy agents were working in that locality. On the 4th or 5th August a considerable number of mines of the submarine type were also laid in the War channel in the White Sea by enemy vessels.

On August 3rd four "C" class submarines left the Nore in tow of tugs for Archangel, en route by the canal system for service in the Baltic. These submarines performed very useful work in those waters during the year 1917.

The increase in minelaying by German submarines gave rise to anxiety that the movements of the Grand Fleet might be hampered by minefields near the bases at a critical moment, and, in the absence of any new minesweepers, the minesweeping force at Scapa was strengthened during July by withdrawing a certain number of trawlers from patrol duty in order to form a minesweeping flotilla; during the latter half of 1916 the Grand Fleet minesweeping force at Scapa or Cromarty comprised two flotillas composed of sloops and gunboats, as well as two flotillas, each consisting of 12 trawlers; in addition one flotilla of paddle minesweepers was based on Granton in the Firth of Forth. These flotillas were all additional to the small local sweeping force of trawlers at the various fleet bases.

On August 18th the Grand Fleet proceeded to sea for a sweep in southern waters. The presence of an unusually large number of submarines in the North Sea - a phenomenon which had been observed shortly before the Jutland Battle - had suggested the possibility of movement on the part of the enemy and a sweep appeared desirable. The Iron Duke, after leaving Scapa Flow, proceeded ahead of the remainder of the Battle Fleet screened by two destroyers to communicate with the Royalist, and at 7.55 p.m., as the ships were about to communicate, a submarine on the starboard bow, about 250 yards off, fired a torpedo, which passed close astern of the screening destroyer Onslaught on that bow. Only one torpedo was seen. Possibly the submarine misjudged the attack, and did not get into the position intended for attacking the Iron Duke, which was proceeding at high speed, and zigzagging, and, therefore, fired at the Onslaught instead. Communication between the Iron Duke and Royalist was deferred until after dark in consequence of this attack; the Fleet was warned by signal.

The squadrons from Scapa were opened out to avoid the submarine, and passed her without further incident, and the Battle Fleet and cruisers concentrated at daylight on the 19th, in the vicinity of the "Long Forties," steering to the southward at a speed of advance of 17 knots. The Battle Cruiser Fleet had been ordered to a position 30 miles ahead of the Battle Fleet. At 5.55 a.m. on the 19th the Nottingham, one of the light cruiser screen ahead of the battle cruisers, whilst zigzagging at 20 knots speed, was hit by two torpedoes in Lat. 55.34 N., Long. 0.12 E. The submarine was not seen, and the torpedoes struck the port side almost simultaneously.

The first report indicated that she had been hit by mines or torpedoes, and, until it was clear that a minefield did not exist, it was prudent for the Fleet to avoid this locality, and course was accordingly reversed until it was ascertained that the damage was due to torpedoes; when this became clear the southward course of the Fleet was shaped to pass to the eastward of the submarine. Meanwhile the Dublin cruised at high speed in the vicinity of the Nottingham for the purpose of keeping the submarine down so as to prevent further attacks. But at 6.26 a.m. the Nottingham was hit by a third torpedo, and it became evident that she could not float much longer. Her boats were lowered, and the majority of the ship's company placed in them. The ship sank at 7.10 a.m., just as the destroyers Penn and Oracle, which had been sent to her assistance, arrived on the scene. These two destroyers picked up all the survivors, except Captain Miller, one officer, and several men who remained on board until the ship sank, and who were rescued by a cutter from the Dublin. Several torpedoes were fired at the Dublin and the two destroyers during their work of rescue, but all fortunately missed.

From 8.24 a.m. onwards Zeppelins were frequently in sight from both the Battle Fleet, and the Battle Cruiser Fleet, and were fired at, but they kept at too long a range for our fire to be effective. The Galatea sighted the first airship at 8.24 a.m., and the second was seen by the Battle Fleet at 9.55 a.m.; at 10 a.m. Commodore Tyrwhitt, who was at sea with the Harwich force, reported himself in position Lat. 52.50 N., Long. 3.38 E., and also being followed by a Zeppelin. He stated later that his force was shadowed by airships during the whole period of daylight on the 19th. Reports were also received from the patrol trawler Ramexo that she had two Zeppelins in sight in Lat. 57 N., Long. 1 E. It was evident that a very large force of airships was out. A total of at least ten was identified by our directional wireless stations and they appeared to stretch right across the North Sea.

At 10.10 a.m. a report was received from submarine E 23, on patrol in the Heligoland Bight, that she had sighted ships of the High Sea Fleet steering west at 9.19 a.m.; the position as received in the signal appeared incorrect, and I rightly assumed it to be Lat. 54.20 N., Long. 5.0 E. Information received earlier from our directional wireless stations also led me to consider that a ship of the High Sea Fleet was in the position named at 5.30 a.m., instead of at 9.19 a.m. On the return of E 23 to Harwich, her captain reported that he had attacked the battle cruiser Derfflinger unsuccessfully at 3.13 a.m. on the 20th. At 5 a.m., in spite of the strong enemy destroyer screen, he succeeded in torpedoing the rear battleship of the first Battle Squadron, a ship of the "Nassau" type. This ship turned for home on being torpedoed, and proceeded under the escort of five destroyers, but at 7.20 a.m. E 23 succeeded in again torpedoing her, and the captain of E 23 was of opinion that the ship was sunk. Subsequent information, however, showed that she reached port in a damaged condition; the persistent action of the captain of E 23 in the face of great opposition, was a fine example of the determined spirit animating our submarine service.

On receipt of the reports from E 23, and from our directional wireless stations, speed was increased, and course shaped to a position at which it was hoped the High Sea Fleet would be met, if the objective of that fleet was a bombardment of the works on the Tyne or in the neighbourhood as appeared possible. My intention was to make for a position in about Lat. 55 N., Long. 0.40 E., where the Fleet would be favourably placed either to engage the enemy before he closed the coast or to cut him off from his bases afterwards. From previous experience of coast raids, I formed the opinion that if that was his objective the bombardment would be carried out either shortly before dusk, or at daylight, in order to facilitate escape afterwards, or approach before, unobserved. In the possible alternative of the movement being designed to cover a landing, the Fleet would also be favourably placed to prevent such an operation. At noon the Battle Fleet was in position Lat. 55.42 N., Long. 1.04 E. steering south-southeast. Submarines were sighted by the cruiser Minotaur at 1.23 p.m., and by the light cruiser Boadicea at 1.38 p.m.; both these ships were in the vicinity of the Battle Fleet which was manoeuvred as necessary to avoid the submarines; this caused some slight delay in the southward movement.

The 11th Submarine Flotilla had been ordered to sea in readiness to meet the Fleet, if required, and during the forenoon of the 19th, was directed to spread on a line running 180 degrees from Lat. 55 N., Long. 0, where the submarines would be clear of our Fleet and would be in a position to attack the enemy's vessels should they proceed towards our coast north of Flamborough Head; in such an event the enemy would be between the Fleet and the submarines.

The Active, with nine destroyers of the newly formed 4th Flotilla in the Humber, which was also at sea, was directed to join the Battle Fleet.

At 1.45 p.m. I received information by wireless that directional wireless stations placed enemy vessels at 12.30 p.m. in a position approximately Lat. 54.30 N., Long. 1.40 E. Our Battle Fleet at 1.45 p.m. was in Lat. 55.15 N., Long. 1.0 E., and the Battle Cruiser Fleet was well ahead. If the High Sea Fleet had continued on the same course after 12.30 p.m. as it had steered between 5.30 a.m. and 12.30 p.m., which would take them to Hartlepool, it was evident that it might be sighted at any moment by the Battle Cruiser Fleet, the distance between the opposing Battle Fleets being only 42 miles; a signal was therefore made to the Battle Fleet that the High Sea Fleet might be encountered at any moment. The meeting appeared to be so certain that I arranged the distribution of gunfire of the Battle Fleet. On the assumption that the enemy would turn to the eastward on meeting us, I directed a concentration of fire of ships that would be ahead of the Iron Duke on deployment, of two ships on one, leaving the Iron Duke to deal with one ship singly, as a compliment to her accurate firing at Jutland. The conditions were eminently favourable to us.

The weather was clear. There seemed to be a very good prospect that we might, on gaining touch with the enemy, find that the Grand Fleet was in a position to cut off the High Sea Fleet from its base, as it was probable that we should be to the eastward, although farther north. Our submarines were also well placed should the enemy elect to make for our coast and try to escape to the northward, where he would have found himself between the Grand Fleet and the submarines. As time passed, however, and no reports of enemy vessels being sighted came in from our light cruisers, it became evident that the High Sea Fleet had turned back, probably owing to the fact that the Zeppelins had warned the German Commander-in-Chief of our presence and movements. On this assumption, at 2.35 p.m. I directed Commodore Tyrwhitt to steer for a position to the northwestward of Terschelling, so that he might be ready to deliver a night attack on the enemy's fleet with the Harwich force.

It seemed fairly certain to me that the enemy would leave a trap behind him in the shape of mines or submarines, or both; and, indeed, the numerous submarines already sighted made it probable that the trap was extensive; it was therefore unwise to pass over the waters which he had occupied unless there was a prospect of bringing the High Sea Fleet to action.

It was clear that if no enemy vessels were in sight by 4 p.m., and if he had turned for home, it would be impossible to bring him to action; I therefore passed a visual signal out at 3.5 p.m. to Sir David Beatty to the effect that his force was to turn 16 points, if nothing was in sight by 4 p.m.

At 3.20 p.m., however, the Rear-Admiral Commanding the 3rd Light Cruiser Squadron reported a submarine in sight, and I signalled to Sir David Beatty to turn at once, as it seemed that my supposition as to the submarines was correct.

At 3.40 p.m. I directed the 5th Battle Squadron and the cruisers ahead to turn. At this time I received information from our directional wireless stations that enemy ships were in Lat. 54.14 N., Long. 2.0 E., at 2.45 p.m. It was evident then that the enemy was returning to his bases, and was far beyond pursuit. I therefore turned the Battle Fleet at 3.56 p.m., when in Lat. 54.40 N., Long. 1.01 E., reversing the course to pass up the searched channel so as to avoid mines.

At 4.52 p.m. the Falmouth of the 3rd Light Cruiser Squadron in Lat. 54.27 N., Long. 1.15 E., was hit by two torpedoes, one right forward, and one right aft. The ship was zigzagging at 23 knots speed at the time, and the submarine was not seen, although the tracks of the torpedoes were visible for about 300 yards on the starboard bow after she had been hit. The Chester, stationed astern of the Falmouth, proceeded at full speed to zigzag in the vicinity with the object of keeping the submarine submerged and preventing further attack. Another torpedo was fired at the Falmouth at 5.14 p.m., but missed.

At 5.20 p.m. the destroyers Pasley, Pelican, and Negro, detached to assist the Falmouth, arrived on the scene and the Falmouth, under their escort, proceeded towards the coast under her own steam, the Chester then leaving to rejoin her squadron to the northward.

At 6.55 p.m. the Pelican sighted a periscope, tried to ram the submarine, but missed. She then dropped six depth charges and reported that the submarine came to the surface almost immediately, and then appeared to sink. Requests for tugs had meanwhile been signalled, and four more destroyers were detached to assist to screen the Falmouth, which was proceeding at five knots. The ship eventually reached the vicinity of Flamborough Head safely, and was there again hit by two more torpedoes fired from a submarine. She still remained afloat, and was towed by four tugs, and escorted by nine destroyers until 8 p.m. on the 20th, when she sank in Lat. 54 N., Long. 0.2 W.

At 2.30 p.m. on the 20th, the destroyer Porpoise reported having rammed a submarine that had attacked the Falmouth.

To return to the Grand Fleet proceedings on the 19th, From 3.10 p.m. onwards frequent reports were received of submarines being sighted. The Phaeton, Dublin (twice), and Southampton all reported submarines in sight between 3.10 and 4.52 p.m., the time at which the Falmouth was torpedoed. At 6 p.m. Sir David Beatty reported that there was a German submarine screen of several boats extending northeast for some 25 miles from Lat. 54.19 N., Long. 1.0 E. At 6.7 p.m. Commodore Tyrwhitt reported that he was following an enemy's force of heavy ships steering east, accompanied by two Zeppelins. A reply was sent giving the position of the Grand Fleet; the conditions for night attack proved to be unfavourable, and at 7.30 p.m. the Commodore reported that he had abandoned the pursuit; he returned with his force to Harwich. At 6.20 p.m. reports received from our directional stations showed that enemy ships were in Lat. 54.16 N., Long. 2.51E. at 4.52 p.m., giving clear evidence that the enemy was returning to his base.

During the passage up the searched channel a number of submarines were sighted and frequent, and in some cases, large alterations of course were necessary to avoid them; if all the reports were correct, the locality indeed seemed to be a hotbed of submarines. Reports of submarines being seen were received between 4 p.m. and dark, from the Galatea, Phaeton, Bellona, Dublin, Southampton, Lion, Royal Sovereign (two submarines), Queen Elizabeth, and Inflexible, the last ship reporting that two torpedoes had been fired at her at 7.50 p.m., and that both had passed close astern; at this time the Battle Fleet and Battle Cruiser Fleet were in company.

Zeppelins were also sighted during the afternoon by the Chatham, Galatea, and Lion, and the trawlers Sea Ranger and Ramexo; the last-named reported having sighted a Zeppelin at a low altitude, and having scored two hits and caused a fire in the forward car.

During the evening the Battle Cruiser Fleet was detached to Rosyth, and the Battle Fleet continued to the northward. Reports of submarines being sighted to the eastward of the Pentland Skerries were received at 5 a.m. and 8.30 p.m. on the 20th, and the Battle Fleet was therefore taken well to the northward to avoid them, and approached the Pentland Firth from a north-easterly direction, arriving without incident between 6.80 and 8 p.m.

The experience of August 19th showed that light cruisers, proceeding at even the highest speed unscreened by destroyers, ran considerable danger from enemy submarines. The enemy's submarine commanders were no doubt increasing in efficiency, and risks, which we could afford to run earlier in the War, were now unjustifiable. Representations were made to the Admiralty to the effect that it was considered that in future light cruisers should be screened by at least one destroyer per ship; the number of destroyers available for the Grand Fleet did not at the time admit of this, but as the total complement of 100 (the number intended to be appropriated to the Fleet) was reached, destroyers could be allotted to most of the light cruisers in the advanced line, provided there were not many absent from the Fleet carrying out extraneous services.

The ease with which the enemy could lay a submarine trap for the Fleet had been demonstrated on the 19th of August; what had constantly puzzled me was that this had not been done very frequently at an earlier stage in the War. Since, however, it had been attempted and with some success, there seemed to be every reason to expect a repetition of the operation, and it was clear that it was unwise to take the Fleet far into southern waters unless an adequate destroyer force was present to act as a submarine screen for all ships. If the circumstances were exceptional and the need very pressing, it would be necessary to accept the risk. There was general agreement on this point between the Flag officers of the Fleet and the Admiralty.

During the month of August the weekly average of the 10th Cruiser Squadron showed: No. of ships intercepted, including trawlers, 112; No, sent in, 35; No. on patrol, 13; No. absent at ports or en route to or from patrols, 10; No. on special service, 0.

The weather at Scapa and in the neighbourhood was foggy and misty during a great part of the month. Much mist or fog was experienced from the 1st to the 6th, the 10th to the 12th, and 13th to 16th.

During the month Grand Fleet submarines were exercised at Scapa Flow in carrying out attacks on ships under way, and the destroyer flotillas were similarly practised in making torpedo attacks, the Battle Fleet divisions being exercised in countering such attacks by turning movements. These exercises were continued for the remainder of the year, and much experience was obtained from them as to the different methods of dealing with attacks by enemy destroyers dinging a Fleet action.

Admiral John Rushworth Jellicoe (1859–1935)

17 - The Submarine Peril

Events were to prove that my period of command of the Grand Fleet was drawing to a close, my transfer to the Admiralty occurring at the end of November 1917.

But before coming to that development something must be said in continuation of the narrative of the work of the Grand Fleet.

During the month of September, 1916, there was not much movement by the Fleet as a whole. On the 4th, the 2nd Battle Cruiser Squadron and 2nd Light Cruiser Squadron, with eleven destroyers, left Rosyth, swept towards the Naze, then down to the southward of the Little Fisher Bank, and back to Rosyth. On the same day three divisions of destroyers from Scapa endeavoured without success to locate a submarine reported by the Talisman to the eastward of the Pentland Skerries. On the 7th a further unsuccessful search for a submarine was carried out in the same locality.

On the 10th the 1st and 4th Light Cruiser Squadrons left Rosyth and Scapa respectively to exchange bases, carrying out a search of the North Sea en route, and on the 20th two light cruisers and four destroyers left Rosyth for a similar sweep to that carried out on the 4th.

On the 22nd numerous reports of submarines to the eastward made it necessary to move the patrol line of the 10th Cruiser Squadron temporarily farther west

On September 20th the Battle Fleet, 2nd Battle Cruiser Squadron, 4th Light Cruiser Squadron, Campania, and the destroyer flotillas left Scapa for a cruise between the Orkneys and Shetland Islands and the Norwegian coast. Three battleships, three cruisers, two light cruisers, and ten destroyers were absent, undergoing refit. Battle exercises were carried out during the cruise. A submarine was reported on the intended track of the fleet on return, and the base was, therefore, approached by another route, the available local patrol vessels being employed to keep the submarine submerged during the entry of the fleet to Scapa.

Submarines were again active during the latter part of the month in the vicinity of the cruising-ground of the 10th Cruiser Squadron, the position of the squadron being shifted for that reason.

On the 26th two light cruisers and four destroyers left Rosyth to search the waters to the southward of the German North Sea minefield, returning on the 28th.

On the same date the yacht Conqueror II, the patrol trawler Sarah Alice, and two British steamers were torpedoed in the Fair Island Channel by enemy submarines. On receipt of the news at Scapa Flow, destroyers were detached from the Grand Fleet flotillas to operate against the submarines, and to strengthen the patrol in these waters.

Early on the 30th the Lion, with the 1st and 2nd Battle Cruiser Squadrons, and the 2nd Light Cruiser Squadron, and accompanied by a destroyer escort, left Rosyth and swept in the direction of the Naze, then turned to the northward and proceeded to Scapa.

During September the cruiser patrols were continuously maintained to the northward of the Shetlands and on the Archangel routes, each patrol consisting of a cruiser and an armed boarding steamer. The submarine patrol, consisting of three submarines, was maintained off the Horn Reef. The enemy had presumably found the patrols inconvenient, and German destroyers on several occasions during the month cruised at night in the area patrolled with a view to interrupting our submarines when recharging their batteries. This was met by a frequent change of position at night. Submarine G 12, when returning from patrol on the 29th, sighted an enemy submarine on the surface, and, being unable to get into position to attack by torpedo, engaged her by gunfire, but did not score any hits before the enemy submarine submerged.

The formation of a new Grand Fleet Submarine Flotilla (the 10th Submarine Flotilla) was begun during the month, the base being the River Tees, and the parent ship the Lucia, with two attendant destroyers. The formation of the 15th Destroyer Flotilla was also commenced, this being the last of the Grand Fleet Flotillas to be formed to complete the total number of Grand Fleet destroyers to 100.

On the 21st the new battle cruiser Repulse, heavily armed and of high speed, but with inadequate protection for a battle cruiser, joined the Fleet at Scapa to work up gunnery and torpedo practices. The armour protection of this ship was about equal to that of the Australia and New Zealand, and she was greatly inferior in this respect to the Lion, and later battle cruisers. As already stated, experience during the War had demonstrated very clearly that our battle cruisers were at a marked disadvantage in engaging German vessels of the same class, unless they were provided with better protection than that given to the Australia and earlier vessels. Proposals were, therefore, forwarded to the Admiralty for adding very considerably to the deck protection of both the Repulse and her sister ship, the Renown. These proposals were approved, and the work carried out at the Fleet bases. Although the ships were much improved by the alteration, they were still far inferior in protection to the German battle cruisers.

On the 23rd a new floating-dock, which had been built on the Tyne, for light cruisers and destroyers, arrived at Invergordon, and was a very useful addition to that most valuable refitting base.

The average weekly results from the 10th Cruiser Squadron during September were: No. of ships intercepted, 135; No. sent in, 45; No. on patrol, 15; No. absent at ports or en route to or from patrol, 9; No. on special service, 0.

The favourable weather and short nights, combined with the large number of vessels maintained on patrol were responsible for the increase in the number of ships intercepted.

The weather as a whole was good during the month. Fog or mist was prevalent on the 3rd, 8th, 23rd, 24th and 27th, and a gale occurred on the 18th. Otherwise the conditions were favourable.

In the early part of October, the activities of the enemy's submarines in the White Sea, which had been considerable during the month of September, became more pronounced. Between October 1st and 5th three Norwegian steamers were sunk in the vicinity of Sletness, and a British vessel and Russian steamer fell victims to U 48, in Lat. 70.14 N., Long. 85.8

E. Some submarines were attacked by Russian destroyers in Lat. 69.45 N., Long. 88.6 E., and it was reported that the attack was successful. The Fearless, now a submarine parent ship, and three submarines started for the White Sea on October 18th from Scapa to operate from Alexandroksk against the hostile submarines. They arrived on the 20th and began operations at once. During their stay in the White Sea, they did not succeed in sinking any enemy submarines, but there was a marked decrease in enemy operations, possibly due to the cramping effect of the presence of our vessels in those waters. The Fearless, with her submarines, left Alexandrovsk on the return passage on November 15th, in order to be clear of these waters before the ice began to form.

On October 2nd the 1st Battle Squadron, some ships of the 2nd Cruiser Squadron, and the 12th Destroyer Flotilla, left Scapa for a cruise to the eastward, returning on the 4th.

On the 7th the Battle Cruiser Fleet left Scapa and swept towards the Naze, thence proceeding to a position to the southwestward of the Little Fisher Bank, in which our submarines engaged in the Horn Reef patrol had reported the presence of trawlers, which had been acting suspiciously. Twelve trawlers flying neutral colours were found there by the 2nd Light Cruiser Squadron; three were selected and sent in for examination, but were found to be in order.

On the same day, the 7th, two light cruisers left Scapa to meet at sea the airships stationed at Longside, near Peterhead, with a view to gaining experience in airships and light cruisers working together. The programme arranged could not be completed owing to bad weather, but was carried out on a subsequent occasion, and some useful hints were gained. This work was undertaken as a preliminary to the airships being detailed to accompany the Fleet to sea when on passage south, as the number of these craft completing in the near future justified such a procedure; although we still lacked airships of the Zeppelin type, it was felt that those of the smaller class might be able to carry out useful reconnaissance work ahead of the Fleet if moving south on the western side of the North Sea. We had already had considerable experience of the value of Zeppelins to the German High Sea Fleet in this respect. That experience had fully confirmed the views put forward in 1913 on this subject at a period when, as Second Sea Lord, the Naval Air Service came under my supervision. These views were expressed on an occasion when the building of a fleet of Zeppelins was being urged on behalf of the Navy.

It was then pointed out with emphasis how great would be the value of such vessels for reconnaissance duty in connection with Fleet movements. At this time the usual conflict was proceeding as to the relative values of Zeppelin and heavier-than-air craft, but the views expressed were that whatever future there might be for the latter as development proceeded, there was no likelihood of their having the radius of action necessary for scouting work in a fleet for some years, whereas the Zeppelin already possessed it. My apology for making mention of this fact is that it controverts the assertion so constantly made that the senior officers in the Navy were not alive to the value of aircraft before the War.

On October 8th, the 2nd Battle Squadron, some cruisers of the 2nd Cruiser Squadron, and destroyers of the 15th and 11th Flotillas, left Scapa to cruise to the eastward, returning on the 10th.

On the 15th, two light cruisers and four destroyers left for a sweep, but were recalled on the 16th owing to bad weather.

On the 17th two light cruisers and four destroyers sailed from Rosyth for a position to the westward of Ekersund, and thence swept down to the Little Fisher Bank and back to Rosyth, without sighting anything of interest.

On the 19th two cruisers, two light cruisers and eight destroyers left the northern bases to spread on a line between Lat. 59.30 N., Long. 1 E., and Lat. 60 N., Long. 4.20 E., and sweep down, in wide zigzags, on a course approximately parallel to the Norwegian coast in order to search for possible enemy raiders; the operation was repeated during daylight hours on two successive days; no enemy vessels were sighted.

On the 22nd the 4th and 5th Battle Squadrons and the 14th and 15th Flotillas left Scapa for a watching and exercise cruise to the eastward, returning on the 24th.

During each of the Battle Squadron cruises carried out during the month of October, the Flag officers were directed to carry out battle exercises based on the tactics employed by the enemy during the Jutland action, with a view to gaining experience in methods designed to meet these tactics; reports on the subject were requested from all Flag officers.

On October 24th a division of destroyers, together with seaplanes, was sent to the Fair Island Channel to operate against enemy submarines reported to be using this passage. No enemy vessels were sighted during the patrol.

On the 26th a submarine was sent into the Skagerrak to operate against an enemy decoy vessel reported in those waters. On the same day the Kildonan Castle, of the 10th Cruiser Squadron, was fired at by a submarine and missed by two torpedoes in Lat. 63.17 N., Long. 18.30 W. The 10th Cruiser Squadron patrol line was consequently moved temporarily to the westward, and trawlers were despatched to the neighbourhood.

On the 28th two light cruisers and four destroyers sailed from Rosyth to carry out a reconnaissance of the waters south of the German North Sea minefield. They returned on the 30th, not having sighted any enemy vessels.

On October 31st the Battle Cruiser Fleet and 13th Flotilla left Rosyth for an observation and exercise cruise in the central and northern positions of the North Sea, and returned without incident on November 3rd.

During the month the Northern patrol north of the Shetlands by one cruiser and one armed boarding-steamer was continued, as were the patrol on the Archangel route, and the submarine patrol off the Horn Reef.

The weekly average for the 10th Cruiser Squadron showed the following figures: - No. of ships intercepted, 74; No. sent in, 25; No. on patrol, 12; No. absent at ports or en route to or from patrol, 12; No. on special service, 0.

Bad weather during the month interfered with the operations of the squadron; gales were experienced on the 10th, 12th, 14th and 25th. There was little fog or mist.

On November 1st I left the Iron Duke at Cromarty and proceeded to the Admiralty at the request of the First Lord,

Mr. Balfour. The visit was the result of letters I had written on the subject of the ever-growing danger of the submarine to our sea communications, and the necessity for the adoption of most energetic measures to deal with this danger. It had been for some time my opinion that unless the Navy could devise effective means, first, to destroy the submarines, and, secondly, to protect our communications more successfully until the submarines could be destroyed, there was undoubted risk of our being forced into making an unsatisfactory peace. From information furnished to me it was evident that the Germans were making special efforts to increase the number of their submarines very largely, and there did not seem to be much prospect, with the methods we were at the time employing, of destroying submarines at a rate at all approaching that of their construction.

So far as I was aware there was an insufficient reserve of food in the country to provide against the consequences of successful action by enemy submarines; and the construction of merchant-ships on an adequate scale to replace those lost had not been taken in hand, this being obviously an essential measure. I had written semi-officially for eighteen months before on the matter. It seemed to me questionable whether our organisation at the Admiralty included a sufficiently numerous and important staff, having as its sole business the work of dealing, rapidly and effectively, with the problem which was assuming such very serious proportions.

It did not appear that new proposals and inventions for dealing with the submarine campaign were being pushed forward with the necessary rapidity, possibly because of the absence of such an organisation, of difficulties connected with labour and materiel; and generally it seemed doubtful whether the dangers confronting us would be successfully combated. The Admiralty had no responsibility either for food supplies or, at that time, for merchant-ship building.

I knew that the First Sea Lord, Sir Henry Jackson, was alive to the danger, and that it caused him much anxiety. We had corresponded very freely on all subjects during his tenure of office at the Admiralty, and I was aware of his views on matters connected with the War, on which we had always been in complete agreement. His direction and assistance in connection with matters concerning the development and employment of the Grand Fleet had been most helpful to me, and invaluable to the nation, and my hope was that in putting forward my views as to the new and serious danger confronting us, and the possible methods of dealing with it, I should be rendering him assistance in combating the menace.

One of my suggestions was the formation of a committee, or department, at the Admiralty under a senior officer, and composed of some of the clever and younger officers who had shown marked ability in studying new ideas. Their sole object would be the development of arrangements for dealing with the submarine warfare against merchant shipping, and the production of the necessary material. I pointed out that our existing methods were not meeting with the success attained at an earlier period, and gave the reasons which, in my opinion, were responsible for this result.

I had also formed and expressed the opinion that the High Sea Fleet would not be risked again in a Fleet action, at any rate, until the submarine campaign against merchant shipping had been fully tried and had failed. So strongly did I hold this view that I suggested to the Admiralty the desirability of reducing the number of destroyers in the Grand Fleet by one flotilla for work against the enemy's submarines in waters where such action had some chance of success.

I pointed out, once again, that offensive action against submarines in the northern part of the North Sea (the only waters in which Grand Fleet destroyers could be used, and yet be available for work with the Fleet in an emergency) was not likely to give satisfactory results, as the submarines could, in the wide expanse of water open to them, always dive and escape. The areas in which destroyers could act more effectively against submarines were comparatively narrow and deep waters; in restricted localities, such as some parts of the English Channel, where the depth did not allow of their resting on the bottom, if hunted. My contention was that it was probably wise to reduce the number of Grand Fleet destroyer flotillas in order to strengthen the force required to deal with the submarine danger, even if this reduction necessitated sending the Grand Fleet to sea short of one battle squadron, should it have to deal with a grave emergency, such as attempted invasion. The alternative, which I felt we could not face, was to run the graver risk of serious disaster from successful submarine warfare on merchant shipping.

It was my firm belief that the High Sea Fleet would not risk a fleet action for some time, and even if this Fleet undertook an operation having as its objective some military advantage, I considered that with the 1st, 2nd and 5th Battle Squadrons (all the ships of which had been fitted with additional deck protection) it could be engaged with every prospect of success, provided always that it was well screened from submarine attack and carefully handled. The only direction, apart from an attack on our sea communications, in which the High Sea Fleet could inflict any material damage on us and which the Grand Fleet could expect to be in a position to prevent lay in attempted invasion. The bombardment of coast towns was an operation which the Grand Fleet could not prevent, unless by some fortunate chance it happened to be at sea and in the right position at the right moment.

The objection which might be raised to this policy, which was otherwise to my mind correct, was the effect on the public mind of the High Sea Fleet being at sea without being brought to action, even if it could achieve no military success by its presence at sea. I recognised very fully the force of this objection, and the responsibility involved in disregarding it. On the other hand, the submarine danger to our shipping was most pressing and should, I felt strongly, be dealt with at all costs, and without delay, since the existence of the armies as well as that of the civil population depended on merchant shipping.

I returned to the Fleet from my visit to the Admiralty on November 5th.

On the 2nd the 2nd Battle Squadron with the 4th Light Cruiser Squadron and 11th Destroyer Flotilla, left Scapa to cruise eastward of the Shetland Islands, returning on November 4th.

On the 3rd the Botha, with four destroyers of the 14th Flotilla, left Scapa for a sweep northward along the Norwegian coast from a position near Udsire Lighthouse on the probable track of enemy submarines returning to their bases. On the same day the Faulknor and six destroyers of the 12th Flotilla from Cromarty carried out a similar sweep to the northward, starting from the vicinity of the Little Fisher Bank. The 1st Light Cruiser Squadron and eight destroyers of the 18th Flotilla from Rosyth supported both forces.

At 1.20 p.m., on November 5th, submarine J 1 on patrol off the Horn Reef, sighted four enemy battleships of the "Kaiser" class in Lat. 56.6 N., Long. 6.53 E. A considerable sea was running, making it difficult to prevent J 1 from breaking surface. The battleships had a strong destroyer screen, and the conditions for attack were very difficult. But Commander Lawrence succeeded, in spite of these difficulties, in firing his four bow torpedoes at a range of 4,000 yards. Two of them took effect on two of the battleships. The battleships turned to the southward, and the destroyers hunted J 1 for a considerable period, but unsuccessfully. It was learned subsequently that the two damaged ships managed to reach port, but this fact does not detract from the great credit attaching to the submarine for her very successful attack under exceedingly difficult conditions. The incident showed, as in previous cases, the efficiency of the German system of underwater protection in their capital ships.

On the 9th submarine G9 left to operate against enemy submarines on their expected tracks.

From the 16th to the 18th very heavy weather was experienced in northern waters; several merchant ships were disabled, and assistance was rendered to them by the ships of the 10th Cruiser Squadron, and by tugs from Scapa. One Admiralty collier foundered at sea on the 17th.

On the 18th the Otway, of the 10th Cruiser Squadron, intercepted the Norwegian steamship Older, which was found to be in charge of a prize crew from a German submarine. She had on board, in addition, survivors of an Italian steamship and a British trawler, sunk by the submarine. The Otway recaptured her, but was not in time to prevent the Germans from exploding several bombs in an attempt to sink her. The attempt did not, however, succeed, and the ship was brought into Stornoway.

During the period up to November 19th, the weekly average of work of the 10th Cruiser Squadron showed the following figures: - No. of ships intercepted, 29; No. sent in, 10; No. on patrol, 13; No. absent, 11; No. on special service, 0.

The weather throughout the period to the 19th November was very bad, and the figures showed a corresponding reduction in the number of ships intercepted.

Gales were experienced on the 4th, 5th, 6th, 12th, 16th, 17th and 18th.

On the 24th, the 1st, 2nd, 4th and 5th Battle Squadrons, 1st and 2nd Cruiser Squadrons, 4th Light Cruiser Squadron, and destroyers proceeded to sea for a cruise in northern waters, during which battle exercises were carried out.

Shortly before the Iron Duke slipped from her buoy, and whilst the remainder of the Battle Fleet was on its way out of harbour, I received a telegram from the First Lord, Mr. Balfour, offering me the post of First Sea Lord, and expressing a hope that I would accept it. I consulted my chief of the Staff, Sir Charles Madden, and he stated his opinion that I ought to accept the post in order to be in a position to put into practice the views I held as to the steps required to deal with the submarine menace to shipping. It was naturally a great blow to leave the Fleet, with which I had been associated since the outbreak of the War, for a position which I knew was the most difficult that a sailor could be called upon to fill in war time.

I replied to Mr. Balfour, saying that I was ready to do whatever was considered best for the Service, and in accordance with the wish expressed in his telegram, agreed to meet him at Rosyth.

I then followed the Fleet to sea in the Iron Duke, and having completed the exercises on the 26th, I turned over the Command of the Fleet to Admiral Sir Cecil Burney (second in command), with directions that the ships should return to the Fleet bases, and I proceeded in the Iron Duke to Rosyth, arriving there on the morning of the 27th.

I met and conferred with Mr. Balfour during the 27th, on the question of taking up the work at the Admiralty, and accepted the appointment. He intimated to me that in that event, it had been decided that Sir David Beatty should succeed to the Command of the Grand Fleet, and informed me also of the other changes in Flag appointments that would be effected. I made suggestions on some of these matters.

Mr. Balfour then returned to London, and I started my preparations for the change of duties and the transfer of command. I was under no delusion as to the difficulty of the task before me. The attacks already made upon the Admiralty in connection with the shipping losses due to submarine warfare, and on the subject of night raids on our coast, which it was impossible to prevent, with the means existing, fully prepared me for what was to come.

I knew then that no fresh measures, involving the production of fresh material, could become effective for a period of at least six to twelve months. Indeed, I was so certain of the course that events would take, that in bidding farewell to the officers and men of the Iron Duke (a very difficult task in view of the intense regret that I felt at leaving them), I said that they must expect to see me the object of the same attacks as those to which my distinguished predecessor. Sir Henry Jackson had been exposed. I was not wrong in this surmise. I left the Iron Duke with a very sad heart on November 28th, 1916, and cannot close this record of the work of the Grand Fleet during my twenty-eight months' service as Commander-in-Chief better than by quoting my farewell memorandum to the Fleet which I loved so well.

"In bidding farewell to the Flag officers, Captains, officers and men of the Fleet which it has been my privilege to command since the commencement of the War, I desire to express my warmest thanks to all ranks for their loyal support during a period which I know must have tried their patience to the breaking-point.

"The disappointment which has so constantly attended the southern movements of the Fleet might well have resulted in a tendency to staleness and a feeling that the strenuous efforts made to maintain the highest state of efficiency were unavailing if the opportunities for testings the result were so seldom provided by our enemy.

"But this is far from being the case. I am proud to be able to say, with absolute confidence, that the spirit of keenness and enthusiasm has constantly grown, and I am convinced that the Fleet gains in efficiency from day to day. We have benefited by experience, and we have turned that experience to good account.

"Whilst leaving the Fleet with feelings of the deepest regret, I do so with the knowledge that officers and men are imbued with that spirit which has carried their forefathers to victory throughout all ages, whenever and wherever they have met the enemies of their country, and whilst giving our present foe full credit for high efficiency, I am perfectly confident that in the Grand Fleet they will meet more than their match, ship for ship in all classes, and that the result will never be for one moment in doubt.

"May your arduous work be crowned with a glorious victory resulting in a just and lasting peace!
"J. R. Jellicoe, Admiral."

- *28-11-16*

Captain Jellicoe (of HMS *Centurion*)

Image: Cigarette card from c. 1897.

Original photograph by Jabez Hughes and Gustav Mullins.

Printed in Great Britain
by Amazon